Napa Valley College
Small Business Development Ctr
1556 1st St, Ste. 103
Napa, CA 94559
(707)253-3210
www.napasbdc.org

LEGAL IN ONLINE ANYTIME 24 hours a day

www.nolo.com

AT THE NOLO.COM SELF-HELP LAW CENTER, YOU'LL FIND

- Nolo's comprehensive Legal Encyclopedia filled with plain-English information on a variety of legal topics
- Nolo's Law Dictionary—legal terms <u>without</u> the legalese
- Auntie Nolo—if you've got questions, Auntie's got answers
- The Law Store—over 200 self-help legal products including Downloadable Software, Books, Form Kits and eGuides
- Legal and product updates
- Frequently Asked Questions
- NoloBriefs, our free monthly email newsletter
- Legal Research Center, for access to state and federal statutes
- Our ever-popular lawyer jokes

Quality LAW BOOKS & SOFTWARE FOR EVERYONE

Nolo's user-friendly products are consistently first-rate. Here's why:

- A dozen in-house legal editors, working with highly skilled authors, ensure that our products are accurate, up-to-date and easy to use
- We continually update every book and software program to keep up with changes in the law
- Our commitment to a more democratic legal system informs all of our work
- We appreciate & listen to your feedback. Please fill out and return the card at the back of this book.

An Important Message to Our Readers

4th edition

Working for Yourself

Law and Taxes for Independent Contractors, Freelancers and Consultants

by Attorney Stephen Fishman

Keeping Up-to-Date

To keep its books up-to-date, Nolo issues new printings and new editions periodically. New printings reflect minor legal changes and technical corrections. New editions contain major legal changes, major text additions or major reorganizations. To find out if a later printing or edition of any Nolo book is available, call Nolo at 510-549-1976 or check our Website at www.nolo.com.

To stay current, follow the "Update" service at our Website: www.nolo.com/lawstore/update/list.cfm. In another effort to help you use Nolo's latest materials, we offer a 35% discount off the purchase of the new edition of your Nolo book if you turn in the cover of an earlier edition. This book was last revised in **August 2002**.

Fourth Edition	AUGUST 2002
Editor	LISA GUERIN
Cover Design	TONI IHARA
Book Design	AMY IHARA
Production	SARAH HINMAN
Illustrations	MARI STEIN
Index	JANET PERLMAN
Proofreading	SHERYL ROSE
Printing	CONSOLIDATED PRINTERS, INC

Fishman, Stephen.
    Working for yourself : law and taxes for independent contractors, freelancers & consultants / by Stephen Fishman.--4th ed.
        p. cm.
    Includes index.
    ISBN 0-87337-854-7
    1. Independent contractors--Legal status, laws, etc.--United States. 2. Independent contractors--Taxation--United States--Popular works. 3. Self-employed--Taxation--Law and legislation--United States--Popular works. I. Title.

KF390.I54 F57   2002
346.7302'4--dc21

2002071773

For information on bulk purchases or corporate premium sales, please contact the Special Sales Department. For academic sales or textbook adoptions, ask for Academic Sales. Call 800-955-4775 or write to Nolo, 950 Parker Street, Berkeley, CA 94710.

Acknowledgments

Many thanks to:

Barbara Kate Repa, Janet Portman, Amy DelPo and Lisa Guerin for their superb editing.

Malcolm Roberts, CPA, for reviewing the tax materials.

Gary Gerard for sharing his experiences as an independent contractor.

The many independent contractors throughout the country who permitted me to interview them.

Janet Perlman for the helpful index.

Sheryl Rose for thorough proofreading.

Sarah Hinman for diligent production work.

Table of Contents

10 The Bane of Self-Employment Taxes

11 Paying Estimated Tax

12 Rules for Salespeople, Drivers and Clothing Producers

13 Taxes for Workers You Hire

14 Recordkeeping and Accounting Made Easy

15 Safeguarding Your Self-Employed Status

21 Help Beyond This Book

A1 Appendix 1: Forms and Documents

Asset Log

Expense Journal

Income Journal

Invoice Form

Application for Employer Identification Number—Form SS4

Request for Taxpayer Identification Number and Certification—Form W-9

A2 Appendix 2: Sample Agreements

General Independent Contractor Agreement

Contract Amendment Form

Nondisclosure Agreement

A3 Appendix 3: Agencies

State Offices Providing Small Business Help

State Unemployment Tax Agencies

State Sales Tax Agencies

Patent and Trademark Depository Libraries

State Trademark Agencies and Statutes

Introduction

This book is a law-and-tax guide for people who either work for themselves or are planning to do so. The business world uses all sorts of terms to describe such people, from self-employed to independent contractor to freelancer to consultant to business owner. All these terms describe the same thing—people who have left the ranks of the wage slaves to strike out on their own.

This book covers all the legal and tax basics self-employed people need to know, from how to organize their businesses to how to pay the right taxes to how to draft contracts with their clients.

This book is intended only for those self-employed people who sell personal services—meaning people such as writers, consultants, artists, photographers, lawyers and doctors. If your business involves selling goods to the public, see *Legal Guide for Starting and Running a Small Business*, by Fred Steingold (Nolo).

As you will discover reading this book—if you haven't discovered it already—being self-employed can be both heaven and hell. There are a lot of rewards and a lot of risks. We hope that this book helps you navigate the risks so that the rewards are rich and plentiful.

Working for Yourself:
The Good, the Bad and the Ugly

Working for yourself can be both financially and spiritually satisfying. Be warned, however, that the lot of the self-employed is not always an easy one. You have to make what can be a difficult transition from having an employer take care of you to handling everything on your own. For example, you won't have a company payroll department to withhold and pay all your taxes for you. Many self-employed people—even those with plenty of clients—get into trouble because they don't run their operations in a businesslike manner. You don't have to start wearing a green eye shade, but you do need to learn a few rudiments of business and tax law. That's the focus of this book.

Spending a few hours now to learn the nuts and bolts of law and taxes for the self-employed can save you innumerable headaches and substantial time and money later on.

Before you delve into the details of law and taxes discussed in the following chapters, read this chapter for an overview of the pros and cons of being self-employed as compared to being an employee. It may help you make an informed decision if you're thinking about striking out on your own—or help confirm that you made the right decision if you're already working for yourself.

A. Working for Yourself: The Good

Being self-employed can give you more freedom and privacy than employees have, and it can result in substantial tax benefits.

1. Independence

When you're self-employed, you are your own boss—with all the risks and rewards that entails. Most self-employed people bask in the freedom that comes from being in business for themselves. They would doubtless agree with the following sentiment expressed by one self-employed person: "I can choose how, when and where to work, for as much or little time as I want. In short, I enjoy working for myself."

The self-employed are masters of their economic fates. The amount of money they make is directly related to the quantity and quality of their work. This is not necessarily the case for employees. The self-employed don't have to ask their bosses for a raise; they go out and find more work.

Moreover, since you're normally not dependent upon a single company for your livelihood, the hiring or firing decisions of any one company don't have the impact on you that they have on employees. One self-employed person explains: "I was laid off six years ago and chose to start my own company rather than sign on for another ride on someone else's rollercoaster. It's scary at first, but I'm now no longer at someone else's mercy."

2. Higher Earnings

You can often earn more when you're self-employed than as an employee in someone else's business. For example, an employee in a public relations firm decided to go out on her own when she learned that the firm billed her time out to clients at $125 per hour while paying her only $17 per hour. She now charges $75 per hour and makes a far better living than she ever did as an employee.

According to *The Wall Street Journal*, self-employed people who provide services are usually paid at least 20% to 40% more per hour than employees performing the same work. This is because hiring firms don't have to pay half of their Social Security taxes, pay unemployment compensation taxes, provide workers' compensation coverage or fund employee benefits like health insurance and sick leave. Of course, how much you're paid is a matter for negotiation between you and your clients. Self-employed people whose skills are in great demand may receive far more than employees doing similar work.

3. Tax Benefits

Being self-employed also provides you with many tax benefits that employees don't have. For example, no federal or state taxes are withheld from your paychecks as they must be for employees. Instead, the self-employed normally pay estimated taxes directly to the IRS four times a year. (See Chapter 10.) This means you can hold on to your hard-earned money longer before you have to turn it over to the IRS. It's up to you to decide how much estimated tax to pay (although there are penalties if you underpay). The lack of withholding combined with control over estimated tax payments can result in improved cash flow for the self-employed.

Even more important, you can take advantage of many business-related tax deductions that are limited or not available at all for employees. When you're self-employed, you can deduct from your income tax any necessary expenses related to your business as long as they are reasonable in amount and ordinarily incurred by businesses of your type. This may include, for example, office expenses (including those for home offices), travel expenses, entertainment and meal expenses, equipment and insurance costs and more. (See Chapter 4.)

In contrast to the numerous deductions available to the self-employed, an employee's work-related deductions are severely limited. Some deductions available to the self-employed may not be taken by employees—for example, an employee may not deduct the cost of commuting to and from work, but a self-employed person who has a main office separate from that of a client may ordinarily deduct this expense. (See Chapter 9.) Even those expenses that are deductible may only be deducted to the extent they add up to more than 2% of the employee's adjusted gross income. This means that most expenses related to employment cannot be fully deducted.

The self-employed can also establish retirement plans, such as SEP-IRAs and Keogh Plans, that have tax advantages. These plans also allow them to shelter a substantial amount of their incomes until they retire. (See Chapter 16.)

Because of these tax benefits, the self-employed often pay less tax than employees who earn similar incomes.

4. More Privacy

If you're seeking to shield yourself from the prying eyes of the government, you'll have far more success if you're self-employed than if you work as an employee. The government uses employers to keep track of employees for a variety of purposes. For example, there is a federal law that requires all employers to report to the Department of Health and Human Services the name, address and Social Security number of each newly hired employee. This information is placed in a huge database that is supposed to be used solely to aid in the collection of overdue child support.

Many states have similar requirements. Some mandate that employers provide them with even more information, such as telephone numbers, dates of birth, and details of insurance coverage provided to new employees.

When you're self-employed, such laws don't apply to you. It's far harder for the government to keep tabs on you or control your life.

B. Working for Yourself: The Bad

Despite the advantages, being self-employed may not be a bed of roses. Here are some of the major drawbacks and pitfalls.

1. No Job Security

As discussed above, one of the best things about being self-employed is that you're on your own. But this can be one of the worst things about it as well.

When you're an employee, you must be paid as long as you have your job, even if your employer's business is slow. This is not the case when you're self-employed. If you don't have business, you don't make any money. As one self-employed person says, "If I fail, I don't eat. I don't have the comfort of punching a timeclock and knowing the check will be there on payday."

2. No Free Benefits

Although not required to by law, employers usually provide their employees with health insurance, paid vacations and paid sick leave. More generous employers may also provide retirement benefits, bonuses and even employee profit sharing.

When you're self-employed, you get no such benefits. You must pay for your own health insurance, often at higher rates than employers are able to pay. (See Chapter 6.) Time lost due to vacations and illness comes directly out of your bottom line. And you must fund your own retirement.

If you don't earn enough money to purchase these benefits yourself, you will have to forgo some or all of them.

3. No Unemployment Insurance Benefits

The self-employed also don't have the safety net provided by unemployment insurance. Hiring firms do not pay unemployment compensation taxes for the self-employed, and self-employed people can't collect unemployment when their work for a client ends.

4. No Workers' Compensation

Employers must generally provide workers' compensation coverage for their employees. Employees injured on the job are entitled to collect workers' compensation benefits even if the injury was their own fault.

Hiring firms do not provide workers' compensation coverage for the self-employed. If a work-related injury is a self-employed person's fault, he or she has no recourse against the hiring firm. (See Chapter 6.)

5. No Free Office Space or Equipment

Employers normally provide their employees with office space or other workplaces and whatever equipment they need to do the job. This is not necessary when a company hires a self-employed person, who must normally provide his or her own workplace and equipment.

6. Few or No Labor Law Protections

A wide array of federal and state laws protect employees from unfair exploitation by employers. Among other things, these laws:

- impose a minimum wage and require many employees to be paid time and a half for overtime
- prohibit discrimination and harassment
- require employers to provide family and medical leave, leave for military service or time off to vote or serve on a jury, and

• protect employees who wish to unionize.

Few such legal protections apply to the self-employed.

7. Complete Business Responsibility

When you're self-employed, you must run your own business. This means, for example, that you'll need to have at least a rudimentary recordkeeping system or hire someone to keep your records for you. (See Chapter 14.) You'll also likely have to file a far more complex tax return than you did when you were an employee. (See Chapter 8.)

8. Others May Discriminate

Because you don't have a guaranteed annual income as employees do, insurers, lenders and others may spurn your business or you may have to pay more than employees do for similar services. It can be particularly difficult, for example, for a self-employed person to obtain disability insurance, particularly if he or she works at home.

Health insurance is easier to get but could cost an arm and a leg.

Life will be more difficult if you want to buy a house because lenders are wary of self-employed borrowers. To prove you can afford a loan, you'll likely have to provide a prospective lender copies of your recent tax returns and a profit and loss statement for your business.

C. Working for Yourself: The Ugly

Unfortunately, the bad aspects of self-employment discussed above do not end this litany of woes. Being self-employed can get downright ugly.

1. Double Social Security Tax

For many, the ugliest and most unfair thing about being self-employed is that they must pay twice as much Social Security and Medicare taxes as employees. Employees pay a 7.65% tax on their salaries, up to the Social Security tax limit ($84,900 in 2002). Employers pay a matching amount. In contrast, self-employed people must pay the entire tax themselves—a whopping 15.3% up to the Social Security tax limit. This is in addition to federal and state income taxes. In practice, the Social Security tax is a little less than 15.3% because of certain deductions, but it still takes a big bite out of what you earn. (See Chapter 10.)

It is possible, however, to avoid paying at least part of this Social Security tax burden by incorporating your business. (See Chapter 2.)

2. Personal Liability for Debts

Employees are not liable for the debts incurred by their employers. An employee may lose his or her job if the employer's business fails, but will owe nothing to the employer's creditors.

This is not necessarily the case when you're self-employed. If you're a sole proprietor or partner in a partnership, you are personally liable for your business debts. You could lose most of what you own if your business fails. However, there are ways to decrease your personal exposure, such as incorporating your business and obtaining insurance. (See Chapters 2 and 6.)

3. Deadbeat Clients

Ugliest of all, you could do lots of business and still fail to earn a living. This is because many self-employed people have great difficulty getting their clients to pay them on time or at all. When you're self-employed, you bear the risk of loss from deadbeat clients. Neither the government nor anyone else is going to help you collect.

Clients who pay late or don't pay at all have driven many self-employed people back to the ranks of the wage slaves. However, there are many strategies you can use to help alleviate payment problems. (See Chapter 7.)

D. How to Use This Book

This book will help you make what's good about self-employment even better, make the bad less daunting and—hopefully—make the ugly aspects a little more attractive.

Exactly which portions of the book you'll need to read now depends on whether you're already self-employed or are just starting out.

1. Starting Up Your Business

If you're just starting out, there are a number of tasks you'll need to complete before or soon after you start doing business. These include:

- choosing the legal form for your business (see Chapter 2)
- choosing a name for your business (see Chapter 3)
- deciding where to set up your office (see Chapter 4)
- obtaining business licenses and permits and a federal taxpayer ID number (see Chapter 5)
- obtaining insurance for your business and yourself (see Chapter 6), and

- setting up at least a rudimentary bookkeeping system (see Chapter 14).

You should read the chapters discussing these tasks first.

2. Ongoing Legal and Tax Issues

Once your business is up and running, there are a number of ongoing legal and tax issues you may have to tackle. These include:

- deciding how to price your services and taking steps to ensure you get paid (see Chapter 7)
- paying estimated taxes (see Chapter 11)
- keeping track of your tax-deductible business expenses (see Chapters 9 and 14)
- taking steps to ensure the IRS doesn't view you as an employee if you're audited (see Chapter 15)
- using written client agreements (see Chapters 18, 19 and 20)
- dealing with ownership of copyrights, patents and trade secrets you create (see Chapter 17)
- deciding how to help fund your retirement (see Chapter 16), and
- dealing with taxes for employees or independent contractors you hire (see Chapter 13).

You can read the appropriate chapters when a problem arises or read them in advance to help avoid problems in the first place. ■

Choosing the Legal Form
for Your Business

As a self-employed person, one of the most important decisions you have to make is what legal form your business will take. There are several alternatives—and the one you choose will have a big impact on how you're taxed, whether you'll be liable for your business's debts and how the IRS and state auditors will treat you.

There are four main forms in which to organize a business:

- sole proprietorship (see Section A)
- corporation (see Section B)
- partnership (see Section C), or
- limited liability company (see Section D).

If you own your business alone, you need not be concerned about partnerships; this business form requires two or more owners. If, like most self-employed workers, you're running a one-person business, your choice is among being a sole proprietor, forming a corporation or forming a limited liability company.

Don't worry too much about making the wrong decision. Your initial choice about how to organize your business is not engraved in stone. You can always switch to another legal form later. It's common, for example, for self-employed people to start out as sole proprietors, then incorporate later when they become better established and start making a substantial income.

WAYS TO ORGANIZE YOUR BUSINESS

Type of Organization	Main Advantages	Main Disadvantages
Sole Proprietorship (See Section A)	• Simple and inexpensive to create and operate. • Owner reports profit or loss on personal tax return.	• Owner personally liable for business debts. • Not a separate legal entity.
C Corporation (See Section B)	• Clients have less risk from government audits. • Owners have limited personal liability for business debts. • Owners can deduct fringe benefits as business expense. • Owners can split corporate profit among owners and corporation, paying lower overall tax rate.	• More expensive to create and operate than sole proprietorship or partnership. • Double taxation threat because the corporation is a separate taxable entity. • No beneficial employment tax treatment.
S Corporation (See Section B)	• Clients have less risk from government audits. • Owners have limited personal liability for business debts. • Owners can use corporate losses to offset income from other status. • Owners can save on employment taxes by taking distributions instead of salary.	• More expensive to create and operate than sole proprietorship. • Fringe benefits for shareholders are limited.
Partnership (See Section C)	• Simple and inexpensive to create and operate. • Owners report profit or loss on personal tax returns.	• Owners personally liable for business debts. • Two or more owners required. • No beneficial employment tax treatment.
Limited Liability Company (See Section D)	• Owners have limited liability for business debts if they participate in management. • Profit and loss can be allocated differently than ownership interests.	• No beneficial employment tax treatment.

Adapted from *Legal Guide for Starting and Running a Small Business*, by Fred S. Steingold (Nolo).

A. Sole Proprietorships

A sole proprietorship is a one-owner business. It is by far the cheapest and easiest way to legally organize your business. You don't have to get permission from the government to be a sole proprietor or pay any fees, except perhaps for a fictitious business name statement or business license. (See Chapter 5.) You just start doing business; if you don't incorporate or have a partner, you automatically are a sole proprietor. If you're already running a one-person business and haven't incorporated, you're a sole proprietor right now.

The majority of self-employed people are sole proprietors. Most sole proprietors run small operations, but a sole proprietor can hire employees and nonemployees, too. Indeed, some one-owner businesses are large operations with many employees.

All in the Family—Almost
You can share ownership of your business with your spouse and still maintain its status as a sole proprietorship. In the eyes of the law, you are both owners of the business—what the IRS calls co-sole proprietors. You can either split the profits from your business (if you and your spouse file separate returns) or put them all into the family pot if you file a joint return. But only a spouse can be a co-sole proprietor. If any other family members share ownership with you, the business must be organized as a partnership, corporation or limited liability company.

1. Tax Concerns

When you're a sole proprietor, you and your business are one and the same for tax purposes. Sole proprietorships don't pay taxes or file tax returns. Instead, you must report the income you earn or losses you incur on your own personal tax return, IRS Form 1040. If you earn a profit, the money is added to any other income you have—for example, interest income or your spouse's income if you're married and file a joint tax return—and that total is taxed. If you incur a loss, you can use it to offset income from other sources.

Although you are taxed on your total income regardless of its source, the IRS does want to know about the profitability of your business. To show whether you have a profit or loss from your sole proprietorship, you must file IRS Schedule C, Profit or Loss From Business, with your tax return. On this form you list all your business income and deductible expenses. (See Chapter 9.) If you have more than one business, you must file a separate Schedule C for each one.

Sole proprietors are not employees of their proprietorships; they are business owners. Their businesses don't pay payroll taxes on a sole proprietor's income or withhold income tax from their compensation. However, sole proprietors do have to pay self-employment taxes—that is, Social Security and Medicare taxes—on their net self-employment income. (See Chapter 10.) These taxes must be paid four times a year (along with income taxes) in the form of estimated taxes. (See Chapter 11.) Clients don't withhold any taxes from a sole proprietor's compensation, but any client who pays a sole proprietor $600 or more in a year must file Form 1099-MISC with the IRS reporting the payment. (See Chapter 9, Section A.)

EXAMPLE: Annie operates a computer consulting business as a sole proprietor—that is, she is the sole owner of the business. She must report all the income she receives from her clients on her individual tax return, IRS Form 1040, and file Schedule C. She need not file a separate tax return for her business. In one recent year, she earned $50,000 from consulting and had $15,000 in business expenses, leaving a net business income of $35,000. She reports her gross profits from consulting and her business expenses on Schedule C. She must add her $35,000 profit to any other income she has and report the total on her Form 1040. She must pay both income and self-employment taxes on this profit.

IRS AUDIT RATES ARE HIGHER FOR SOLE PROPRIETORS

As the following chart shows, among businesses, sole proprietors generally are most likely to be audited by the IRS. Only corporations with assets over $1 million are audited more often than sole proprietors earning less than $25,000 or more than $100,000; only corporations with $250,000 or more in assets are audited more than sole proprietors earning $25,000 to $100,00.

This undoubtedly reflects the IRS's belief that sole proprietors habitually underreport their income, take deductions to which they're not entitled or otherwise cheat on their taxes.

The IRS is particularly suspicious of sole proprietors who report very small incomes from their businesses. This is shown by the high audit rates for sole proprietors with incomes below $25,000.

However, because the chances of being audited are still relatively low, this factor alone should not dictate your choice of business form.

	1998 Audit Rate	1999 Audit Rate
Sole Proprietors		
Income under $25,000	2.69%	2.43%
$25,000 to $100,000	1.30%	0.93%
$100,000 and over	2.40%	1.48%
Partnerships	0.43%	0.33%
S Corporations	0.81%	0.55%
C Corporations		
Assets under $250,000	0.46%	0.29%
$250,000 to $1 million	1.68%	1.10%
$1 million to $5 million	4.93%	2.96%

2. Liability Concerns

One concern many business owners have is liability—that is, whether and to what extent they are responsible for paying their business's debts and paying judgments entered against their business in a lawsuit.

a. Business debts

When you're a sole proprietor, you are personally liable for all the debts of your business. This means that a business creditor—a person or company to whom you owe money for items you use in your business—can go after all your assets, both business and personal. This may include, for example, your personal bank accounts, your car and even your house. Similarly, a personal creditor—a person or company to whom you owe money for personal items—can go after your business assets, such as business bank accounts and equipment.

> **EXAMPLE:** Arnie, a sole proprietor consultant, fails to pay $5,000 to a supplier. The supplier sues him in small claims court and wins a $5,000 judgment. As a sole proprietor, Arnie is personally liable for this judgment. This means the supplier can not only tap Arnie's business bank account, but his personal savings accounts as well. And the supplier can also go after Arnie's personal assets such as his car and home.

Fortunately, however, some of your personal property is safe from the reach of creditors. How much of your property is protected depends on the state in which you live. For example, depending on how much they are worth, creditors may not be allowed to take your car, your business tools or your home and furnishings.

The fact that most of what you own is fair game to satisfy all debts is probably the main drawback of setting up your business as a sole proprietorship. However, bankruptcy is always an option if your debts get out of control.

A MINI-COURSE ON BANKRUPTCY

By filing for bankruptcy, you can partly or wholly wipe out your debts and get a fresh financial start. There are two types of bankruptcy for individuals.

- Chapter 7 bankruptcy is the more familiar liquidation bankruptcy, in which many of your debts are wiped out completely without any further repayment. In exchange, you might have to surrender some of your property so it can be sold to pay your creditors. Most people who file for Chapter 7 bankruptcy don't have anything to turn over to their creditors, however. The whole process takes about three to six months and commonly requires only one trip to the courthouse. You can probably do it yourself, without a lawyer.

- Chapter 13 bankruptcy is a reorganization bankruptcy in which you rearrange your financial affairs, repay a portion of your debts and put yourself back on your financial feet. You repay your debts through a Chapter 13 plan. Under a typical plan, you make monthly payments to the bankruptcy court for three to five years. The money is distributed to your creditors. If you finish your repayment plan, any remaining unpaid balance on the unsecured debts is wiped out.

For a complete discussion of bankruptcy and the types and amounts of property that your creditors can't reach, see:

- *How to File for Chapter 7 Bankruptcy,* by Stephen Elias, Albin Renauer, Robin Leonard & Kathleen Michon and
- *Chapter 13 Bankruptcy: Repay Your Debts,* by Robin Leonard.
(Both are published by Nolo.)

b. Lawsuits

If you're a sole proprietor, you'll also be personally liable for business-related lawsuits—for example, if someone slips and falls at your business location and sues for damages. Fortunately, you can obtain insurance to protect yourself against these types of risks. (See Chapter 6.)

3. Audit Concerns

If you are a self-employed person who does work for a client, you are generally considered an independent contractor (IC) of the client. In some cases, however, a self-employed person's relationship to a client will have qualities that make it look more like an employer-employee relationship. When this happens, the government will call you an employee of the client—whether or not you and the client view the relationship that way. This employee label can have serious tax consequences—both for you and for your client.

Because of these disastrous consequences—which include heavy fines and back taxes—most companies will only hire self-employed people whom they are certain will be viewed by the government as independent contractors and not as employees. One thing the client will look at is what sort of business entity you are.

A disadvantage of the sole proprietorship form is that it won't help you establish that you're self-employed in the eyes of the IRS or state auditors. Sole proprietors who provide services can look a lot like employees—especially if they work on their own without assistants and deposit their compensation in their personal bank account. After all, this is exactly what employees do. For this reason, some hiring firms prefer to hire self-employed people who have incorporated their businesses. (See Section B.)

B. Corporations

The word corporation usually conjures up images of huge businesses such as General Motors or IBM. However, a business doesn't have to be large to be a corporation. Virtually any business can be a corporation, even if it has only one owner. Indeed, most corporations have only a few owners; such small corporations are often called "closely held."

Relatively few self-employed people are incorporated, but this doesn't mean you shouldn't consider this form for your business. Incorporating your business can result in tax savings, limit your liability for business debts and even help you get clients.

1. What Is a Corporation?

A corporation is a legal form in which you can organize and conduct a business and share in the profits or losses. Unlike a sole proprietorship, it has a legal existence distinct from its owners. It can hold title to property, sue and be sued, have bank accounts, borrow money, hire employees and do anything else in the business world that a human being can do.

In theory, every corporation consists of three groups:
- those who direct the overall business, called directors
- those who run the business day-to-day, called officers, and
- those who just invest in the business, called shareholders.

However, in the case of a small business corporation, these three groups often boil down to the same person—that is, a single person can direct and run the corporation and own all the corporate stock. So if you incorporate your one-person business, you don't have to go out and recruit and pay a board of directors or officers.

2. Your Employment Status

When you incorporate your business, you automatically become an employee of your corporation if you continue to work in the business, whether full time or part time. This is so even if you're the only shareholder and are not subject to the direction and control of anybody else. In effect, you wear two hats—you're both an owner and an employee of the corporation.

> **EXAMPLE:** Ellen, an independent truck driver, forms a one-person trucking corporation, Ellen's Trucking, Inc. She owns all the stock and runs the business. The corporation hires her as an employee with the title of president.

When you have incorporated your business, clients hire your corporation, not you personally. You will sign any written agreement on behalf of your corporation. When you're paid, the client should issue the check to your corporation and you should deposit it in your corporate bank account, not your personal account. You can then pay the money to yourself in the form of salary, bonus or dividends. The method you choose to pay yourself can have important tax consequences. (See Section B5.)

Social Security and Medicare taxes must be withheld from any employee salary your corporation pays you and money must be paid to the IRS just as for any employee. (See Chapter 8, Section A.) However, your total Social Security and Medicare taxes are about the same as if you were a sole proprietor. They're just paid from two different accounts; half are paid by your corporation and half are withheld from your salary. Since all the money is yours, there is no practical difference from being a sole proprietor. Some additional state payroll taxes will be due, however—mostly state unemployment taxes. (See Chapter 8, Section A.)

You can also have your corporation provide you with employee fringe benefits such as health insurance and pension benefits. (See Section 6d.)

SELF-EMPLOYED BY ANY OTHER NAME

Strictly speaking, when you incorporate your business, you are no longer self-employed; you are an employee of your corporation. Your corporation is neither legally self-employed nor an employee of the clients or customers for whom it provides services or produces products. Only individual human beings can be self-employed or employees.

However, people who own single-shareholder corporations and sell services to clients still often refer to themselves as self-employed when they communicate with clients and customers and other self-employed people. This is understandable since their employee status is mainly a legal technicality.

---

3. Audit Risks

Many potential clients are fearful of hiring self-employed people because they are afraid they could get in trouble if the IRS audits them and claims the workers should have been treated as employees. (See Chapter 15.) For years, tax experts have believed that firms that hire corporations have a much smaller chance of having worker classification problems with the IRS than firms that hire sole proprietors to do the same work. This is because taking the time and trouble to incorporate is strong evidence that a worker is operating an independent business.

The IRS confirmed this view in a manual issued in 1996 to train IRS auditors on how to determine the status of workers. (See Chapter 15.) The manual provides that an incorporated worker will usually not be treated as an employee of the hiring firm, but instead as an employee of the worker's corporation.

Because of this clear direction from the IRS, some hiring firms try to avoid hiring sole proprietors or partnerships and deal with incorporated businesses only. Others give preference to a corporation if they have a choice between hiring a sole proprietor and a corporation. The ability to get more business may alone justify the time and expense involved in incorporating.

Incorporating may be particularly helpful if you're a computer programmer, systems analyst, engineer or drafter, or if you perform similar technical services. Because special IRS rules make it harder for firms that hire such workers to win IRS worker classification audits, hiring firms generally classify them as employees. But they may make an exception if you're incorporated and they are able to hire your corporation instead of hiring you personally.

However, don't get the idea that you and your clients need not worry about the IRS at all if you incorporate. The IRS also directs that an incorporated worker may be reclassified as an employee of the hiring firm if the worker does not follow corporate formalities or otherwise abuses the corporate form. IRS auditors may disregard your corporate status and find that you're a hiring firm's employee if you act like one—for example, if you:

- deposit your earnings directly into your personal bank account instead of putting them into a separate corporate account
- fail to file tax returns for your corporation
- don't issue yourself stock, or
- fail to follow other corporate formalities, such as holding an annual meeting or keeping corporate records. (See Section B8.)

IRS DOCKS DOC, BUT NOT M.D., INC.

One case from 1995 shows why many clients prefer to hire corporations rather than sole proprietors. An outpatient surgery center hired two doctors to work as administrators. They both performed the same services. However, one of the doctors had formed a medical corporation of which he was an employee. The surgery center signed a written contract with the corporation, not the doctor. It also paid the doctor's corporation, not the doctor. The other doctor was a sole proprietor and had no written contract with the center.

The court concluded that the incorporated doctor was not an employee of the surgery center, but the unincorporated doctor was an employee. As a result, the center had to pay substantial back taxes and penalties for the unincorporated doctor, but not for the doctor who was incorporated. (*Idaho Ambucare Center v. U.S.*, 57 F.3d 752 (9th Cir. 1995).)

4. Liability Concerns

The main reason many business owners consider forming a corporation is to avoid personal liability for business debts and lawsuits. While incorporating your business can insulate you from liability to a certain extent, the protection is not nearly as great as most people think.

a. Business debts

Corporations were created to enable people to invest in businesses without risking all their personal assets if the business failed or became unable to pay its debts. In theory, corporation owners are not personally liable for corporate debts or lawsuits. That is, they can lose what they invested in the corporation, but corporate creditors can't go after their personal assets such as their personal bank accounts or homes.

This theory holds true where large corporations are concerned. If you buy stock in IBM, for example, you don't have to worry about IBM's creditors suing you. But it often doesn't work that way for small corporations. Major creditors (like banks) are probably not going to let you shield your personal assets by incorporating. Instead, they will likely demand that you personally guarantee business loans or extensions of credit—that is, sign a legally enforceable document pledging your personal assets to pay the debt if your business assets fall short. This means that you will be personally liable for the debt, just as if you were a sole proprietor. (See Section A.)

You can avoid having to make a personal guarantee for some business debts. These will most likely be routine and small debts. It's not likely, for example, that your office supply store will make you personally guarantee that your corporation will pay for its purchases. But, of course, if it gets wise to the fact that your business is not paying its bills, it won't extend you any more credit.

b. Lawsuits

Being incorporated can also shield you from personal liability for some types of business-related lawsuits. For example, you can avoid being personally liable if an employee or self-employed person you hire accidentally harms someone while working for you.

> **EXAMPLE:** Jane, a graphic designer, has incorporated her business. She is the sole shareholder and president of Jane's Graphics, Inc. Her corporation employs Bill as an assistant. He runs over and injures a pedestrian, Steve, while delivering some designs to a client. Steve sues the corporation and obtains a judgment against

it. Since Jane's business is a corporation, she is not personally liable for the damages. Steve can collect against Jane's corporate bank accounts and even force her to sell her corporation's assets, but can't go after her personal assets such as her personal bank accounts or house.

However, as a practical matter, incorporating is no substitute for a good insurance policy protecting you from the cost of lawsuits. As the above example shows, even if you incorporate, all the assets of your business will be available to satisfy any court judgment. Your corporate assets will probably amount to a large portion of your total net worth.

In addition, you can't use a corporation to shield yourself from personal liability for your own professional negligence. (See Section B10c—and see Chapter 6 for details on obtaining liability insurance.)

5. Basics of Corporate Taxation

When it comes to federal income tax, there are two very different types of corporations:

- C corporations, sometimes called regular corporations (see Section 6), and
- S corporations, also called small business corporations (see Section 7).

Basically, C corporations pay taxes and S corporations don't. You have the option of forming either type of corporation. Each has its benefits and drawbacks. Generally, S corporations are best for small businesses that have little income or suffer losses. C corporations are often advantageous for very successful businesses with substantial

profits. You can start out as an S corporation and switch to a C corporation later, or vice versa.

 If, after reading this chapter, you're not sure whether a C or S corporation is best for you, consult an accountant or other tax professional for help. (See Chapter 21.)

As explained below, you can save money on taxes by incorporating. There are some less tangible benefits as well. For one thing, small corporations are audited much less often than sole proprietorships. And, even when small corporations are audited, the IRS seems to take a less rigorous look at their tax deductions than it does for sole proprietors.

 For additional information on corporate taxation, see:
- *Tax Savvy for Small Business,* by Frederick W. Daily (Nolo)
- IRS Publication 542, *Tax Information on Corporations,* and
- IRS Publication 589, *Tax Information on S Corporations.*

You can obtain these IRS publications free by calling the IRS at: 800-TAX-FORM; if you have a computer, you can also download them from the IRS website at www.irs.gov.

6. Taxes for C Corporations

When you form a corporation, it automatically becomes a C corporation for federal tax purposes. C corporations are treated separately from their owners for tax purposes. C corporations must pay income taxes on their net income and file their own tax returns with the IRS using either Form 1120 or Form 1120-A. They also have their own income tax rates, which are lower than individual rates at some income levels. C corporations generally take the same deductions as sole proprietorships to determine their net profits, but can take some additional deductions as well. This separate tax identity is a unique attribute of C corporations and can lead to tax savings.

a. Income splitting

When you form a C corporation, you take charge of two separate taxpayers: your corporation and yourself. You don't pay personal income tax on income your incorporated business earns until it is distributed to you in the form of salary, bonuses or dividends. This allows you to split the income your business earns with your corporation. You can save on income tax this way because corporate tax rates can be lower than your personal tax rate. A C corporation pays less income tax than an individual on the first $75,000 of taxable income. (See the chart in Section 6C below.)

You can keep up to $250,000 of your business earnings in your corporation without penalty—that is, you can let it stay in the corporate bank account. You can use this money to expand your business, buy equipment or to pay yourself employee benefits such as health insurance and pension benefits. However, if you keep more than $250,000, you'll become subject to an extra 39.6%

tax called the accumulated earnings tax. This tax is intended to discourage you from sheltering too much money in your corporation.

There is another substantial tax benefit to income splitting: you don't have to pay Social Security and Medicare taxes, also called employment taxes, on profits you retain in your corporation. This is a 15.3% tax; so, for example, if you retain $10,000 in your corporation rather than paying it to yourself as salary, you'll save $1,530 in taxes.

> **EXAMPLE:** Betty owns and operates her own incorporated construction contracting business. In one year, the corporation has a net profit of $20,000 after paying Betty a healthy $100,000 salary. Rather than pay herself the $20,000 in the form of additional salary or bonuses, Betty decides to leave the money in her corporation. She uses the money to buy equipment and pay salaries of her employees. The corporation pays only a 15% tax on these retained earnings. Had Betty taken the $20,000 as salary, she would have had to pay most of it to the government: 36% as income tax and 15.3% as employment tax.

b. Consultants and other professionals

Income splitting is usually not a viable option if you're a consultant or engage in certain other occupations involving professional services. The IRS calls corporations formed by such people personal service corporations. These corporations are required to pay corporate tax at a special flat 35% rate.

Corporations formed by self-employed consultants are personal service corporations if all of the corporation's stock is owned by consultants who are corporate employees. Consulting means getting paid just to give a client your advice or counsel. You're not a consultant if you get paid only if the client buys something from you or from someone else through you. Unfortunately, huge numbers of self-employed people qualify as consultants.

> **EXAMPLE:** Acme Corporation hires Data Analysis, Inc., a C corporation solely owned by Tony, a data analyst, to determine its data processing needs. Tony, who is an employee of his corporation, studies Acme's business and recommends the type of data and information its employees need. Tony doesn't provide Acme with computer hardware or software; he just makes recommendations about how Acme's data processing system should be designed.
>
> Tony is considered a consultant and his corporation is a personal service corporation because all the stock is owned by consultant-employees—that is, by Tony. The corporation will be subject to a flat 35% tax rate.

A corporation will also qualify as a personal service corporation if all the stock is owned by corporate employees performing the following activities or professions:

- accounting
- engineering
- law
- health services—including doctors, nurses, dentists or other health care professionals
- performing arts, or
- actuarial science.

Because the 35% tax rate for personal service corporations is so high, their owners will usually end up paying more taxes for leaving money in the corporation than for taking it out of the business in the form of salary, bonuses and fringe benefits and paying taxes on it at their individual tax rates. Individual rates are lower than the 35% personal service corporation tax rate at income levels below $141,250 for individuals and $179,950 for married people filing joint returns. (See the chart below).

> **EXAMPLE:** Max, a self-employed engineer, forms his own corporation; it qualifies as a personal service corporation because he owns all the stock and is the corporation's employee. His business earned $100,000 in one recent year. If Max takes all the earnings out of his corporation in the form of salary, he'll pay a maximum 30% individual income tax. But if he leaves any money in his corporation, it will be taxed at the 35% personal service corporation tax rate.

If your corporation qualifies as a personal service corporation and you think you might not be able to take all the profits out of the business, consider electing S corporation status. This way, all corporate profits will automatically pass to you each year and you'll avoid corporate taxes altogether. (See Section B7.)

c. Comparison of tax rates

The following chart offers a comparison of the tax rates for individuals, corporations and personal service corporations.

The individual income tax brackets shown above are adjusted annually for inflation. This table shows the 2002 brackets. For the current brackets, see IRS Publication 505, Tax Withholding and Estimated Tax. You can obtain a copy free by calling the IRS at: 800-TAX-FORM; if you have a computer, you can download it from the IRS website at www.irs.gov.

d. Fringe benefits

The other significant tax benefit of forming a C corporation is that your corporation can provide you—its employee—with fringe benefits, then deduct the entire cost from the corporation's income as a business expense. No other form of business entity can do this.

Possible employee fringe benefits include:

2000 INDIVIDUAL AND CORPORATE TAX RATES

Taxable Income	Individual Rate (Single)	Individual Rate (Married Filing Jointly)	Corporate Rate (Other than personal service corporations)	Personal Service Corporation Rate
Up to $6,000	10%	10%	15%	35%
$6,001–$12,000	15%	10%	15%	35%
$12,001–$27,950	15%	15%	15%	35%
$27,951–$46,701	27%	15%	15%	35%
$46,701–$50,000	27%	27%	15%	35%
$50,001–$67,700	27%	27%	25%	35%
$67,701–$75,000	30%	27%	34%	35%
$75,001–$100,000	30%	27%	34%	35%
$100,001–$112,850	30%	27%	39%	35%
$112,851–$141,250	30%	30%	39%	35%
$141,251–$171,950	30%	35%	39%	35%
$171,951–$307,050	35%	35%	39%	35%
$307,051–$335,00	38.6%	38.6%	39%	35%
$335,000–$10,000,000	38.6%	38.6%	34%	35%

- health insurance for you and your family members
- disability insurance
- reimbursement of medical expenses not covered by insurance
- deferred compensation plans
- group term life insurance
- retirement plans, and
- death benefit payments up to $5,000.

You need not include the value of premiums or other payments your corporation makes for these benefits in your personal income for income tax purposes. With health insurance costs skyrocketing, the ability to fully deduct these expenses is one of the best reasons to form a C corporation.

EXAMPLE: Marilyn incorporates her marketing business and is its only employee. Marilyn's corporation provides her with health insurance for her and her family at a cost of $6,000 per year. The entire cost can be deducted from the corporation's income for corporate income tax purposes, but is not included as income on Marilyn's personal tax return.

In 2002, sole proprietors, S corporation owners and partners in partnerships were allowed to deduct 70% of their health insurance premiums from their personal income tax. Starting in 2003 and later, this amount increases to 100%. This deduction applies to health insurance for the self-em-porployed worker and his or her spouse and dependents. This means that unincorporated self-employed people and S corporation owners will be on an equal footing with C corporations, at least in terms of deducting health insurance premiums. However, C corporations still retain an important advantage in the area of health costs: A C corpo-

ration can establish a medical reimbursement plan that reimburses employees for medical expenses not covered by insurance. These costs can be fully deducted by the C corporation as a business expense. In contrast, if an unincorporated self-employed person or S corporation owner pays for uninsured health expenses out of his or her own

THE BUGABOO OF DOUBLE TAXATION

When you're a sole proprietor and you want to take money out of your business for personal use, you can simply write yourself a check. Such a transfer has no tax impact because all of your sole proprietorship profits are taxed to you personally. It makes no difference whether you leave the money in the business or put it in your personal bank account.

Things are very different when you form a C corporation. Any direct payment of your corporation's profits to you will be considered a dividend by the IRS and taxed twice. First, the corporation will pay corporate income tax on the profit and then you'll pay personal income tax on it. This is called double taxation.

However, this problem rarely arises with small corporations. Ordinarily, you'll be an employee of your corporation and the salary, benefits and bonuses you receive will be deductible expenses for corporate income tax purposes. If you handle things right, your employee compensation will eat up all the corporate profits so there's no taxable income left on which your corporation will have to pay income tax. You'll only pay income tax once on your employee compensation.

EXAMPLE: Al has incorporated his consulting business. He owns all the stock and is the company's president and sole employee. In one recent year, the corporation earned $100,000 in profits. During that year, Al's corporation paid him an $80,000 salary and a $20,000 Christmas bonus. The salary and bonus are tax-deductible corporate business expenses, leaving the corporation with a net profit of zero. As a result, Al's corporation pays no income taxes. Al simply pays personal income tax on the income he received from the corporation, just as any other employee would.

The only time you might have a problem with double taxation is when your business profits are so great you can't reasonably pay them all to yourself in the form of employee compensation. The IRS only allows corporate owner-employees to pay themselves a reasonable salary for work they actually perform. Any amounts that are deemed unreasonable are treated as disguised dividends by the IRS and are subject to double taxation. One way to avoid this is to leave the excess profits in your corporation and distribute them to yourself as salary, bonus or benefits in future years.

pocket, the personal income tax deduction is limited to amounts exceeding 7.5% of adjusted gross income.

e. Interest-free loans

Yet another benefit of forming a C corporation is that the shareholders can borrow up to $10,000 from the corporation free of interest. If you borrow any more than that, however, you must either pay interest or pay tax on the amount of interest you should have paid. The interest rate is determined by IRS tables. No other form of business entity offers this benefit.

Borrowing money from your corporation is a very attractive option because the loan is not taxable income to you. However, shareholder loans must be true loans. As proof of the loan's veracity, you should sign a promissory note obligating you to repay it on a specific date or in regular installments. The loan should also be secured by your personal property, such as your house or car.

7. Taxes for S Corporations

When you incorporate, you have the option of having your corporation taxed as an S corporation for federal income tax purposes. An S corporation is taxed like a sole proprietorship. Unlike a C corporation, it is not a separate taxpaying entity. Instead, the corporate income and losses are passed through directly to the shareholders—that is, you and anyone else who owns your business along with you. The shareholders must split the taxable profit according to their shares of stock ownership and report that income on their individual tax returns.

An S corporation normally pays no taxes, but must file an information return with the IRS on Form 1120S, indicating how much the business earned or lost and each shareholder's portion of the corporate income or loss.

> **EXAMPLE:** Alice owns ABC Programming, Inc., an S corporation, and is its sole shareholder and sole employee. In one year, ABC earned $100,000 in gross income and had $90,000 in deductions, including an $80,000 salary for Alice. The corporation's $10,000 net profit is passed through directly to Alice, who must report it as income on her personal tax return. The S corporation files an information return with the IRS on Form 1120S, but pays no income taxes itself.

S corporations have become very popular with small business owners in recent years. Owning an S corporation can give you the best of both worlds. You're taxed as a sole proprietor, which is simpler than having a C corporation and is particularly helpful when you're first starting out and have little business income (or perhaps even losses). At the same time, you still have the limited liability of a corporation owner. And there's one added benefit: You can save on self-employment taxes by setting up an S corporation.

a. Deducting business losses

You must report income or loss from an S corporation on your individual tax return. This means that if your business has a loss, you can deduct it from income from other sources, including your spouse's income if you're married and file a joint return. You can't do this with a C corporation because it's a separate taxpaying entity; its losses must be subtracted from its income and can't be directly passed on to you. The ability to deduct business losses on your personal tax return may be particularly helpful when you're first starting out, if you have incurred business losses you can use to reduce your total taxable income.

EXAMPLE: Jack and Johanna are a married couple who file a joint income tax return. Johanna earns $80,000 a year from her job. Jack quits his job as an employee-salesperson and becomes self-employed. He forms an S corporation with himself as the sole share-holder and only employee. In his first year in business his company earns $20,000 and has $40,000 in expenses. Jack and Johanna report this $20,000 loss on their joint tax return and subtract it from their total taxable income. Since Johanna's $80,000 salary puts them in the 27% marginal income tax bracket (see Section 6c), they've saved $5,400 in income tax (27% x $20,000).

b. No income splitting

When you operate an S corporation, you can't split your income between two separate taxpay-ing entities as you can with a C corporation. If your business does well, income splitting can re-duce your federal income taxes because C corpo-rations may pay less tax than individuals on prof-its up to $75,000. (See Section 6a.) (Whether C corporations actually pay less tax or not depends on their exact income—for example, they pay more than married taxpayers on amounts up to $12,000, but less on amounts from $12,001 to $75,000; see the chart in Section 6c for more de-tails.)

But the inability to split your income between yourself and your S corporation may be a draw-back only in theory. Income splitting is a viable option only if your business earns enough money

for you to leave some in your corporate bank ac-count, rather than distributing it all to yourself in the form of salary, bonuses and benefits. Many self-employed people don't make enough money to even consider income splitting—particularly when they're first starting out. If you start making so much money that you want to split income, you can always convert your S corporation to a C corporation.

c. Self-employment tax

A little-known tax benefit of forming an S corpo-ration is that it can save you Social Security and Medicare tax. This is a flat 15.3% tax on your first $84,900 in income in 2002; the ceiling is adjusted annually for inflation. If you earn more than that amount, you pay a 2.9% Medicare tax on the excess.

If you're a sole proprietor, partner in a partner-ship or limited liability company member, all the income you receive from your business is subject to these taxes, called self-employment taxes. (See Chapter 10.) If you incorporate your business and you are an employee of your corporation, the same 15.3% tax must be paid. You pay half out of your employee compensation and your corpora-tion pays the other half.

Whether you are a sole proprietor, partner in a partnership, limited liability company member or employee of your C corporation, you must pay Social Security and Medicare taxes on all the in-come you take home.

Only S corporations offer you a way to take home some money without paying these taxes. You report your corporation's earnings on your personal tax return and you must pay Social Secu-rity and Medicare taxes on any employee salary your S corporation pays you. You do not, how-ever, have to pay such tax on distributions from your S corporation—that is, on the net profits that pass through the corporation to you personally. The larger your distribution, the less Social Secu-rity and Medicare tax you'll pay.

EXAMPLE: Mel, a consultant, has formed an S corporation of which he's the sole shareholder and only employee. In one year, his corporation had a net income of $50,000. If Mel pays this entire amount to himself as employee salary, he and his corporation will have to pay Social Security and Medicare tax on all $50,000—a total tax of $7,650.

Instead, Mel decides to pay himself only a $30,000 salary. The remaining $20,000 is passed through the S corporation and reported as an S corporation distribution on Mel's personal income tax return, not employee salary. No Social Security or Medicare tax need be paid on this amount. Mel pays only $4,590 in Social Security and Medicare taxes instead of $7,650—a tax saving of $3,060.

Theoretically, if you took no salary at all, you would not owe any Social Security and Medicare taxes. As you might expect, however, this is not allowed. The IRS requires S corporation shareholder-employees to pay themselves a reasonable salary—at least what other businesses pay for similar services.

When you reduce your Social Security tax in this way, you might receive smaller Social Security benefits when you retire, since benefits are based on your contributions. However, you can more than offset this by putting the money you save into a tax-advantaged retirement plan such as an IRA, SEP-IRA or Keogh Plan. You'll probably earn more money from your contributions to such plans than you'd collect from making a similar contribution to Social Security. In addition, your contributions to such plans are usually tax deductible and you can start taking the money out when you reach age 59 1/2. In contrast, you can't collect Social Security until you're at least 62.

d. S corporation rules

There are some IRS rules on who can establish an S corporation and how these corporations must be operated. For example:

- an S corporation can only have 75 shareholders
- none of the shareholders can be nonresident aliens—that is, noncitizens who don't live in the United States
- an S corporation can have only one class of stock—for example, you can't create preferred stock giving some shareholders special rights, and
- the shareholders can only be individuals, estates or certain trusts—a corporation can't be an S corporation shareholder.

If you're running a one-person business, are a U.S. citizen or live in the U.S. and will be the only shareholder, these restrictions will not affect your S corporation operations at all.

e. How to elect S corporation status

To establish an S corporation, you must first form a regular corporation under your state law. (See Section B9.) Then you file Form 2553 with the IRS. If you want your corporation to start off as an S corporation, you must file the form within 75 days of the start of the tax year for your business.

f. State tax rules

Check with your state's corporation office to find out how an S corporation files and pays state taxes. Typically, states impose a minimum annual corporate tax or franchise fee. You may also face a state corporation tax on S corporation income—for example, California imposes a 1.5% tax on S corporation profits in addition to a minimum annual franchise tax of $800. However, you can deduct any state and local taxes from your federal income taxes as business expenses.

8. Disadvantages of the Corporate Form

There are some disadvantages to incorporating. You'll have to pay some taxes and fees that other business entities don't pay. And you'll have to maintain some minimal corporate formalities that will take some time and effort.

a. Corporate formalities

The IRS and state corporation laws require corporations to hold annual shareholder meetings and document important decisions with corporate minutes, resolutions or written consents signed by the directors or shareholders. Fortunately, this is usually not a substantial burden for small businesses with only one or a few shareholders and directors. They usually dispense with holding real annual meetings. Instead, the secretary of the corporation prepares minutes for a meeting that takes place only on paper. There are also standard minute and consent forms you can use to ratify important corporate decisions.

If you're audited and the IRS discovers that you have failed to comply with corporate formalities, you may face drastic consequences. For example, if you fail to document important tax decisions and tax elections with corporate minutes or signed consents, you may lose crucial tax benefits and risk substantial penalties. Even worse, if you neglect these basic formalities, the IRS or a court may conclude that your corporation is a sham—and you may lose the limited liability afforded by your corporate status. This could leave you personally liable for corporate debts.

In addition, banks, trust, escrow and title companies, landlords and others often insist on a copy of a board or shareholder resolution approving a corporate transaction with that institution, such as borrowing money or renting property.

 For information on handling corporate formalities in a streamlined manner, see *The Corporate Minutes Book: The Legal Guide to Taking Care of Corporate Business*, by Anthony Mancuso (Nolo).

b. More complex bookkeeping

It is absolutely necessary that you maintain a separate corporate bank account if you incorporate. You'll need to keep a more complex set of books than you would as a sole proprietor. You'll also need to file a somewhat more complex tax return, or file two returns if you form a C corporation. And, since you'll be an employee of your corporation, you'll need to pay yourself a salary and file employment tax returns. (See Chapter 8.) All this costs time and money.

 You'll probably want to use the services of an accountant or bookkeeper, at least when you first start out. Such a seasoned pro may be able to set up a bookkeeping system for you, make employment tax payments, provide guidance about tax deductions and prepare your tax returns.

 If you have a computer, you can also use accounting software packages for small businesses, such as *QuickBooks, Mind Your Own Business, Peachtree Accounting* and many others.

c. Some increased taxes and fees

Finally, there are some fees and taxes you'll have to pay if you incorporate that are not required if you're a sole proprietor. For example, since you'll be an employee of your corporation, it will have to provide unemployment compensation for you.

(See Chapter 9.) The cost varies from state to state, but is at least several hundred dollars per year.

You'll also have to pay a fee to your state to form your corporation and you may have to pay additional fees throughout its existence. In most states, the fees are about $100 to $300. At least one state—California—imposes much higher fees. In California, you must pay the state $900 to incorporate (although small corporations may pay $600 instead). You also have to pay a minimum $800 franchise tax to the state every year, even if your corporation has no profits. Fortunately, you can deduct any state and local fees and taxes as business expenses for your federal income taxes.

9. Forming a Corporation

You create a corporation by filing the necessary forms and paying the required fees with your appropriate state agency—usually the Secretary of State or Corporations Commissioner. Each state specifies the forms to use and the filing cost.

You'll also need to choose a name for your corporation (see Chapter 3), adopt corporate bylaws, issue stock and set up your corporate records. This all sounds complicated, but it really isn't that difficult to do yourself. You can obtain preprinted articles, bylaws and stock certificates and simply fill in the blanks.

For detailed guidance on forming a corporation in any of the 50 states, see *Incorporate Your Business: A 50-State Legal Guide to Forming a Corporation* (Nolo). If you want to incorporate in California, see *How to Form Your Own California Corporation* (Nolo). Both are written by Anthony Mancuso.

THERE'S NO PLACE LIKE HOME FOR INCORPORATING

People who live in high-tax states such as California and New York often hear that they can save money by incorporating in low-tax states such as Nevada or Delaware.

This is a myth. You won't save a dime by incorporating outside your own state. If you form an out-of-state corporation, you will have to qualify to do business in your home state anyway.

This process is similar to incorporating in your state, and it costs the same. You also will have to pay any state corporate income taxes levied in your home state for income earned there. Even if another state has more modern or flexible corporation laws, these mostly favor large, publicly-held corporations, not the small closely-held corporations self-employed people form.

10. Professional Corporations

You may be required to form a special kind of corporation called a professional corporation or professional service corporation if you're involved in certain types of professions. The list of professionals who must form professional corporations varies from state to state, but usually includes:

- accountants
- engineers
- healthcare professionals such as doctors, dentists, nurses, physical therapists, optometrists, opticians and speech pathologists
- lawyers
- psychologists
- social workers, and
- veterinarians.

Call your state's corporate filing office, usually the Secretary of State or your Corporations Commissioner, to see who is covered in your state.

a. Ownership requirements

Typically, a professional corporation must be organized for the sole purpose of performing professional services, and all shareholders must be licensed to render that service. For example, in a medical corporation, all the shareholders must be licensed physicians.

b. Formation requirements

Special forms and procedures must be used to establish a professional corporation—for example, you might be required to obtain a certificate of registration from the government agency regulating your profession, such as the state bar association. Special language will also have to be included in your articles of incorporation.

c. Limits on limited liability

In most states, you can't use a professional corporation to avoid personal liability for your malpractice or negligence—that is, your failure to exercise your professional responsibilities with a reasonable amount of care.

> **EXAMPLE:** Janet, a civil engineer, forms a professional corporation of which she is the sole shareholder. She designs a bridge that collapses, killing dozens of commuters. Even though Janet is incorporated, she is personally liable (along with her corporation) for any damages caused by her negligence in designing the bridge. Janet's personal assets are at risk along with those of her corporation.

You can usually obtain additional business insurance to protect you against these types of risks, but it can be expensive. (See Chapter 6.)

However, if you're a professional involved in a group practice with other professionals, incorporating will shield you from personal liability for malpractice committed by other members of the group.

> **EXAMPLE:** Marcus is a doctor involved in an incorporated medical practice with Susan, Florence and Louis. One of Florence's patients claims she committed malpractice and sues her personally and the group. While both the group and Florence are liable, Marcus is not personally liable for Florence's malpractice. This means his personal assets are not at risk.

COMPARE AND CONTRAST: PROFESSIONAL SERVICE CORPORATIONS

Corporations formed by workers in the fields of consulting, health, law, engineering, architecture, accounting or actuarial science constitute professional service corporations for federal tax purposes if all the stock is owned by employees who perform professional services for the corporation.

Such corporations are subject to a flat 35% corporate income tax. The IRS will apply this tax rate regardless of whether the individuals involved are organized as a professional corporation or a regular corporation under state law.

C. Partnerships

If you are not the sole owner of your business, you can't be a sole proprietor. Instead, you automatically become a partner in a partnership unless you incorporate or form a limited liability company. However, if you co-own your business only with your spouse, you can both still be sole proprietors. (See Section A.)

A partnership is much the same as a sole proprietorship except there are two or more owners. Like a sole proprietorship, a partnership is legally inseparable from the owners (the partners). Unlike corporations, partnerships do not pay taxes, although they file an annual tax form. Instead, partnership income and losses are passed through the partnership directly to the partners and reported on the partners' individual federal tax returns. Partners must file IRS Schedule E with their returns, showing their partnership income and deductions.

Like sole proprietors, partners are neither employees nor independent contractors of their partnership; they are self-employed business owners. A partnership does not pay payroll taxes on the partners' income or withhold income tax. Like sole proprietors, partners must pay income taxes (see Chapter 9) and self-employment taxes (see Chapter 10) on their partnership income.

 For a detailed discussion of partnerships including how to write partnership agreements, see *The Partnership Book,* by Denis Clifford and Ralph Warner (Nolo).

1. Ownership

The main difference between a partnership and a sole proprietorship is that one or more people own the business along with you. This means that, among other things, you have to decide:

- how each partner will share in the partnership profits or losses
- how partnership decisions will be made
- what the duties of each partner are
- what happens if a partner leaves or dies, and
- how disputes will be resolved.

Although not required by law, you should have a written partnership agreement answering these and other questions.

2. Personal Liability

Partners are personally liable for all partnership debts and lawsuits, just like sole proprietors. (See Section A.) This means you'll be personally liable for business debts your partners incurred, whether you knew about them or not.

PARTNERSHIPS COMPARED WITH CORPORATIONS

Partnerships are somewhat cheaper to form and operate than corporations. You don't have to comply with formalities, such as holding annual meetings, or pay registration fees.

However, the fact that you open yourself up to greater liability than in a corporation is a huge drawback. Also, some prospective clients may prefer to hire corporations rather than partnerships because they think they'll face fewer problems with IRS and other government audits. (See Section B3.)

3. Limited Partnerships

A limited partnership is a special kind of partnership with two types of partners. One or more general partners run the partnership business. The other partners are called limited partners—they invest in the partnership but don't help run it. The limited partners are a lot like corporate shareholders in that they aren't personally liable for the partnership's debts. The general partners are treated just like partners in normal partnerships and are liable for all partnership debts and lawsuits.

Limited partnerships are most commonly used for real estate and similar investments. Self-employed people rarely form them. If there are people who want to invest in your business but don't want to work in it or have any personal liability, you'd probably be better off forming a corporation and selling them shares. That way, you'll have the limited liability afforded by corporate status. (See Section B4.)

4. Registered Limited Liability Partnerships

In all states, professionals may set up a special type of partnership called a registered limited liability partnership (RLLP). In some states, including California, certain types of professionals are not allowed to form limited liability companies (LLCs), so RLLPs were established as an alternative.

RLLPs give their partner-owners the same type of limited liability as owners of professional corporations: The partners remain personally liable for their own malpractice, but receive limited liability for any malpractice by other partners in the firm. In addition, in most states the RLLP partners receive personal liability protection from business debts and other type of lawsuits, such as slip-and-fall suits.

RLLPs are limited to professionals in certain occupations—typically people who work in the medical, legal and accounting fields, as well as a few other professions in which a special professional-client relationship is assumed to exist. The list of professionals who may form an RLLP in a particular state is normally the same as the list of those eligible to form a professional corporation.

At least two partners are needed to form an RLLP, and the partners must usually be licensed in the same or related professions.

RLLPs are taxed like any other partnership—that is, they are pass-through tax entities. The owners are taxed on all profits on their individual income tax returns at their individual tax rates. The RLLP itself is not taxed on profits.

For more information in RLLPs, look up your state RLLP law. You can find it on the Internet through Nolo's Legal Research Center at www.nolo.com/research/index.html. Click on your state and then either do a search or browse your state's code to find the RLLP act. You can also try calling your secretary of state or LLC filing office for further information.

D. Limited Liability Companies

The limited liability company, or LLC, is the newest type of business form in the United States. An LLC is taxed like a sole proprietorship or partnership but provides its owners with the same limited liability as a corporation. LLCs have become extremely popular with self-employed people because they are simpler and easier to run than corporations.

For a complete discussion of limited liability companies, see *Form Your Own Limited Liability Company,* by Anthony Mancuso (Nolo).

1. LLC Owners

When LLCs first began in the mid-1990s, most states required that they have two or more owners (or "members"), which made life difficult for people running one-person businesses. This is no longer the case. As of 2002, only Massachusetts requires two or more owners for LLCs.

If you live in Massachusetts and your business only consists of yourself, there is a way around the multi-owner rule. You can have your spouse, or a trusted friend or business associate, fill the second owner slot. You can then provide in your LLC operating agreement that this person has no voting power, leaving you in sole control.

Generally speaking, you are considered a business owner, not an employee, when you form an LLC. If, however, you receive a guaranteed salary or other form of guaranteed pay from the LLC (instead of or in addition to a share in the LLC's profits), then you will be considered an employee of the LLC. For example, if an LLC owner is guaranteed $10,000 per year regardless of profits, the owner is treated as an employee of the LLC, which means the $10,000 is subject to withholding and other employment taxes.

In some states, people involved in certain professions are not allowed to form regular LLCs. Instead, they must form a "professional" LLC and comply with special rules. Typically, these rules provide that only licensed professionals may own a membership interest in the professional LLC, and require each member to carry a specified amount of malpractice insurance. These restrictions usually apply to doctors and other licensed health care professionals, lawyers, accountants and, in some states, engineers.

In a few states, however, professionals such as these are not allowed to form LLCs at all. These states include California and Rhode Island.

Even if you are allowed to form an LLC, doing so may not be advantageous if you are a professional and practice with others, rather than by yourself. This is because LLC laws in most states do not protect an LLC owner from personally liability for the malpractice of another professional in the practice. Thus, if you form an LLC, you could end up being liable for the malpractice of your co-owners. You'd be better off forming a professional corporation or RLLP, both of which will shield you from liability for the malpractice of your co-owners.

2. Tax Treatment

IRS rules permit LLC owners to decide for themselves how they want their LLC to be taxed. An LLC can be taxed as a pass-through entity—like a sole proprietorship, partnership or S corporation—or as a regular C corporation.

a. Pass-through entity

Ordinarily, LLCs are pass-through entities. This means that they pay no taxes themselves. Instead, all profits or losses are passed through the LLC and reported on the LLC members' individual tax returns. This is the same as for a sole proprietorship, S corporation or partnership.

If the LLC has only one member, the IRS treats it as a sole proprietorship for tax purposes. The members' profits, losses and deductions are reported on his or her Schedule C, the same as for any sole proprietor. (See Section A1.)

If the LLC has two or more members, it must prepare and file each year the same tax form used by a partnership—IRS Form 1065, Partnership Return of Income—showing the allocation of profits, losses, credits and deductions passed through to the members. The LLC must also prepare and distribute to each member a Schedule K-1 form showing the member's allocations.

b. Taxation as a C corporation

LLCs have the option of being taxed as a regular C corporation. You can make this election by filing IRS Form 8832 and checking the appropriate box. If you wish to start your LLC out with this tax status, you must file the form within 75 days of the date your LLC Articles of Organization are filed. LLCs that elect corporate tax status must file the same corporate tax returns as a regular C corporation. The LLC pays income taxes on profits left in the business at corporate income tax rates, which can be lower than personal rates. (See Section B6.)

When an LLC chooses to be taxed as a corporation, all of the owners who work for it will become corporate employees. As such, they will be subject to employment taxes, and the LLC must withhold income tax from their pay. The LLC must also pay state and federal unemployment taxes for each owner-employee.

Of course, if you want to be taxed as a C corporation, you can form a C corporation instead of an LLC. The only reason to form an LLC instead of a C corporation in this instance is that an LLC is somewhat simpler and easier to run.

3. Liability Concerns

LLC company owners, called members, enjoy the same limited liability from business debts and lawsuits as corporation owners. You won't be liable for business debts unless you personally guarantee them. (See Section B4.)

4. Pros and Cons

LLCs appear to be a clear favorite over partnerships since they offer the same tax benefits, but also provide limited liability. They are also a serious alternative to forming a corporation, since they offer the same limited liability as a corporation along with some tax advantages.

Whether an LLC is right for you depends on whether the advantages of an LLC outweigh the disadvantages for your business.

a. Advantages of LLCs

LLCs provide the same limited liability as a corporation; however, such "limited liability" is often more mythical than real. (See Sections B4 and B10.)

Setting up an LLC takes about the same amount of time and money as setting up a corporation, but thereafter an LLC is simpler and easier to run. With a corporation, you must hold and record regular and special shareholder meetings to transact important corporate business. Even if you're the only corporate owner, you need to document your decisions. This isn't required for an LLC.

LLCs allow more flexibility in allocating profits and losses among the business's owners than a corporation can. The owners of an S corporation must pay taxes on profits or get the benefits of losses in proportion to their stock ownership. For example, if there are two shareholders and each own 50% of the stock, they must each pay tax on 50% of the corporation's profits or get the benefits of 50% of the losses. In contrast, if you form an LLC, you have near total flexibility on how to allocate profits and losses among the owners—for example, one owner could get 75% of the profits and the other 25%. Of course, this will be useful only if two or more people own your business.

Moreover, an S corporation has less flexibility than an LLC to use borrowed business money to increase the tax deductions of the owners on their

---

CHOOSING A FORM OF BUSINESS

There is no one best business form—and choosing the one that will work best for you can be difficult. It all depends on your goals and preferences. The following chart may help you analyze which business form best furthers your own personal goals.

Goal	Preferred Form of Business
Limit your personal liability	C or S corporation, LLC
Save on Social Security taxes	S corporation
Retain earnings in business	C corporation
Provide tax-deductible benefits to employees, including yourself	C corporation
Deduct losses from your personal taxes	S corporation, LLC, Sole proprietorship, Partnership
Easiest and cheapest to form and operate	Sole proprietorship, Partnership
Avoid state and federal unemployment taxes	Sole proprietorship, LLC, Partnership
Simplest tax returns	Sole proprietorship, Partnership
Added credibility for your business	S or C corporation
Benefit from lower corporate tax rates	C corporation
Distribute high profits	S corporation, LLC, Sole proprietorship, Partnership

annual individual tax returns and lower the tax bite when the business is ultimately sold.

A C corporation cannot allocate profits and losses to shareholders at all. Shareholders get a financial return from the corporation by receiving corporate dividends or a share of the corporate assets when it is sold or liquidated.

LLCs don't have to comply with the rules limiting who can form and own an S corporation. (See Section B7d.)

And finally, LLC members are not employees of the LLC, so the LLC doesn't have to pay federal and state unemployment tax for them. When you form a corporation, you are an employee of the corporation and such taxes must be paid.

b. Disadvantages of LLCs

Perhaps the biggest drawback of LLCs is that they don't offer the opportunity to save on self-employment taxes as an S corporation does. LLC members who actively manage the business must pay self-employment tax on all the income they receive from the LLC—whether in the form of salary or distributions. In contrast, you can save on self-employment taxes by forming an S corporation because S corporation distributions—as opposed to salaries—are not subject to self-employment tax. (See Section B7.)

Moreover, money you retain in a S corporation or C corporation is not subject to self-employment taxes. This is not the case with an LLC that is treated as a pass-through entity. Whether or not you distribute your LLC profits to yourself or leave them in your company, you must pay self-employment taxes on your entire share of LLC profits.

Finally, clients who hire LLCs and pay them more than $600 per year must file Form 1099-MISC with the IRS reporting the amount of the payment. (This requirement doesn't apply only if the LLC has opted to be taxed as a corporation.) Generally speaking, clients do not have to file Form 1099-MISC when they hire a corporation. For this reason, some clients prefer to hire corporations instead of LLCs because they can avoid filing the 1099-MISC form altogether. Clients don't like filing the forms because they often lead to audits.

5. Forming an LLC

To form an LLC, you must file Articles of Organization with your state government. Your company's name will have to include the words "limited liability company" or "LLC" or a similar phrase as set forth in your state law. You should also create a written operating agreement, which is similar to a partnership agreement. (See Section C.)

For a complete explanation of how to form limited liability companies, see *Form Your Own Limited Liability Company* by Anthony Mancuso (Nolo). ■

Choosing and Protecting Your Business Name

This chapter will help you choose a name for your business. This is something you need to do right after you decide on the legal form of your business. (See Chapter 2). You'll need to know what your business name will be to establish bank accounts, print stationery and market your business to others.

Business names are used in different contexts, and the legal rules governing them differ depending on how they are used. A business name may be the name you use:

- to identify your business on your business checking account, invoices, business cards, contracts and letterhead; this is called a trade name or business name
- to market your services or goods; this is called a service mark or trademark, and
- to identify your company or yourself on the Internet; this is called an Internet domain name.

You may be able to use a different name in each of these contexts or use the same or a similar name.

A. Choosing a Trade Name

Your trade name is the name you use to identify your business when you open a business bank account, sign a contract or sue someone in the name of your business. If, like the vast majority of self-employed people, you're a sole proprietor (see Chapter 2, Section A), you can simply use your own name as your business name. For example, Roger Davis calls his consulting business Roger Davis Consulting.

However, you have the option of using a name other than your own as your business name. When a sole proprietor uses a name other than his or her own name, it's called a fictitious business name, assumed name or dba—short for "doing business as."

EXAMPLE: Roseann Zeiss quits her job with a public relations firm and sets up her own public relations business. Roseann is a sole proprietor. She could call her company Roseann Zeiss. She decides to call it AAA Publicity instead so she'll come first in her local business telephone directory.

Self-employed people often prefer to use assumed names instead of their personal names for their businesses to get a jumpstart on marketing. An assumed name can sound jazzier, help identify what your business does or make you seem more businesslike. But there is an added benefit that can be even more useful: It helps to establish your status as an independent contractor. Employees, obviously, don't use business names.

1. Choosing an Assumed Name

Use some care in choosing an assumed name. Avoid using a name that is very similar to that of a local or regional competitor or a large national company in your field. If it is so similar to a name that is already being used that it will confuse the public, you could be sued under state and federal unfair competition laws. If you lose, you may be required to change the name and even pay damages.

Also, make sure your name is not very similar to any famous business name, even if the name is used by a company in a different field—for example, McDonald's, Proctor & Gamble, Honda and the like. Companies with famous names are usually fanatical about protecting them.

Check local business directories, Yellow Pages and other records to see if someone is already using the name you want. (See Section D1.)

2. Registering an Assumed Name

Any person who uses a name other than a surname to identify a business must register the name with the state or county as an assumed or fictitious name. If you fail to register, you'll have all sorts of problems. For example, you may not be able to open a bank account in your business name. You also may be barred from suing on a contract signed with the name.

To register, you usually file a certificate with the county clerk (most likely at your county courthouse) stating who is doing business under the name. In many states, you must publish the statement in a local newspaper. This is intended to help creditors identify the person behind an assumed business name. This makes it easier to track down those people who are in the habit of changing their business names to confuse and avoid creditors.

Some communities have newspapers that specialize in publishing such legal notices. Some states require, instead of or in addition to publication, that you file the statement with the state department of revenue or some other state agency.

Contact your county clerk and ask about the registration requirements in your locale. You'll have to fill out a simple form and pay a fee—usually between $15 and $50. The county clerk will normally check to see if any identical or very similar names have already been registered in the county. If so, you'll have to use another name. It's a good idea to think of several possible names before you attempt to register.

ADDITIONS TO A SURNAME MAY REQUIRE REGISTRATION

You never have to file a fictitious business name statement if you use your full legal name as your business name—for example, if John Smith uses "John Smith" as his business name. However, some states require you to register your name if you use words in addition to your full name—for example, registration might be required if John Smith used "The Smith Group" as his business name. Ask your county clerk about your state's requirements.

---

3. Naming a Corporation or Limited Liability Company

If you form a corporation or limited liability company, you must get permission to use your corporate name by registering it with your Secretary of State or similar official.

a. Registering a corporation name

To register a corporate name, you must follow these three steps:

- **Step 1. Select a permissible name.** All but three states—Maine, Nevada and Wyoming—require you to include a word or its abbreviation indicating corporate status, such as "corporation," "incorporated," "company" or "limited." Several states also require that the name be in English or Roman characters.

- **Step 2. Clear your name.** Next you must make sure that your corporate name is distinguishable from any corporate name already registered in your state. Your state won't register a corporate name that too closely mimics a name already on file. The secretary of state or other corporate filing agency will do a search for you prior to authorizing the use of your name. In about half the states, you may phone to check on the availability of a name in advance. In the others, you must write to request a search. Often you may request a search of more than one name at a time.

- **Step 3. Reserve your corporate name.** A corporation can usually reserve a name before incorporating if the name otherwise qualifies for registration. This freezes out other would-be registrants from claiming that name or names that are deceptively similar during the period of reservation, usually 120 days. Most states permit you to extend the reservation for one or more additional 120-day periods for additional fees.

The reservation process involves sending an application for reservation to the Secretary of State, or the designated office, with a fee. Some states even permit you to reserve a corporate name over the telephone. You can find out your state's procedures by calling the secretary of state or corporate commissioner.

b. Registering a limited liability company name

Registering a name for a limited liability company (LLC) is very similar to registering a corporate name. You must choose a name that conforms with your state's LLC requirements. Most states require you to use the words Limited Liability Company, Limited Company or their abbreviations in your name.

You then call your state LLC filing office and ask personnel there to do a search to see if the name or names you've chosen are available. Most states allow you to reserve LLC names for 30 to 120 days by paying a small fee, usually no more than $50.

For a detailed discussion of LLC name requirements, see *Form Your Own Limited Liability Company*, by Anthony Mancuso (Nolo).

4. Legal Effect of Registering a Name

People often think that once they have complied with all the registration requirements for their trade name, they have the right to use it for all purposes. This isn't so. There are two very different contexts in which a business name may be used.

For bank accounts, creditors and potential lawsuits, the formal name of the business or trade name is used. However, a business may also use a name as a trademark or service mark to market its goods or services.

The registration requirements only control the formal business or trade name. Registering an as-

sumed, corporate or LLC name gives you no ownership rights in the name—that is, you can't prevent others from using it. If someone else is the first to use your name as a mark, it doesn't make any difference whether you or they have previously registered it as an assumed or corporate or LLC name. They will still have the exclusive right to use the name in the marketplace.

Simply put, if the name you have registered was already in use or federally registered as a trademark or service mark, you will have to limit your use of the name to your checkbook and bank account. The minute you try to use the name in connection with marketing your goods or services, you risk infringing the existing trademark or service mark.

If your business name figures in your future marketing plans, you must make sure no one else is using the name as a trademark in addition to complying with the name registration requirements. (See Section B.)

If you plan to market your goods or services on the Internet, then you'll also want to check to see whether someone else has already taken your proposed name as their domain name, which would mean, at the least, that you'd have to use a slightly modified name to do business in cyberspace. (See Section C.)

B. Choosing a Trademark

A trademark is a distinctive word, phrase, logo or other graphic symbol that's used to distinguish one product from another—for example, Ford cars and trucks, Kellogg's cornflakes, IBM computers and Microsoft software.

A service mark is similar to a trademark, except that trademarks promote products while service marks promote services. Some familiar service marks include: McDonald's (fast-food service), Kinko's (photocopying service), Blockbusters (video rental service), CBS's stylized eye in a circle (television network service) and the Olympic Games' multicolored interlocking circles (international sporting event).

The word trademark is also a generic term used to describe the entire broad body of state and federal law that covers how businesses distinguish their products and services from the competition. Each state has its own set of laws establishing when and how trademarks can be protected. There is also a federal trademark law called the Lanham Act (15 U.S.C. § 1050 and following), which applies in all 50 states. Generally, state trademark laws are relied upon for marks used only within one particular state, while the Lanham Act is used to protect marks for products that are sold in more than one state or across territorial or national borders.

If, like many self-employed people, you operate within a single state, you'll have to rely primarily on your state trademark law. But if you do business in more than one state, you can use either the federal or state law. The various trademark laws don't differ greatly except that some state laws allow trademark owners to collect greater damages from infringers than does federal law.

For a detailed discussion of trademarks, see *Trademark: Legal Care for Your Business and Product Name*, by Stephen Elias (Nolo).

1. Trade Names Are Not Trademarks

Your trade name is neither a trademark nor a service mark and is not entitled to trademark protection unless you use it to identify a particular product or service that you produce and sell to the public. Businesses often use shortened versions of their trade names as trademarks—for example, Apple Computer Corporation uses the name Apple as a trademark on its line of computer products.

A trade name acts like a trademark when it is used in such a way that it creates a separate commercial impression—in other words, when it acts to identify a product or service. This can some-

times be hard to figure out, especially when comparing trade names and service marks, because they often both appear in similar places—on letterheads, advertising copy, signs and displays. But some general principles apply:

- If the full name, address and phone are used, it's probably a trade name.
- If a shortened version of the trade name is used, especially with a design or logo beside or incorporating it, the trade name becomes a trademark.

EXAMPLE: Joe, a self-employed computer programmer, calls his unincorporated business Acme Software Development and files a fictitious business name statement with his county clerk. When he uses the name Acme Software Development along with his office address on his stationery, it is just a trade name, not a trademark. However, Joe develops a software utility program that he calls Acme Tools and markets over the Internet. Acme Tools is a trademark.

2. Selecting a Trademark

Not all trademarks are treated equally by the law. The best trademarks are "distinctive"—that is, they stand out in a customer's mind because they are inherently memorable. The more distinctive or "strong" a trademark is, the more legal protection it will receive. Less distinctive or "weak" marks may be entitled to little or no legal protection. Obviously, it is much better to have a strong trademark than a weak one.

Good examples of distinctive marks are arbitrary, fanciful or coined names such as Kodak and Xerox. Examples of poorly chosen marks include:

- personal names, including nicknames, first names, surnames and initials
- marks that describe the attributes of the product or service or its geographic location—for example, marks such as Quick Printing and Oregon Marketing Research

are initially weak and subject to few legal protections until they have been in use long enough to be easily recognized by customers, and

- names with bad translations, unfortunate homonyms (sound-alikes) or unintended connotations—for example, the French soft drink called Pschitt had to be renamed for the U.S. market.

Generally, selecting a mark begins with brainstorming for general ideas. After you have selected several possible marks, the next step is often to use formal or informal market research techniques to see how the potential marks will be accepted by consumers. Next, you have to conduct a trademark search, to find out whether the same or similar marks are already being used.

3. Registering a Trademark

If you use all or part of your business name or any other name as a trademark or service mark, consider registering it. Registration is not mandatory, but it's a good idea: it makes it easier for you to protect your mark against would-be copiers and puts others on notice that the mark is already taken.

If you do business only in one state, register your mark with your state trademark office. Most local service businesses that don't do business across state lines or sell to interstate travelers fall into this category.

If you do business in more than one state, register with the U.S. Patent and Trademark Office in Washington, DC.

To register, you must fill out an application and pay a fee. Be prepared to work with your state or federal trademark officials to get your registration approved. (See the Appendix for a list of state trademark agencies.)

The USPTO has an outstanding website at www.uspto.gov. It contains a good deal of basic information about trademarks and trademark reg-

istration. You can register your trademark online using the Trademark Electronic Application System (TEAS). TEAS allows you to fill out a trademark registration form and check it for completeness over the Internet. You then submit the form directly to the USPTO over the Internet, making an official filing online.

If you don't want to use the Internet, you can call the USPTO at 800-786-9199 and order a number of useful publications about trademarks and trademark registration.

INTENT TO USE REGISTRATION

If you intend to use a trademark on a product or for a service sold in more than one state in the near future, you can reserve the right to use the mark by filing an intent to use registration with the U.S. Patent and Trademark Office (PTO).

If the mark is approved, you have six months to actually use the mark on a product sold to the public and file papers with the PTO describing the use, with an accompanying $100 fee. If necessary, this period may be increased by five additional six-month periods if you have a good explanation for each extension

The ownership becomes effective when you put the mark in use and complete the application process, but ownership will be deemed to have begun on the date you filed the application.

You should promptly file an intent to use registration as soon as you have definitely selected a trademark for a forthcoming product. Your competitors are also trying to come up with good trademarks, and they may be considering using a mark similar to the one you want.

For step-by-step guidance on how to register a trademark, see *Trademark: Legal Care for Your Business and Product Name*, by Stephen Elias (Nolo).

4. Trademark Notice

The owner of a trademark that has been registered with the U.S. Patent and Trademark Office (PTO) is entitled to use a special symbol along with the trademark. This symbol notifies the world of the registration. Use of trademark notices is not mandatory, but makes it much easier for the trademark owner to collect damages in case of infringement. It also deters others from using the mark.

The most commonly used notice for trademarks registered with the PTO is an "R" in a circle—®—but "Reg. U.S. Pat. & T.M. Off." may also be used. The "TM" superscript—™—may be used to denote marks that have been registered on a state basis only or marks that are in use but have not yet officially been registered by the PTO.

Do not use the copyright symbol, or ©, with a mark. It has absolutely nothing to do with trademarks.

5. Enforcing Trademark Rights

Depending on the strength of the mark and whether and where it has been registered, a trademark owner may be able to bring a court action to prevent others from using the same or similar marks on competing or related products.

Trademark infringement occurs when an alleged infringer uses a mark that is likely to cause consumers to confuse the infringer's products with the trademark owner's products. A mark need not be identical to one already in use to infringe upon the owner's rights. If the proposed mark is similar enough to the earlier mark to risk confusing the average consumer, its use will likely be infringement.

COURT CLAMPS DOWN ON COPYCATS

A Sandusky, Ohio, insurance agent invented the term "securance"—a contraction of the words security and insurance—and used it as a service mark to market his insurance services on his stationery, billboard and newspaper advertising and giveaway items such as calendars and pencils. He registered the mark with the State of Ohio and the U.S. Patent & Trademark Office.

Four years later, the Nationwide Mutual Insurance Co. began using the word as its own service mark in its national advertising.

The agent sued the insurer for trademark infringement and won. The court held that the agent had the exclusive right to use the word securance to identify insurance services in the geographic areas in which he did business, since he had been the first to use it. The court ordered the insurer to stop using securance in its advertising in the entire state of Ohio. (*Younker v. Nationwide Mut. Ins. Co.*, 191 N.E.2d 145 (1963).)

C. Choosing an Internet Domain Name

There are millions of business-related sites on the Web. Most national businesses have a website, as do a huge number of small and medium sized businesses offering all types of products and services. Many self-employed people have websites as well.

If you want to create a website, you'll have to choose an Internet domain name, the site's address on the Web.

For a discussion of Internet domain names, see *Domain Names: How to Choose and Protect a Great Name for Your Website*, by attorneys Patti Gima and Stephen Elias (Nolo).

1. What Is a Domain Name?

Every business on the Web has a domain name—a unique address that computers understand. If you enter a particular domain name in a Web browser, the computer will link your computer with the Website connected with the domain name you entered.

Most World Wide Web business addresses consist of two main sections: a beginning section containing the letters http://www and a section containing the domain name itself. For example, the domain name for Nolo's website is www.nolo.com.

2. Clearing a Domain Name

Because each domain name must be unique—so that all the computers attached to the Internet can find it—it is impossible for two different businesses to have the same domain name. If somebody is already using a name you want, you likely won't be able to use it.

It's easy to find out if someone is already using a domain name you want to use. Go to the website www.netsol.com and type in the name you want to use. Then click on "Go." The website will tell you if the name is available or if it is already taken, in which case it will suggest alternatives. Another website can tell you who owns the name you want: www.netsol.com/cgi-bin/whois/whois. Type the domain name in the search field and you will be given access to the registration records for the domain name. These will give the name and contact information for the name owner. It might be possible to purchase the name from the person or company that has it.

3. Registering a Domain Name

If you register your domain name, no one else can use it for the same purpose on the Internet.

Registering a domain name is very easy. There are several private companies that will register a name for you. You just go to one of their websites, type in the name you want and provide your contact information and a credit card number. Two of the best known registration services are Network Solutions, Inc. at www.netsol.com and register.com at www.register.com.

The registration fees these services charge vary, so you might want to check several to see which will give you the best deal.

D. Conducting a Name Search

Before choosing a trade name, trademark or domain name, conduct a name search to see if someone in a related business is already using the same or a very similar name. If the name you want is already in use, choose a different name. Obviously, you don't want to spend money on marketing and advertising a name or mark only to discover it infringes another name or mark and must be changed.

The amount of time and money you should put into such a search depends on the nature of your business and your plans for expansion.

1. Local Searches

If you only do business locally, you can feel reasonably safe if you search for conflicting names at the state and local levels. Check telephone books and business directories for the cities in which you plan to do business, as well as for surrounding areas. Many public libraries have excellent phone book collections. While at the library, look at trade magazines for your industry and compilations of names of related businesses. The reference librarian should be able to help you find these resources.

Also, call your local county clerk's office to ask how you can check assumed business name filings. In most states, assumed or fictitious business name statements are filed with the county clerk's office. Generally, you must go in and check the files in person. It takes just a few minutes to do this. Don't forget to do a search in each county in which you will be doing business.

To make sure no corporation registered in your state is already using the name, call the state office where corporations are registered—usually the Secretary of State or Corporations. Workers there may do a name search for you over the phone or may require that you send a letter requesting a search.

Finally, check the records of your state trademark agency to see if a similar name has already been registered. Many agencies will do a search for you by phone, either free or for a small charge; some require you to request a search by mail. (See Appendix 3 for a list of state trademark agencies.)

2. National Searches

If you intend to do business regionally or nationally, you'll need to do a more widespread national search, generally called a trademark search. A national search is also necessary if you plan to establish a presence on the Internet because you'll be sending your business name all over the country.

You can hire a search firm to do a trademark search for you, or you can do one yourself.

a. Hiring a search firm

Traditionally, most trademark searches were conducted by specialized trademark search firms at the behest of trademark attorneys who were handling the trademark registration process. Even today, some of the largest trademark search firms refuse to conduct searches for anyone but a lawyer. But most search firms aren't so choosy—they'll conduct a search for anyone willing to pay them.

The services provided by various trademark search firms, and the fees they charge for different types of searches, vary considerably. For this reason, it pays to shop around and compare the services and prices being offered.

You can find a trademark search firm by:

- looking in the Yellow Pages under trademark consultants or information brokers
- consulting a legal journal or magazine, which will usually contain ads for search firms, or
- doing an Internet search.

THE ROLE OF ATTORNEYS IN TRADEMARK SEARCHES

If you decide to hire a trademark attorney to advise you on the choice and registration of a trademark or service mark, the attorney will be able to arrange for the trademark search. Some attorneys do it themselves, but most farm the search out to a search firm.

Once the report comes back from the search firm, the attorney will interpret it for you and advise you on whether to go ahead with your proposed mark. Although you are getting considerably more in this attorney package than you'll get from a search service, it will cost you.

---

b. Doing a search on your own

Many resources are available to help you do all or part of a trademark search yourself, including:

- The U.S. Patent and Trademark Office online trademark database, which may be accessed for free from the USPTO website at www.uspto.gov.

- Numerous private trademark search companies, which will do a search for you for a fee. You can find a list of these on the Yahoo Internet directory at: http://dir.yahoo.com/Business_and_Economy/Business_to_Business/Law/Intellectual_Property/Trademarks/Services/.
- Patent and Trademark Depository Libraries (PTDLs) located throughout the country. Using a Patent and Trademark Depository

Library (PTDL) to do your own federal trademark search involves the least cash outlay, but will cost you in time and transportation expenses unless you live or work close to one. (See Appendix 3 for contact information.)

 For more on trademark searches, see *Trademark: Legal Care for Your Business and Product Name*, by Stephen Elias (Nolo). ■

Home Alone or Outside Office?

When you're self-employed, you have the option of working from home or from an outside office. This chapter covers the pros and cons of working from home, paying special attention to zoning and other restrictions and the home office tax deduction.

A. Pros and Cons of Working at Home

Legally, it makes little difference whether you work at home or in an outside office. The basic legal issues discussed in this book, such as deciding whether to operate as a sole proprietor or corporation, picking a name for your business and collecting from clients, are the same whether you run your business from your garage or from the top floor of a high-rise office building.

Your choice may affect whether you can deduct your office expenses (see Section D), but otherwise, your taxes are the same whether you work at home or in an office.

The issues to consider in deciding whether to work at home are more practical than legal: whether you can afford to pay office rent, factors that may make a home office more convenient (such as avoiding a commute) and whether working at home will disrupt your home or neighborhood.

1. Benefits of Working at Home

Working at home is popular among the self-employed because it can save time and money and improve productivity.

a. No office rent expenses

For many self-employed people, the greatest benefit of working at home is that you don't have to pay rent for an office. Office rents vary enormously depending upon the area, but you'll likely have to pay a few hundred dollars for even a small office. In large cities, you may have to spend much more. Look at the commercial real estate advertising section in your Sunday newspaper to get an idea of the going rates.

You can use the money you save in office rent to expand your business or pay your living expenses. It's true that you can deduct your office rent as a business expense (see Chapter 9), but you may be able to deduct home office expenses as well (see Section D). Keep in mind, however, that you can't deduct all your rent—and the amount you'd save in taxes depends on your tax bracket. (See Chapter 9.)

One way to reduce the costs of office space is to obtain it from a client. Many clients are willing to provide outside workers with desk space. This is particularly likely if having you around will make life easier for them. Some clients may even offer to provide you with office space at no cost to you. However, to safeguard your self-employed status, it's best that you pay something for the space. It doesn't have to be much. You can charge the client slightly more for your services to cover the cost. The client shouldn't mind arranging things this way—it will help the client if the IRS conducts an audit and questions your status.

b. No commuting time or expenses

Working at home means you don't have to commute to an outside office every day. In 2002, the IRS allowed a commuting expense deduction of 36.5 cents per mile. Using this figure, if working at home allows you to drive 6,000 fewer miles per year (500 miles per month) you'd save $2,190 per year.

Not having to commute saves you not only money, but also time. If you commute just 30 minutes each day, you're spending 120 hours each year behind the wheel of your car. That's three full 40-hour weeks that you could use earning money in your home office.

c. You can deduct home office expenses

If you arrange things right, you can deduct your home office expenses—including a portion of your home rent or mortgage payment, utilities and other expenses.

The home office deduction is particularly valuable if you rent your home. It enables you to deduct a portion of what is likely your largest single expense (your rent) an item that is ordinarily not deductible.

d. You can deduct some commuting costs

When you have an outside office, you can't deduct your commuting expenses—that is, what it costs to get from your home to your office and back again. However, if your main office is at home, you may deduct the cost of driving from home to meet clients or to other locations to conduct business.

e. Benefits other than money

Of course, the benefits of working at home are not just monetary. For many self-employed people, they are outweighed by other factors such as the increased flexibility they have over their daily schedule. You can, if you wish, work in the evenings or late at night in your pajamas—something that can be difficult to do if you're renting an office!

When you work at home, it's also easier to deal with childcare problems and household chores and errands. You may also have more contact with your family.

2. Drawbacks of Working at Home

There are potential drawbacks to working from home—for example, it may not help you project a professional image. Even worse, working at home might be against the law where you live. How-ever, there are usually things you can do to avoid or ameliorate the problems.

a. Clients don't take you seriously

The major problem many self-employed people who work at home say they have is that clients don't take them seriously. Some clients may be reluctant to deal with a home-based businessperson. This can make it harder for you to get your business established.

However, there are many things you can do to help create and maintain a professional image. For example:

- obtain a separate telephone line for your business and use it only for business calls
- use an answering service to answer your business phone when you're not home
- obtain and use professional-looking business cards, envelopes and stationery
- hold meetings at clients' offices instead of at your home
- rent a mailbox to receive your business mail instead of using your home address
- use an assumed name for your business rather than your own name (see Chapter 3), and
- consider incorporating or forming a limited liability company so that clients will be hiring a business, not you personally (see Chapter 2).

b. Restrictions on home-based businesses

Another major problem for the home-based self-employed is restrictions on home businesses imposed by cities, condominium associations and deed restrictions. It may actually be illegal for you to work at home. (See Section C.)

c. Obtaining services can be difficult

Businesses that provide services to businesses sometimes discriminate against those who work at home. For example, UPS charges more for deliveries to a home business than to one at an outside business office. And many temporary agencies won't deal with a home-based business because they're afraid they won't get paid.

d. Lack of security

Your home is likely not as secure an environment as an office building that is filled with people, has burglar alarms, employs security guards and even has hidden security cameras. If you're handling large amounts of cash or other highly valuable items, you may prefer to work in a more secure outside office than at home.

However, there are many commonsense precautions you can take to make your home office more secure—for example:

- rent a post office box to receive your mail instead of having it delivered to your home
- don't let equipment servicers or vendors visit without an appointment
- obtain good locks and use them, and
- if you have a separate business phone line, don't alert people to your absence with a message on the answering machine such as "I won't be here for a week."

e. Isolation, interruptions and other factors

Finally, some people have trouble adapting to working at home because of the isolation. They miss the social interaction of a formal office setting. However, renting an outside office where you'll be all by yourself won't necessarily end the isolation problem.

In contrast, other self-employed people find it difficult to get any work done at home because of a lack of privacy and because of interruptions from children and other family members. Others gain weight because the refrigerator is always nearby or end up watching television instead of working.

However, most of the millions of self-employed people who work at home are not fazed by these problems.

3. Businesses Well Suited to Home Offices

Home offices can work well for any business that is normally done in a simple office setting. This includes a multitude of service businesses—for example:

- desktop publishing
- accounting and bookkeeping
- computer programming
- consulting
- writing
- telemarketing
- graphic artwork
- information brokering, and
- financial planning.

A home office is also an ideal choice for businesses in which most of the work is done at clients' offices or other outside locations—for example:

- building contracting
- traveling sales
- house and carpet cleaning
- home repair work
- courier or limousine service
- piano tuning
- pool cleaning
- hazardous waste inspection, and
- catering.

4. Businesses Poorly Suited to Home Offices

Any business that will disrupt your home or neighborhood is not well suited for the home. These include businesses that generate substantial amounts of noise, pollution or waste.

A home office is not your best choice if substantial numbers of clients or customers must visit you in your office. This could cause traffic and parking problems in your neighborhood and cause neighbors to complain. One possible solution to this problem is to rent an office part time or by the hour just to meet clients. Such rentals are available in many cities and will be cheaper than renting a full-time office. Look in your Yellow Pages under office rentals or "business identity programs."

You may also have problems if your business requires you to store a substantial amount of inventory. However, you can still spend most of your time at home by renting a separate storage space for your inventory.

Finally, a home office may not work well if you need to have several employees working with you. This could cause parking problems in your neighborhood and space problems in your home. Moreover, many local zoning laws prevent home businesses from having more than one or two employees. One way around this problem is to allow your employees to work in their own homes.

B. Pros and Cons of an Outside Office

Having an outside office can avoid the problems discussed in the previous section. It can help establish your credibility and provide a more professional setting for meeting clients or customers than a home office.

Renting an outside office will also help establish that you are self-employed if you're audited by the IRS or your state tax department. (See Chapter 15.)

An outside office also helps you to keep your home and work lives separate and may enable you to work more efficiently.

The drawbacks of an outside office are the flipside of the benefits of having a home office. (See Section A.) You must pay rent for your office and drive to and from it every day. You won't be entitled to a home office deduction, although you can deduct your outside office rent, utilities and other expenses. You also lose much of the flexibility afforded by a home office.

C. Restrictions on Home-Based Businesses

If, like millions of self-employed people, you plan to work at home, you may have potential problems with your local zoning laws or with land use restrictions in your lease or condominium rules. You should investigate these potential problems before you open your home office. Even if your community is unfriendly to home offices, there are many things you can do to avoid difficulties.

1. Zoning Restrictions

Municipalities have the legal right to establish rules about what types of activities can be carried out in different geographical areas. For example, they often establish commercial zones for stores and offices, industrial zones for factories and residential zones for houses and apartments.

Some communities—Houston, for example— have no zoning restrictions at all. However, most do, and they often include laws limiting the kinds of businesses you can conduct in a residential zone. The purpose of these restrictions is to help maintain the peace and quiet of residential neighborhoods.

Fortunately, the growing trend across the country is to permit home businesses. Many cities—Los Angeles and Phoenix, for example—have recently updated their zoning laws to permit many home businesses. However, some communities remain hostile to home businesses.

a. Research your local zoning ordinance

Your first step to determine whether you might have a problem working at home is to carefully read your local zoning ordinance. Get a copy from your city or county clerk's office or your public library.

Zoning ordinances are worded in many different ways to limit businesses in residential areas. Some are extremely vague, allowing "customary home-based occupations." Others allow homeowners to use their houses for a broad but, unfortunately, not very specific list of business purposes—for example, "professions and domestic occupations, crafts and services." Still others contain a detailed list of approved occupations, such as "law, dentistry, medicine, music lessons, photography, cabinetmaking."

Ordinances that permit home-based businesses typically include detailed regulations on how you can carry out your business activities. These regulations vary widely, but the most common limit your use of on-street signs, limit car and truck traffic and restrict the number of employees who can work at your house on a regular basis; some prohibit employees altogether. Some ordinances also limit the percentage of your home's floorspace that can be devoted to your business. Again, study your ordinance carefully to see how these rules apply to you.

If you read your ordinance and still aren't sure whether your business is allowed, you may be tempted to discuss the matter with zoning or planning officials. However, until you figure out what the rules and politics of your locality are, it may be best to do this without identifying and calling attention to yourself. For example, have a friend who lives nearby make inquiries.

HARD LOBBYING CAN PAY OFF

If your town has an unduly restrictive zoning ordinance, you can try to get it changed. For example, a self-employed person in the town of Melbourne, Florida, was surprised to discover that his local zoning ordinance barred home-based businesses. He decided to try to change the law.

He sent letters to his local public officials, but got no response. He then reviewed the zoning ordinances favoring home offices from nearby communities and drafted an ordinance of his own that he presented to the city council. He enlisted support from a local home business association and got a major story about his battle printed in the local newspaper.

After several hearings, the city council voted unanimously to amend the zoning ordinance to allow home offices.

b. Determine the attitude toward enforcement

Even if your locality has a restrictive zoning law on the books, you won't necessarily have problems. In most communities, such laws are rarely enforced unless one of your neighbors complains to local officials. Complaints usually occur because you make lots of noise or have large numbers of clients, employees or delivery people coming and going, causing parking or traffic problems. If you're unobtrusive—for example, you work quietly in your home office all day and rarely receive business visitors—it's not likely your neighbors will complain.

Unfortunately, some communities are extremely hostile toward home businesses and actively try to prevent them. This is most likely to be the case if you live in an upscale purely residential community. Even if you're unobtrusive, these communities may bar you from working at home if they discover what you're up to. If you live in such a community, you may want to consider moving. Otherwise you'll really need to keep your head down to avoid discovery.

To determine your community's enforcement style, talk to your local chamber of commerce and other self-employed people you know in your town. Friends or neighbors who are actively involved with your local government may also be knowledgeable.

KEEPING YOUR HOME BUSINESS UNOBTRUSIVE

There are many ways to help keep your home business as unobtrusive as possible in the interest of warding off neighbor complaints. For example, if you get a lot of deliveries, arrange for mail and packages to be received by a private mailbox service such as Mail Boxes, Etc. Don't put your home address on your stationery and business cards.

Also, try to visit your clients in their offices instead of having them come to your home office.

A husband and wife team of psychiatrists who ran a 24-hour group therapy practice in a quiet neighborhood of Victorian homes provide a perfect example of how to get neighbors to complain about a home office: they paved every inch of their yard for parking and installed huge lights to illuminate the entire property.

---

c. Inform your neighbors

Good neighbor relations are the key to avoiding problems with zoning. Tell your neighbors about your plans to start a home business so they'll know what to expect and will have the chance to air their concerns. Explain that there are advantages to you working at home—for example, having someone home during the day should improve security for the neighborhood. You might even offer to meet a neighbor's repairperson or accept his or her packages.

If any of your neighbors are retired, try to be particularly helpful to them. Retired people who stay at home all day are more likely to complain about a home office than neighbors who work during the day.

On the other hand, if your relations with your neighbors are already shaky or you happen to be surrounded by unreasonable people, you may be better off not telling them you work at home. If you're inconspicuous, they may never know what you're doing.

d. If your neighbors complain

If your neighbors complain about your home office, you'll probably have to deal with your local zoning bureaucracy. If local zoning officials decide you should close your home business, they'll first send you a letter ordering you to do so. If you ignore this and any subsequent letters, they may file a civil lawsuit against you seeking an injunction—that is, a court order prohibiting you from violating the zoning ordinance by operating your home business. If you violate such an injunction, a judge can fine you or even put you in jail.

Don't ignore the problem; it won't go away. Immediately after receiving the first letter from zoning officials, talk with the person at city hall who administers the zoning law—usually someone in the zoning or planning department. City officials may drop the matter if you'll agree to make your home business less obtrusive.

If this doesn't work, you can apply to your planning or zoning board for a variance allowing you to violate the zoning ordinance. To obtain such a variance, you'll need to show that your business does no harm to your neighborhood and that relocation would deprive you of your livelihood. Be prepared to answer the objections of unhappy neighbors who may be at the planning commission meeting loudly opposing the proposed variance.

You can also try to get your city council or zoning board to change the local zoning ordinance. You'll probably have to lobby some city council members or planning commissioners. It will be useful to enlist the support of the local chamber of commerce and other business groups. Try to enlist the support of your neighbors as well—for example, have as many of them as possible sign a petition favoring the zoning change. Many people with home offices are organizing on local, state and national levels to lobby for new zoning laws permitting home offices.

Two national membership organizations pushing for changes may be able to give you advice.

- American Association of Home-Based Businesses, P.O. Box 10023, Rockville, MD 20849-0023; fax: 301-963-7042, Internet: www.aahbb.org, and
- Home Office Association of America, P.O. Box 51, Sagapohack, NY 11962; 800-809-4622, fax: 212-286-4646, Internet: www.hoaa.com.

Finally, you can take the matter to court, claiming that the local zoning ordinance is invalid or that the city has misinterpreted it. You'll probably need the help of a lawyer familiar with zoning matters to do this. (See Chapter 21.)

HOME-BASED ENTREPRENEUR FIGHTS CITY HALL—AND WINS

Many self-employed people have successfully fought decisions that their home businesses violate local zoning laws. For example, Judy ran a theatrical costume business from her home in Los Angeles for several years. She never received any complaints from her neighbors about her business, but someone with a grudge against her alerted the Los Angeles Building Department that Judy was operating a home business in violation of the Los Angeles zoning ordinance.

The Building Department sent an inspector to look at her property. He handed her an order on the spot requiring her to stop doing business at home. Judy decided to fight rather than switch her office location. She applied for a zoning variance from the Los Angeles Planning Commission, but was turned down after a hearing.

Refusing to take no for an answer, Judy appealed to the Los Angeles Zoning Appeals Board. She went to work to make sure she was prepared for the appeal. She enlisted the support of her neighbors. She was head of the Neighborhood Watch—a group of volunteers dedicated to keeping the locale safe—so she already knew most of them. Nearly 140 neighbors signed a petition urging the board to permit her home office; several also wrote letters to the board.

Judy drew a map of her property and took pictures to show that her home business did not disrupt the neighborhood. She also conducted a neighborhood traffic survey, which showed that her business did not increase traffic in the neighborhood substantially.

The appeals board was so impressed by her evidence that it granted one of the first variances ever given to a home office in Los Angeles.

For detailed guidance on how to handle neighbor disputes, including disputes over home-based businesses, see *Neighbor Law*, by Cora Jordan (Nolo).

2. Private Land Use Restrictions

The government uses zoning laws to restrict how you can use your property. However, there may also be private restrictions on how you can use your home.

Depending on the part of the country in which you live, use restrictions are commonly found in:

- property deeds
- homeowner association rules, and
- leases.

a. Property deed restrictions

Property deeds often contain restrictions, called restrictive covenants, limiting how you can use your property. Restrictive covenants often bar or limit the use of home offices.

You can find out if your property is subject to such restrictions by reading your title insurance policy or checking your deed. If your neighbors believe you're violating these restrictions, they can take court action to stop you. Such restrictions are usually enforced by the courts unless they are unreasonable or the character of the neighborhood has changed so much since they were written that it makes no sense to enforce them.

b. Homeowners' association rules

One in six Americans lives in a planned community with a homeowners' association. When you buy property in such a development, you automatically become a member of the homeowners' association and become subject to its rules, which are usually set forth in a lengthy document called Covenants, Conditions and Restrictions, or CC&Rs for short. CC&Rs often regulate, in minute detail, what you can do on, in and to your property. The homeowners' association is in charge of modifying and enforcing these rules.

The CC&Rs for many developments specifically bar home offices. The homeowners' association may be able to impose fines and other penalties against you if your business violates the rules. It could also sue you in court to get money damages or other penalties. Some homeowners' associations are very strict about enforcing their rules against home businesses; others are much less so.

Carefully study the CC&Rs before you buy into a condominium, planned development or cooperative to see if home offices are prohibited. If so, you may want to buy somewhere else.

If you're already in a development that bars home offices, you may be able to avoid problems if you're unobtrusive and your neighbors are unaware you have a home office. However, the best course may be to seek to change the CC&Rs. Most homeowner associations rule through a board of directors whose members are elected by all the members of the association. Lobby members of the board about changing the rules to permit home offices. If that fails, you and like-minded neighbors could try to get seats on the board and gain a voice in policymaking.

c. Lease restrictions

If you're a renter, check your lease before you start your home business. Many standard lease forms prohibit tenants from conducting a business on the premises—or prohibit certain types of businesses. Your landlord could evict you if you violate such a lease provision. However, most landlords don't want to evict their tenants. Most don't care what you do on your premises as long as it doesn't disturb your neighbors or cause damage. Keep up good neighbor relations to prevent complaints. (See Section C.)

However, if you have business visitors, your landlord may require you to obtain liability insurance in case a visitor has an accident such as a trip or fall on the premises. (See Chapter 6.)

D. Deducting Your Home Office Expenses

If you elect to work from home, the federal government is prepared to help you out by allowing you to deduct your home office expenses from your taxes. This is so whether you own your home or apartment or are a renter. Although this tax deduction is commonly called the home office deduction, it is not limited to home offices. You can also take it if, for example, you have a workshop or studio at home.

If you've heard stories about how difficult it is to qualify for the home office deduction and felt it wasn't worth the trouble, you can breathe more easily. Changes in the tax law that took effect in 1999 make it much easier for many self-employed people to qualify for the deduction. Even if you haven't qualified for the deduction in the past, you may be entitled to it now.

Because some people claim that the home office deduction is an audit flag for the IRS, many self-employed people who may qualify for it are afraid to take it. Although taking the home office deduction might increase your chance of being audited, the chances are still relatively small. Also, you have nothing to fear from an audit if you're entitled to the deduction.

However, if you intend to take the deduction, you should also make the effort to understand the requirements and set up your home office so as to satisfy them. Before you start moving your furniture around, read on.

SIDELINE BUSINESS MAY QUALIFY FOR OFFICE DEDUCTION

You don't have to work full time in a business to qualify for the home office deduction. If you satisfy the requirements, you can take the deduction for a sideline business you run from a home office. However, the total amount you deduct cannot exceed your income from the business.

EXAMPLE: Barbara works full time as an editor for a publishing company. An avid bowler, she also spends about 15 hours a week writing and publishing a bowling newsletter. She does all the work on the newsletter from an office in her apartment. Barbara may take the home office deduction. But she can't deduct more than she earns as income from the newsletter.

1. Regular and Exclusive Business Use

You can't take the home office deduction unless you regularly use part of your home exclusively for a trade or business.

Unfortunately, the IRS doesn't offer a satisfactory definition of regular use to guide you. The agency has decreed only that you must use a portion of your home for business on a continuing basis—not just for occasional or incidental business. You'll likely satisfy this test if you use your home office a few hours each day.

Exclusive use means that you use a portion of your home *only* for business. If you use part of your home as your business office and also use that part for personal purposes, you cannot meet the exclusive use test and do not take the home office deduction.

EXAMPLE: Johnny, an accountant, has a den at home furnished with a desk, chair, bookshelf, filing cabinet and bed. He uses the desk and chair for both business and personal reasons. The bookshelf contains both personal and business books. And the filing cabinet contains both personal and business files. Johnny can't claim a business deduction for the den since it is not used exclusively for business purposes.

You needn't devote an entire separate room in your home to your business. But some part of the room must be used exclusively for business.

EXAMPLE: Paul, an accountant, keeps his desk, chair, bookshelf and filing cabinet in one part of his den and uses them exclusively for business. The remainder of the room—one-third of the space—is used to store a bed for house guests. Paul can take a home office deduction for the two-thirds of the room used exclusively as an office.

As a practical matter, the IRS isn't going to make a surprise inspection of your home to see whether you're complying with these requirements. However, complying with the rules from the beginning avoids having to lie to the IRS if you are audited.

This means, simply, that you'll have to arrange your furniture and belongings so as to devote a portion of your home exclusively to your home office. The more space you use exclusively for business, the more your home office deduction will be worth. (See Section D.)

Although not explicitly required by law, it's a good idea to physically separate the space you use for business from the rest of the room. For example, if you use part of your living room as an office, separate it from the rest of the room with room dividers or bookcases.

2. Qualifying for the Deduction

Unfortunately, satisfying the requirement of using your home office regularly and exclusively for business is only half the battle.

You must also meet one of these three requirements:

- your home office must be your principal place of business

- you must meet clients or customers at home, or
- you must use a separate structure on your property exclusively for business purposes.

WAYS TO SOLIDIFY HOME OFFICE DEDUCTION

Here are some ways to convince the IRS that you qualify for the home office deduction.

- Take a picture of your home office and draw up a diagram showing your home office as a portion of your home.
- Have all your business mail sent to your home office.
- Use your home office address on all your business cards, stationery and advertising.
- Obtain a separate phoneline for your business and keep that phone in your home office. The tax law helps you do this by allowing you to deduct the monthly fee for a second phone line in your home if you use it for business. You can't deduct the monthly fee for a single phone line, even if you use it partly for business; however, you can deduct the cost of business calls you place from that line. Having a separate business phone will also make it easier for you to keep track of your business phone expenses.
- Encourage clients or customers to regularly visit your home office and keep a log of their visits.
- To make the most of the time you spend in your home office, communicate with clients by phone, fax or electronic mail instead of going to their offices. Use a mail or messenger service to deliver your work to customers.
- Keep a log of the time you spend working in your home office. This doesn't have to be fancy; notes on your calendar will do.

3. Home as Principal Place of Business

The most common way to qualify for the home office deduction is to use your home as your principal place of business. Indeed, due to changes in the tax laws that took effect in 1999, most self-employed people will be able to qualify for the home office deduction on this basis.

a. If you do most of your work at home

If, like many self-employed people, you do all or most of your work in your home office, your home is clearly your principal place of business, and you'll have no trouble at all qualifying for the home office deduction. This would be the case, for example, for a writer who does most of his or her writing at home or a salesperson who sells by phone and makes most of his or her sales calls from home.

b. If you do only administrative work at home

Of course, many people who work for themselves spend the bulk of their time working away from home. This is the case, for example, for:

- building contractors who work primarily on building sites
- doctors who work primarily in hospitals
- travelling salespeople who visit clients at their places of business, and
- house painters, gardeners and home repair people who work primarily in their customers' homes.

Fortunately, the legal changes that took effect in 1999 make it possible for such people to qualify for the home office deduction. Under the new rules, your home office will qualify as your principal place of business, even if you work primarily outside your home, if:

- you use the office to conduct administrative or management activities for your business, and
- there is no other fixed location where you conduct such activities.

What this means is that, to qualify for the home office deduction, your home office need no longer be the place where you generate most of your business income. It's sufficient that you regularly use it to administer or manage your business—for example, keep your books, schedule appointments, do research and order supplies. As long as you have no other fixed location where you do such things—for example, an outside office—you'll get the deduction.

Because of these rules, most self-employed people qualify for the home office deduction. All you have to do is set up a home office that you regularly use to manage or administer your business. Even if you spend most of your work time away from home, you can still find plenty of business-related work to do in your home office.

EXAMPLE: Sally, a handyperson, performs home repair work for clients in their homes. She also has a home office which she uses regularly and exclusively to keep her books, arrange appointments and order supplies. Sally is entitled to a home office deduction.

4. Meeting Clients or Customers at Home

Even if your home office is not your principal place of business, you may deduct your expenses for the part of your home used exclusively to meet with clients, customers or patients. You must physically meet with others at home; phoning them from home is not sufficient. And the meetings must be a regular part of your business; occasional meetings don't qualify.

There is no numerical standard for how often you must meet clients at home for those meetings to be considered regular. However, the IRS has indicated that meeting clients one or two days a week is sufficient. Exclusive use means you use the space where you meet clients only for business. You are free to use the space for business purposes other than meeting clients—for example, doing your business bookkeeping or other paperwork. But you cannot use the space for personal purposes such as watching television.

EXAMPLE: June, an attorney, works three days a week in her city office and two days in her home office which she uses only for business. She meets clients at her home office at least once a week. Since she regularly meets clients at her home office, it qualifies for the home office deduction. This is so even though her city office is her principal place of business.

If you want to qualify for this deduction, encourage clients or customers to visit you at home. Keep a log or appointment book showing all their visits.

5. Using a Separate Structure for Business

You can also deduct expenses for a separate free-standing structure, such as a studio, garage or barn, if you use it exclusively and regularly for your business. The structure does not have to be your principal place of business or a place where you meet patients, clients or customers.

As always where the home office deduction is involved, exclusive use means you use the structure only for business—for example, you can't use it to store gardening equipment or as a guest house. Regular use is not precisely defined, but it's probably sufficient for you to use the structure 10 or 15 hours a week.

EXAMPLE: Deborah is a freelance graphic designer. She has her main office in an industrial park, but also works every weekend in a small studio in her back yard. Since she uses the studio regularly and exclusively for her design work, it qualifies for the home office deduction.

STORING INVENTORY OR PRODUCT SAMPLES AT HOME

You can take the home office deduction if you're in the business of selling retail or wholesale products and you store inventory or product samples at home.

To qualify, you can't have an office or other business location outside your home. And you must store your inventory at a particular place in your home—for example, a garage, closet or bedroom. You can't move your inventory from one room to the other. You don't have to use the storage space exclusively to store your inventory to take the deduction. It's sufficient that you regularly use it for that purpose.

EXAMPLE: Janet sells costume jewelry door to door. She rents a home and regularly uses half of her attached garage to store her jewelry inventory and also uses it to park her Harley Davidson motorcycle. Janet can deduct the expenses for the storage space even though she does not use her garage exclusively to store inventory. Her garage accounts for 20% of the total floor space of her house. Since she uses only half of the garage for storing inventory, she may deduct one half of this, or 10%, of her rent and certain other expenses.

6. Amount of Deduction

To figure out the amount of the home office deduction, you need to determine what percentage of your home is used for business. To do this, divide the square footage of your home office by the total square footage of your home. For example, if your home is 1,600 square feet and you use 400 square feet for your home office, 25% of the total area is used for business.

Or if all the rooms in your home are about the same size, figure the business portion by dividing the number of rooms used for business by the number of rooms in the home. For example, if you use one room in a five-room house for business, 20% of the area is used for business. Claiming 20% to 25% of your home as a home office is perfectly acceptable. However, claiming anything over 40% will likely raise questions with the IRS unless you store inventory at home.

The home office deduction is not one deduction, but many. You are entitled to deduct from your gross income your home office use percentage of:

- your rent if you rent your home, or
- depreciation, mortgage interest and property taxes if you own your home.

In addition, owners and renters may deduct this same percentage of other expenses for keeping up and running an entire home. The IRS calls these indirect expenses.

They include:

- utility expenses for electricity, gas, heating oil and trash removal
- homeowner's or renter's insurance
- home maintenance expenses that benefit your entire home including your home office, such as roof and furnace repairs and exterior painting
- condominium association fees
- snow removal expenses
- casualty losses if your home is damaged—for example, in a storm, and
- security system costs.

You may also deduct the entire cost of expenses just for your home office. The IRS calls these direct expenses. They include, for example, painting your home office or paying someone to clean it. If you pay a housekeeper to clean your entire house, you may deduct your business use percentage of the expense.

> **EXAMPLE:** Jean rents a 1,600 square foot apartment and uses a 400 square foot bedroom as a home office for her consulting business. Her percentage of business use is 25% (400 divided by 1,600). She pays $12,000 in annual rent and has a $1,200 utility bill for the year. She also spent $200 to paint her home office. She is entitled to deduct 25% of her rent and utilities and the entire painting expense for a total home office deduction of $3,500.

Be sure to keep copies of all your bills and receipts for home office expenses—for example, keep:

- IRS Form 1098 sent by whoever holds your mortgage, showing the interest you paid on your mortgage for the year
- property tax bills and your canceled checks
- utility bills, insurance bills and receipts for payments for repairs to your office area, along with your canceled checks paying for these items, and
- a copy of your lease and your canceled rent checks, if you're a renter.

The home office deduction can be very valuable if you're a renter because you get to deduct part of your rent—a substantial expense that is ordinarily not deductible. If you own your home, the home office deduction is worth less because you're already allowed to deduct your mortgage interest and property taxes.

Taking the home office deduction won't increase your income tax deductions for these items, but it will allow you to deduct them from your self-employment taxes. You'll save $153 in self-employment taxes for every $1,000 in mortgage interest and property taxes you deduct. You'll also be able to deduct a portion of repairs, utility bills, cleaning and maintenance costs and depreciation.

DEPRECIATING OFFICE FURNITURE AND OTHER PERSONAL PROPERTY

Whether or not you qualify for or take the home office deduction, you can depreciate or expense under Section 179 the cost of office furniture, computers, copiers, fax machines and other personal property you use for your business and keep at home. These costs are deducted directly on your Schedule C, Profit or Loss From Business. They don't have to be listed on the special tax form used for the home office deduction.

If you use the property for both business and personal reasons, the IRS requires you to keep records showing when the item was used for business and when for personal reasons—for example, a diary or log with the dates, times and reason the item was used. (See Chapter 14, Section A.)

---

a.   Profit limit for deductions

There is an important limitation on the home office deduction: it may not exceed the net profit you earn from your home office.

Determining this amount can be complex.

First, you have to figure out how much money you earn from using your home office. If you do all your work at home, this will be 100% of your business income. But if you work in several locations, you must determine the part of your gross income that came from working in your home office. To do this, consider how much time you spend in your home office and elsewhere and the type of work you do in each location.

Then, subtract from this amount:

- the business percentage of your otherwise deductible mortgage interest and real estate taxes; you'll only have these expenses if you own your home, and
- business expenses that are not attributable to the business use of your home—for example, supplies, depreciation of business equipment, business phone, advertising or salaries.

The remainder is your profit—the most you can deduct for using your home office.

EXAMPLE: Sam runs a part-time consulting business out of his home office, which occupies 20% of his home. In one recent year, his gross income from the business was $6,000. He does all his consulting work at home, so this entire amount is attributable to his home office. He determines how much of his home office expenses he may deduct as follows:

- First, he subtracts 20% of his home mortgage interest and property taxes from his $6,000 gross income. This is $3,000, so he has $3,000 left.
- Next, he subtracts his business expenses other than for the use of his home office. These amount to $2,000, so he is left with $1,000.

Sam may only deduct $1,000 of home office expenses. These expenses totaled $2,000 for the year, so Sam has $1,000 left over that he may not deduct for the year. He may deduct this amount next year if he has sufficient income from his business.

You can carry over any excess in home office deductibles and deduct them in the first year in which your business earns a profit. However, whether or not your business incurs a loss, you can still deduct all your home mortgage interest and property taxes because you're a homeowner.

b. Special concerns for homeowners

If you're not careful when you take the home office deduction, you may have to pay extra taxes when you sell your home.

Ordinarily, any profit you make when you sell your home—up to $250,000 for single taxpayers and $500,000 for married taxpayers filing jointly—is not taxable. However, if you take the home office deduction, this rule does not apply to the portion of your house that you use for business. Instead, your old house is treated as two separate properties for tax purposes.

You'll have to pay 20% capital gains tax on the profit you earn from the portion of your house used as a home office. For example, if 20% of your house was used as a home office, you'd have to pay tax on 20% of the profit you earn when you sell your home. If your home has gone up in value dramatically since you bought it, you'll have a huge tax bill.

You'll also have to pay tax on any depreciation you took on your home office.

To avoid this tax trap, you must use your entire home as your principal residence for at least two of the five years preceding the year of sale. In other words, you can't take the home office deduction for those two years. So if you plan on moving, it's best not to use a home office (or at least, not to take the deduction) for least two years before the date of sale.

If you want to be able to move on short notice without worrying about taxes, don't take the home office deduction.

7. IRS Reporting Requirements

All unincorporated taxpayers who take the home office deduction must file IRS Form 8829 with their tax returns. Renters who take the deduction must also file Form 1099-MISC with the IRS.

a. IRS Form 8829

If you qualify for the home office deduction and are a sole proprietor or partner in a partnership, you must file IRS Form 8829, Expenses for Business Use of Your Home, along with your personal tax return. The form alerts the IRS that you're taking the deduction and shows how you calculated it. You should file this form even if you're not allowed to deduct your home office expenses because your business has no profits. By filing, you can apply the deduction to a future year in which you earn a profit.

If you organize your business as an S corporation instead of a sole proprietorship or partnership, you don't have to file Form 8829. (See Chapter 2, Section B.) This is one of the major advantages of forming an S corporation. Filing Form 8829 calls your home office deduction to the attention of the IRS. If you can avoid filing it, you are less likely to face an audit.

 For additional information, see IRS Publication 587, *Business Use of Your Home.* You can obtain this and all other IRS publications by calling the IRS at 800-TAX-FORM, visiting your local IRS office or downloading the publications from the IRS Internet site at www.irs.gov.

b. Filing requirement for renters

If you're a renter and take the home office deduction, you should file an IRS Form 1099-MISC each year reporting the amount of your rental payments attributable to your home office.

> **EXAMPLE:** Bill rents a house and takes the home office deduction. He spends $12,000 per year on rent and uses 25% of his house as a home office. He should file a Form 1099 reporting $3,000 of his rental payments.

You should file three copies of Form 1099:

- File one copy with the IRS by February 28
- Give one copy to your landlord by January 31, and
- File one copy with your state tax department, if your state has income taxes. (See Chapter 9.)

Your landlord may not appreciate receiving a Form 1099 from you, but it will definitely be helpful if you're audited by the IRS and your home office deduction is questioned. It helps to show that you were really conducting a business out of your home.

Form 1099 is not required if your landlord is a corporation. Form 1099 need not be filed for payments to corporations. A Form 1099 is also not required in the unlikely event that your rental payments for your home office total less than $600 for the year. ■

Obtaining Licenses, Permits and Numbers

Once you've decided how to organize and name your business, you'll need to obtain any necessary licenses, permits and numbers. This can be a bit of a pain and may require you to fill out paperwork and pay some fees, but it's worth it. You can face fines and other penalties if you don't satisfy the government requirements.

Also, having all required business licenses helps you look like an independent businessperson instead of an employee. Some potential clients or customers may even ask for copies of your licenses, permits or numbers before agreeing to hire you—they know this information will help them if they're audited by the IRS or other government agencies.

A. Business Licenses

The type of business licenses and permits that you need (if any) depends on the kind of work you do and where you do it. You may have to get licenses or permits from the federal, state and local governments. Professional organizations, other self-employed people and your local chamber of commerce may all be able to give you information on licensing requirements for your business.

1. Federal Licenses and Permits

The federal government doesn't require licenses or permits for most small businesses. One notable exception, however, is the trucking industry. Trucking companies must be licensed by the Interstate Commerce Commission. License requirements are also imposed on investment advisors by the Securities and Exchange Commission.

2. State Requirements

A few states require all businesses to obtain state business licenses. These are required in addition to local licenses.

Most states don't issue or require general business licenses. However, all states require special licenses for people who work in certain occupations. Doctors, lawyers, architects, nurses and engineers must be licensed in every state. Most states require licenses for other occupations that require extensive training or that expose consumers to potential hazards or fraud—for example, most states license barbers, bill collectors, building contractors, tax preparers, insurance agents, cosmetologists, real estate agents or brokers and auto mechanics. Your state may require licenses for other occupations, too.

Procedures for obtaining a license vary from state to state and occupation to occupation. You may have to meet specific educational requirements or have training or experience in the field. You may even have to pass a written examination. Of course, you'll have to pay a license fee. Some states may also require that you have liability insurance before you can be issued a license. (See Chapter 6.)

If your state government discovers that you're doing business without a required license, various bad things can happen to you. You'll undoubtedly be ordered to stop doing business. You may also be fined. And depending on your occupation, failure to obtain a license may be a crime—a misdemeanor or even a felony.

Many states have agencies designated to help businesses get started. This is the first place you should call to obtain information on your state's license requirements. These agencies often have free or inexpensive publications that discuss licensing rules.

Also, most state agencies have sites on the Internet which may contain information about licensing requirements. A good place to start an Internet search for such information is at www.statelocalgov.net/index.cfm. Also, the Library of Congress maintains a list of state government websites at http://lcweb.loc.gov/global/state/stategov.html#meta.

3. Local Requirements

Many cities, counties and municipalities require business licenses or permits for all businesses—even one-person home-based operations. Usually, you just have to pay a fee to get such licenses; they are simply a tax in disguise. Other cities have no license requirements at all, or exempt very small businesses.

If you're doing business within a city's limits, you'll need to contact your city government. If you're in an unincorporated area, you'll need to contact your county government. If you're doing business in more than one city or county, you may have to get a license in each one.

To find out what to do, call the appropriate local official in charge of business licensing. This is often the city or county clerk, planning or zoning department, city tax office, building and safety department or public works department. More than one local license may be needed, so you may have to deal with more than one local agency. Your local chamber of commerce may be able to direct you to the agency or person to contact.

To obtain a license, you'll be required to fill out an application and pay a fee. Fees vary from locality to locality—from as little as $15 to several hundred dollars. Fees are often based on your projected gross revenues—for example, 10 cents per $1,000 of revenue. You'll be required to renew your license and pay an additional fee, usually every year. It's also likely that you'll be required to post your license at your place of business.

Many self-employed people, particularly those who work at home, never bother to get a local business license. If your local government discovers you're running an unlicensed business, it may fine you and bar you from doing business until you obtain a license.

 Problems for the Home-Based Self-Employed

If you work at home, be careful about applying for a local business license. You'll have to provide your business address to obtain one. Before granting a license, many cities first check to see whether the area in which your business is located is zoned for business. If your local zoning ordinance bars home offices in your neighborhood, you could be in for trouble. (See Chapter 4.)

B. Obtaining an Employer Identification Number

A federal employer identification number, or EIN, is a nine-digit number the IRS assigns to businesses for tax filing and reporting purposes. The IRS uses the EIN to identify the taxpayer.

1. When an EIN Is Required

Use your EIN on all business tax returns, checks and other documents you send to the IRS. Your state tax authority may also require your EIN on state tax forms.

a. Sole proprietors

If you're a sole proprietor, you must have an EIN to:

- hire employees
- have a Keogh retirement plan (see Chapter 16)
- buy or inherit an existing business that you operate as a sole proprietorship
- incorporate or form a partnership, or
- file for bankruptcy.

Also, some banks require you to have an EIN before they'll set up a bank account for your business.

If, like most self-employed people, you're a sole proprietor and don't have any employees or a

Keogh plan, you don't have to obtain an EIN; you can use your Social Security number instead. Note that sole proprietors without employees are permitted to obtain EINs and you should do so. Using an EIN instead of your Social Security number on your tax returns and payments helps to show that you're an independent businessperson—in other words, an independent contractor and not an employee. This will make you more attractive to prospective clients.

b. Corporations, partnerships and limited liability companies

You must have an EIN if you form a corporation, partnership or limited liability company. An EIN is also required if you were formerly a sole proprietor and form any of these entities.

2. Obtaining an EIN

EINs are free and easy to obtain. You can get one by filing IRS Form SS-4, Application for Employer Identification Number, with the IRS. Filling out the form is simple—it has detailed instructions.

Note these possible trouble spots.

- **Space 1:** List your full legal name if you're a sole proprietor. If you've incorporated, list the corporation's name—the name on your articles of incorporation or similar document establishing your corporation.
- **Space 7:** Leave this space blank if you're a sole proprietor.
- **Space 11:** For most self-employed people, the closing month of the tax year is December. (See Chapter 8, Section A.)
- **Space 12:** If you don't plan to hire any employees, enter "N/A" in this space.

a. Applying by mail

You can obtain your EIN by mailing the completed SS-4 to the appropriate IRS service center listed in the form's instructions. The IRS will mail the EIN to you in about a month.

b. Applying by phone

If you need an EIN right away, you can get it over the phone by using the IRS's Tele-TIN program. Here's what to do.

- Fill out the SS-4 form.
- Call the IRS at 866-816-2065; an IRS representative will take the information off your SS-4 and assign you an EIN which you can start using immediately.
- Write your EIN in the upper right-hand corner of the SS-4 and sign and date the form.
- Mail or fax the signed SS-4 within 24 hours to the Tele-TIN unit at the IRS service center address for your state; the addresses are provided in the SS-4 instructions or the IRS representative can give you the fax number.

C. Sales Tax Permits

Almost all states and many municipalities impose sales taxes of some kind. The only states without sales tax are Alaska, Delaware, Montana, New Hampshire and Oregon. However, many cities, counties and boroughs in Alaska have their own local sales taxes. In addition, the other four states impose sales-type taxes on certain types of business transactions.

In some states, sales tax is imposed on sellers, who then have the option of passing the tax along to their purchasers. In other states, the tax is imposed directly on the purchaser, and the seller is responsible for collecting the tax and remitting it to the state. In a few states, sellers and purchasers share sales tax.

1. Selling Products or Services

If you sell tangible personal property—things you can hold in your hand—to the public, you'll most likely have to pay sales taxes. All states that have sales taxes impose them on sales of goods or products to end users.

IRS FORM SS-4

Form **SS-4**
(Rev. December 2001)
Department of the Treasury
Internal Revenue Service

Application for Employer Identification Number

(For use by employers, corporations, partnerships, trusts, estates, churches, government agencies, Indian tribal entities, certain individuals, and others.)

▶ See separate instructions for each line.　▶ Keep a copy for your records.

EIN

OMB No. 1545-0003

Type or print clearly.

1 Legal name of entity (or individual) for whom the EIN is being requested
Harry Flashman

2 Trade name of business (if different from name on line 1)

3 Executor, trustee, "care of" name

4a Mailing address (room, apt., suite no. and street, or P.O. box)
555 Main St.

5a Street address (if different) (Do not enter a P.O. box.)

4b City, state, and ZIP code
Ann Arbor, MI 48104

5b City, state, and ZIP code

6 County and state where principal business is located
Washenaw

7a Name of principal officer, general partner, grantor, owner, or trustor
Harry Flashman

7b SSN, ITIN, or EIN

8a Type of entity (check only one box)
[X] Sole proprietor (SSN) ___123 45 6789___
[ ] Partnership
[ ] Corporation (enter form number to be filed) ▶ _____
[ ] Personal service corp.
[ ] Church or church-controlled organization
[ ] Other nonprofit organization (specify) ▶ _____
[ ] Other (specify) ▶

[ ] Estate (SSN of decedent) _____
[ ] Plan administrator (SSN) _____
[ ] Trust (SSN of grantor) _____
[ ] National Guard　[ ] State/local government
[ ] Farmers' cooperative　[ ] Federal government/military
[ ] REMIC　[ ] Indian tribal governments/enterprises
Group Exemption Number (GEN) ▶ _____

8b If a corporation, name the state or foreign country (if applicable) where incorporated

State

Foreign country

9 **Reason for applying** (check only one box)
[ ] Started new business (specify type) ▶_____

[X] Hired employees (Check the box and see line 12.)
[ ] Compliance with IRS withholding regulations
[ ] Other (specify) ▶

[ ] Banking purpose (specify purpose) ▶ _____
[ ] Changed type of organization (specify new type) ▶ _____
[ ] Purchased going business
[ ] Created a trust (specify type) ▶ _____
[ ] Created a pension plan (specify type) ▶ _____

10 Date business started or acquired (month, day, year)
Aug. 1, 2002

11 Closing month of accounting year
December

12 First date wages or annuities were paid or will be paid (month, day, year). **Note:** If applicant is a withholding agent, enter date income will first be paid to nonresident alien. (month, day, year) . . . .▶ Sept. 1, 2002

13 Highest number of employees expected in the next 12 months. **Note:** If the applicant does not expect to have any employees during the period, enter "-0-." . . . .▶

Agricultural	Household	Other
	1	

14 Check **one** box that best describes the principal activity of your business.
[ ] Construction　[ ] Rental & leasing　[ ] Transportation & warehousing
[ ] Real estate　[ ] Manufacturing　[ ] Finance & insurance
[ ] Health care & social assistance　[ ] Wholesale–agent/broker
[ ] Accommodation & food service　[X] Wholesale–other　[ ] Retail
[ ] Other (specify)　Consulting

15 Indicate principal line of merchandise sold; specific construction work done; products produced; or services provided.

16a Has the applicant ever applied for an employer identification number for this or any other business? . . . . . [ ] Yes　[X] No
Note: If "Yes," please complete lines 16b and 16c.

16b If you checked "Yes" on line 16a, give applicant's legal name and trade name shown on prior application if different from line 1 or 2 above.
Legal name ▶　Trade name ▶

16c Approximate date when, and city and state where, the application was filed. Enter previous employer identification number if known.
Approximate date when filed (mo., day, year)　City and state where filed　Previous EIN

Third Party Designee

Complete this section **only** if you want to authorize the named individual to receive the entity's EIN and answer questions about the completion of this form.

Designee's name

Address and ZIP code

Designee's telephone number (include area code)
(　)

Designee's fax number (include area code)
(　)

Under penalties of perjury, I declare that I have examined this application, and to the best of my knowledge and belief, it is true, correct, and complete.

Name and title (type or print clearly) ▶ Harry Flashman, Owner

Signature ▶ *Harry Flashman*　Date ▶ August 15, 2002

Applicant's telephone number (include area code)
(315)555-5555

Applicant's fax number (include area code)
(315)554-5555

For Privacy Act and Paperwork Reduction Act Notice, see separate instructions.　Cat. No. 16055N　Form **SS-4** (Rev. 12-2001)

On the other hand, if you only provide services to clients or customers—that is, you don't sell or transfer any type of personal property—you probably don't have to worry about sales taxes because most states don't tax services at all or only tax certain specified services. Notable exceptions are Hawaii, New Mexico and South Dakota, which impose sales taxes on all services, subject to certain exceptions.

Determining whether you're selling property or providing a service can be difficult because the two are often involved in the same transaction. For example, a piano tuner may have to replace some piano wire to tune a piano, or a dentist may provide a patient with a gold filling in the process of filling a tooth. In these instances, many state taxing authorities look at the true object of the transaction to determine if sales tax will be assessed. That is, they look at whether the main purpose of the transaction is to provide the consumer with a service or to sell property. It seems clear that the main purpose of hiring a piano tuner or dentist is to obtain a service—that is, a tuned piano or filled tooth. The property used to provide the service is incidental.

2. Contacting Your State Sales Tax Department

Each state's sales tax requirements are unique. A product or service taxable in one state may be tax-free in another. The only way to find out if the products or services you provide are subject to sales taxes is to contact your state sales tax department. (See Appendix 3 for a list of state sales tax offices.) If you don't understand the requirements, seek help from a tax pro. (See Chapter 21.)

3. Obtaining a State Sales Tax Permit

If the products or services you provide are subject to sales tax, you'll have to fill out an application to obtain a state sales tax permit. Complete and mail the application before you make a taxable sale. Many states impose penalties if you make a sale before you obtain a sales tax permit. Generally, you pay sales taxes four times a year, but you might have to pay them monthly if you make lots of sales. Be sure to collect all the taxes due. If you fail to do so, you can be held personally liable for the full amount of uncollected tax.

⚠️ Keep a Stern Lookout

States constantly change their sales tax laws, so be on the lookout for changes affecting your business. Professional organizations and your state chamber of commerce can be good sources of information on your state's sales tax rules. ∎

Insuring Your Business and Yourself

Most employees don't need to worry much about health or liability insurance or insurance for business property; their employers take care of their insurance needs. Unfortunately, this is not the case when you're self-employed. Self-employed people must purchase all their insurance themselves, and they usually need more coverage than employees. Insurance is the single greatest expense for many of the self-employed.

The best time to obtain insurance is when you first become self-employed or even before you quit your job to do so. Insurance is cheapest and easiest to obtain before you have a problem. Don't wait until you become ill, are being sued or have business property damaged or stolen to start thinking about insurance. By then it may be too late. And even if you're able to obtain insurance, it will likely not provide coverage for your pre-existing condition or problem.

 For more information on insurance, see *The Buyer's Guide to Business Insurance*, by Don Bury and Larry Heischman (Oasis Press), 1-800-228-2275, www.psi-research.com/oasis.htm.

A. Health Insurance

Health insurance pays at least part of your doctor, hospital and prescription expenses if you or a family member get sick. When you're self-employed, you have to obtain your own health insurance. Your clients or customers need not and will not provide it for you. Even if you're in perfect health, you should obtain health insurance. Medical costs for even relatively minor illnesses or injuries can be huge.

And if you're uninsured, the reality is that you may have difficulty finding a doctor or hospital willing to treat you. A recent study by the Harvard School of Public Health found that 45% of uninsured people had trouble getting adequate healthcare.

Although the laws of most states prevent an insurer from denying you coverage because you or a family member have a pre-existing medical problem, it can still be very difficult for self-employed people to obtain affordable health insurance if you or a family member have a chronic or serious illness. Some people who would like to quit their jobs and go into business for themselves refrain from doing so because they're afraid they won't be able to get health insurance.

The availability and cost of health insurance depends on many factors; some are within your control and others are not. Among the factors you have no control over are:

- your age and gender
- your health history, and
- where you live.

The most important factors over which you do have control are whether you obtain a group or individual policy and the type of plan you purchase.

1. Group and Individual Policies

You can obtain health insurance either through a group or as an individual. Group policies insure all members of the group. Insurers prefer to cover large groups because the risks and administrative costs are spread over many people.

Industry trade associations, professional groups and similar membership organizations can act as groups, so you can often obtain a group policy by joining one of them. There is a professional group or trade association for virtually every occupation. If you don't know of a group you can join, ask other self-employed people in your field. Most of these organizations have websites, so you may be able to find one using a search engine such as Google at www.google.com. You can also ask your local library if it has a book with a list of professional associations in your area. For example, thousands of membership organizations are listed in the *Directory of Organizations* (Gale Research).

You may also be able to obtain health insurance by joining your local chamber of commerce.

Finally, there are national membership organizations for the self-employed that provide insurance, such as the National Association of the Self-Employed, which you can reach at: 800-232-6273, www.nase.org. Other organizations set up specifically to provide health and other insurance benefits to members include the Support Services Alliance, 800-836-4772, www.ssainfo.com; and the Small Business Service Bureau, 800-343-0939, www.sbsb.com.

In addition, several states have formed cooperatives that small business owners may join to obtain group health insurance coverage. These are called Cooperatives for Health Insurance Purchasing (or CHIPs, for short). To find out if your state offers a CHIP, call the Institute for Health Policy Solutions at: 202-789-1491, or visit their website at www.ihps.org.

Individual coverage is typically 25% to 30% more expensive than group coverage, and individual coverage limits are usually lower than those offered under group coverage. For example, a group health insurance policy often does not impose any limit on the total benefits paid during your lifetime, while individual coverage often limits total lifetime benefits to one or two million dollars. With the skyrocketing costs of medical care, you can reach the limit surprisingly quickly if you have a chronic illness.

PORTABILITY LAW DOESN'T HELP SELF-EMPLOYED

In late 1996, Congress passed a law making employee health insurance portable—that is, employees who go from one job where they had group health coverage to another company that has health insurance can't be denied coverage solely because of their health status, claims history or medical condition.

The employer's health insurer can now exclude coverage for an employee's pre-existing medical condition for 12 months at most. A pre-existing condition is defined as one for which the employee received treatment within six months before the enrollment date in the new plan. The law took effect July 1, 1997. Unfortunately, the law does nothing for the millions of uninsured Americans or for people in business for themselves—that is, the self-employed.

2. Types of Plans

A bewildering array of health insurance plans are available, with a bewildering amount of lingo in their policies. As a self-employed person, you will most likely be able to choose among traditional and managed care plans.

The type of plan that will be best for you depends on how much money you can afford to spend for health insurance, your prior health history, which plans are available in your area and will accept you and how important choice of doctors is to you. It's best to shop around and investigate as many different plans as possible, since costs and benefits vary widely.

a. Traditional plans

The traditional form of health insurance is now becoming increasingly rare. In this type of fee for service plan, you're allowed to go to any doctor or hospital you choose. Either you or your doctor submit a claim to the insurer for reimbursement of the cost. However, the plan will pay only for care that is medically necessary and covered by the plan.

These plans typically require you to pay a deductible and a co-payment—that is, to pay a portion of your medical bills out of your own pocket before your insurance kicks in to cover expenses.

The deductible can be anywhere from $100 to several thousand dollars. Ordinarily, the deductible accumulates throughout the calendar year. This means any medical bills you pay from January 1 to December 31 count toward your deductible for that year; on New Year's Day, you start again at zero. Once you have met your deductible, your insurer starts paying benefits.

The co-payment is usually 20%, although 10% or 30% co-payments are not uncommon.

The higher the deductible and co-payment, the lower your premiums will be. However, if you get sick, you'll have to pay a substantial amount out of your own pocket. For example, if you have a policy with a $1,000 deductible and a 20% co-payment, you'll have to pay the first $1,000 of your yearly medical expenses yourself; thereafter, the insurer will pay 80% of the cost and you'll have to pay the other 20%. If you incur $5,000 in medical expenses under such a plan, you'd have to pay $1,800 of the cost yourself.

If you have a substantial medical bill—and a serious illness could cost several hundred thousand dollars—a 20% co-payment will be a real hardship. To avoid this, most insurance plans change their co-insurance percentages to 100% after you've incurred a certain amount of paid expenses for the year. This is called the out-of-pocket maximum.

b. Managed care

Managed care has become the norm in the United States. Under a managed care plan, instead of paying for each service you receive separately, your coverage is paid for in advance. Managed care is usually cheaper than a traditional plan, but you get a more limited choice of doctors and hospitals.

- **Health maintenance organizations.** Often called HMOs, these are prepaid health programs that require you to use doctors and hospitals that are part of the organization. Some HMOs employ their own doctors and run their own hospitals, while others are affiliated with private physicians. With an HMO, you get your medical care for a fixed price. Ordinarily you don't pay a deductible, but you may be charged a small co-payment—$10 or $15—for certain services. However, you can't go to a doctor or hospital outside the plan except in a medical emergency.

  HMOs often offer the lowest premiums around, but these savings come at a price. When you're in an HMO, your primary care doctor is in complete control of your care. You can't visit a specialist without a referral from another doctor. HMOs often discourage referrals to expensive specialists; your primary doctor's compensation from the HMO may even be reduced if he or she refers you to someone else.

  And many HMOs require you to get prior approval for any treatment you get. They also have detailed guidelines governing your care. For example, HMO rules may not allow you to be given experimental treatments, such as bone marrow transplants, if you get cancer.

- **Preferred provider organization plans.** Also called PPOs, these plans are a cross between traditional fee for service plans and HMOs. PPOs establish networks of doctors and hospitals that agree to provide care at a price that is usually lower than would be available outside the plan. You obtain full benefits only if you go to a doctor or hospital within the network. You are permitted go to a doctor or hospital outside the network, but you'll usually be required to pay a deductible and co-payment.

- **Point of service plans.** Point of service plans are similar to PPOs, except that you ordinarily have a primary care physician who is in charge of your medical care. PPOs generally don't require this.

3. Comparing Plans

Comparing health insurance plans can be confusing. Be sure to read the plan literature carefully. If you don't understand something, ask for an explanation. Compare the plans' coverage and costs.

No plan covers everything. HMOs typically provide broader coverage than fee for service plans. Most plans don't cover eyeglasses, hearing aids or cosmetic surgery. However, you may pay for such items with funds from a Medical Savings Account. (See Section 4.) Look carefully to see what medical expenses are covered. Expenses to check include:

- inpatient hospital services
- outpatient surgery
- physician visits in the hospital
- office visits
- skilled nursing care
- medical tests and x-rays
- prescription drugs
- mental health care
- drug and alcohol abuse treatment
- home health care visits
- rehabilitation facility care
- physical therapy
- hospice care
- maternity care
- preventive care and checkups, and
- well-baby care

See if the plan excludes pre-existing conditions or specific illnesses.

Next, compare the amount of the premium and the deductible or co-payment for each plan you consider. Just as important as the premium, however, is the maximum amount the plan will pay.

You should seek a benefit limit of at least $1 million. Beware of plans that advertise a high benefit ceiling but have a much lower benefit limit per claim or a lower maximum benefit per year.

Finally, see what type of hoops the plan requires you to jump through to get treatment. You may be required to get advance authorization for treatment or obtain a second opinion before you're allowed to have surgery. To save money, more and more traditional plans are imposing these types of restrictions usually associated with managed care.

If you're looking for a new plan but want to continue with your current doctor, make sure he or she belongs to the plan you're considering. Ask for your doctor's opinion about the various plans before you sign up. Most doctors belong to several plans and can tell you which are easy to deal with and which are Byzantine bureaucracies.

4. Archer Medical Savings Accounts

In 1997, the federal government began a pilot program allowing self-employed people to establish medical savings accounts, or MSAs. In 2000, these were renamed Archer MSAs in honor of a congressman who championed them. Archer MSAs represent the most radical change in health care financing in the last 50 years and are a real boon for the self-employed. If you are unhappy with the health coverage you have now, or you don't have any coverage at all, you should seriously consider establishing an Archer MSA.

Archer MSAs are designed to be used by self-employed people who purchase health insurance with a high deductible—that is, they must pay a substantial amount themselves before the insurance kicks in. (See the chart below.) Companies with 50 or fewer employees may also establish Archer MSAs for their workers.

When you purchase health insurance with a high deductible, you pay lower premiums. You can use the money you save on premiums—or money from any other source—to establish an

Archer MSA, which is similar to an IRA. You set up an Archer MSA with a bank or other financial institution. Your contributions to the account are tax deductible and you don't have to pay tax on the interest you earn on the money in your account.

2002 DEDUCTIBLES FOR ARCHER MSAs

Type of Health Coverage	Minimum Annual Deductible	Maximum Annual Deductible
Self-only	$1,650	$2,500
Family	$3,300	$6,050

These deductibles are adjusted annually for inflation. For the latest amounts, contact an Archer MSA insurer or review IRS Publication 969, *Medical Savings Accounts*. You can obtain this and all other IRS publications by calling 800-TAX-FORM, visiting your local IRS office or downloading them from the IRS Internet site at www.irs.gov.

---

a. Withdrawing Archer MSA funds

If you or a family member becomes sick, you can withdraw your money from the Archer MSA to pay your deductible or any other medical expenses. You pay no federal tax on Archer MSA withdrawals you use to pay medical expenses. Equally importantly, you can use your Archer MSA funds to pay any "qualified medical expense" under tax rules. Qualified medical expenses include all the things normally covered by health insurance (such as doctor and hospital bills and prescriptions). But they also include many things normally not covered by health insurance—for example, acupuncture, chiropractors, eyeglasses and contact lenses, dental treatment, fertility treatment, laser eye surgery and treatment for learning disabilities. You can find a complete list of qualified medical expenses in IRS Publication 502, *Medical and Dental Expenses.* However health insurance premiums may not be paid with Archer MSA funds, even though they are listed in Publication 502.

> **EXAMPLE:** Jane, a self-employed consultant and single mother, obtains health insurance coverage with a $2,000 deductible. She sets up an Archer MSA at her bank and deposits $1,500 every year for three years. She deducts each $1,500 contribution from her gross income for the year for income tax purposes. Jane pays no taxes on the interest she earns on the money in her account, which is invested in a money market fund. By the end of three years, she has $5,500 in the account. Jane becomes ill after the third year and is hospitalized. She withdraws $2,000 from her Archer MSA to pay her deductible. She also withdraws $3,000 to pay for speech therapy for her son, which is not covered by her health insurance. She pays no federal tax on these withdrawals.

However, if you withdraw funds from your Archer MSA to use for something other than medical expenses, you must pay the regular income tax on the withdrawals plus a 15% penalty. For example, if you were in the 27% income tax bracket, you'd have to pay a 42% tax on your withdrawals.

Once you reach the age of 65, or become disabled, you can withdraw your Archer MSA funds for any reason without penalty. You will have to pay regular income tax on the withdrawals only if you use them for nonmedical expenses.

If you enjoy good health while you have your Archer MSA and don't have to make many withdrawals, you may end up with a substantial amount in your account—and you can withdraw it without penalty for any purpose once you turn 65. In effect, an Archer MSA can serve as a supplemental retirement account, much like an additional IRA.

b. Tax reporting of Archer MSA withdrawals

When you withdraw money from your Archer MSA, your trustee (the institution handling your account) must report the amount of the withdrawal to the IRS. You must also report the amount on your annual tax return. This reporting is required even if you use the money you withdraw to pay for medical expenses, and so don't have to pay taxes on it. The IRS has created a special tax form for this—Form 8853.

You are supposed to keep a record of the name and address of each person or company whose bills you pay with funds from your Archer MSA, along with the amount and date of payment. You need not file these records with your tax return. Just keep them with your tax records.

c. Limit on contributions

Contributions to Archer MSAs are subject to an annual limitation, which is a percentage of your health plan deductible. If you have individual coverage, you may contribute up to 65% of your deductible. If you have family coverage, you may contribute up to 75% of your deductible each year. In addition, self-employed people may not contribute more than they earn from their businesses each year. These maximums are prorated during the initial year based on the number of months the Archer MSA is effective.

> **EXAMPLE:** Barry is self-employed and obtains individual health coverage with a $2,000 deductible. He can contribute up to $1,300 to an MSA each year (65% of $2,000), provided he earns at least this much from his business.

You have until April 15 of the current year to make a tax deductible Archer MSA contribution for the previous year. It's up to you to decide how much to contribute to your Archer MSA, up to the contribution limit. You can contribute nothing if you wish. However, financial experts advise you to contribute at least enough over the first five years to cover the amount of your deductible. You can contribute monthly or make a lump sum contribution. Also, it's up to you to decide how your account will be invested—it can be in a savings account, money market account, mutual fund or other investment vehicle. Typically, the money is invested in money market funds.

d. How to open an Archer MSA

You can't have an Archer MSA if you're covered by other health insurance—for example, if your spouse has family coverage for you from his or her job. So you may have to change your existing coverage.

To participate in the Archer MSA program, you need two things:

- a high-deductible health plan, and
- an Archer MSA account.

If you already have a high-deductible health plan that meets the criteria, you can immediately establish an Archer MSA with any bank, insurance company or financial institution that offers an MSA product. However, most traditional high-deductible health plans don't meet the criteria: either the deductible is too low or the cap on out of pocket expenses is too high. To qualify, the policy must have a cap on the out of pocket expenses you must pay of $5,850 for families and $3,200 for singles; the IRS adjusts these caps annually for inflation. Check your policy carefully to see if it meets these requirements.

An Archer MSA must be established with a trustee. Any person, insurance company, bank or financial institution already approved by the IRS to be a trustee or custodian of an IRA is approved automatically to serve as an Archer MSA trustee. Others have applied and been approved under IRS procedures for Archer MSAs.

If you're not insured by a qualifying high-deductible health plan, you must enroll in such a plan before setting up an Archer MSA. You may obtain coverage from an HMO, PPO or traditional plan. Some health insurers administer both the health plan and the Archer MSA; others have a bank or other financial institution handle the account separately.

Whoever administers your account will usually give you a checkbook or debit card to use to withdraw funds from the account.

Archer MSAs are not very well known—indeed, many insurance brokers have never heard of them—so you may have to do some searching to find an insurer. However, over 25 insurers are now offering Archer MSAs—including Blue Cross and Blue Shield in some states. In addition to Blue Cross and Blue Shield, some of the insurers most actively pursuing Archer MSA customers are:

- American Health Value; 800-914-3248; www.americanhealthvalue.com
- Fortis Health, Inc.; 888-846-3672; www.etdbw.com/fh/fortishealth/index.jsp
- Golden Rule Insurance Co.; 800-589-8911; www.goldenrule.com
- Mutual of Omaha Insurance Co.; 800-775-6000; www.mutualofomaha.com
- Trustmark Insurance Co.; 800-366-6663; www.trustmarkinsurance.com

You can find lists of insurers offering Archer MSA coverage and banks and other financial institutions offering trustee services at a website maintained by the Council for Affordable Health Insurance. The URL is: www.cahi.org/msaresources.htm. A list of insurance brokers who claim to be knowledgeable about Archer MSAs can be found at www.room100.com/naabcrr/.

Look at the plans offered by several companies to see which offers the best deal. Compare how much the set-up and service fees are, how the account is invested and whether you're allowed to move your Archer MSA to another trustee without losing your coverage.

e. Advantages for the self-employed

MSAs appear to be a very good deal, particularly if you're young or in good health and don't go to the doctor often or take many expensive medications. You can purchase a health plan with a high deductible, pay lower premiums and have the security of knowing you can dip into your MSA if you get sick and have to pay the deductible or other uncovered medical expenses.

But if you don't tap into the money, it will keep on accumulating free of taxes. You also get the benefit of deducting your Archer MSA contributions from your income taxes. And you can use your Archer MSA funds to pay for many health-related expenses that aren't covered by traditional health insurance.

ARCHER MSAs PAINT PRETTY PICTURE FOR GRAPHIC ARTIST

Martin, an Indiana-based self-employed graphic artist, lost his health insurance when his wife was laid off in 1997. He opened an Archer MSA and obtained health insurance for himself and his family with a high $3,200 family deductible. He pays $100 per month into his Archer MSA and deducts this $1,200 from his income tax each year. Fortunately, Martin and his family are extremely healthy, rarely go to the doctor and don't take expensive medications. As a result, Martin has made few withdrawals from his Archer MSA. He has accumulated over $6,000 in his account to date.

f. Time limits on the program

Archer MSAs were originally established as a four-year pilot program. They were scheduled to end at the end of 2000. As this book went to press,

Congress had extended the program to the end of 2003. There seems to be a very good chance that the program will be extended beyond that date. Indeed, in 2002, the Bush Administration introduced legislation to greatly expand the Archer MSA program. If you're using this book after 2003, check to see if you can still get an Archer MSA. Even if the Archer MSA program is terminated, those who already have MSAs will be able to continue to use and contribute to their accounts. For this reason, you may wish to set up an Archer MSA as soon as possible.

5. Insurance From a Former Job

If you're laid off or quit, and your employer provided you with group health insurance coverage, you may be able to keep your old health insurance coverage for a limited period of time. A federal workplace law called COBRA—short for Consolidated Omnibus Budget Reconciliation Act—requires your former employer to offer you and your spouse and dependents continuing insurance coverage if you lose your job for any reason other than being fired or resigning on account of gross misconduct.

The law applies to all employers with 20 or more employees. Your employer's health plan administrator is supposed to inform you within 14 days after you leave your job that you can continue your coverage. Coverage must be offered regardless of any pre-existing medical conditions you have. You have 60 days after receiving the notice to decide whether to obtain the continuing coverage. If you elect to obtain this coverage, it's retroactive to the date you left your job.

You usually have to pay for this coverage yourself. Your employer may charge you up to 102% of what it pays for the coverage; the extra 2% is for administrative costs. However, some employees who are laid off are able to negotiate free coverage for a time as part of a severance package.

Your coverage can last for anywhere from 18 to 36 months, depending on the reason why you left your job. At the end of that time, you have the right to convert to an individual policy. However, such a policy will likely be much more expensive than your employer's group policy.

Employers and health insurance plan administrators who violate COBRA can be fined. Unfortunately, the law generally cannot be enforced by any means other than a complex and expensive lawsuit. Such lawsuits are usually brought only by large groups of former employees who can afford to share the legal fees involved. If you run into problems claiming COBRA benefits, you can try calling your state Labor Department or IRS office; both agencies administer COBRA.

Many states have laws similar to COBRA that are easier to enforce and, more importantly, usually provide broader benefits and apply to smaller employers than does COBRA. These laws vary greatly from state to state. Contact your state insurance department for more information.

B. Disability Insurance

Disability insurance is designed to replace the income you lose if you become so sick or injured that you're unable to work for a lengthy period or never able to work again.

HOW IMPORTANT IS DISABILITY INSURANCE?

Disability insurers have compiled some very scary statistics in an attempt to show that disability insurance is absolutely essential. But is it really? If you work in a physically demanding occupation such as homebuilding or roofing, you may have a good chance of injuring yourself some time during your working life. But if you do office work, your chances of being disabled to such an extent that you are unable to work at all are much lower—particularly if you work at home and don't commute to work. Only you can decide whether to get disability insurance. But many self-employed people do just fine without it.

Disability insurance pays you a monthly benefit if you're unable to work. The cost of disability insurance depends on many factors:

- **The amount of coverage you obtain.** The maximum benefit you can obtain is usually two-thirds of your income. You can also obtain a smaller benefit and pay a smaller premium. At a minimum, try to obtain a benefit large enough to pay your monthly mortgage costs or rent and other fixed expenses.
- **The term of your coverage.** Some disability insurance plans offer only short-term benefits; the periods range from 13 weeks to five years. More expensive long-term plans pay you until you turn 65 or pay indefinitely. If you can afford it, a long-term policy is best.

- **The elimination period.** Most policies require you to wait a while after you become disabled before you start getting benefits. These elimination periods range from 30 to 730 days. A 90-day period is most common.
- **The nature of your work.** The amount of your premiums will also depend on the nature of your work. People in hazardous occupations—construction, for example—pay more than people with relatively safe jobs.
- **How your policy defines disability.** More expensive plans pay you full benefits if you can't work in your particular occupation, even if you may be able to do other types of work. Less expensive plans pay you only if you are unable to work in any occupation for which you're suited.
- **Your health.** Your current health is also an important factor. Usually, some type of physical exam will be required. If you smoke or suffer from a pre-existing medical condition, be prepared to pay more and search harder for coverage.

Unfortunately, it can be very difficult for self-employed people to obtain disability insurance. Many disability insurers don't like to issue policies to the self-employed because their incomes often fluctuate dramatically and they may not be able to pay their premiums. Also, because the self-employed don't have employers to supervise them and verify they're disabled, it can be difficult for an insurer to know for sure whether they're really unable to work. This is a particular problem if you work at home. Some insurers won't issue a disability policy to anyone who works more than half time at home.

Many insurers will not issue you a policy until you've been self-employed for at least six months. They want to see how much money you've earned during this period so they'll know whether you can afford the cost of premiums.

You'll have an easier time obtaining disability coverage if you can show an insurer that you're operating a successful, established business—for example, if you have:

- employees
- long-term contracts with clients
- a detailed financial forecast statement showing how much money you expect your business to earn in future years, and
- good credit references.

If you're still employed, try to obtain an individual disability policy before you quit your job and become self-employed.

If you're already self-employed, try to obtain group coverage though a professional organization or trade group. If this doesn't work, you'll have to obtain a individual policy.

There are five main disability insurers: Chubb Group of Insurance Companies, Northwestern Mutual Life Insurance Company, Paul Revere Life Insurance Company, Provident Life & Accident Insurance Company and UNUM Life Insurance Company of America. Try to get quotes from them all. You can likely find them listed in your local Yellow Pages under insurance. If not, check out their websites or find local insurance agents who represent them.

You can find a directory of many other companies that offer disability coverage on the Internet site maintained by the Health Insurance Association of America, an industry trade group. The Internet address is: www.hiaa.org/consumer/disability_dir.html.

C. Business Property Insurance

Business property insurance helps compensate for loss to your business assets: computers, office furniture, equipment and supplies. If, for example, your office burns down or is burglarized and all your business equipment is lost, your business property insurance will pay you a sum of money. Three main factors determine the cost of such insurance: the policy limits, policy type and scope of coverage.

1. Policy Limits

All policies have a maximum limit on how much you will be paid, no matter how great your loss. The greater your policy limit, the more expensive the insurance will be.

2. Replacement or Cash Value Coverage

Property insurance can pay you the cost of replacing your property or its actual present cash value. A replacement cost policy will replace your property at current prices regardless of what you paid for it. An actual cash value policy will only pay you what your property was worth when it was lost or destroyed. If the item has depreciated in value, you may obtain far less than the amount needed to replace it. A replacement cost policy is always preferable, but costs more than a cash value policy.

3. Scope of Coverage

Business property insurance comes in one of two forms: Named Peril and Special Form.

Named Peril policies only cover you for the types of harm listed in the policy. For example, the cheapest type of named peril policy only covers losses caused by fire, lightning, explosion, windstorm, hail, smoke, aircraft, vehicles, riot, vandalism, sprinkler leaks, sinkholes and volcanoes.

In contrast, a Special Form policy will cover you for anything except for certain perils that are specifically excluded—for example, earthquakes. Special Form policies cost somewhat more, but may be worth it.

Before you purchase business property insurance, take an inventory of all your business property and estimate how much it would cost you to replace it if it was lost, destroyed, damaged or stolen. Obtain replacement value business property coverage with a policy limit equal to this amount. If you can't afford that much coverage, consider a policy with a higher deductible. This is usually much wiser than obtaining coverage with a lower policy limit. If you insure your property for less than its full value, you won't be covered if you suffer a total loss.

Losses from earthquakes and floods normally aren't covered by business property policies. Earthquake insurance can be obtained through a separate policy or as an endorsement to your business property coverage. Flood insurance is usually handled through a separate policy called Difference in Conditions. Unfortunately, if you live in a part of the country where these hazards are common, such insurance can be expensive.

CHEAP INSURANCE FOR YOUR COMPUTER

If the only valuable business equipment you have is a computer, you may only need computer insurance. A company called Safeware will insure your computer equipment against any type of loss except theft of computer equipment left in an unattended car. The rates are based on the replacement cost of your computers—not their present cash value—and are quite reasonable. You can contact Safeware at: 800-848-3469. You can also apply online at www.safeware.com.

---

4. If You Work at Home

If you work at home, there are several ways to obtain insurance coverage for your business property.

- **Homeowner's policies.** If you have homeowner's insurance, take a careful look at your policy. It may provide you with a limited amount of insurance for business property—usually no more than $2,500 for property damaged or lost in your home and $250 away from your home. Computer equipment may not be covered at all. If you have very little business property, this might be enough coverage for you.

- **Homeowner's insurance endorsements.** You can double the amount of business property covered by your homeowner's policy by purchasing an endorsement—for example, increasing your coverage from $2,500 to $5,000. The cost is usually only about $20 per year. However, these endorsements typically are available only for businesses that generate $5,000 or less in annual income.

- **In-home policies.** The insurance industry has created a special policy for people who work at home. These in-home business policies insure your business property at a single location for up to $10,000. The cost is usually around $200 per year. For an additional premium, the policy includes liability coverage ranging from $300,000 to $1 million. Liability premium costs are based on how much coverage you buy. There's also coverage available to protect against lost valuable papers, records, accounts receivable, off-site business property and equipment.

- **BOP policies.** Business owner's packaged policies (or BOPs for short) are for businesses not based at home or for larger home-based businesses. Such policies combine both property and liability coverage in a single policy. BOPs are more expensive than in-home policies, but provide the most comprehensive coverage available for small businesses.

- **Business property policies.** Some policies just cover your business property. This might be a good idea if you have extremely valuable business equipment.

5. If You Rent an Office

If you rent an office outside your home, read your lease carefully to see if it requires you to carry insurance. Many commercial landlords require their tenants to carry insurance to cover damage the tenant does to the premises and injuries suffered by clients and other visitors.

The lease may specify how much insurance you must carry. Your best bet will probably be to get a BOP policy providing both property and liability coverage. Your landlord will probably require you to submit proof that you have insurance—for example, a photocopy of the first page of your policy.

D. Liability Insurance

Liability insurance protects you when you're sued for something you did or failed to do that injured another person or damaged some property. It pays the legal fees for defending such lawsuits and any settlement or judgment against you up to the amount of the policy, as well as the injured person's medical bills. In our lawsuit-happy society, such insurance is often a must.

There are two very different types of liability insurance:

- general liability insurance, and
- professional liability insurance.

You may need both types of coverage.

INCORPORATING PROVIDES SOME LAWSUIT PROTECTION

Incorporating your business gives you some protection from lawsuits, but not as much as you may think. For example, incorporating may protect your personal assets from lawsuits by people who are injured on your premises, but it won't protect you from personal liability if someone is injured or damaged because of your malpractice or negligence—that is, your failure to exercise your professional responsibilities with a reasonable amount of care.

Also, unless you have a decent insurance policy, all the assets of your incorporated business—which will probably amount to a large portion of your net worth—can be taken to satisfy a court judgment obtained by an injured person. (See Chapter 2.)

---

1. General Liability Insurance

General liability insurance provides coverage for the types of lawsuits any business owner could face. For example, this type of insurance protects you if a client visiting your home office slips on the newly washed floor and shatters her elbow, or you knock over and shatter an heirloom vase while visiting a client in his home.

You definitely need this coverage if clients or customers visit your office. If you already have a homeowners' or renters' insurance policy, don't assume you're covered for these types of claims. Such policies ordinarily don't provide coverage for injuries to business visitors unless you obtain and pay for a special endorsement.

You also need general liability insurance if you do any part of your work away from your office—for example, in clients' offices or homes. You could injure someone or damage property while working there.

On the other hand, if you have little or no contact with the public, you may not need such insurance. For example, a freelance writer who works at home and never receives business visitors probably wouldn't need general liability coverage.

However, whether you want it or not, some clients may require you to carry liability insurance as a condition of doing business with you. Many clients are afraid that if you injure someone while working for them and you don't have insurance, the injured person will sue them instead. This fear is well founded: lawyers always go after the deepest pockets—the person with insurance or money to pay a judgment. You might think this means you'd be better off with no insurance at all because people won't sue you, but this is not necessarily the case. If you have money or property, there's a good chance you'll get sued. Liability insurance will protect you from losing everything you own.

Luckily, general liability insurance is not terribly expensive; you can usually obtain it for a few hundred dollars per year. You can purchase such coverage:

- as part of a package policy such as a business owner's package or BOP policy, or
- by obtaining a separate general liability insurance policy known as a commercial general liability or CGL policy; this will probably cost the most, but will give you higher policy limits—that is, more coverage.

If you work at home, you may also be able to add an endorsement to your homeowner's policy covering injuries to business visitors.

2. Professional Liability Insurance

General liability insurance does not cover professional negligence—that is, claims for damages caused because of an alleged error or omission in the way you perform your services. You need a separate professional liability insurance policy, also known as errors and omissions or E & O

coverage. Some types of workers—doctors and lawyers, for example—are required by state law to obtain such insurance.

EXAMPLE: Susan, an architect, designs a factory building that collapses, costing her client a fortune in damages and lost business. The client claims that Susan's design for the building was faulty and sues her for the economic losses it suffered. Susan's general liability policy won't cover such a claim. She needs a special E & O policy for architects.

Common types of professional liability insurance policies cover the following types of workers:

- accountants
- architects
- attorneys
- doctors
- engineers
- insurance agents and brokers
- pension plan fiduciaries, and
- stockbrokers.

You can obtain E & O coverage for many other occupations as well if you're willing to pay the price. Because of the growing number of professional negligence suits and the huge costs of litigation, such insurance tends to be expensive, ranging from several hundred to several thousand dollars per year. The premiums you'll have to pay depend on many factors, including:

- the claims history for your type of business; insurance costs more for businesses that generate lots of lawsuits
- the size of your business; the more work you do, the more opportunity there is for you to make a mistake resulting in a lawsuit
- your knowledge and experience in your field (less experienced self-employed people are more likely to make mistakes), and
- the size of your clients' businesses; mistakes involving large businesses will likely result in larger lawsuits than those involving small businesses.

If you need E & O insurance, the first place to look is a professional association. Many of them arrange for special deals with insurers offering lower rates; those that don't can at least steer you to a good insurer.

HOME-BASED ARCHITECT GETS LIABILITY INSURANCE

Mel, an architect, recently left a job with a large architectural firm in San Francisco and set up his own architecture business, designing homes and small commercial offices. He works out of an office in a detached studio in his backyard. It soon dawned on Mel that he needed liability insurance.

First, Mel needed general liability insurance because clients, delivery people and other business visitors come and go from his home office every week. Mel could be subject to a huge lawsuit if, for example, a client was injured after slipping on a roller skate left by Mel's son. Mel called his homeowner's insurer and obtained an endorsement to his existing homeowner's policy covering injuries to business visitors and insuring up to $25,000 worth of his business equipment. He had to pay an additional $150 annual premium for $500,000 in liability coverage.

Mel also needed E & O insurance because he could also be subject to a lawsuit for professional negligence if a problem occurred with one of his buildings. He shopped around and decided to purchase coverage through the American Institute of Architects in Washington, DC—a leading membership organization for architects. Mel obtained a one million dollar architect liability policy for $3,300 per year.

E. Car Insurance

If, like most self-employed people, you use your automobile for business as well as personal use— for example, visiting clients or transporting supplies in addition to grocery shopping—you need to make certain that your automobile insurance will protect you from accidents that may occur while on business. The personal automobile policy you already have may also cover your business use of your car. On the other hand, it may specifically exclude coverage if you use your car on business.

Review your policy and discuss the matter with your insurance agent or auto insurer. You may need to purchase a separate business auto insurance policy or obtain a special endorsement covering your business use. Whatever you do, make sure your insurer knows you use your car for business, not just for private use or driving to and from your office. If you do not inform your company about this, it may cancel your coverage if a claim occurs that reflects a business use—for example, you get into an accident while on a business trip.

If you keep one or more cars strictly for business use, you will definitely need a separate business automobile policy. You may be able to purchase such a policy from your personal auto insurer.

F. Workers' Compensation Insurance

Each state has its own workers' compensation system that is designed to provide replacement income and cover medical expenses for employees who suffer work-related injuries or illnesses. To pay for this, employers are required to pay for workers' compensation insurance for their employees, through either a state fund or a private insurance company.

Before the first workers' compensation laws were adopted about 80 years ago, an employee injured on the job had only one recourse: to sue the employer in court for negligence—a difficult, time-consuming and expensive process. The workers' compensation laws changed all this by establishing a no-fault system. Injured employees gave up their rights to sue in court. In return, employees became entitled to receive compensation without having to prove that the employer caused the injury. In exchange for paying for workers' compensation insurance, employers were spared having to defend lawsuits by injured employees and paying out damages.

1. Restricted to Employees

Workers' compensation is for employees, not self-employed people (independent contractors). If you qualify as an independent contractor under your state's workers' compensation insurance law, your clients or customers need not provide you with workers' compensation coverage. Each state has its own test to determine if a worker qualifies as an employee or independent contractor for workers' compensation purposes.

For detailed information on how states classify workers for workers' compensation purposes, see *Hiring Independent Contractors: The Employer's Legal Guide,* by Stephen Fishman (Nolo).

You should satisfy your state's test if you act to preserve your status as an independent contractor. (See Chapter 15.) However, whether you're an independent contractor or employee for workers' compensation purposes is the client's determination to make, not yours.

2. Your Worker Status

Not having to provide you with workers' compensation coverage saves your clients a lot of money, but also presents them with a problem: If you're injured while working on a client's behalf, you

could file a workers' compensation claim and allege that you're really the client's employee. If you prevail on your claim, you can collect workers' compensation benefits even if your injuries were completely your own fault. Fines and penalties can also be imposed against your client by the state workers' compensation agency if it determines that the client misclassified you as an independent contractor.

Many hiring firms respond to these fears by requiring you to obtain your own workers' compensation coverage, even if you don't want it. They're afraid that if you don't have your own coverage, you'll file a workers' compensation claim against them if you're injured on the job. Also, many workers' compensation insurers require hiring firms to pay additional premiums for any independent contractors they hire that don't have their own workers' compensation coverage.

3. If You Have Employees

Even if your clients don't require you to have it, you must obtain workers' compensation coverage if you have employees. However, if you have only a few employees, you might not need to obtain workers' compensation coverage. The work-

STATE EMPLOYEE MINIMUMS FOR WORKERS' COMPENSATION		
Workers' Comp not required if you have two or fewer employees	**Workers' Comp not required if you have three or fewer employees**	**Workers' Comp not required if you have four or fewer employees**
Arkansas	Florida	Alabama
Georgia	Rhode Island	Mississippi
Michigan	South Carolina	Missouri
New Mexico		Tennessee
North Carolina		
Virginia		
Wisconsin		

ers' compensation laws of about one-third of the states exclude many small employers. (See the chart on the previous page.)

Many knowledgeable clients will want to see proof that you have workers' compensation insurance for your employees before they hire you. The reason for their adamance is that your state law will probably require your client to provide the insurance if you don't. The purpose of these laws is to prevent employers from avoiding paying for workers' compensation insurance by subcontracting work out to independent contractors who don't insure their employees.

4. Obtaining Coverage

Most small businesses buy insurance through a state fund or from a private insurance carrier.

In the following states, you must purchase coverage from the state fund: Nevada, North Dakota, Ohio, Washington and West Virginia.

In a number of states, you have a choice of buying coverage from either the state or a private insurance company. They include: Arizona, California, Colorado, Hawaii, Idaho, Kentucky, Maine, Maryland, Louisiana, Michigan, Minnesota, Missouri, Montana, New Mexico, New York, Oklahoma, Oregon, Pennsylvania, Rhode Island, Utah and Texas.

If private insurance is an option in your state, you may be able to save money on premiums by coordinating workers' compensation coverage with property damage and liability insurance. (See Sections C and D.)

5. Cost of Coverage

The cost of workers' compensation varies from state to state. What you will have to pay depends upon a number of factors, including:
- the size of your payroll
- the nature of your work, and

SUING YOUR CLIENTS FOR NEGLIGENCE

Even if you have your own workers' compensation insurance, you can still sue a hiring firm for damages if its negligence caused or contributed to a work-related injury. Since you're not the hiring firm's employee, the workers' compensation provisions barring lawsuits by injured employees won't apply to you. The damages available through a lawsuit may far exceed the modest workers' compensation benefits to which you may be entitled.

EXAMPLE: Trish, a self-employed trucker, contracts to haul produce for the Acme Produce Co. Trish is self-employed and Acme does not provide her with workers' compensation insurance. At Acme's insistence, however, Trish obtains her own workers' compensation coverage. Trish loses her little finger when an Acme employee negligently drops a load of asparagus on her hand. Since Trish is self-employed, she can sue Acme in court for negligence even though she has workers' compensation insurance. If she can prove Acme's negligence, Trish can collect damages for her lost wages, medical expenses and her pain and suffering as well. These damages could far exceed the modest workers' compensation benefits Trish may be entitled to for losing her finger.

However, if you receive workers' compensation benefits and also obtain damages from the person that caused the injury, you may have to reimburse your workers' compensation insurer for any amounts it paid for your medical care. Your insurer might also be able to bring its own lawsuit against your client.

• how many claims have been filed in the past by your employees.

As you might expect, it costs far more to insure employees in hazardous occupations such as construction than to insure those who work in relatively safe jobs such as clerical work. It might cost $200 to $300 a year to insure a clerical worker and perhaps ten times as much to insure a construction worker or roofer.

G. Other Types of Insurance

There are several other types of insurance policies that may be useful for self-employed people:

• business interruption insurance, designed to replace the income you lose if your business property is damaged or destroyed due to fire or other disasters and you're forced to close, relocate or cut your business back while you recover and rebuild

• electronic data processing or EDP insurance, which compensates you for the cost of reconstructing the data you lose when your computer equipment is damaged or destroyed, and

• product liability insurance, which covers liability for injuries caused by products you design, manufacture or sell.

If you're interested in such coverage, talk to several agents who have experience dealing with self-employed people in your field. Professional and trade organizations may also be able to give you helpful advice.

H. Ways to Find and Save Money on Insurance

There are a number of things you can do to make it easier to find and pay for insurance.

1. Seek Out Group Plans

For many self-employed people, the cheapest and easiest way to obtain insurance is through a professional organization, trade association or similar membership organization.

There are hundreds of such organizations representing every conceivable occupation—for example, the American Society of Home Inspectors, the Association of Independent Video and Filmmakers and the Graphic Artists Guild.

There are also national membership organizations that allow all types of self-employed people to join—for example, the National Association of the Self Employed and the Home Office Association of America. Many of these organizations give their members access to group health and business insurance. Because these organizations have many members, they can often negotiate cheaper rates with insurers than you can yourself. Your local chamber of commerce or alumni association may also offer insurance benefits.

If you don't know the name and address of an organization you may be eligible to join, ask other self-employed people or check out the *Encyclopedia of Associations* (Gale Research); it should be available in your public library. Also, many of these organizations have websites on the Internet, so you may be able to find the one you want by doing an Internet search. (See Chapter 21.)

2. Buying From an Insurance Company

If you're unable to arrange coverage through a group, try to purchase insurance from one of the growing number of companies that sell policies directly to the public rather than using insurance agents or brokers. These companies can usually offer you lower rates because they don't have to pay commissions to insurance agents. Other self-employed people may be able to recommend a company to you, or you can find them listed in the Yellow Pages under insurance.

BE WARY OF INSURANCE AGENTS

Insurance agents or brokers can be a useful source of information. The terms agent and broker mean different things in different parts of the country, however. In some states, an agent is a person who represents a specific insurance company and a broker is a person who is free to sell insurance offered by various companies. Elsewhere, the term insurance agent is used more broadly to cover both types of representatives. If you want to use an agent, find one who is familiar with businesses such as yours and who represents more than one insurer.

However, be wary about what any agent tells you. Insurance agents are salespeople who earn their livings by selling insurance policies to the public, for which they are paid commissions by insurance companies. The more insurance they sell you, the more money they make. Agents often recommend insurance from companies paying the highest commissions, whether or not it's the cheapest or best policy for you. If you use an agent, try to get quotes from more than one and compare them with the coverage you can obtain through a professional organization or by dealing directly with an insurer.

---

3. Comparison Shop

Insurance costs vary widely from company to company. You may be able to save a lot by shopping around. Also, review your coverage and rates periodically. Insurance costs go up and down periodically. If you're shopping for insurance during a time when prices are low, try lock-

ing in a low rate by signing up for a contract for three or more years.

4. Increase Your Deductibles

Your premiums will be lower if you obtain policies with high deductibles. For example, the difference between a $250 and $500 deductible may be 10% in premium costs, and the difference between a $500 and $1,000 deductible may save you an additional 3% to 5%.

5. Find a Comprehensive Package

It's often cheaper to purchase a comprehensive insurance package that contains many types of coverage than to buy coverage piecemeal from several companies. Many insurers offer special policies for small business owners, also called BOP policies, that combine liability coverage against injuries to clients or customers or damage to their property while on your premises with fire and theft coverage and business interruption insurance.

6. Use the Internet

You can obtain a great deal of information about insurance from your computer. Insurance companies, agents and organizations all have their own sites. Some good places to start an Internet search about insurance are:

- **Health Insurance Association of America.** This is a nationwide trade association of over 250 health insurers. Its Internet site contains useful articles on all aspects of health insurance and directories of disability and long-term health insurance providers. The Internet address is www.hiaa.org.
- **Quotesmith.** This company provides free quotes from hundreds of insurance companies. The Internet address is www.quotesmith.com.

CHECK ON AN INSURER'S FINANCIAL HEALTH

Several insurance companies have gone broke in recent years. If this happens and you have a loss covered by a policy, you may only receive a small part of the coverage you paid for—or none at all. The best way to avoid this is to obtain coverage from an insurer that is in good financial health.

You can check out insurers' financial status in these standard reference works, which rate insurance companies for financial solvency:

- *Best's Insurance Reports* (Property-Casualty Insurance Section)
- *Moody's Bank and Financial Manual* (Volume 2)
- *Duff & Phelps* (Insurance Company Claims-Paying Ability Rating Guide), and
- *Standard & Poor's.*

An insurance agent should be able to give you the latest rating from these publications. They may also be available in your public library.

If you have access to the Internet, you can obtain insurance company ratings from Standard & Poor's and Duff & Phelps for free on the Insurance News Network, an Internet site maintained by the Independent Insurance Agents of America. The Internet address is www.insure.com.

- **Quicken.com.** The massive Quicken.com website provides lots of information about insurance, as well as insurance price quotes. You can find it at www.quicken.com/insurance.
- **Insure.com.** This website contains a good deal of basic information on all forms of insurance and will link you to other websites from which you can obtain insurance quotes and apply for insurance online. The Web address is www.insure.com.
- **Yahoo! Insurance Center.** This website also provides much information on insurance and online quotes. It can also help you locate insurance agents and brokers. The URL is http://insurance.yahoo.com/.

7. Deduct Your Business Insurance Costs

You can deduct the premiums for any type of insurance you obtain for your business from your income taxes. This includes business property insurance, liability insurance, insurance for business vehicles and workers' compensation insurance.

The premiums for health insurance you obtain for yourself are deductible if you're a sole proprietor, partner in a partnership or S corporation owner. They are also deductible if you form a C corporation and it provides insurance for you as its employee. (See Chapter 2.)

Car insurance and homeowners' or renters' insurance premiums are deductible to the extent you use your car or home for business. (See Chapter 9.)

However, you may not deduct premiums for life or disability insurance for yourself. But, if you become disabled, the disability insurance benefits you receive are not taxable. ■

Pricing Your Services and Getting Paid

Two difficult problems self-employed workers face are deciding how much to charge clients and getting paid for their services. This chapter will help you figure out how to set your fees and give you ideas about what to do when clients or customers don't pay what they owe you.

A. Pricing Your Services

New and experienced self-employed people alike are often perplexed about how much to charge. No book can tell you how much your services are worth, but this section gives you some factors to consider in making this determination.

1. How the Self-Employed Are Paid

There are no legal rules controlling how (or how much) you are paid. It is entirely a matter for negotiation between you and your clients. The method you choose will be determined by the customs and practices in your particular field, your personal preferences and those of your clients. Some clients insist on paying all self-employed people they hire a particular way—for example, a fixed fee. Others are more flexible. Many self-employed people also have strong preferences for particular payment methods—for example, some insist on always being paid by the hour.

When you're first starting out, you may wish to try several different payment methods with different clients to see which works best for you. However, if the customary practices in your field dictate a particular payment method, you may have no choice in the matter. Other self-employed workers and professional organizations can give you information on the practices in your particular field.

This section provides an overview of the more common payment methods for the self-employed. However, these are by no means the only ways you can be paid. Other methods are used in some fields—for example, freelance writers are often paid a fixed amount for each word they write.

 For more information on payment methods and setting fees, see:
- *Selling Your Services*, by Robert Bly (Henry Holt), and
- *The Contract and Fee Setting Guide for Consultants and Professionals,* by Howard Shenson (John Wiley & Sons).

a. Fixed fee

In a fixed fee agreement, you charge a set amount for an entire project. Your fixed fee can include all your expenses—for example, materials costs, travel expenses, phone and fax expenses and photocopying charges—or you can bill them separately to the client.

Most clients like fixed fee agreements because they know exactly what they'll have to pay for your services. However, fixed fees can be risky for you. If you underestimate the time and expense required to complete the project, you could earn much less than your work was worth or even lose money. Many self-employed people refuse to use fixed fees for this reason. For example, one self-employed technical writer always charges by the hour because she says she's never had a project that didn't last longer than both she and the client thought it would.

> **EXAMPLE:** Ellen, a graphic artist, agrees to design a series of book covers for the Scrivener & Sons Publishing Co. Her fixed price contract provides that she'll be paid $5,000 for all the covers. Ellen estimates that the project will take 75 hours at most, so she would earn at least $66 per hour, more than her normal hourly rate of $50 per hour.
>
> However, due to the publisher's exacting standards and demands for revisions, the project ends up taking Ellen 125 hours. As a result, she earns only $40 per hour for the project—far less than what she would have charged had she billed by the hour.

Although fixed fee agreements can be risky, they can also be very rewarding if you work efficiently and you accurately estimate how much time and money a project will take. Surveys of the self-employed have consistently found that fixed fee agreements are more profitable than other types of contracts. For example, a study recently conducted by the hosts of the consultant's forum on the America Online service found that self-employed people who charged fixed fees earned on average 150% more than those who charged by the hour for the same services. A similar survey conducted by a trade journal called *The Professional Consultant* found that self-employed people charging fixed fees earned 95% more than their colleagues who charged by the hour or day.

REDUCING THE RISKS OF FIXED FEES

There are several ways to reduce the risks involved in charging a fixed fee.

- First and foremost, carefully and thoroughly define the scope of the project in writing before determining your fee. If this will take a substantial amount of time, you may wish to charge the client a flat fee or hourly rate to compensate you for the work involved in this assessment process.

- Leave some room for error or surprises when you calculate your fee—that is, charge the client as if the project will take a bit longer than you think it will.

- Consider placing a cap on the total number of hours you'll work on the project. Once the cap is reached, you and the client must negotiate new payment terms. For example, the client might increase your fixed fee or agree to pay you by the hour until the project is finished.

- Make sure your agreement with the client contains a provision allowing you to renegotiate your price if the client makes changes or the project takes longer than you estimated. (See Chapter 19.)

b. Unit of time

It's safer for you to be paid for your time—that is, by the number of hours or days you spend on a project—rather than a fixed fee. This is especially true if you are unsure how long or difficult the project will be or if the client is likely to demand substantial changes midstream. Many self-employed people refuse to work any other way. This method of payment is customary in many fields, including law and accounting.

However, clients are often nervous about paying by the hour. They're afraid you'll spread out the project for as long as possible to earn more money. Clients will often seek to place a limit on the total number of hours you can spend on the project. This way, they limit the total amount they'll have to spend. Others will require you to provide a time estimate. If you do this, be sure to call the client before spending more time on the project than you estimated.

As with fixed fees, it's a good idea to leave some margin for error when you provide a time estimate. One self-employed person says she determines how many hours a job will take by first deciding how long it should take, doubling that number and then adding 25%. You may not need to go to this extreme, but it's wise to be conservative when estimating the time any project will require.

c. Fixed and hourly fee combinations

You can also combine a fixed fee with an hourly payment. This arrangement allows you to reduce the risk that you'll be underpaid—if you can't accurately estimate how much time or effort some part of the project might take, you can charge by the hour for that work, while charging a fixed fee for the rest of the project. For example, if your work involves some tasks that are essentially mechanical and others that are highly creative, you can probably accurately estimate how long the mechanical work will take but may have great difficulty estimating how much time the creative work will require. You can reduce the risk of underpayment by charging a fixed fee for the mechanical work and billing by the hour for the creative work.

EXAMPLE: Bruno, a freelance graphic artist, is hired by Scrivener & Sons Publishing Co. to produce the cover for its new detective thriller, *And Then You Die*. Bruno has absolutely no idea how long it will take him to come up with an acceptable design for the cover. He charges Scrivener $75 per hour for this design work. Once a design is accepted, however, Bruno knows exactly how long it will take him to produce a camera-ready version. He charges Scrivener a fixed fee of $1,000 for this humdrum production work.

d. Retainer agreements

With a retainer agreement, you receive a fixed fee up front in return for promising to be available to work a certain number of hours for the client each month or to perform a specified task. Often, the client pays a lump sum retainer fee at the outset of the agreement; or you can be paid on a regular schedule—for example, monthly, quarterly or annually.

EXAMPLE: Jean, an accountant, agrees to perform up to 20 hours of accounting services for Acme Corp. every month, for which Acme pays her $1,500 per month.

Many self-employed people like retainer agreements because they provide a guaranteed source of income. But in return for this security, you usually have to charge somewhat less than you do when paid on a per project basis. Also, retainer agreements can contradict your work status. If you spend most of your time working for a single client, the IRS may view you as that client's employee. (See Chapter 15.)

e. Performance billing

Perhaps the riskiest form of billing is performance billing, also known as charging a contingency fee. Basically, this means you get paid according to the value of the results you achieve for a client. If you get poor results, you may receive little or nothing. Clients generally favor this type of arrangement because they don't have to pay you if your services don't benefit them. Using this type of fee arrangement can help you get business if a client is skeptical that you'll perform as promised or if you're providing a new service with benefits that are not generally understood.

This type of fee arrangement is used most often for sales or marketing projects in which the fee is based on a percentage of the increased business.

EXAMPLE: Alice, a marketing consultant, contracts to perform marketing services for Acme Corp. to help increase its sales. Acme agrees to pay her 25% of the total increase in gross sales over the next 12 months. If sales don't go up, Alice gets nothing.

Some self-employed people reduce the risks involved in performance billing by requiring their clients to pay them a minimum amount regardless of the results they achieve. For example, a contract might provide that a sales trainer would receive $5,000 for providing training services plus 10% of the increase in the client's sales for a specified number of months after the training program.

If you use a performance contract, don't tie your compensation to the client's profits. Clients can easily manipulate their profits—and therefore reduce your compensation—through accounting gimmicks. Use a standard that is easier to measure and harder to manipulate, such as the client's gross sales or some measurable cost saving.

f. Commissions

Self-employed people who sell products or services are often paid by commission—that is, a set amount for each sale they make. Many independent sales representatives, brokers, distributors and agents are paid on a commission basis.

EXAMPLE: Mark is a self-employed salesperson who sells industrial filters. He receives a commission from the filter manufacturer for each filter he sells. The commission is equal to 20% of the price of the filter.

If you're a good salesperson, you can earn far more on commission than with any other payment method. But if business is poor, your earnings will suffer.

2. Determining Your Hourly Rate

However you're paid, you need to determine how much to charge per hour. This is so even if you're paid a fixed fee for an entire project. To determine the fixed fee you should charge, you must estimate how many hours the job will take, multiply the total by your hourly rate, then add the amount of your expenses. Knowing how much you should earn per hour will also help you know whether a retainer agreement or performance billing is cost effective or whether a sales commission is fair.

If you're experienced in your field, you probably already know what to charge because you are familiar with market conditions. However, if you're just starting out, you may have no idea what you can or should charge. If you're in this boat, try using a two-step approach to determine your hourly rate:

- calculate what your rate should be based on your expenses, then
- investigate the marketplace to see if you should adjust your rate up or down.

a. Hourly rate based on expenses

A standard formula for determining an hourly rate requires you to add together your labor and overhead costs, add the profit you want to earn, then divide the total by your hours worked. This is the absolute minimum you must charge to pay your expenses, pay yourself a salary and earn a profit. Depending on market conditions, you may be able to charge more for your services or you might have to charge less. (See Section A2c.)

To determine how much your labor is worth, pick a figure for your annual salary. This can be what you earned for doing similar work when you were an employee, what other employees earn for similar work or how much you'd like to earn.

Next, compute your annual overhead. Overhead includes all the costs you incur to do business—for example:

- rent and utilities
- business insurance
- stationery and supplies
- postage and delivery costs
- office equipment and furniture
- clerical help
- travel expenses
- professional association memberships
- legal and accounting fees
- telephone expenses
- business-related meals and entertainment, and
- advertising and marketing costs—for example, the cost of a Yellow Pages ad or brochure.

Overhead also includes the cost of your fringe benefits, such as medical insurance, disability insurance and retirement fund money. Also include your income and self-employment taxes.

If you're just starting out, you'll have to estimate these expenses or ask other self-employed people to give you some idea of their overhead costs.

You're also entitled to earn a profit over and above your labor and overhead expenses. Your salary is part of your costs—it does not include profit. Profit is the reward you get for taking the risks of being in business for yourself. It also provides money you can use to expand and develop your business. Profit is usually expressed as a percentage of total costs. There is no standard profit percentage, but a 10% to 20% profit is common.

Finally, you must determine how many hours you'll work and get paid for during the year. Assume you'll work a 40-hour week for purposes of this calculation, although you may end up working more than this. If you want to take a two-week vacation, you'll have a maximum of 2,000 billable hours (50 weeks x 40 hours). If you want to take a longer vacation, you'll have fewer billable hours.

However, you'll probably spend at least 25% to 35% of your time on tasks such as bookkeeping and billing, marketing your services, upgrading your skills and doing other things you can't bill to clients. This means you'll likely have at most 1,300 to 1,500 hours for which you can get paid each year—if you factor in two vacation weeks away from work.

EXAMPLE: Sam, a self-employed computer programmer, earned a $50,000 salary as an employee and wants to receive at least the same salary. He estimates that his annual overhead amounts to $20,000 per year. He wants to earn a 10% profit and estimates he'll have 1,500 billable hours each year. To determine his hourly rate, Sam must:

- add his salary and overhead together: $50,000 + $20,000 = $70,000
- multiply this total by his 10% profit margin and add the amount to his salary and overhead: $70,000 x 10% = $7,000; $70,000 + $7,000 = $77,000, and
- divide the total by his annual billable hours: $77,000 ÷ 1,500 = $51.33.

Sam determines that his hourly rate should be $51.33. He rounds this off to $50. However, depending on market conditions, Sam might end up charging more or less.

b. Hourly rate worksheet

You can use the following worksheet to calculate your hourly rate.

HOURLY RATE WORKSHEET

Annual salary you want to earn   ————————

Desired Profit %   ————————

Billable hours per year   ————————

Yearly Expenses

- Marketing   ————————

- Travel   ————————

- Legal and accounting costs   ————————

- Insurance   ————————

- Supplies   ————————

- Rent   ————————

- Utilities   ————————

- Telephone   ————————

- Professional association memberships   ————————

- Business meals and entertainment   ————————

- Other   ————————

Total Expenses   ————————

Calculation:

- Step 1: Salary + Expenses = X   ————————

- Step 2: X x Profit % = Y   ————————

- Step 3: X + Y = Z   ————————

- Step 4: Z ÷ Billable Hours = Hourly Rate   ————————

A CALCULATING SHORTCUT

An easier but less accurate way to calculate your hourly rate is to find out what hourly salary you'd likely receive if you were to provide your services as an employee in someone else's business and multiply this by 2.5 or 3. This is a much cruder way business management experts have developed to calculate how much money you need to earn to pay your expenses, salary and earn a profit.

EXAMPLE: Betty, a freelance word processor, knows that employees performing the same work receive $15 per hour. She should charge $37.50 to $45 per hour.

If you don't know what employees receive for doing work similar to yours, try calling several employment agencies in your area and ask what you'd earn per hour as an employee.

You can also obtain salary information for virtually every conceivable occupation from *The Occupational Outlook Handbook*, published by the U.S. Department of Labor. You should be able to find it in your public library.

c.   Investigate the marketplace

It's not enough to calculate how much you'd like to earn per hour. You also have to determine whether this figure is realistic. This requires you to do a little sleuthing to find out what other self-employed people are charging for similar services and what the clients you'd like to work for are willing to pay. There are many ways to gather this information.

- Contact a professional organization or trade association for your field. It may be able to tell you what other self-employed people are charging in your area.
- Some professional organizations even publish pricing guides. For example, the National Writers Union publishes the *National Writers Union Guide to Freelance Rates & Standard Practice* (Writer's Digest Books), which lists rates for all types of freelance writing assignments. And the Graphic Artists Guild puts out a *Handbook of Pricing & Ethical Guidelines* for freelance graphic artists.
- Ask other self-employed people what they charge. If you have a computer and modem, you can communicate pricing concerns with other self-employed people on commercial online services such as Compuserve and America Online or on the World Wide Web. (See Chapter 21, Section E.)
- Talk with potential clients and customers—for example, attend trade shows and business conventions.

3.   Experimenting With Charging

Pricing is an art, not an exact science. There are no magic formulas. And nostrums you often hear, such as "charge whatever the market will bear," are not very helpful. The best way—indeed, the only way—to discover how to charge and how much to charge is to experiment. Try out different payment methods and fee structures with different clients and see which work best for you.

You may discover that you will not likely get your ideal hourly rate because other self-employed people are charging less in your area. However, if you're highly skilled and performing work of unusually high quality, don't be afraid to ask for more than other self-employed people with lesser skills charge. Lowballing your fees won't necessarily get you business. Many potential clients believe they get what they pay for and are willing to pay more for quality work.

One approach is to start out charging a fee that is at the lower end of the spectrum for self-employed people performing similar services, then gradually increase it until you start meeting price resistance. Over time, you should be able to find a payment method and fee structure that enables you to get enough work and that adequately compensates for your services.

THE SELF-EMPLOYED SHOULD BE PAID MORE THAN EMPLOYEES

Don't be afraid to ask for more per hour than employees earn for doing similar work. Self-employed people should be paid more than an employee. Unlike employees, the self-employed are not provided with employee benefits such as health insurance, vacations, sick leave or retirement plans. Nor do hiring firms have to pay payroll taxes for them. This saves a hiring firm a bundle—employee benefits and payroll taxes add at least 20% to 40% to employers' payroll costs. You also have many business expenses employees don't have, such as office rent, supplies and marketing costs.

In addition, in our economic system, people in business for themselves are supposed to earn more than employees because they take much greater risks. Unlike most employees, self-employed workers don't get paid if business is bad. It's only fair, then, that they should be paid more than employees when business is good.

B. Getting Paid

Hiring firms normally pay their employees like clockwork. Employers know that if they don't pay on time, their employees can get the state labor department to investigate and fine them. Also, employers usually depend upon their employees for the daily operation of their businesses, so they need to keep the workforce as content as possible.

Unfortunately, no similar incentives encourage hiring firms to pay the self-employed. Many self-employed people have trouble getting paid by their clients. Some hiring firms feel free to pay outside workers late; some never pay at all. Sometimes this is because of cashflow problems, but often it's because hiring firms know that the self-employed often don't have the time, money or will to force them to pay on time. One computer consultant complains that delaying payment is an almost automatic response for a lot of companies. They seem to figure that if you don't nag, you don't really want to get paid.

As an independent businessperson, it's entirely up to you to take whatever steps are appropriate and necessary to get paid. No government agency will help you. Here are some strategies you can use to get clients to pay on time—or at least pay you eventually.

1. Avoiding Payment Problems

Taking a healthy dose of preventative medicine before you sign on with a client can help you eliminate, or at least reduce, payment problems.

a. Use written agreements

If you only have an oral agreement with a client who fails to pay you, it can be very hard to collect what you're owed. Without a writing to contradict him or her, the client can claim you didn't perform as agreed or can easily dispute the amount due. Unless you have witnesses to support your version of the oral agreement, it will be just your word against the client's. At the very least, you should have a writing containing a description of the services you agree to perform, the deadline for performance and the payment terms. (See Chapter 19.)

b. Find out if a purchase order is required

A purchase order is a document a client uses to authorize you to be paid for your services. (See Chapter 20, Section D.) Some clients will not pay you unless you have a signed purchase order, even if you already have a signed contract. Find out whether your client uses purchase orders and obtain one before you start work to avoid payment problems later on.

c. Ask for a down payment

If you're dealing with a new client or one who has money problems, ask for a down payment before you begin work. Some self-employed people refer to such a payment as a retainer. This will show that the client is serious about paying you. And even if the client doesn't pay you in full, you'll at least have obtained something. Some self-employed people ask for as much as one-third to one-half of their fees in advance.

d. Use periodic payment schedules

For projects lasting more than a couple of months, try using payment schedules that require the client to pay you in stages—for example, one-third when you begin work, one-third when you complete half your work and one-third when you finish the entire project. Complex projects can be divided into phases or milestones with a payment due when you complete each phase.

If a client misses a payment, you can stop work. If you're never paid in full, you'll at least have obtained partial payment, so the entire project won't be a dead loss. A staged payment schedule will also improve your cashflow.

e. Check clients' credit

The most effective way to avoid payment problems is to not deal with clients who have bad credit histories. A company that habitually fails to pay other creditors will likely give you payment problems as well. If you're dealing with a well-established company or government agency that is clearly solvent, you may forego a credit check. But if you've never heard of the company, a credit check is prudent.

The most effective way to check a client's credit is to obtain a credit report from a credit reporting agency. Dun & Bradstreet, the premier credit reporting agency for businesses, maintains a database containing credit information on millions of companies. You can obtain a credit report on any company in Dun & Bradstreet's database by calling: 800-234-3867. The report will be faxed to you the same day or mailed. You can also obtain reports via your computer from Dun & Bradstreet's Internet site at: www.dnb.com.

A basic Dun & Bradstreet credit report, called a credit scoring information report, costs $54.50. It contains information on the company's payment history and financial condition. It will also tell you whether the company has had any lawsuits, judgments or liens filed against it and whether it has ever filed for bankruptcy. Dun & Bradstreet also assigns a credit rating, to help you predict which companies will pay slowly or not at all.

A cheaper but more time-consuming way to check a potential client's credit is to ask the client to provide you with credit information and references. This is better than nothing, but may not give you an accurate picture—potential clients may try to avoid tipping you off about their financial problems by giving you the names of references who have not had problems with them.

Credit checks are routine these days, so your request for credit credentials is not likely to drive away business. Be wary of any potential client that refuses to give you credit information. Provide the client with a request for credit information such as the following.

REQUEST FOR CREDIT INFORMATION

Andre Bocuse Consulting Services
123 4th Street
Marred Vista, CA 90000
555-1234

Please provide the following information so we can extend credit for our services. All responses will be held in confidence. Please mail this form to the address shown below, or fax it to 100-555-1222. Thank you.

1. Company Name _____

   Address _____

   _____

2. Contact person _____

3. Federal Tax ID No. _____

4. Type of Business _____

5. Number of employees _____

6. Date business established _____

7. Check one of the following forms of business.

☐ **Corporation**   **State of incorporation** _____

Names, titles and addresses of your three chief corporate officers:

Name: _____
Address: _____
          _____
          _____

Name: _____
Address: _____
          _____
          _____

Name: _____
Address: _____
          _____
          _____

☐ **Partnership**

Names and addresses of the partners:

Name: _____
Address: _____
          _____
          _____

Name: _____
Address: _____
          _____
          _____

Name: _____

Address: _____

_____

_____

_____

☐ **Limited Liability Company**

Name: _____

Address: _____

_____

_____

Name: _____

Address: _____

_____

_____

Names and addresses of the owners:

Name: _____

Address: _____

_____

_____

Name: _____

Address: _____

_____

_____

Name: _____

Address: _____

_____

_____

☐ **Sole Proprietorship**

8. Purchase order required? Yes ☐ No ☐

9. Bank References

Bank #1

Account # _____ Phone: _____

Contact Person: _____

Address: _____

_____

Bank #2

Account # _____ Phone: _____

Contact Person: _____

Address: _____

_____

10. Please provide the following information for three vendors you use regularly:

Reference #1

Name: _____

Address: _____

_____

Phone: _____

Reference #2

Name: _____

Address: _____

_____

Phone: _____

Reference #3

Name: _____

Address: _____

_____

Phone: _____

My company and I authorize the disclosure and release of any credit-related information based on this document to Andre Bocuse Consulting.

Authorized Signature:

_____

Printed Name:

_____

Title: _____

Date: _____

Call the accounting department of the credit references listed and ask if the company has experienced any payment problems with the client. Accounting departments are typically asked for this information and will usually provide it freely.

If a credit report or your own investigation reveals that a potential client has a bad credit history or is in financial trouble, you may prefer not to do business with it. However, you may not be able to afford to work only for clients with perfect credit records. If you want to go ahead and do the work, obtain as much money up front as possible and be on the lookout for payment prob-

lems. If the client is a corporation or limited liability company, you may seek to have its owners sign a personal guaranty. (See Section B1g.)

f. Checking form of ownership

Your investigation of a potential client should include determining how its business is legally organized. This could have a big impact on your ability to collect a judgment against if it fails to pay you.

If you win a lawsuit against a client that fails to pay you, the court will order the client to pay you a specified sum of money. This is known as a court judgment. Unfortunately, if the client fails or refuses to pay the judgment, the court will not help you collect it. You've got to do it yourself or hire someone to help you. However, there are many legal tools you can use to collect a court judgment. For example, you can file liens on the client's property that make it impossible for the client to sell the property without paying you, get hold of the client's bank accounts and even have business or personal property such as the client's car seized by local law enforcement and sold.

Your ability to collect a court judgment may be helped—or severely hindered—by the way the client's business is legally organized.

- If the client is a sole proprietorship—that is, individually owns the business—he or she is personally liable for any debts the business owes you. This means the proprietor's own personal assets—as well as those of the business—are available to satisfy the debt. For example, both the proprietor's business and personal bank accounts may be tapped to pay you.

- If the client is a partner in a partnership, you can go after the personal assets of all the general partners. Be sure to get all their names before you start work. If the partnership is a limited partnership, you can't touch the assets of the limited partners, so don't worry about getting their names.

- If the client is a corporation, you could have big problems collecting a judgment. You normally can't go after the personal assets of a corporation's owners, such as the personal bank accounts of the shareholders and officers. Instead, you're limited to collecting from the corporation's assets. If the corporation is insolvent or goes out of business, there may be no assets to collect.

- If the client is a limited liability company, its owners will normally not be personally liable for any debts the business incurred, just as if it were a corporation.

WHAT'S IN A NAME? A LOT

Often, you can tell how a potential client's business is legally organized just by looking at its name.

If it's a corporation, its name will normally be followed by the words Incorporated, Corporation, Company or Limited; or the abbreviations Inc., Corp., Co. or Ltd.

Partnerships often have the words Partnership or Partners in their name, but not always. A limited liability company will usually have the words Limited Liability Company, Limited Company or the abbreviations L.C., LLC or Ltd. Co. in its name. Sole proprietors often use their own names, but they don't have to do so. They may use fictitious business names or dbas that are completely different from their own names.

---

g. Obtaining personal guarantees

If you're worried about the credit-worthiness of a new or small incorporated client or limited liability company, you may ask its owners to sign a personal guarantee. A person who signs a personal guarantee, known as a guarantor, promises to pay someone else's debt. This is the same as co-signing a loan. A guarantor who doesn't pay can be sued for the amount of the debt by the person to whom the money is owed.

You can ask for a personal guaranty from the officers or owners of a company you're afraid will not pay you. The guarantee legally obligates them to pay your fee if the company doesn't pay it. This means that if the client fails to pay you, you can sue not only the client, but the guarantors as well—and you can go after their personal assets if you obtain a court judgment.

EXAMPLE: Albert, a self-employed consultant, contracts to perform services for Melt, Inc., a company involved in the highly competitive ice cream business. Melt is a corporation owned primarily by Barbara, a multi-millionaire. Albert's contract contains a personal guaranty requiring Barbara to pay him if the corporation doesn't.

Melt goes broke when botulism is discovered in its ice cream and the company fails to pay Albert. Albert files a lawsuit against Barbara, and easily obtains a judgment on the basis of the personal guaranty. When Barbara refuses to pay, Albert gets a court order enabling him to tap into one of her fat bank accounts and is paid in full.

Having a personal guaranty will not only help you collect a judgment, it will also help prevent payment problems. The guarantors will have a strong incentive to make sure you're paid in full and on time. By doing so, they safeguard their personal assets from being snatched away.

Not many self-employed people ever think about asking for personal guarantees, so some clients may be taken aback if you do so. Explain that you need the added protection so you can extend the credit the client seeks. Also, note that signing a guaranty presents no risk at all to the business's owners as long as you're paid on time. You might also give the client a choice: the business's owners can either provide you with a personal guaranty or give you a substantial down payment up front.

A personal guaranty can be a separate document, but the easiest way to create one is to include a guaranty clause at the end of your contract with the client.

EXAMPLE: Andre Bocuse, a self-employed consultant, agrees to perform consulting services for Acme Corporation, a one-person corporation owned by Joe Jones. Because Andre has never worked for Acme before and is worried about being paid, he asks Joe Jones to sign a personal guaranty. This way he knows he can go after Jones' personal assets if Acme doesn't pay up. He adds the following clause to the end of his contract with Acme and has Jones sign it:

In consideration of Andre Bocuse entering into this Agreement with Acme Corporation, I personally guarantee the performance of all of the contractual obligations undertaken by Acme Corporation, including complete and timely payment of all sums due Andre Bocuse under the Agreement.

—————————————————
Joe Jones

2. Sending Invoices to Your Clients

Send invoices to your clients as soon as you complete work. You don't have to wait until the end of the month. Create a standard invoice to use with all your clients. If you have a computer, accounting or invoice programs can create invoices for you. You can also choose to have your own invoices printed.

Your invoice should contain:

- your company name, address and phone number
- the client's name
- an invoice number
- the date
- the client's purchase order number or contract number, if any
- the terms of payment
- the time period covered by the invoice

- a brief description of the services you performed; if you're billing by the hour, list the number of hours expended and the hourly rate
- if you're billing separately for expenses or materials, the amounts of these items
- the total amount due, and
- your signature.

Include a self-addressed return envelope with your invoice. This tiny investment can help speed up payment.

Make at least two copies of each invoice: one for the client and one for your records. You may also want to make a third copy to keep in an unpaid invoices folder so you can keep track of when payments are overdue. (See Section B3.)

Following is an example of a self-employed worker's invoice.

a. Terms of payment

The terms of payment is one of the most important items in your invoice. It sets the ultimate deadline by which the client must pay you. This varies from industry to industry and will also vary from client to client. Thirty days is common, but some clients will want longer—45, 60 or even 90 days.

Obviously, the shorter the payment period, the better off you'll be. This is something you should discuss with the client before you agree to take a job. Some self-employed people ask for payment within 15 days or immediately after the services are completed. However, some clients' accounting departments aren't set up to meet such short deadlines.

INVOICE

JOHN SMITH
1000 GRUB STREET
MARRED VISTA, CA 90000
510-555-5555

Date: **4/30/20XX**

Invoice Number: **103**

Your Order Number: **A62034**

Terms: **Net 30**

Time period of: **4/1/20XX-4/30/20XX**

To: Susan Elroy
      Accounting Department
      Acme Widget Company
      10400 Long Highway
      Marred Vista, CA 90000

Services:

Consulting services of John Smith on thermal analysis of Zotz 650 control unit. 50 hours @ $100.00 per hour.

Subtotal: $5,000

Material Costs: None

Expenses: 0

TOTAL AMOUNT OF THIS INVOICE: $5,000

Signed by: *John Smith*

If you have a written client agreement, it should indicate how long the client has to pay you. (See Chapter 19, Section A3.)

The standard way to indicate the payment terms in your invoice is to use the word Net followed by the number of days the client has to pay after receipt of the invoice. For example, Net 30 means you want full payment in 30 days.

Some self-employed people offer discounts to clients or customers that pay quickly. A common discount is 2% for payment within ten days after the invoice is received. If such a discount can get a slow-paying client to pay you quickly, it's worth it. You're always better off getting 98% of what you're owed right away than having to wait months for payment in full.

If you decide to offer a discount, indicate on your invoice the percentage followed by the number of days the client has to pay to receive the discount—for example, 2% 10 means the client can deduct 2% of the total due if it pays you within ten days. State your discount before the normal payment terms—for example, 2% 10 Net 30 means the client gets a 2% discount if it pays within ten days, but the full amount must be paid within 30 days.

b. Charging late fees

One way to get clients to pay on time is to charge late fees for overdue payments. One consultant was experiencing major problems with late paying clients—40% of his clients were over 30 days late in paying him. After he began charging a late fee, the number dropped to 5%.

However, late fees don't always work; some clients simply refuse to pay them. Not paying a late fee when required in your invoice is a breach of contract by the client, but it's usually not worth the trouble to go to court to collect a late fee.

If you wish to charge a late fee, make sure it's mentioned in your agreement. You should also clearly state the amount of your late fee on all your invoices. For example, your invoices should include the phrase: "Accounts not paid within terms are subject to a ____% monthly finance charge."

The late fee is normally expressed as a monthly interest or monthly finance charge.

State Restrictions on Late Fees

Your state might have restrictions on how much you can charge as a late fee. You'll have to investigate your state laws to find out. Check the index to the annotated statutes for your state— sometimes called a code—available in any law library. (See Chapter 21, Section D.) Look under the terms interest, usury or finance charges. Your professional or trade organization may also have helpful information.

No matter what state you live in, you can safely charge as a late fee at least as much as banks charge businesses to borrow money. Find out the current bank interest rate by calling your bank or looking in the business section of your local newspaper.

The math takes two parts. First, divide the annual interest rate by 12 to determine your monthly interest rate.

> **EXAMPLE:** Sam, a self-employed consultant, decides to start charging clients a late fee for overdue payments. He knows banks are charging 12% interest per year on borrowed money and decides to charge the same. He divides this rate by 12 to determine his monthly interest rate: 1%.

Then, multiply the monthly rate by the amount due to determine the amount of the monthly late fee.

> **EXAMPLE:** Acme Corp. is 30 days late paying Sam a $10,000 fee. Sam multiples this amount by his 1% finance charge to determine his late fee: $100 (.01 x $10,000). He adds this

amount to Acme's account balance. He does this every month the payment is late.

3. Collecting Overdue Accounts

If your invoice isn't paid on time, act quickly to collect. Clients who consistently pay late or do not pay at all can put you out of business. More-over, experience shows that the longer a client fails to pay, the less likely it is that you'll ever be paid.

a. When an account is overdue

Money that your clients or customers owe you is called an account receivable. Keep track of the age of your accounts receivable so you know when a client's payment is late and how late it is.

Many computer accounting programs can keep track of the age of your accounts receivable. However, there is a simple way to do this without a computer. Make an extra copy of each of your invoices and keep them in a folder or notebook marked Unpaid Invoices. When a client pays you, throw away the applicable invoice. By looking in this notebook, you can tell exactly which clients haven't paid and how late their payments are.

Consider a client late if it fails to pay you within ten days after the due date on your in-voice. At this point, you should contact the client and find out why you haven't been paid.

⚠ Find Out Where Clients Bank
When a client pays you by check, make a note of the name and address of the bank and the account number and place it in your client file. This information will come in very handy if you ever have to collect a judgment against the client.

b. Contacting the client

Don't rely on collection letters. A phone call will have far more impact. Unfortunately, it can often be hard to get clients to return your collection calls. To reduce the time you spend playing phone tag, ask what time the client will be in and call back then. If you leave a phone message, state the time of day you receive return calls—for example, every afternoon from 1 p.m. to 5 p.m. If you can't reach the client by phone, try sending faxes. One self-employed worker even reports good success from sending telegrams to nonpaying clients.

c. Your first collection call

During your first collection call, you want to either solve a problem that has arisen or handle a stalled payment. Write down who said what during this and each subsequent phone call.

Prepare before you make your call. You should know exactly how much the client owes you and have a copy of your invoice and any purchase order in front of you when you dial the phone. Also, make sure you speak with the appropriate person. In large companies, this may be someone in the accounts payable department or purchasing department; in small companies, it could be the owner.

Politely inform the client that its payment to you is past due. About 80% of the time, late payments are caused by problems with invoices—for example, your client didn't receive an invoice or misplaced or didn't understand it. You may simply have to send another invoice or provide a brief explanation of why you charged as you did.

On the other hand, some clients may refuse to pay you because they are dissatisfied with your services or charges. In this event, schedule a meeting with the client as soon as possible to work out the problem. If the client is dissatisfied with only part of your work, ask for partial payment immediately.

Other clients may be satisfied with your services but not have the money to pay you. They may want an extension of time to pay or ask to work out a payment plan with you—for example, pay a certain amount every two weeks until the balance is paid. If such a client seems sincere about paying you, try to work out a reasonable payment plan. You are likely to get paid eventually this way—and you may also get repeat business from the client. If you agree to any new payment terms, set them forth in a confirming letter and send it to the client. The letter should state how much you'll be paid and by when. Keep a copy in your files.

SAMPLE CONFIRMING LETTER

April 15, 20XX
Sue Jones, President
Acme Corporation
123 Main Street
Marred Vista, CA 90000

Re: Your contract # 1234
    Invoice # 102

Dear Sue:

Thank you for your offer to submit $500 per month to pay off your company's outstanding balance on the above account.

As agreed, I am willing to accept $500 monthly payments for four months until this debt is satisfied. The payments are due on the first of each month, beginning May 1, 20XX and continuing monthly through August 1, 20XX.

As long as the payments are timely made, I will withhold all further action.

Thank you for your cooperation.

Very truly yours,

Andre Bocuse

SAMPLE CONFIRMING LETTER

August 1, 20XX
John Anderson
200 Grub Street
Albany, NY 10000

Re: My Invoice # 102

Dear John:

As we orally agreed, I'm willing to accept $4,500 as a full and complete settlement of your account.

This sum must be paid by September 1, 20XX or this offer will become void.

Thank you for your cooperation and I look forward to receiving payment.

Very truly yours,

Yolanda Allende

Some clients may offer to pay a part of what they owe if you'll accept it as full payment. Although it may be galling to agree to this, it may make more economic sense than fighting with the client for full payment. If you orally agree to this, send the client a confirming letter setting forth the new payment terms. Keep a copy for yourself.

BEWARE OF PAYMENT IN FULL CHECKS

Be careful about accepting and depositing checks that have the words Payment in Full or something similar written on them. If the client owes you more than the face value of the check, you may be barred from collecting the additional amount.

Where there's a dispute about how much the client owes you, depositing a full payment check usually means that you accept the check in complete satisfaction of the debt. Crossing out the words Payment in Full generally won't help you. You'll still be prevented from suing for the balance once you deposit the check.

However, several states have changed this rule to help creditors. In these states, you normally can cash a full payment check and still preserve your right to sue for the balance by writing the words Under Protest or Without Prejudice on your endorsement. These states include Alabama, Delaware, Massachusetts, Minnesota, Missouri, New Hampshire, New York, Ohio, Rhode Island, South Carolina, South Dakota, West Virginia and Wisconsin.

Californians may cross out the full payment language, cash the check and sue for the balance. However, the client may be able to get around this by sending a written notice that cashing the check means it was accepted as payment in full. (Calif. Civil Code Section 1526.) Luckily, few clients are aware of this rule, so crossing out the full payment language usually works just fine.

d. Subsequent collection efforts

If you haven't received payment after more than a month and a first reminder, send the client another invoice marked Second Notice. Call the client and send invoices monthly. If you've been dealing with someone other than the owner of the company, don't hesitate to call the owner. Explain that cashflow is important to your company and that you can't afford to carry this receivable any longer.

Be persistent. When it comes to collecting debts, the squeaky wheel usually gets the money. A client with a faltering business and many creditors who has the money to pay just one debt will likely pay the creditor who has made the most fuss.

At this point, you should feel free to stop all work for the client and not hand over any work you've completed but not yet delivered. You'll go broke fast if you keep working for people who don't pay you.

However, don't cross the line into harassing the client; that could get you into legal trouble.

DON'T HARASS DEADBEAT CLIENTS

No matter how angry you are at a client who fails to pay you, don't harass him or her.

Harassment includes:

- threatening or using physical force if the client doesn't pay
- using obscene or profane language
- threatening to sue the client when you really don't intend to do so
- threatening to have the client arrested
- phoning the client early in the morning or late at night
- causing a phone to ring repeatedly or continuously to annoy the client, or
- communicating with the client unreasonably often.

Many states have laws prohibiting these types of collection practices. And even in states that don't have specific laws against it, court decisions often penalize businesses that harass debtors. A client could sue you for engaging in this kind of activity. Use your common sense and deal with the client in a businesslike manner, however much he or she owes you—and however agitated that debt makes you feel.

4. If a Client Won't Pay

If a client refuses to pay or keeps breaking promises to pay, you must decide whether to write off the debt or take further action. If the client has gone out of business or is unable to pay you anything, either now or in the future, your best option may be to write off the debt. There's no point in spending time and money trying to get blood from a turnip.

But if the client is solvent, you should seriously consider:

- taking legal action against the client yourself

- hiring an attorney to take legal action against the client, or
- hiring a collection agency.

a. Sending a final demand letter

Before you start any type of legal action against a client, send a final demand letter to the client informing him or her that you will sue if you don't receive payment by a certain date. Many clients will pay you voluntarily after receiving such a letter—they don't want to be dragged into court and have their credit ratings damaged if you obtain a judgment against them.

In your letter, state how much the client owes you and inform the client that you'll take court action if full payment isn't received by a specific date. Here is an example of such a letter.

SAMPLE FINAL DEMAND LETTER

April 24, 20XX
Dick Denius
123 Grub Street
Anytown, AK 12345
Re: Your account number: 678

Dear Mr. Denius:

Your outstanding balance of $6,000 is over 120 days old.

If you do not make full payment by 5/15/20XX, a lawsuit will be filed against you. A recorded judgment will be a lien against your property and can only have an adverse effect on your credit rating.

I hope to hear from you immediately so that this matter can be resolved without filing a lawsuit.

Very truly yours,
Natalie Kalmus

b. Suing in small claims court

All states have a wonderful mechanism that helps businesses collect small debts: small claims court. Small claims courts are set up to resolve disputes involving relatively modest amounts of money. The limit is normally between $2,000 and $7,500, depending on the state in which you file your lawsuit. If you're owed more than the limit, you can still sue in small claims court for the limit and waive your right to collect the rest.

Small claims court is particularly well suited to collecting small debts because it's inexpensive and usually fairly quick. In fact, debt collection cases are by far the most common type of cases heard in small claims court.

You don't need a lawyer to go to small claims court. Indeed, a few states—including California, New York and Michigan—bar lawyers from small claims court.

For detailed advice about how to handle a small claims court suit, see *Everybody's Guide to Small Claims Court* (National and California Editions), by Ralph Warner (Nolo).

You begin a small claims lawsuit by filing a document called a complaint or statement of claim. These forms are available from your local small claims court clerk and are easy to fill out. You may also be asked to attach a copy of your written agreement, if you have one. You then notify the client, now known as the defendant, of your lawsuit. Depending on your state, the notice can be delivered by certified mail or by a process server. Many clients pay up when they receive a complaint because they don't want to go to court.

A hearing date is then set. If the client doesn't show up in court, you'll win by default. A substantial percentage of clients don't contest claims for unpaid fees in court because they know they owe the money and can't win. If the client does attend the court session, you present your case to a judge or court commissioner under rules that encourage a minimum of legal and procedural formality. Be sure to bring all your documentation to court, including your invoices, client agreement and correspondence with the client.

Unfortunately, getting a small claims judgment against a client doesn't guarantee you'll be paid. Many clients will automatically pay a judgment you obtain against them, but others will refuse to pay. The court will not collect your judgment for you. You've got to do it yourself or hire someone to help you.

BIG FEE, SMALL CLAIM

Gary, a freelance translator, recently contracted with the San Francisco office of a national brokerage firm to perform translating services on a rush basis. He completed the work on time and faxed it to the company with his invoice. The client failed to pay the invoice within 30 days.

Over the next three months, Gary sent the company a stream of collection letters demanding payment, but never heard a word. He finally got sick of waiting and decided to sue the client. He was owed $3,000, well within the $5,000 California small claims court limit, so filed his suit in the San Francisco small claims court.

He then had the San Francisco County Sheriff's Department serve his complaint on the client at its office. The next day he received a fax from the company's legal department at its New York headquarters apologizing for the delay in payment and promising to pay at once. He received a check within a few days.

c. Suing in other courts

If the client owes you substantially more than the small claims court limit for your state, you may wish to sue in a formal state trial court, usually called the municipal court or superior court. Debt collection cases are usually very simple, so you can often handle them yourself or hire a lawyer for the very limited purpose of giving you advice on legal points or helping with strategy. In truth, few collection cases ever go to trial. Usually, the defendant either reaches a settlement with you before trial or fails to show up in court and loses by default.

 For detailed guidance on how to represent yourself in courts other than small claims courts, see *Represent Yourself in Court: How to Prepare and Try a Winning Case*, by Paul Bergman and Sara Berman-Barrett (Nolo). This book explains how to handle a civil case yourself, without a lawyer, from start to finish.

d. Arbitration

Before you think about suing the client in court, look at your contract to see whether it contains an arbitration clause. If your contract has such a clause, you'll be barred from suing the client in small claims or any other court. This is not necessarily a bad thing. Arbitration is similar to small claims court in that it's intended to be speedy, inexpensive and informal. The main difference is that an arbitrator, not a judge, rules on the case. An arbitrator's judgment can be entered with a court and enforced just like a regular court judgment. (See Chapter 21, Section A1.)

e. Hiring an attorney

Hiring an attorney to sue a client for an unpaid bill is usually not worth the expense involved unless the debt is very large and you know the client can pay. However, it can be effective to have a lawyer send a letter to a client. Some clients take communications from lawyers more seriously than they take a letter you write on your own. Some lawyers are willing to do this for a nominal charge. (See Chapter 21, Section B.)

f. Hiring a collection agency

Collection agencies specialize in collecting debts. You don't pay them anything. Instead, they take a slice of the money they collect. This can range from 15% to 50% depending on the size, age and type of debts involved. Collection agencies can be particularly good at tracking down skips—people who hide from their creditors.

Sicking a collection agency on a client will likely alienate the client and mean that you will not get any repeat business from him or her. Use this alternative only if you don't want to work for a particular client again.

You may have trouble finding an agency to deal with you if you only have a few debts, particularly if they're small. Try to get a referral to a good collection agency from colleagues or a professional organization or trade group. Ask for references before hiring any agency; call them to make sure the agency checks out. It's also advisable to get a fee agreement in writing.

5. Deducting Bad Debts From Income Taxes

In a few situations, you can deduct the value of an unpaid debt from your income taxes. This is called a bad debt deduction. Unfortunately, if you're like the vast majority of self-employed people—a cash-basis taxpayer who sells services to your clients—you can't claim a bad debt deduction if a client fails to pay you. Since you don't report income until it is actually received, you aren't considered to have an economic loss when a client fails to pay.

EXAMPLE: Bill, a self-employed consultant, works 50 hours for a client and bills $2,500. The client never pays. Bill cannot deduct the $2,500 loss from his income taxes. Since Bill is a cash-basis taxpayer, he never reported the $2,500 as income because he never received it. As far as the IRS is concerned, this means Bill has no economic loss.

This rule seems absurd—you've lost the value of your time and energy when a client fails to pay you for your services—but it's strictly enforced by the IRS.

The only time a business can deduct a bad debt is if it actually lost cash on the account or it previously reported income from sale of the item. Few self-employed people give out cash, and only businesses using the complex accrual method of accounting report income from a sale for which no payment is received. (See Chapter 14, Section C.) There's no point in trying to switch to the accrual method to deduct bad debts. You won't reduce your taxes since the bad debt deduction merely wipes out a sale you previously reported as income. ■

Taxes and the Self-Employed

Employees typically don't need to worry much about taxes. All or most of their taxes are withheld from their paychecks by their employers and paid directly to the IRS and state tax department. The employer calculates how much to withhold. The employee's only responsibility is to file a tax return with the IRS and state tax department each year.

But when you become self-employed, your tax life changes dramatically. You have no employer to pay your taxes for you; you must pay them directly to the IRS and your state. This requires periodic tax filings you probably never made before—and it will be up to you to calculate how much you owe. To make these filings, you'll also need to keep accurate records of your business income and expenses. And the tax return you must file each year will likely be more complicated than the ones you filed when you were an employee.

This chapter provides an overview of the brave new world of taxation you are about to enter as a self-employed worker and explains some ways to deal with it efficiently.

A. Tax Basics for the Self-Employed

All levels of government—federal, state and local—impose taxes. You need to be familiar with the requirements for each.

1. Federal Taxes

The federal government puts the biggest tax bite on the self-employed. When you're in business for yourself, the federal government may impose a number of taxes on you.

These federal taxes include:

- income taxes
- self-employment taxes
- estimated taxes, and
- employment taxes.

a. Income taxes

Everyone who earns more than a minimum amount must pay income taxes. Unless you're one of the few self-employed people who have formed a C corporation, you'll have to pay personal income tax on the profits your business earns. Fortunately, you may be able to take advantage of a number of business-related deductions to reduce your taxable income when you're self-employed. (See Chapter 9.)

By April 15 of each year, you'll have to file an annual income tax return with the IRS showing your income and deductions for the previous year and how much estimated tax you've paid. You must file IRS Form 1040 and include a special tax form in which you list all your business income and deductible expenses. Most self-employed people use IRS Schedule C, Profit or Loss From Business.

Tax matters are more complicated if you incorporate your business. If you form a C corporation, it will have to file its own tax return and pay taxes on its profits. You'll be an employee of your corporation; you'll have to file a personal tax return and pay income tax on the salary your corporation paid you. (See Chapter 2, Section B.)

b. Self-employment taxes

Self-employed people are entitled to Social Security and Medicare benefits when they retire, just like employees. And just like employees, they have to pay Social Security and Medicare taxes to help fund these programs. These taxes are called self-employment taxes, or SE taxes. You must pay SE taxes if your net yearly earnings from self-employment are $400 or more. When you file your annual tax return, you must include IRS Form SE, showing how much SE tax you were required to pay. (See Chapter 10, Section E.)

c. Estimated taxes

Federal income and self-employment taxes are pay-as-you-go taxes. You must pay these taxes as you earn or receive income during the year. Unlike employees, who usually have their income and Social Security and Medicare tax withheld from their pay by their employers, self-employed people normally pay their income and Social Security and Medicare taxes directly to the IRS. These tax payments, called estimated taxes, are usually made four times every year on IRS Form 1040-ES—on April 15, June 15, September 15 and January 15. You have to figure out how much to pay; the IRS won't do it for you. (See Chapter 11, Section B.)

d. Employment taxes

Finally, if you hire employees to help you in your business, you'll have to pay federal employment taxes. These consist of half your employees' Social Security and Medicare taxes and all of the federal unemployment tax. You must also withhold half your employees' Social Security and Medicare taxes and all their income taxes from their paychecks. You must pay these taxes monthly, by making federal tax deposits at specified banks. You may also deposit them directly with the IRS electronically.

When you have employees, you'll have to keep lots of records and file quarterly and annual employment tax returns with the IRS. (See Chapter 13, Section B.)

When you hire other self-employed people, however, you don't have to pay any employment taxes. You need only report payments over $600 for business-related services to the IRS and to your state tax department if your state has income taxes. (See Chapter 13, Section C.)

2. State Taxes

Life would be too simple if you were only required to pay federal taxes. States get into the act as well, imposing their own taxes to fund their governments.

a. Income taxes

All states except Alaska, Florida, Nevada, South Dakota, Texas, Washington and Wyoming impose income taxes on the self-employed. New Hampshire and Tennessee impose income taxes on dividend and interest income only. Some states simply charge you a percentage of the federal income tax you have to pay for the year—for example, Vermont residents must pay 24% of the amount of their federal income taxes. Most other states charge a percentage of the income shown on your federal income return. Depending on the state in which you live, these percentages range anywhere from 3% to 11%.

In most states, you have to pay your state income taxes during the year in the form of estimated taxes. These are usually paid at the same time you pay your federal estimated taxes.

You'll also have to file an annual state income tax return with your state tax department. In all but six states—Arkansas, Delaware, Hawaii, Iowa, Louisiana and Virginia—the return must be filed by April 15, the same deadline as your federal tax return. (See Section A4.)

If you're incorporated, your corporation will likely have to pay state income taxes and file its own state income tax return.

Each state has its own income tax forms and procedures. Contact your state tax department to learn about your state's requirements and obtain the forms. (See Appendix 3 for a list of state tax offices.)

b. Employment taxes

If you live in a state with income taxes and have employees, you'll likely have to withhold state income taxes from their paychecks and pay the money over to your state tax department. You'll also have to provide your employees with unemployment compensation insurance by paying state unemployment taxes to your state unemployment compensation agency. (See Chapter 13, Section B2.)

c. Sales taxes

Almost all states and many municipalities impose sales taxes of some kind. The only states without sales tax are Alaska, Delaware, Montana, New Hampshire and Oregon.

All states that have sales taxes impose them on sales of goods or products to end users. If you only provide services to clients or customers, you probably don't have to worry about sales taxes because most states don't tax services at all or only tax certain specified services. Notable exceptions are Hawaii, New Mexico and South Dakota—all of which impose sales taxes on all services, subject to certain exceptions.

If the products or services you provide are subject to sales tax, you'll have to fill out an application to obtain a state sales tax number. Many states impose penalties if you make a sale before you obtain a sales tax number. Generally, you pay sales taxes four times a year, but you might have to pay monthly if you make lots of sales.

d. Other state taxes

Various states impose a hodgepodge of other taxes on businesses. These are too numerous and diverse to summarize here.

For example:

- Nevada imposes a Business Privilege Tax of $100 per year per employee.
- Hawaii imposes a general excise tax on businesses ranging from .5% to 4% of the gross receipts businesses earn.
- Michigan has a Single Business Tax of 2% on businesses with gross receipts over $250,000.

Contact your state tax department for information on these and other similar taxes your state might impose.

3. Local Taxes

You might have to pay local business taxes in addition to federal and state taxes. For example, many municipalities have their own sales taxes which you may have to pay to a local tax agency.

Some cities and counties also impose property taxes on business equipment or furniture. You may be required to file a list of such property with local tax officials, along with cost and depreciation information. Some cities also have a tax on business inventory. This is why many retail businesses have inventory sales: they want to reduce their stock on hand before the inventory tax date.

A few large cities—for example, New York City—impose their own income taxes. Some also charge annual business registration fees or business taxes.

Your local chamber of commerce should be able to give you good information on your local taxes. You can also contact your local tax department.

4. Calendar of Important Tax Dates

The following calendar shows you important tax dates during the year. If you're one of the few self-employed people who uses a fiscal year instead of a calendar year as your tax year, these dates will be different. (See Chapter 14, Section C.) If you have employees, you must make additional tax filings during the year. (See Chapter 13, Section B.)

The dates listed below represent the last day you have to take the action described. If any of the dates fall on a holiday or weekend, you have until the next business day to take the action.

TAX CALENDAR

Date	Action
January 15	Your last estimated tax payment for the previous year is due.
January 31	If you file your tax return by now, you don't have to make the January 15 estimated tax payment. (See Chapter 11.) If you hired independent contractors last year, you must provide them with Form 1099-MISC.
February 28	If you hired independent contractors last year, you must file all your 1099s with the IRS.
March 15	Corporations must file federal income tax returns.
April 15	Your individual tax return must be filed with the IRS and any tax due paid. Or, you can pay the tax due and file for an extension of time to file your return. You must make your first estimated tax payment for the year. Partnerships must file information tax return. State, individual income tax returns due in all states except Arkansas, Delaware, Hawaii, Iowa, Louisiana and Virginia.
April 20	Individual income tax returns due in Hawaii.
April 30	Individual income tax returns due in Delaware, Iowa and Virginia.
May 15	Individual income tax returns due in Arkansas and Louisiana.
June 15	Make your second estimated tax payment for the year.
September 15	Make your third estimated tax payment for the year.

B. Handling Your Taxes

Many self-employed people take care of their taxes completely by themselves. Others hire tax professionals to take care of everything for them. Many more are somewhere in between. Your approach will depend on how complex your tax affairs are and whether you have the time, energy and desire to do some or all of the work yourself.

Self-employed workers commonly use three different approaches in preparing their taxes.

Self-employed people whose tax affairs are relatively simple can easily handle all their tax work themselves, particularly if they're comfortable using computers and accounting and tax preparation computer programs.

EXAMPLE: Steve, a freelance writer, does all his taxes himself. Like most self-employed workers, he is a sole proprietor and does all the work in his writing business himself—that is, he does not hire employees or independent contractors to help him. As a writer, he works at home and doesn't need much in the way of equipment or supplies. He has few business expenses to track other than his home office expenses.

He has a computer and easily keeps track of his income and expenses by using a simple computer accounting program. He also uses a computer tax preparation program to prepare his tax returns. He estimates he spends no more than one hour per month on bookkeeping and perhaps five hours to prepare his annual tax return.

On the other hand, self-employed people with larger businesses often hire tax pros to do all the work for them. This may be a particularly good idea if you incorporate your business or have employees.

EXAMPLE: Carol, a software tester, has formed a C corporation and has two employees. Her tax affairs are much more complicated than Steve's. She must file tax returns both for herself and her corporation. She must also withhold employment taxes from her own pay and her employees' pay and file quarterly and annual employment tax returns with the IRS and state of California.

Her bookkeeping requirements are also more complex than those of a sole proprietor like Steve. Carol does none of her tax work herself. She hires an accountant to do her bookkeeping and prepare her tax returns and uses a payroll service to calculate and pay the employment taxes for herself and her employees.

Even if you have a fairly complex tax return and want a tax pro to prepare it for you, you can still save money by doing some work yourself such as routine bookkeeping.

EXAMPLE: Gary, a self-employed translator, is a sole proprietor like Steve. However, unlike Steve, he hires independent contractor translators to work for him. He has to keep track of his payments to the independent contractors and report them to the IRS and his state tax department. He also rents an outside office and must keep track of this and other business expenses. A trained engineer with a mathematical bent, he does all his bookkeeping himself using a manual system. However, he hires an accountant to prepare his annual tax return, including some rather complex business deductions like depreciating his business equipment.

1. Doing the Work Yourself

The more tax work you do yourself, the less money you'll have to pay a tax pro such as an enrolled agent or certified public accountant (CPA) to help you through. This will not only save you cash, but also will give you more personal control over your financial life. The subject of taxes might seem daunting, but you don't need to become a CPA to take care of your own tax needs. Nor do you have to do everything yourself—for example, you can hire a tax pro to prepare your annual tax return or to advise you if you encounter a particularly difficult problem.

You can do some or all of the following tasks yourself.

a. Bookkeeping

Even if you do hire a tax pro to prepare your tax returns, you'll save money if you keep good records. Tax pros have many horror stories about clients who come in with plastic bags or shoe boxes filled with a jumble of receipts and canceled checks. As you might expect, these people end up paying much more than those who have a complete and accurate set of income and expense records. It is not difficult to set up and maintain a bookkeeping system for your business. You should do so when you first start business. (Chapter 14, Section A describes a simple bookkeeping system adequate for most self-employed people. Chapter 9 provides an overview of the business tax deductions you'll need to track.)

b. Paying Estimated Taxes

If your business makes money, you'll need to pay estimated taxes during the year. It's usually not too difficult to calculate what you owe and send in your money. You may have to make estimated tax payments soon after you start doing business, so don't delay this task. (See Chapter 11.)

If you live in one of the 43 states with income taxes—that is, all states but Alaska, Florida, Nevada, South Dakota, Texas, Washington and Wyoming—call your state tax department to find out whether you must make estimated tax payments. (See Appendix 3 for contact details.)

c. Paying state and local taxes

You may have to pay various state and local taxes, such as a gross receipts tax, sales tax or personal property tax. (See Section A2.) This is an area where seeking guidance from a tax pro can be very helpful, particularly if the expert is familiar with businesses similar to yours. He or she can advise you as to whether you must pay any of these taxes. Otherwise, you'll need to contact your state tax department and local tax office for information. However, once you learn about the requirements and obtain the proper forms, it's usually not difficult to compute these taxes on your own.

d. Filing your annual tax returns

The most difficult and time-consuming tax-related task you'll face is filing your annual tax return. This involves determining and adding up all your deductible expenses for the year and subtracting them from your gross income to determine your taxable income.

As you probably know, your federal tax return is due by April 15. If you live in one of the states that has income taxes, you'll have to file a state income tax return as well. These are also due by April 15 except in six states that have later dates. (See the chart in Section A4.)

One way to make your life easier is to hire a tax pro to prepare your returns the first year you're in business. You can then use those returns as a guide when you do your own returns in future years.

TAXES AT THE TOUCH OF A BUTTON

Many self-employed people do their tax returns themselves. If your business is small, it's usually not that difficult. This task is made much easier by the availability of many excellent publications and computer programs.

Having a computer will make preparing your tax returns much easier. Several tax preparation programs are available that contain all the forms you'll need. These programs not only do all your tax calculations for you, but they also contain online tax help and questionnaires you can complete to figure out what forms to use.

The programs automatically put the information and numbers you type into the proper blanks on the forms. When you're done, the program prints out your completed tax forms. All you have to do by hand is sign the forms and put them in the mail. If you don't want to use the mail, you can even file your taxes electronically. Most tax packages also have additional programs you can purchase for your state taxes.

Two of the most highly regarded tax preparation programs are *TurboTax* and *Kiplinger Taxcut*. There are versions of *TurboTax* specially designed for small business owners.

If you don't have a computer, there are several tax preparation guides that are published each year that provide much better guidance than the IRS instructions that come with your tax forms. These include *Consumer Reports' Guide to Income Tax* (Consumer Reports) and *The Ernst and Young Tax Guide* (John Wiley & Sons).

e. Paying employment taxes

If you have employees, your tax life will be much more complicated than if you work alone or just hire independent contractors. You'll need to file both annual and quarterly employment tax returns. You're also required to withhold part of your employees' pay and send it to the IRS along with a contribution of your own. (See Chapter 13, Section B.)

This is an area where many business owners seek outside help, since calculating withholding can be complex. Many use an accountant or payroll tax service to perform these tasks. However, if you have a computer, accounting programs such as *QuickBooks* and *PeachTree Accounting* can calculate your employee withholding and prepare employment tax returns.

 If you handle your taxes yourself, you'll likely want to obtain a more detailed book specifically on taxation. Many excellent books are available. One of the best of these tax guides is *Tax Savvy for Small Business*, by Frederick W. Daily (Nolo).

The IRS also has publications on every conceivable tax topic. These are free, but can be difficult to understand. IRS Publication 910, *Guide to Free Tax Services*, contains a list of these publications and many of the most useful ones are cited in the following chapters. One that you should obtain is Publication 334, *Tax Guide for Small Business*. You can obtain these and all other IRS publications by calling the IRS at 800-TAX-FORM, visiting your local IRS office or downloading them from the IRS's Internet site at www.irs.gov.

2. Hiring a Tax Pro

Instead of doing the work yourself, you can hire a tax professional to perform some or all of it for you. A tax pro can also provide guidance to help you make key tax decisions, such as choosing the best set-up for your business and helping you deal with the IRS if you get into tax trouble. (See Section C.)

a. Types of tax pros

There are several different types of tax pros. They differ widely in training, experience and cost.

Tax preparers. As the name implies, tax preparers prepare tax returns. The largest tax preparation firm is H & R Block, but many mom and pop operations open for business in store-front offices during tax time. In most states, anybody can be a tax preparer; no licensing is required. Most tax preparers don't have the training or experience to handle taxes for businesses and so are probably not a wise choice.

Enrolled agents. Enrolled agents or EAs are tax advisors and preparers who are licensed by the IRS. They have to have at least five years of experience and pass a difficult test. EAs are often the best choice for self-employed workers. They can often do as good a job as a certified public accountant, but charge less. Many also offer bookkeeping and accounting assistance.

Certified Public Accountants. Certified public accountants, or CPAs, are licensed and regulated by each state. They undergo lengthy training and must pass a comprehensive exam. CPAs represent the high end of the tax pro spectrum. In addition to preparing tax returns, they perform sophisticated accounting and tax work. Large businesses routinely hire CPAs for tax help. However, if you're running a one-person business, you may not require a CPA's expertise—you might do just as well with a less expensive EA.

Tax attorneys. Tax attorneys are lawyers who specialize in tax matters. The only time you'll ever need a tax attorney is if you get into serious trouble with the IRS or another tax agency and need legal representation before the IRS or in court. Some tax attorneys also give tax advice, but they are usually too expensive for small businesses. You're probably better off hiring a CPA if you need specialized tax help.

b. Finding a tax pro

The best way to find a tax pro is to obtain referrals from business associates, friends or professional associations. If none of these sources can give you a suitable lead, try contacting the National Association of Enrolled Agents (301-212-9608) or one of its state affiliates. You can find a listing of affiliates at the NAEA website at www.naea.org. Local CPA societies can give you referrals to local CPAs. You can also find tax pros in the telephone book under "Accountants, Tax Return."

Your relationship with your tax pro will be one of your most important business relationships. Be picky about the person you choose. Talk with at least three tax pros before hiring one. You want a tax pro who takes the time to listen to you, answers your questions fully and in plain English, seems knowledgeable and makes you feel comfortable. Make sure the tax pro works frequently with small businesses. It can also be helpful if the tax pro already has clients in businesses similar to yours. A tax pro already familiar with the tax problems posed by your type of business can often give you the best advice for the least money.

c. Tax pros' fees

Ask about a tax pro's fees before hiring him or her and, to avoid misunderstandings, obtain a written fee agreement before any work begins.

Most tax pros charge by the hour. Hourly rates vary widely depending on where you live and on the type of tax pro you hire. Enrolled agents often charge $25 to $50 per hour. CPAs typically charge about $100 per hour. Some tax pros charge a flat fee for specific services—for example, preparing a tax return.

These fees are rarely set in stone; you can usually negotiate. You'll be able to get the best possible deal if you hire a tax pro after the tax season when he or she is less busy—that is, during the summer or fall.

C. IRS Audits

In an audit, the IRS examines you, your business, your tax returns and the records used to create the returns. If an IRS auditor determines you didn't pay enough tax, you'll have to pay the amount due plus interest and penalties.

Historically, the self-employed have had a much higher chance of being audited by the IRS than employees. This is still true (see the chart below), but all IRS audit rates have gone down dramatically in recent years. For example, in 1993 the IRS audited 3.9% of sole proprietors with incomes of $100,000 or more. In 1999, this figure fell to 1.48%. The reasons for this drop include reductions in the IRS's staff, a growing number of tax returns being filed and a new IRS emphasis on taxpayer service rather than enforcement.

Due to these extremely low audit rates (which are somewhat misleading—see the sidebar below), some people now believe that they no longer need to fear the IRS. As a result, many self-employed people have become very aggressive about taking tax deductions or gotten lax in their record keeping.

However, the IRS plans on making a comeback. In 2001, the IRS restructured itself into four operating divisions. By far the largest of these is the Small Business and Self-Employed Operating Division, with about 39,000 employees. This division will handle most micro-businesses, unincorporated sole proprietors, partnerships and people with part-time or sideline businesses. With an increase in funding, the IRS planned to increase the number of audits by 100,000 per year by 2002. As in the past, the IRS will doubtless play particularly close attention to self-employed people—the IRS believes they are far more likely to cheat on their taxes than employees. IRS statistics show that, while 83% of all taxpayers don't cheat on their taxes, only 51% of the self-employed are similarly law abiding.

The moral is that you need to take the IRS seriously. This doesn't mean you shouldn't take all the deductions to which you're legally entitled. But it does mean that you must understand the rules and be able to back up your deductions with proper records.

COMPARING **IRS** AUDIT RATES OF EMPLOYEES WITH SOLE PROPRIETORS		
	1998 Audit Rate	**1999 Audit Rate**
Employees		
Income under $25,000	0.58%	0.37%
$25,000 to $50,000	0.36%	0.21%
$50,000 to $100,000	0.37%	0.23%
$100,000 and over	1.14%	0.84%
Sole Proprietors Filing Schedule C		
Income under $25,000	2.69%	2.43%
$25,000 to $100,000	1.30%	0.93%
$100,000 and over	2.40%	1.48%

These audit rates, compiled by the IRS itself, are misleading. They don't include the millions of IRS computer-based reviews of taxpayer returns—often called "invisible audits." For example, under the IRS information reporting program, IRS computers will compare the amounts reported as income on a sole proprietor's Schedule C with the amounts the proprietor's clients reported paying the proprietor when they filed their 1099 forms with the IRS. If there is a discrepancy, the proprietor will be sent a letter asking that it be explained or stating that additional tax is due and must be paid. If the IRS included these and other types of invisible audits in its calculations, reported audit rates would be three to four times higher.

1. Audit Time Limit

As a general rule, the law allows the IRS to audit a tax return up to 36 months after it's filed. This means you normally don't have to worry about audits for tax returns you filed more than three years ago. The IRS calls the years during which it can audit you "open years."

2. Type of Audit

The IRS auditor will seek to interview you. If, like most self-employed people, you're a sole proprietor and gross less than $100,000 per year, the auditor will probably request that you come to the local IRS office for the audit. Office audits usually last from two to four hours. In an office audit, a typical business taxpayer is typically hit for additional taxes averaging $4,000.

However, if your business is a corporation, partnership or sole proprietorship grossing more than $100,000 per year, the IRS will usually want to conduct the audit at your place of business. This is known as a field audit. You're entitled to request that the audit be conducted elsewhere—for example, the IRS office or the office of your attorney or accountant. Explain that your business will be disrupted if the auditor comes there. This is usually a good idea because you don't want an IRS auditor snooping around your business premises.

Field audits are conducted by IRS revenue agents, who are much better trained than IRS office auditors. They are more thorough than office audits—that is, a field auditor will spend more time on the audit and look at more records than an office auditor. As a result, these audits usually result in a larger tax bite. The typical field audit costs a business about $17,000.

3. What the Auditor Does

IRS auditors look primarily at two issues: whether you've under-reported your income and whether you've claimed tax deductions to which you're not entitled—for example, claimed that nondeductible personal expenses were deductible business expenses. Using a separate bank account for your business expenses will help convince the auditor that you're not mixing your personal bills with your business expenses.

The auditor will want to see the business records you used to prepare your tax returns, including your books, check registers, canceled checks and receipts. The auditor will also ask to see your records supporting your business tax deductions—for example, a record of the miles you've driven your car if you took a deduction for business use of your car.

IRS auditors can also obtain your bank records, either from you or your bank, and check them to see if your deposits match the income you reported on your tax return. If the total of all your deposits is larger than your reported income, the auditor will assume you failed to report all your income, unless you can show that the deposits you didn't include in your tax return weren't income—for example, that they were loans, inheritances, or transfers from other accounts. This is why you need to keep good records of your income. (See Chapter 14, Section A.)

An IRS auditor may also investigate whether you really qualify as an independent contractor or should have been classified as an employee by your clients or customers. (See Chapter 15.)

4. Handling Audits

You have the legal right to take anyone along with you to help during an audit—a bookkeeper, tax pro or even an attorney. If you've hired a tax pro to prepare your returns, it can be helpful for him or her to attend the audit to help explain your business receipts and records and to explain how the returns were prepared. Some tax pros include free audit services as part of a tax preparation package.

However, if you prepared your tax returns yourself, you can probably deal with an office audit yourself. It could cost more to hire a tax pro to represent you in an office audit than the IRS is likely to bill you. If you're worried that some serious irregularity will come to light—for example, you've taken a huge deduction and can't produce a receipt or canceled check to verify it—consult with a tax pro before the audit.

No matter who prepared your tax returns, it usually makes sense to have a tax pro represent you in a field audit, since these can result in very substantial assessments.

 For a detailed discussion of IRS small business audits, see *Tax Savvy for Small Business,* by Frederick W. Daily (Nolo). ■

Reducing Your Income Taxes

If you're like the vast majority of self-employed people, you must pay personal federal income tax on the net profit you earn from your business activities. This is true whether you're legally organized as a sole proprietor, S corporation, partnership or limited liability company. The only exception is if you've formed a C corporation. (See Chapter 2, Section B.)

The key phrase here is "net profit." You are entitled to deduct the total amount of your business-related expenses from your gross income—that is, all the money or the value of other items you receive from your clients or customers. You pay income tax on your resulting net profit, not your gross self-employment income.

> **EXAMPLE:** Karen, a sole proprietor, earned $50,000 this year from her consulting business. Fortunately, she doesn't have to pay income tax on the entire $50,000. She qualifies for several business-related tax deductions, including a $5,000 home office deduction (see Chapter 4) and a $10,000 deduction for equipment expenses (see Section D). She deducts these amounts from her $50,000 gross income to arrive at her net profit: $35,000. She only pays income tax on that amount.

This chapter provides an overview of the many business-related federal income tax deductions that are available to reduce your gross profits and so reduce the amount of income tax you have to pay. It is a good introduction to this complex subject, but you may need more detailed information.

Most States Have Income Taxes, Too

All states except Alaska, Florida, Nevada, South Dakota, Texas, Washington and Wyoming also impose personal income taxes on the self-employed. (New Hampshire and Tennessee only impose income taxes on dividend and interest income.) If you're incorporated, your corporation will likely have to pay state income taxes as well. Contact your state tax department for income tax information and the appropriate forms. (See the Appendix for a list of state income tax offices.)

 For a more detailed treatment of income taxes, see:

- *Tax Savvy for Small Business*, by Frederick W. Daily (Nolo).

In addition, many IRS publications dealing with income tax issues are mentioned below. You can obtain a free copy of any IRS publication by calling 800-TAX FORM or contacting your local IRS office. You can also download the publications from the IRS Internet site at www.irs.gov. (See Chapter 21, Section E.)

A. Income Reporting

Employers deduct income tax from their employees' paychecks and remit and report it to the IRS. They give all their employees an IRS Form W-2, Wage and Tax Statement, showing wages and withholding for the year. Employees must file a copy of the W-2 with their income tax returns so that the IRS can compare the amount of income they report with the amounts their employers claim they were paid.

When you're self employed, no income tax is withheld from your compensation and you don't receive a W-2 form. However, this does not mean that the IRS doesn't have at least some idea of how much money you've made. If a client pays you $600 or more over the course of a year, the client must complete and file IRS Form 1099-MISC reporting the payments.

The client must complete and file a copy of Form 1099 with:

- the IRS
- your state tax office (if your state has income tax), and
- you.

To make sure you're not underreporting your income, IRS computers check the amounts listed on your 1099 forms against the amount of income you report on your tax return. If the amounts don't match, you have a good chance of being flagged for an audit.

1. When Form 1099 Is Not Required

Your clients need not file any 1099 form if you've incorporated your business and the client hires your corporation, not you personally. This is one reason clients often prefer to hire incorporated businesses. The IRS uses Form 1099 as an important audit lead. If a company files more 1099 forms than average for its type of business, the IRS often concludes that it must be misclassifying employees as independent contractors and may conduct an audit.

Although 1099s generally need not be filed for corporations, there are two exceptions to this rule. If you are an incorporated doctor and perform business-related services for a patient, your corporation must file a 1099. The same rule applies to incorporated lawyers who perform business services for a client.

Form 1099 is not required when you perform services for a person who is not engaged in a business, such as a homeowner or patient. Nor are they required to report payments to you solely for merchandise or inventory. (See Chapter 13, Section C1.)

2. What to Do With Your 1099 Forms

You should receive all your 1099 forms for the previous year by January 31 of the current year. Check the amount of compensation your clients say they paid you in each Form 1099 against your own records, to make sure they are consistent. If there is a mistake, call the client immediately and request a corrected Form 1099. Insist that a corrected Form 1099 be filed with the IRS. You don't want the IRS to think you've been paid more than you really were.

You don't have to file your 1099 forms with your tax returns. Just keep them in your records.

1099s MAY BE SENT ELECTRONICALLY

Starting in 2002, hiring firms may send 1099s to independent contractors electronically—that is, by e-mail. But they may do this only if you agree to it. If you don't agree they must deliver them by mail or in person. If you have an e-mail account, you may as well agree to get your forms electronically. You'll probably get your 1099s faster. Indeed, you may wish to ask your clients to send your 1099s by e-mail—they will probably be glad to comply. Be sure to save your 1099s. If you get them by e-mail, print them out and file them away.

3. If You Don't Receive a Form 1099

It's not unusual for clients to fail to file required 1099 forms. This may be unintentional—for example, the client may not understand the rules or may be negligent. On the other hand, some clients purposefully fail to file 1099 forms because they don't want the IRS to know they're hiring independent contractors.

If, by January 31, you don't receive a Form 1099 from a client who paid you more than $600 for business-related services the prior year, call the client and ask for it. If the client still does not produce the form, don't worry about it. It's not your duty to see that 1099 forms are filed. This is your client's responsibility. The IRS will not impose any fines or penalties on you if a client fails to file a Form 1099. It may, however, impose a $100 fine on the client—and exact far more severe penalties if an IRS audit reveals that the client should have classified you as an employee.

Whether or not you receive a Form 1099, it is your duty to report all the self-employment income you earn each year to the IRS. If you're audited by the IRS, it will, among other things, examine your bank records to make sure you haven't underreported your income. If you have underreported, you'll have to pay back taxes, fines and penalties.

YOUR REPORTED INCOME MUST JIBE WITH YOUR 1099 FORMS

It's very important that the self-employment income you report in your tax return be at least equal to that reported to the IRS on the 1099 forms your clients send in. If a client reimbursed you for expenses such as travel, be sure to check and see if the Form 1099 the client provides you includes this amount. Some clients routinely include expense reimbursements on their 1099 forms, others do not.

If a Form 1099 includes expenses, you must report the entire amount as income on your tax return. You then deduct the amount of the expense reimbursement as your own business expense on your Schedule C. This way, your net self-employment income will come out right.

B. Introduction to Income Tax Deductions

A deduction is an expense or the value of an item that you can subtract from your gross income to determine your taxable income—that is, the amount you earn that is subject to taxation. The more deductions you have, the lower your taxable income and the less income tax you pay. When people speak of taking a deduction or deducting an expense from their income taxes, they mean that they subtract it from their gross incomes.

Most of the work involved in doing your taxes will go into determining what deductions you can take, how much you can take and when you can take them. You don't have to become an income tax expert. But even if you have a tax pro prepare your tax returns, you need to have a basic understanding of what expenses are deductible so that you can keep proper records. This takes some time, but it's worth it. There's no point in working hard to earn a good income only to turn most of the money over to the government.

1. What You Can Deduct

Virtually any expense is deductible as long as it is:

- ordinary and necessary
- directly related to your business, and
- for a reasonable amount.

a. Ordinary and necessary expenses

An expense qualifies as ordinary and necessary if it is common, accepted, helpful and appropriate for your business or profession. An expense doesn't have to be indispensable to be necessary; it need only help your business in some way, even in a minor way. It's usually fairly easy to tell if an expense passes this test.

EXAMPLE: Bill, a freelance writer, hires a research assistant for a new book he's writing about ancient Athens and pays her $15 an hour. This is clearly a deductible business expense. Hiring research assistants is a common and accepted practice among professional writers. The assistant's fee is an ordinary and necessary expense for Bill's writing business.

EXAMPLE: Bill, the freelance writer, visits a masseuse every week to work on his bad back. Bill claims the cost as a business expense, reasoning that avoiding back pain helps him concentrate on his writing. This is clearly not an ordinary or customary expense for a freelance writer and the IRS would not likely allow it as a business expense.

b. Expense must be related to your business

An expense must be related to your business to be deductible. That is, you must use the item you buy for your business in some way. For example, the cost of a personal computer is a deductible business expense if you use the computer to write business reports.

You cannot deduct purely personal expenses as business expenses. The cost of a personal computer is not deductible if you use it just to play computer games. If you buy something for both personal and business reasons, you may deduct the business portion of the expense. For example, if you buy a cellular phone and use it half the time for business calls and half the time for personal calls, you can deduct half the cost of the phone as a business expense.

However, the IRS requires you to keep records showing when the item was used for business and when for personal reasons. One acceptable form of record would be a diary or log with the dates, times and reason the item was used. (See Chapter 14, Section A.) This kind of record-keeping can be burdensome and may not be worth the trouble if the item isn't very valuable.

To avoid having to keep such records, try to use items either only for business or only for personal use. For example, if you can afford it, purchase two computers and use one solely for your business and one for playing games and other personal uses.

c. Deductions must be reasonable

There is usually no limit on how much you can deduct as long as it's not more than you actually spend and the amount is reasonable. Certain areas are hot buttons for the IRS—especially entertainment, travel and meal expenses. The IRS won't allow such expenses to the extent it considers them lavish. (See Section G.)

Also, if the amount of your deductions is very large relative to your income, your chance of being audited goes up dramatically. One recent analysis of almost 1,300 tax returns found that you are at high risk for an audit if your business deductions exceed 63% of your revenues. You're relatively safe so long as your deductions are less than 52% of your revenue. If you have extremely large deductions, make sure you can document them in case you're audited. (See Chapter 14, Section A3.)

d. Common deductions for the self-employed

Self-employed workers typically are entitled to take a number of income tax deductions. The most common include:

- advertising costs—for example, the cost of a Yellow Pages advertisement or brochure
- attorney and accounting fees for your business
- bank fees for your business bank account
- business start-up costs
- car and truck expenses (see Section E)
- costs of renting or leasing vehicles, machinery, equipment and other property used in your business
- depreciation of business assets (see Section D2)
- education expenses—for example, the cost of attending professional seminars or classes required to keep up a professional license
- expenses for the business use of your home (see Chapter 4)
- fees you pay to other self-employed workers you hire to help your business—for example, the cost of paying a marketing consultant to advise you on how to get more clients

- health insurance for yourself and your family (see Section H)
- insurance for your business—for example, liability, workers' compensation and business property insurance (see Chapter 6)
- interest on business loans and debts—for example, interest you pay for a bank loan you use to expand your business
- license fees—for example, fees for a local business license or occupational license (see Chapter 5)
- office expenses, such as office supplies
- office utilities
- postage
- professional association dues
- professional or business books you need for your business
- repairs and maintenance for business equipment such as a photocopier or fax machine
- retirement plan contributions (see Section H3)
- software you buy for your business (see Section D3)
- subscriptions for professional or business publications
- travel, meals and entertainment (see Sections F and G), and
- wages and benefits you provide your employees.

INVENTORY IS NOT A BUSINESS EXPENSE

If you make or buy goods to sell, you are entitled to deduct the cost of those goods actually sold on your tax return. This is what you spent for the goods or their actual market value (if they've declined in value since you bought them).

However, money spent for goods to sell is not treated as a business expense. Instead, you deduct the cost of goods you've sold from your business receipts to determine your gross profit from the business. Your business expenses are then deducted from your gross profit to determine your net profit, which is taxed.

Businesses that make, buy or sell goods must determine the value of their inventories at the beginning and the end of each tax year using an IRS-approved accounting method. Conducting inventories can be burdensome. Many self-employed people don't have to worry about inventories because they sell personal services to their clients or customers. For example, doctors, lawyers, carpenters and painters usually do not keep inventories of goods. However, if in addition to selling your services, you also regularly charge clients for materials and supplies, you must maintain an inventory for tax purposes.

For more information on inventories, see the Cost of Goods Sold section in Chapter 7 of IRS Publication 334, *Tax Guide for Small Businesses*, IRS Publication 538, *Accounting Periods and Methods* and Publication 970, *Application to Use LIFO Inventory Method*.

You can obtain these and all other IRS publications by calling the IRS at 800-TAX-FORM, visiting your local IRS office or downloading the publications from the IRS Internet site at www.irs.gov.

2. When to Deduct

Some expenses can be deducted all at once; others have to be deducted over a number of years. It all depends on how long the item you purchase can reasonably be expected to last—what the IRS calls its useful life.

a. Current expenses

The cost of anything you buy for your business that has a useful life of less than one year must be fully deducted in the year it is purchased. This includes, for example, rent, telephone and utility bills, photocopying costs and postage and other ordinary business operating costs. Such items are called current expenses.

b. Capital expenses

Certain types of costs are considered part of your investment in your business rather than operating costs. These are called capital expenses. Subject to an important exception for a certain amount of personal property (see Section D1), you cannot deduct the full value of such expenses in the year you incur them. Instead, you must spread the cost over several years and deduct part of it each year.

There are two main categories of capital expenses. They include:

- the cost of any asset you will use in your business that has a useful life of more than one year—for example, equipment, vehicles, books, furniture, machinery and patents (see Section D2), and
- business start-up costs, such as fees for doing market research or attorney and accounting fees paid to set up your business.

3. Businesses That Lose Money

If the money you spend on your business exceeds your business income for the year, your business incurs a loss. This isn't as bad as it sounds because you can use a business loss to offset other income you may have—for example, interest income or your spouse's income if you file jointly. You can even accumulate your losses and apply them to reduce your income taxes in future or past years.

 For detailed information on deducting business losses, see IRS Publication 536, *Net Operating Losses*. You can obtain this and all other IRS publications by calling the IRS at 800-TAX-FORM, visiting your local IRS office or downloading the publications from the IRS Internet site at www.irs.gov.

a. Recurring losses

If you keep incurring losses year after year, you need to be very concerned about running afoul of the hobby loss rule. This tax law could cost you a fortune in additional income taxes.

The IRS created the hobby loss rule to prevent taxpayers from entering into ventures primarily to incur expenses they could deduct from their other incomes. The rule halts this form of tax avoidance by allowing you to take a business expense deduction only if your venture qualifies as a business. Ventures that don't qualify as businesses are called hobbies. If the IRS views what you do as a hobby, there will be severe limits on what expenses you can deduct.

A venture is a business if you engage in it to make a profit. It's not necessary that you earn a profit every year. All that is required is that your main reason for doing what you do is to make a profit. A hobby is any activity you engage in mainly for a reason other than making a profit—for example, to incur deductible expenses or just to have fun.

The IRS can't read your mind to determine whether you want to earn a profit. And it certainly isn't going to take your word for it. Instead, it looks to see whether you do actually earn a profit, or whether you behave as if you want to earn a profit.

b. Profit test

You don't have to worry about the IRS labeling your business as a hobby if you earn a profit from it in any three of five consecutive years. If your venture passes this test, the IRS presumes it is carried on for profit.

You have a profit when the gross income from an activity exceeds the deductions you take for it. You don't have to earn a big profit to satisfy this test. Careful year-end planning can help your business show a profit for the year. For example, if clients owe you money, press for payment before the end of the year. Also, put off paying expenses or buying new equipment until the new year.

A loss for one or two years isn't fatal. But do everything possible to avoid showing losses for three consecutive years. This will definitely set the IRS computers to whirring and increase your chance of being audited. If you are audited, the hobby loss issue will definitely be raised.

c. Behavior test

If you keep incurring losses and can't satisfy the profit test, you by no means have to throw in the towel and treat your venture as a hobby. You can continue to treat it as a business and fully deduct your losses. However, you must take steps that will convince the IRS your business isn't a hobby if you're audited.

You must be able to convince the IRS that earning a profit—not having fun or accumulating tax deductions—is the primary motive for what you do. This can be particularly difficult if you're engaged in an activity that could objectively be considered fun—for example, creating artwork, photography or writing—but it can still be done. People who have incurred losses for seven, eight or nine years in a row have convinced the IRS they were running a business.

LOSING GOLFER SCORES HOLE-IN-ONE IN TAX COURT

Donald, a Chicago high school gym teacher, decided to become a golf pro when he turned 40. He became a member of the Professional Golfers of America, which entitled him to compete in certain professional tournaments. Donald kept his teaching job, but played in various professional tournaments during the summer. His expenses exceeded his income from golfing for five straight years.

Year	Golf Earnings	Golf Expenses	Losses
1978	$ 0	$2,538	$2,538
1979	148	1,332	1,184
1980	400	4,672	4,272
1981	904	4,167	3,263
1982	1,458	8,061	6,603

The IRS sought to disallow the losses for 1981 and 1982, claiming that golf was a hobby for Donald. Donald appealed to the Tax Court and won.

The court held that Donald played golf to make a profit, not just to have fun. He carefully detailed the expenses he incurred for each tournament he entered and recorded the prize money available. He attended a business course for golfers, and assisted a professional golfer from whom he also took lessons. He practiced every day, up to 12 hours during the summer; he also traveled frequently to Florida during the winter to play. Although his costs increased over the years, his winnings steadily increased each year as well. The court concluded that, although Donald obviously enjoyed golfing, he honestly wanted to earn a profit from it. (*Kimbrough v. Commissioner,* 55 TCM. 730 (1988).)

You must show the IRS that your behavior is consistent with that of a person who really wants to make money. There are many ways to accomplish this.

First and foremost, you must show that you carry on your enterprise in a businesslike manner—for example, you:

- maintain a separate checking account for your business (see Chapter 14, Section A)
- keep good business records (see Chapter 14, Section A2)
- make some effort to market your services— for example, have business cards and, if appropriate, a Yellow Pages or similar advertisement
- have business stationery and cards printed
- obtain a federal employer identification number (see Chapter 5)
- secure all necessary business licenses and permits (see Chapter 5)
- have a separate phone line for your business if you work at home
- join professional organizations and associations, and
- develop expertise in your field by attending educational seminars and similar activities.

You should also draw up a business plan with forecasts of revenue and expenses. This will also be a big help if you try to borrow money for your business.

 For detailed guidance on how to create a business plan, see *How to Write a Business Plan*, by Mike McKeever (Nolo).

The more time and effort you put into the activity, the more it will look like you want to make money. So try to devote as much time as possible to your business and keep a log showing the time you spend on it.

It's also helpful to consult with experts in your field and follow their advice about how to modify your operations to increase sales and cut costs. Be sure to document your efforts.

EXAMPLE: Otto, a professional artist, has incurred losses from his business for the past three years. He consults with Cindy, a prominent art gallery owner, about how he can sell more of his work. He writes down her recommendations and then documents his efforts to follow them—for example, he visits art shows around the country and talks with a number of gallery owners about representing his work.

You'll have an easier time convincing the IRS that your venture is a business if you earn a profit in at least some years. It's also very helpful if you've earned profits from similar businesses in the past.

d. Tax effect

If the IRS determines your venture is a hobby, you'll lose valuable deductions and your income tax burden will increase. Unlike business expenses, expenses for a hobby are personal expenses that you can deduct only from income from the hobby. They can't be applied to your other income, such as your or your spouse's salary or interest income.

EXAMPLE: Bill holds a full-time job as a college geology teacher and also paints part time and shows his work in art galleries. The IRS has decided that painting is a hobby for Bill, since he's never earned a profit from it. In one year, Bill spent $2,000 on the painting hobby, but earned only $500 from the sale of one painting. His expenses can only be deducted from the $500 income derived from painting. This wipes out the $500, but Bill cannot apply the remainder to his other income. Because of the hobby loss rule, Bill has lost $1,500 worth of tax deductions.

4. Tax Savings From Deductions

Only part of any deduction will end up as an income tax saving—for example, a $5,000 tax deduction will not result in a $5,000 income tax saving.

How much you'll save depends on your tax rate. The tax law assigns a percentage income tax rate to specified income levels. People with high incomes pay income tax at a higher rate than those with lower incomes. These percentage rates are called tax brackets.

To determine how much income tax a deduction will save you, you need to know your marginal tax bracket. This is the tax bracket in which the last dollar you earn falls. It's the rate at which any additional income you earn would be taxed. The income tax brackets are adjusted each year for inflation.

 For the current brackets, see IRS Publication 505, *Tax Withholding and Estimated Tax.* You can obtain this and all other IRS publications by calling the IRS at 800-TAX-FORM, visiting your local IRS office or downloading the publications from the IRS Internet site at www.irs.gov.

2002 TAX BRACKETS

Tax Bracket	Income If Married Filing Joint Return	Income If Single
10%	Up to $12,000	Up to $6,000
15%	From $12,001 to $46,700	$6,001 to $27,950
27%	$46,701 to $112,850	$27,951 to $67,700
30%	$112,851 to $171,950	$67,701 to $141,250
35%	$181,951 to $307,050	$141,251 to $307,050
38.6%	On all over $307,051	On all over $307,050

The table on the previous page shows the tax brackets for 2002. For example, if you were single and earned $50,000 in 2002, your marginal tax bracket was 27%—that is, you had to pay 27 cents in income tax for every additional dollar you earned.

To determine how much tax a deduction will save you, multiply the amount of the deduction by your marginal tax bracket. If your marginal tax bracket is 27%, you will save 27 cents in income taxes for every dollar you are able to claim as a deductible business expense.

> **EXAMPLE:** Barry, a single self-employed consultant, earned $50,000 in 2002 and was therefore in the 27% marginal tax bracket. He was able to take a $5,000 home office deduction. (See Chapter 4.) His actual income tax saving was 27% of the $5,000 deduction, or $1,350.

You can also deduct most business-related expenses from your income for self-employment tax purposes. (See Chapter 10.)

The effective self-employment tax rate is about 12% on net self-employment income up to the Social Security tax cap ($84,900 in 2002). (See Chapter 10.)

In addition, you may deduct your business expenses from your state income tax. State income taxes rates vary, but they average about 6%. (However, Alaska, Florida, Nevada, South Dakota, Texas, Washington and Wyoming don't have income taxes.)

When you add all this together, you can see the true value of a business tax deduction. For example, if you're in the 27% federal income tax bracket, a business deduction is roughly worth 27% + 12% + 6% = 45%. So you end up deducting about 45% of the cost of your business expenses from your state and federal taxes. If, for example, you buy a $1,000 computer for your business, you may deduct about $450 of the cost from your taxes. That's a whopping tax savings. In effect, the government is paying for almost half of your business expenses. This is why it's so important to take all the business deductions to which you're entitled.

C. Business Use of Your Home

Many self-employed people work from home, particularly when they're starting out. If you can meet some strict requirements, you're allowed to deduct your expenses for the business use of part of your home. This is commonly called the home office deduction. (See Chapter 4.)

D. Deducting the Cost of Business Assets

One of the nice things about being self-employed is that you can deduct the money you spend for things you use to help produce income for your business—for example, computers, calculators and office furniture. You can take a full deduction whether you pay cash for an asset or buy on credit.

If you qualify for the Section 179 deduction discussed below, you can deduct the entire cost of these items in the year you pay for them. Otherwise, you have to deduct the cost over a period of years—a process called depreciation.

The rules for deducting business assets can be complex, but it's worth spending the time to understand them. After all, by allowing these deductions, the U.S. government is in effect offering to help you pay for your equipment and other business assets. All you have to do is take advantage of the offer.

SPECIAL 9/11 TAX RELIEF FOR NEW YORKERS

Congress passed a new tax law in March, 2002, that gives special tax relief to taxpayers in the Lower Manhattan area of New York City—the area devastated by the 9/11 attacks and collapse of the World Trade Center. Self-employed people who have their workplaces in this area are entitled to increased depreciation and Section 179 deductions and various tax credits. For detailed information, see IRS Publication 3920, *Tax Relief for Victims of Terrorist Attacks*. You can obtain this and all other IRS publications by calling the IRS at 800-TAX-FORM, visiting your local IRS office or downloading the publication from the IRS website at www.irs.gov.

1. Section 179 Deduction

If you learn only one section number in the tax code, it should be Section 179. It is one of the greatest tax boons for small businesspeople. Section 179 permits you to deduct a large amount of your business asset purchases in the year you make them, rather than having to depreciate them over several years. (See Section D2.) This is called first year expensing or Section 179 expensing. It allows you to get a big tax deduction all at once, rather than taking it a little at a time.

> **EXAMPLE:** Ginger buys a $8,000 photocopy machine for her business. She can use Section 179 to deduct the entire $8,000 expense from her income taxes for the year.

It's up to you to decide whether to use Section 179. It may not always be in your best interests to do so. (See Section D2.) If you do use it, you can't change your mind later and decide to use depreciation instead.

a. Property that can be deducted

You can use Section 179 to deduct the cost of any tangible personal property you use for your business that the IRS has determined will last more than one year—for example, computers, business equipment and office furniture. (See Section D3.) Special rules apply to cars. (See Section D3.) You can't use Section 179 for land, buildings or intangible personal property such as patents, copyrights and trademarks.

If you use property both for business and personal purposes, you may deduct under Section 179 only if you use it for business purposes more than half the time. The amount of your deduction is reduced by the percentage of personal use. You'll need to keep records showing your business use of such property. (See Chapter 14.)

If you use an item for business less than half the time, you must depreciate it. (See Section D2.)

b. Deduction limit

There is a limit on the total amount of business expenses you can deduct each year using Section 179. In 2002, the limit is $24,000. In 2003 and after, it is $25,000.

This dollar limit applies to all your businesses together, not to each business you own and run. You do not have to claim the full amount. It's up to you to decide how much of the cost of prop-

erty you want to deduct. But you don't lose out on the remainder; you can depreciate any cost you do not deduct under Section 179. (See Section D2.)

If you purchase more than one item of Section 179 property during the year, you can divide the deduction among all the items in any way, as long as the total deduction is not more than the Section 179 limit. It's usually best to apply Section 179 to property that has the longest useful life and therefore the longest depreciation period. This reduces the total time you have to wait to get your deductions. (See Section D2c.)

> **EXAMPLE:** In 2002, Ben, a self-employed consultant, buys for his business an $11,000 computer, an $11,000 copier and $11,000 in office furniture. The total for all these purchases is $33,000—more than the $24,000 Section 179 limit for 2002. He can divide his Section 179 deduction among these items any way he wants. The copier and computer would have to be depreciated over five years, but the furniture over seven years. He should apply Section 179 to the furniture first and then to the computer or copier. Any portion of the cost of the copier or computer that exceeds the Section 179 limit can be depreciated over five years. This way, he avoids having to wait seven years to get his full deduction for the furniture.

c. Limit on Section 179 deduction

You can't use Section 179 to deduct more in one year than the total of your profit from all of your businesses and your salary, if you have a job in addition to your business. If you're married and file a joint tax return, you can include your spouse's salary and business income in this total as well. You can't count investment income—for example, interest you earn on your savings.

You can't use Section 179 to reduce your taxable income below zero. But you can carry to the next tax year any amount you cannot use as a Section 179 deduction and possibly deduct it then.

> **EXAMPLE:** In 2002, Amelia earned a $5,000 profit from her engineering consulting business and $10,000 from a part-time job. She spent $17,000 for computer equipment. She can use Section 179 to deduct $15,000 of this expense for 2000 and deduct the remaining $2,000 the next year.

In the unlikely event that you buy over $200,000 of Section 179 property in a year, your deduction is reduced by one dollar for every dollar you spend over that amount.

d. Minimum period of business use

When you deduct an asset under Section 179, you must continue to use it for business at least 50% of the time for as many years it would have been depreciated. (See Section D2c.) For example, if you use Section 179 for a computer, you must use it for business at least 50% of the time for five years, because computers have a five-year depreciation period.

If you don't meet these rules, you'll have to report as income part of the deduction you took under Section 179 in the prior year. This is called recapture.

 For more information, see IRS Publication 334, *Tax Guide for Small Business, Chapter 12, Depreciation.* You can obtain this and all other IRS publications by calling the IRS at 800-TAX-FORM, visiting your local IRS office or downloading the publications from the IRS Internet site at www.irs.gov.

2. Depreciation

Because it provides a big tax deduction immediately, most small business owners look first to Section 179 to deduct asset costs.

However, you must use depreciation instead if you:

- don't qualify to use Section 179—for example, you want to deduct the cost of a building or a patent, or
- use up your Section 179 deduction for the year.

Depreciation involves deducting the cost of a business asset a little at a time over a period of years. This means it will take you much longer to get your full deduction than under Section 179. However, this isn't always a bad thing. Indeed, you may be better off in the long run using depreciation instead of Section 179 if you expect to earn more in future years than you will in the current year. Remember that the value of a deduction depends on your income tax bracket. If you're in the 15% bracket, a $1,000 deduction is worth only $150. If you're in the 30% bracket, it's worth $300. (See Section B4.) So spreading out a deduction until you're in a higher tax bracket can make sense.

EXAMPLE: Marie, a self-employed consultant, buys a $5,000 photocopier for her business in 2003. She elects to depreciate the copier instead of using the Section 179 deduction. This way, she can deduct a portion of the cost from her gross income each year for the next six years. Marie is only in the 15% tax bracket in 2003, but expects to be in the 30% bracket in 2004.

The following chart shows how much more money Marie saves by taking depreciation and deducting a portion of the copier's cost over six years rather than taking a Section 179 deduction for the entire cost in one year. Marie is using the straight line depreciation method, which produces the same deduction every year, except the first and last. (See Section D2d.)

You may also prefer to use depreciation rather than Section 179 if you want to puff up your business income for the year. This can help you get a bank loan or help your business show a profit instead of incurring a loss—and therefore, avoid running afoul of the hobby loss limitations. (See Section B3.)

a. What must be depreciated

Whether you must depreciate an item depends on how long it can reasonably be expected to last— what the IRS calls its useful life. Depreciation is used to deduct the cost of any asset you buy for your business that has a useful life of more than one year—for example, buildings, equipment, machinery, patents, trademarks, copyrights and furniture. Land cannot be depreciated because it doesn't wear out. The IRS, not you, decides the useful life of your assets. (See Section D2c.)

You can also depreciate the cost of major repairs that increase the value or extend the life of an asset—for example, the cost of a major upgrade to make your computer run faster. However, you have to deduct normal repairs or maintenance in the year they're incurred as a business expense.

b. Mixed use property

If you use property for both business and personal purposes, you can take depreciation only for the business use of the asset. Unlike the Section 179 deduction, you don't have to use an item more than half the time for business to depreciate it.

COMPARISON OF DEDUCTIONS: SECTION 179 AND DEPRECIATION

Year	Marie's Marginal Tax Rate	Tax Savings Using Section 179 Deduction	Tax Savings Using Depreciation Deduction
2003	15%	$750 (15% x $5,000, the cost of the copier)	$75 (15% x $500 of copier's $5,000 cost)
2004	30%	0	$300 (30% x $1,000)
2005	30%	0	$300 (30% x $1,000)
2006	30%	0	$300 (30% x $1,000)
2007	30%	0	$300 (30% x $1,000)
2008	30%	0	$150 (30% x $500)
TOTAL		$750	$1,425

EXAMPLE: Carl uses his photocopier 75% of the time for personal reasons and 25% for business. He can depreciate 25% of the cost of the copier.

Keep a diary or log with the dates, times and reason the property was used to distinguish between the two uses. (See Chapter 14, Section A.)

c. Depreciation period

The depreciation period—called the recovery period by the IRS—begins when you start using the asset and lasts for the entire estimated useful life of the asset. The tax code has assigned an estimated useful life for all types of business assets, ranging from 3 to 39 years. Most of the assets you buy for your business will probably have an estimated useful life of five or seven years.

If you need to know the depreciation period for an asset not included in this table, see IRS Publication 534, *Depreciation,* for a complete listing. You can obtain this and all other IRS publications by calling the IRS at 800-TAX-FORM, visiting your local IRS office or downloading the publications from the IRS Internet site at www.irs.gov.

You are free to continue using property after its estimated useful life expires, but you can't deduct any more depreciation.

d. Calculating depreciation

You can use three different methods to calculate the depreciation deduction: straight line or one of two accelerated depreciation methods. Once you choose your method, you're stuck with it for the entire life of the asset.

In addition, you must use the same method for all property of the same kind purchased during the year. For example, if you use the straight line method to depreciate a computer, you must use that method to depreciate all other computers you purchase during the year for your business.

The straight line method requires you to deduct an equal amount each year over the useful life of an asset. However, you ordinarily deduct only a half-year's worth of depreciation in the first year. You make up for this by adding an extra year of depreciation at the end.

EXAMPLE: Sally buys a $1,000 fax machine for her business in 2003. It has a useful life of five years. (See the chart in Section D2c.) Using the straight line method, she would de-

ASSET DEPRECIATION PERIODS

Type of Property	Recovery Period
Computer software (software that comes with your computer is not separately depreciable unless you're separately billed for it)	3 years
Office machinery (computers and peripherals, calculators, copiers, typewriters)	5 years
Autos and light trucks	5 years
Construction and research equipment	5 years
Office furniture	7 years
Residential buildings	27.5 years
Nonresidential buildings purchased before 5/12/93	31.5 years
Nonresidential buildings purchased after 5/12/93	39 years

preciate the asset over six years. Her annual depreciation deductions are as follows:

2003	$100
2004–2007	$800 ($200 each year)
2008	$100
TOTAL	$1,000

Most small businesses use one of two types of accelerated depreciation: the double declining balance method or the 150% declining balance method. The advantage to these methods is that they provide larger depreciation deductions in the earlier years and smaller ones later on. The double declining balance method starts out by giving you double the deduction you'd get for the first full year with the straight line method. The 150% declining balance method gives you one and one-half times the straight line deduction.

EXAMPLE: Sally decides to use the fastest accelerated depreciation method to depreciate her $1,000 fax machine—the double declining balance method. Her annual depreciation deductions are as follows:

2003	$400
2004	$240
2005	$144
2006	$108
2007	$108
TOTAL	$1,000

However, using accelerated depreciation is not necessarily a good idea if you expect your income to go up in future years. There are also some restrictions on when you can use accelerated depreciation. For example, you can't use it for cars, computers and certain other property that is used for business less than 50% of the time. (See Section D3.)

Determining which depreciation method is best for you and calculating how much depreciation you can deduct is a complex task usually best left to an accountant. If you want to do it yourself, seriously consider obtaining a tax prepa-ration computer program that can help you do the calculations. (See Chapter 8.)

e. 30% Bonus Depreciation Deduction

In the wake of the 9/11 tragedy and the ensuing recession, Congress revised the depreciation rules to give businesses an additional depreciation deduction. Under these rules, taxpayers get an additional "bonus" 30% depreciation deduction for property purchased between September 11, 2001 and September 10, 2004 and placed into service (that is, used for business purposes) before 2005. The 30% is deducted from the "adjusted basis" (usually the cost) of the property. You can take it in addition to normal depreciation.

EXAMPLE: Stan purchases and places in service $50,000 worth of equipment for his construction business in 2003. He gets a bonus depreciation deduction of $15,000 in 2003 (30% of $50,000) and depreciates the remaining cost of the equipment—$35,000—in 2003 and later years under the normal depreciation rules.

If you want to take the Section 179 deduction discussed in Section D1 you can combine it with the 30% bonus depreciation and regular depreciation, in that order.

EXAMPLE: Stan purchases and places in service $50,000 worth of equipment for his construction business in 2003. First, he may take a $25,000 Section 179 deduction—that is, he may deduct this entire amount from his income. Next, he may take a 30% bonus depreciation deduction on the remaining $25,000 of the equipment cost—this amounts to a $7,500 deduction (30% of $25,000). Finally, he may deduct the remaining $17,500 ($25,000 minus $7,500) of the original equipment cost in 2003 and later under the normal depreciation rules.

Of course, if you purchase business property during the year for an amount equal to or less than the Section 179 deduction ($24,000 in 2002 and $25,000 in 2003 and later), you can't use the 30% bonus because you'll have nothing left to depreciate. But the 30% bonus is a great boon to self-employed people who purchase business property worth more than the Section 179 deduction—it allows them to deduct a lot of the cost in the first year.

The 30% bonus depreciation deduction will be applied automatically to all taxpayers who qualify for it. However, the deduction is optional. You need not take it if you don't want to. You can elect not to take the deduction by attaching a note to your tax return. It may be advantageous to do this if you expect your income to go up substantially in future years, which would place you in a higher tax bracket.

If you do take the deduction, you may only use it for property with a depreciation life of 20 years or less. This includes most types of property self-employed people buy for their business, such as office equipment and computers (see Section D2). You may also use it for computer software that does not come with your computer.

If you filed your taxes for 2001 before the 30% bonus provision was enacted in March, 2002, you obviously weren't aware of the bonus. You may file an amended return for 2001 to take the depreciation bonus for any qualifying business property you purchased between September 11, 2001 and December 31, 2001.

For more information, see IRS Publication 534, *Depreciation*. You can obtain this and all other IRS publications by calling the IRS at 800-TAX-FORM, visiting your local IRS office or downloading the publications from the IRS Internet site at www.irs.gov.

3. Cars, Computers and Cellular Phones

The IRS imposes special rules on certain items that can easily be used for personal as well as business purposes. These items, called listed property, include:

- cars, boats, airplanes and other vehicles (see Section E for rules on mileage and vehicle expenses)
- computers
- cellular phones, and
- any other property generally used for entertainment, recreation or amusement—for example, VCRs, cameras and camcorders.

The IRS fears that taxpayers might use listed property items for personal reasons but claim business deductions for them. For this reason, you're required to document your business use of listed property. You can satisfy this requirement by keeping a logbook showing when and how the property is used. (See Chapter 14, Section A.)

a. Exception to recordkeeping rule

You normally have to document your use of listed property even if you use it 100% for business. However, there is an exception to this rule: If you use listed property only for business and keep it at your business location, you need not comply with the recordkeeping requirement. This includes listed property you keep at your home office if the office qualifies for the home office deduction. (See Section C.)

> **EXAMPLE:** John, a freelance writer, works full time in his home office which he uses exclusively for writing. The office is clearly his principal place of business and qualifies for the home office deduction. He buys a $4,000 computer for his office and uses it exclusively for his writing business. He does not have to keep records showing how he uses the computer.

b. Depreciating listed property

If you use listed property for business more than 50% of the time, you can depreciate it just like any other property. However, if you use it 50% or less of the time for business, you must use the straight line depreciation method and an especially long recovery period. If you start out using accelerated depreciation and your business use drops to 50% or less, you have to switch to the straight line method and pay taxes on the benefits of the prior years of accelerated depreciation.

E. Car Expenses

Most self-employed people do at least some driving related to business—for example, to visit clients or customers, to pick up or deliver work, to obtain business supplies or to attend seminars. Of course, driving costs money—and you are allowed to deduct your driving expenses when you use your car, van, pickup or panel truck for business.

There are two ways to calculate the car expense deduction. You can:

- use the standard mileage rate, which requires relatively little recordkeeping, or
- deduct your actual expenses, which requires much more recordkeeping but might give you a larger deduction.

If you own a late model car worth more than $15,000, you'll usually get a larger deduction by using the actual expense method because the standard mileage rate doesn't include enough for depreciation of new cars. On the other hand, the standard mileage rate will be better if you have an inexpensive or old car and put in a lot of business mileage.

Either way, you'll need to keep records showing how many miles you drive your car for business during the year—also called business miles. Keep a mileage logbook for this purpose. (See Chapter 14, Section A2c.)

 Commuting Expenses Are Not Deductible

You usually cannot deduct commuting expenses—that is, the cost involved in getting to and from work. However, if your main office is at home, you may deduct the cost of driving to meet clients. This is one of the advantages of having a home office. (See Chapter 4.)

1. Standard Mileage Rate

The easiest way to deduct car expenses is to take the standard mileage rate. When you use this method, you need only keep track of how many business miles you drive, not the actual expenses for your car such as gas or repairs.

You can use the standard mileage rate only for a car that you own. You must choose to use it in the first year you start using your car for your business. In later years, you can choose to use the standard mileage rate or actual expenses.

Each year, the IRS sets the standard mileage rate—a specified amount of money you can deduct for each business mile you drive. In 2002, for example, the rate was 36.5 cents per mile. To figure your deduction, multiply your business miles by the standard mileage rate for the year.

> **EXAMPLE:** Ed, a self-employed salesperson, drove his car 10,000 miles for business in 2002. To determine his car expense deduction, he simply multiplies the total business miles he drove by 36.5 cents. This gives him a $3,650 deduction (36.5 cents x 10,000 = $3,650).

If you choose to take the standard mileage rate, you cannot deduct actual operating expenses—for example, depreciation or Section 179 deduction, maintenance and repairs, gasoline and its taxes, oil, insurance and vehicle registration fees. These costs are already factored into the standard mileage rate.

You can deduct any business-related parking fees and tolls—for example, a parking fee you have to pay when you visit a client's office. But you cannot deduct fees you pay to park your car at your place of work.

2. Actual Expenses

Instead of taking the standard mileage rate, you can elect to deduct the actual expenses of using your car for business. To do this, deduct the actual cost of depreciation for your car (subject to limitations), interest payments on a car loan, lease fees, rental fees, license fees, garage rent, repairs, gas, oil, tires and insurance. The total deductible amount is based on the percentage of time you use your car for business. You can also deduct the full amount of any business-related parking fees and tolls.

Deducting all these items will take more time and effort than using the standard mileage rate because you'll need to keep records of all your expenses. However, it may provide you with a larger deduction than the standard rate.

EXAMPLE: Sam drives his $20,000 car 15,000 miles for business in 2002, and doesn't drive it at all for personal use. If he took the standard mileage deduction, he could deduct $5,475 from his income taxes (36.5 cents x 15,000 = $5,475). Instead, however, he takes the actual expense deduction. He keeps careful records of all his costs for gas, oil, repairs, parking, insurance and depreciation. These amount to $7,000 for the year. He gets an extra $1,525 deduction by using the actual expense method.

a. Mixed uses

If you use your car for both business and personal purposes, you must also divide your expenses between business and personal use.

EXAMPLE: In one recent year Laura, a salesperson, drove her car 10,000 miles for her business and 10,000 miles for personal purposes. She can deduct 50% of the actual costs of operating her car.

If you only own one car, you normally can't claim to use it only for business. An IRS auditor is not likely to believe that you walk or take public transportation everywhere except when you're on business. You might convince the IRS to accept your deduction if you live in a place with developed transportation systems, such as Chicago, New York City or San Francisco, and drive your car only when you go out of town on business.

b. Expense records required

When you deduct actual car expenses, you must keep records of the costs of operating your car. This includes not only the number of business miles and total miles you drive, but also gas, repair, parking, insurance and similar costs. (See Chapter 14.) If this seems to be too much trouble, use the standard mileage rate. That way, you'll only have to keep track of how many business miles you drive, not what you spend for gas and similar expenses.

c. Limits on depreciation deductions

Regardless of how much you spend for an automobile, your depreciation deduction is strictly limited. For example, for cars purchased in 2000, the annual depreciation deduction is limited to a maximum of $3,060 the first year, $5,000 the second year, $2,950 the third year and $1,775 thereafter.

If you purchased a car between September 11, 2001 and September 10, 2004 and placed it into service (used it in your business) before 2005, the first year's deduction cap is $7,660. This is a $4,600 increase over the old cap and is part of the new 30% bonus depreciation deduction discussed in Section D2e. However, if you choose not to take the bonus depreciation deduction or your car doesn't qualify for it, the first year deduction cap is $3,060.

There is no point in using Section 179 to write off a car because the limit is the same as under the regular depreciation rules. For example, if you purchased a $20,000 car in 2002, you'd only be allowed to write off $7,060 of the cost for the first year. Writing the car off under Section 179 instead of depreciating the cost will not increase your deduction. It will only use up $7,060 of your $24,000 Section 179 deduction for 2002 and mean you can't use Section 179 to write off that amount of other personal property. Save Section 179 for other items not subject to these restrictions.

d. Leasing a car

If you lease a car that you use in your business, you can deduct the part of each lease payment that goes toward the business use of the car. However, you cannot deduct any part of a lease payment that is for commuting or personal use of the car.

Leasing companies typically require you to make an advance or down payment to lease a car. You must spread such payments over the entire lease period for purposes of deducting their cost. You cannot deduct any payments you make to buy a car, even if the payments are called lease payments.

When you lease a car, you cannot use the standard rate method to deduct your expenses for gas, oil, maintenance and repairs, license fees and insurance. You must use the actual expense method and keep records of your expenses.

⚠ Tax Whammy for Luxury Cars

If you lease what the IRS considers to be a luxury car for more than 30 days, you may have to add an inclusion amount to your income.

This addition makes up for the fact that the lease payments on a luxury car are higher than on a lower priced car. The inclusion amount, listed in IRS leasing tables, is usually quite small. For example, if you leased a $40,000 car in 2001 and used it 100% for business, you'd have to add $206 to your income for the first lease year.

The government doesn't want to subsidize people who lease expensive cars. A luxury car is currently defined as one with a fair market value of more than $15,500.

📖 For more information about the rules for claiming car expenses, see IRS Publication 463, *Travel, Entertainment, Gift and Car Expenses*. You can obtain this and all other IRS publications by calling the IRS at 800-TAX-FORM, visiting your local IRS office or downloading the publications from the IRS Internet site at www.irs.gov.

F. Travel Expenses

If you travel for your business, you can deduct your airfare, hotel bills and other expenses. If you plan your trip right, you can even mix business with pleasure and still get a deduction for your airfare. However, IRS auditors closely scrutinize these deductions. Many taxpayers claim them without complying with the copious rules the IRS imposes. To avoid unwanted attention, you need to understand the limitations on this deduction and keep proper records.

1. Travel Within the United States

Some business people seems to think they have the right to deduct the cost of any trip they take. This is not the case. You can deduct a trip within the United States only if:

- it's primarily for business
- you travel outside your city limits, and
- you're away at least overnight or long enough to require a stop for sleep or rest.

a. Business purpose of trip

For your trip to be deductible, you must spend more than half of your time on activities that can reasonably be expected to help advance your business.

Acceptable activities include:

- visiting or working with clients or customers
- attending trade shows, or
- attending professional seminars or business conventions where the agenda is clearly connected to your business.

Business does not include sightseeing or recreation that you attend by yourself or with family or friends, nor does it include personal investment seminars or political events.

Use common sense before claiming a trip is for business. The IRS will likely question any trip that doesn't have some logical connection to your business. For example, if you build houses in Alaska, an IRS auditor would probably be skeptical about a deduction for a trip you took to Florida to learn about new home air conditioning techniques.

To repeat, if your trip within the United States is not primarily for business, none of your travel expenses are deductible. But you can still deduct expenses you incur on your trip that are directly related to your business—for example, the cost of making long distance phone calls to your office or clients while on vacation.

b. Travel outside city limits

You don't have to travel any set distance to get a travel expense deduction. However, you can't take this deduction if you just spend the night in a motel across town. You must travel outside your city limits. If you don't live in a city, you must go outside the general area where your business is located.

c. Sleep or rest

Finally, you must stay away overnight or at least long enough to require a stop for sleep or rest. You cannot satisfy the rest requirement by merely napping in your car.

EXAMPLE: Phyllis, a self-employed salesperson based in Los Angeles, flies to San Francisco to meet potential clients, spends the night in a hotel and returns home the following day. Her trip is a deductible travel expense.

EXAMPLE: Andre, a self-employed truck driver, leaves his workplace on a regularly scheduled roundtrip between San Francisco and Los Angeles and returns home 18 hours later. During the run, he has six hours off at a turnaround point where he eats two meals and rents a hotel room to get some sleep before starting the return trip. Andre can deduct his meal and hotel expenses as travel expenses.

d. Combining business with pleasure

Provided that your trip is primarily for business, you can tack on a vacation to the end of the trip, make a side trip purely for fun or go to the theater and still deduct your entire airfare. What you spend while having fun is not deductible, but you can deduct your expenses while on business.

EXAMPLE: Bill flies to Miami for a four-day business meeting. He then spends three days in Miami swimming and enjoying the sights. Since Bill spent over half his time on business—four days out of seven—the cost of his flight is entirely deductible, as are his hotel and meal costs during the business meeting. He may not deduct his hotel, meal or other expenses during his vacation days.

2. Foreign Travel

The rules differ if you travel outside the United States, and are in some ways more lenient. However, you must have a legitimate business reason for your foreign trip. A sudden desire to investigate a foreign business won't qualify; you can't deduct business expenses for a business unless you're already involved in it.

a. Trips lasting no more than seven days

If you're away no more than seven days and you spend the majority of your time on business, you can deduct all of your travel costs.

However, even if your trip was primarily a vacation, you can deduct your airfare and other transportation costs as long as at least part of the trip was for business. You can also deduct your expenses while on business. For this reason, it's often best to limit business-related foreign travel to seven days.

> **EXAMPLE:** Jennifer flies to London for a two-day business meeting. She then spends five days sightseeing. She can deduct the entire cost of her airfare, and the portion of her hotel and meals she spent while attending the meeting.

b. Trips lasting more than seven days

More stringent rules apply if your foreign trip lasts more than one week. To get a full deduction for your expenses, you must spend at least 75% of your time away on business.

If you spend less than 75% of your time on business, you must determine the percentage of your time spent on business by counting the number of business days and the number of personal days. You can only deduct the percentage of your travel costs that relates to business days. A business day is any day you have to spend at a particular place on business or in which you spend four or more hours on business matters. Days spent traveling to and from your destination also count as business days.

> **EXAMPLE:** Sam flies to London and stays 14 days. He spends seven days on business and seven days sightseeing. He therefore spent 50% of his time on business. He can deduct half of his travel costs.

c. Foreign conventions

Different rules apply if you attend a convention outside North America. In such cases, a deduction is allowed only if:

- the meeting has a definite, clear connection to your business, and
- it's reasonable for the convention to be held outside North America—for example, if all those attending are plumbers from New York, it would be hard to justify a convention in Tahiti.

3. Travel on Cruise Ships

Forget about getting a tax deduction for a pleasure cruise. However, you may be able to deduct part of the cost of a cruise if you attend a business convention, seminars or similar meetings directly related to your business while onboard. Personal investment or financial planning seminars don't qualify.

But there is a major restriction: You must travel on a U.S.-registered ship that stops only in ports in the United States or its possessions, such as Puerto Rico or the U.S. Virgin Islands. Not many cruise ships are registered in the United States, so you'll likely have trouble finding a cruise that qualifies. If a cruise sponsor promises you'll be able to deduct your trip, investigate carefully to make sure it meets these requirements.

If you go on a cruise that is deductible, you must file with your tax return a signed note from the meeting or seminar sponsor listing the business meetings scheduled each day aboard ship and certifying how many hours you spent in attendance. Your annual deduction for cruising is limited to $2,000.

4. Taking Your Family With You

You generally can't deduct the expense of taking your spouse, children or others along with you on a business trip or to a business convention. The only deductions allowed are for expenses of a spouse or other person who is your employee and has a genuine business reason for going on a trip with you. Typing notes or assisting in entertaining customers are not enough to warrant a deduction; the work must be essential. For example, if you hire your son as a salesperson for your product or service and he calls on prospective customers during the trip, both your expenses and his expenses are deductible.

When you travel with your family, you deduct your business expenses as if you were traveling alone. However, the fact that your family is with you doesn't mean you have to reduce your deductions. For example, if you drive to your destination, you can deduct the entire cost of the drive, even if your family rides along with you. Similarly, you can deduct the full cost of a single hotel room even if you obtain a larger, more expensive room for your whole family.

5. Deductible Expenses

You can deduct virtually all of your expenses when you travel on business, including:

- airfare to and from your destination
- hotel or other lodging expenses
- taxi, public transportation and car rental expenses
- telephone and fax expenses

- the cost of shipping your personal luggage or samples, displays or other things you need for your business
- computer rental fees
- laundry and dry cleaning expenses, and
- tips you pay on any of the other costs.

However, only 50% of the cost of meals is deductible. The IRS imposes this limitation based on the reasoning that you would have eaten had you stayed home. You cannot deduct expenses for personal sightseeing or recreation.

You must keep good records of your expenses. (See Chapter 14, Section A.)

G. Entertainment and Meal Expenses

Depending on the nature of your business, you may find it helpful or even necessary to entertain clients, customers, suppliers, employees, other self-employed people, professional advisors, investors and other business associates. It's often easier to do business in a nonbusiness setting. Entertainment includes, for example, going to restaurants, the theater, concerts, sporting events and nightclubs, throwing parties and boating, hunting or fishing outings.

In the past, you could deduct entertainment expenses even if business was never discussed. For example, if you took a client to a restaurant, you could deduct the cost even if you spent the whole time drinking martinis and talking about sports. This is no longer the case. To deduct an entertainment expense, you must discuss business either before, during or after the entertainment.

The IRS doesn't have spies lurking about in restaurants, theaters or other places of entertainment, so it has no way of knowing whether you really discussed business with a client or other business associate. You're pretty much on the honor system here. However, be aware that the IRS closely scrutinizes this deduction because many taxpayers cheat when taking it. You'll have to comply with stringent recordkeeping requirements. (See Chapter 14, Section 3A.)

1. Discussing Business During Entertainment

You're entitled to deduct part of the cost of entertaining a client or other business associate if you have an active business discussion during the entertainment aimed at obtaining income or other benefits. You don't have to spend the entire time talking business, but the main character of the meal or other event must be business.

> **EXAMPLE:** Ivan, a self-employed consultant, takes a prospective client to a restaurant where they discuss and finalize the terms of a contract for Ivan's consulting services. Ivan can deduct the cost of the meal as an entertainment expense.

The IRS will not believe you discussed business if the entertainment occurred in a place where it is difficult or impossible to talk business because of distractions—for example, at a nightclub, theater, or sporting event; or at an essentially social gathering such as a cocktail party.

On the other hand, the IRS will presume you discussed business if a meal or entertainment

took place in a clear business setting—for example, a catered lunch at your office.

2. Discussing Business Before or After Entertainment

You are also entitled to deduct the full expense of an entertainment event if you have a substantial business discussion with a client or other business associate before or after it. This requires that you have a meeting, negotiation or other business transaction designed to help you get income or some other specific business benefit.

Generally, the entertainment should occur on the same day as the business discussion. However, if your business guests are from out of town, the entertainment can occur the day before or the day after.

The entertainment doesn't have to be shorter than your business discussions, but you can't spend only a small fraction of your total time on business. You can deduct entertainment expenses at places such as nightclubs, sporting events or theaters.

> **EXAMPLE:** Following lengthy contract negotiations at a prospective client's office, you take the client to a baseball game to unwind. The cost of the tickets is a deductible business expense.

3. 50% Deduction Limit

You can deduct only entertainment expenses you have paid. If a client picks up the tab, you obviously get no deduction. If you split the expense, you may deduct only what you paid.

Moreover, you're allowed to deduct only 50% of your expenses—for example, if you spend $50 for a meal in a restaurant, you can only deduct $25. However, you must keep track of all you spend and report the entire amount on your tax return. The cost of transportation to and from a

business meal or other entertainment is not subject to the 50% limit.

You can deduct the cost of entertaining your spouse and the client's spouse only if it's impractical to entertain the client without his or her spouse and your spouse joins the party because the client's spouse is attending.

If you entertain a client or other business associate while away from home on business, you can deduct the cost either as a travel or entertainment expense, but not both.

CHAMPAGNE AND CAVIAR MIGHT NOT BE DEDUCTIBLE

Your entertainment expenses must be reasonable to be fully deductible. You can't deduct entertainment expenses if the IRS considers them lavish or extravagant. There is no dollar limit on what is reasonable. Nor are you necessarily barred from entertaining at deluxe restaurants, hotels, nightclubs or resorts.

Whether your expenses will be considered reasonable depends on the particular facts and circumstances—for example, a $250 expense for dinner with a client and two business associates at a fancy restaurant would likely be considered reasonable if you closed a substantial business deal during the meal. Since there are no concrete guidelines, you have to use common sense.

 For additional information, see IRS Publication 463, *Travel, Entertainment and Gift Expenses*. You can obtain this and all other IRS publications by calling the IRS at 800-TAX-FORM, visiting your local IRS office or downloading the publications from the IRS Internet site at www.irs.gov.

H. Health Insurance Deduction

Self-employed people must pay for their own health insurance. If you don't make a lot of money, this can be tough. Fortunately, there are some specific tax deductions designed to help you.

1. Deducting Health Insurance Premiums

If you're a sole proprietor, partner in a partnership, owner of an S corporation or member of a limited liability company, you may deduct a portion of the cost of health insurance covering you, your spouse and your dependents. However, this deduction can't exceed the net profit from your business. The amount of this deduction is 70% of insurance costs in 2002, and 100% of such costs in subsequent years.

> **EXAMPLE:** Bob, a self-employed political consultant, earned $50,000 in net profits from his business during 2003. He spent $3,000 on health insurance for himself and his family. He may deduct this entire amount from his income taxes for the year.

You can't take this deduction if you're an employee and are eligible for health insurance through your employer, or your spouse is employed and you're eligible for coverage through his or her employer.

If you form a C corporation, it may deduct the entire cost of health insurance it provides you and any other employees. (See Chapter 2, Section B.)

2. Medical Savings Accounts

In 1997, the federal government instituted a pilot program allowing medical savings accounts, or Archer MSAs. Archer MSAs are designed to be used by self-employed people who purchase health insurance with a high deductible. (See Chapter 6.)

I. Deducting Start-Up Costs

Expenses you incur before you actually start your business—for example, license fees, fictitious business name registration fees, advertising costs, attorney and accounting fees, travel expenses, market research and office supplies expenses— are deductible from your federal income taxes. These expenses are called business start-up costs. You must deduct them in equal amounts over the first 60 months you're in business, a process called amortization.

> **EXAMPLE:** Bill decides to start a freelance public relations business. Before he opens his office and takes on any clients, he spends $6,000 on license fees, advertising, attorney and accounting fees and office supply expenses. He can't deduct all $6,000 in start-up costs at once. Instead, he can deduct only $100 per month for the first 60 months he's in business—that is, a maximum of $1,200 per year.

You can avoid having to stretch out these deductions over 60 months and instead deduct all of them in the first year you're in business if you:

- delay paying start-up costs until you open your doors and start serving clients or customers, or
- start your business on a very small scale and avoid incurring start-up expenses until you've made some money; it doesn't have to be a lot.

For more information on business start-up costs, see IRS Publication 535, *Business Expenses*. You can obtain a free copy by calling the IRS at 800-TAX-FORM or by calling or visiting your local IRS office. You can also download a copy from the IRS Internet site at www.irs.gov. ■

The Bane of Self-Employment Taxes

All Americans who work in the private sector are required to pay taxes to help support the Social Security and Medicare systems. Although these taxes are paid to the IRS, they are entirely separate from federal income taxes.

Employees have their Social Security and Medicare taxes directly deducted from their paychecks by their employers, who must make matching contributions. Such taxes are usually referred to as FICA taxes.

But if you're self-employed, your clients or customers will not pay or withhold your Social Security and Medicare taxes. You must pay them to the IRS yourself. When self-employed workers pay these taxes, they are called self-employment taxes or SE taxes. This chapter shows you how to determine how much SE tax you must pay.

Low Income, No Tax

If your net income from your business for the year is less than $400, you don't have to pay any self-employment taxes. You can skip this chapter.

For additional information on self-employment taxes, see IRS Publication 533, *Self-Employment Tax*. You can obtain this and all other IRS publications by calling the IRS at 800-TAX-FORM, visiting your local IRS office or downloading them from the IRS Internet site at www.irs.gov.

A. Who Must Pay

Sole proprietors, partners in partnerships and members of limited liability companies must all pay SE taxes if their net earnings from self-employment for the year are $400 or more.

Corporations do not pay SE taxes. However, if you're incorporated and work in your business, you are an employee of your corporation and will ordinarily be paid a salary. Instead of paying SE taxes, you must pay FICA taxes on your salary just like any other employee. Half of your Social Security and Medicare taxes must be withheld from your salary and half paid by your corporation. (See Chapter 6.)

B. SE Tax Rates

The self-employment tax consists of a 12.4% Social Security tax and a 2.9% Medicare tax for a total tax of 15.3%. But in practice, the bite it takes is smaller because of certain deductions. (See Section C.)

The SE tax is a flat tax—that is, the tax rate is the same no matter what your income level. However, there is an income ceiling on the Social Security portion of the tax. You need not pay the 12.4% Social Security tax on your net self-employment earnings that exceed the ceiling amount. If the ceiling didn't exist, people with higher incomes would end up paying far more than they could ever get back as Social Security benefits. The Social Security tax ceiling is adjusted annually for inflation. In 2002, the ceiling was $84,900.

However, there is no similar limit for Medicare: you must pay the 2.9% Medicare tax on your entire net self-employment income, no matter how large. Congress enacted this rule a few years ago to save Medicare from bankruptcy.

> **EXAMPLE:** Mona, a self-employed consultant, earned $150,000 in net self-employment income in 2002. She must pay both Social Security and Medicare taxes on the first $84,900 of her income—a 15.3% tax. She only pays the 2.9% Medicare tax on her remaining $65,100 in income.

C. Earnings Subject to Self-Employment Tax

You pay self-employment taxes on your net self-employment income, not your entire income. To determine your net self-employment income, you first figure the net income you've earned from your business. Your net business income includes all your income from your business, minus all business deductions allowed for income tax purposes. However, you can't deduct retirement contributions you make for yourself to a Keogh or SEP plan or the self-employed health insurance deduction. (See Chapter 9, Section H.) If you're a sole proprietor, as are most self-employed people, use IRS Schedule C, Profit or Loss From Business, to determine your net business income.

If you have more than one business, combine the net income or loss from them all. If you have a job in addition to your business, your employee income is not included in your self-employment income. (See Section F.) Nor do you include investment income, such as interest you earn on your savings.

You then get one more valuable deduction before finally determining your net self-employment income. You're allowed to deduct 7.65% from your total net business income. This is intended to help ease the SE tax burden on the self-employed. To do this, multiply your net business income by 92.35% or .9235.

EXAMPLE: Billie, a self-employed consultant, earned $70,000 from her business and had $20,000 in business expenses, leaving a net business income of $50,000. She multiplies this amount by .9235 to determine her net self-employment income, which is $46,175. This is the amount on which Billie must pay SE tax.

Because of this extra deduction, the "real" self-employment tax rate is about 12% rather than the official rate of 15.3%.

The fact that you can deduct business expenses from your SE income makes them doubly valuable: They will not only reduce your income taxes, but your SE taxes as well.

S CORPORATION STATUS: A WAY AROUND THE SE TAX THICKET

As a person in business for yourself, you may be able to take advantage of an important wrinkle in the SE tax rules: Distributions from S corporations to their owners are not subject to SE taxes. This is so even though such distributions are included in your income for income tax purposes.

If you incorporate your business and elect to become an S corporation, you may distribute part of your corporation's earnings to yourself without paying SE taxes on them. You can't distribute all your earnings to yourself this way, however, because your S corporation must pay you a reasonable salary on which FICA taxes must be paid. (See Chapter 2, Section B7.)

D. Computing the SE Tax

It's easy to compute the amount of your SE tax. First, determine your net self-employment income as described above. If your net self-employment income is below the Social Security tax ceiling—$84,900 in 2002—multiply it by 15.3% or .153.

EXAMPLE: Mark, a self-employed consultant, had $50,000 in net self-employment income in 2002. He must multiply this by .153 to determine his SE tax, which is $7,650.

If your net self-employment income is more than the Social Security tax ceiling, things are a bit more complicated. Multiply your income up to the ceiling by 12.4% and all of your income by the 2.9% Medicare tax; then add both amounts together to determine your total SE tax.

EXAMPLE: Martha had $100,000 in net self-employment income in 2000. She multiplies the first $84,900 of this amount by the 12.4% Social Security tax, resulting in a tax of $10,527. She then multiplies her entire $100,000 income by the 2.9% Medicare tax, resulting in a $2,900 tax. She adds these amounts together to determine her total SE tax, which is $13,427.

In another effort to make the SE tax burden a little lighter for the self-employed, the IRS allows you to deduct half of the amount of your SE taxes from your business income for income tax purposes. For example, if you pay $10,000 in SE taxes, you can deduct $5,000 from your gross income when you determine your taxable income.

E. Paying and Reporting SE Taxes

Pay SE taxes directly to the IRS during the year as part of your estimated taxes. You have the option of either:

- paying the same amount in tax as you paid the previous year, or
- estimating what your income will be this year and basing your estimated tax payments on that. (See Chapter 11, Section B.)

When you file your annual tax return, you must include IRS Form SE, Self-Employment Tax, along with your income tax return. This form shows the IRS how much SE tax you were required to pay for the year. You file only one Form SE no matter how many unincorporated businesses you own. Add the SE tax to your income taxes on your income tax return, Form 1040, to determine your total tax.

Even if you do not owe any income tax, you must still complete Form 1040 and Schedule SE if you owe $400 or more in SE taxes.

F. Outside Employment

If, in addition to being self-employed, you have an outside job in which you're classified as an employee and have Social Security and Medicare taxes withheld from your wages, you must pay the Social Security tax on your wages first. If your wages are at least equal to the Social Security tax ceiling, you won't have to pay the 12.4% Social Security tax on your SE income. But no matter how much you earn from your job, you'll have to pay the 2.9% Medicare tax on all your SE income.

EXAMPLE: Anne earned $90,000 in employee wages and $10,000 in self-employment income from a business in 2002. She did not have to pay Social Security taxes on her earnings above the $84,900 Social Security tax ceiling for the year. Her employer withheld 7.65% in Social Security taxes up to $84,900 of her wages and 1.45% (the Medicare portion of an employee's FICA taxes) on her earnings between $84,900 and $90,000. Anne also had to pay the 2.9% Medicare portion of the SE tax—but not the 12.4% Social Security tax—on her $10,000 in self-employment earnings.

However, if your employee wages are lower than the Social Security tax ceiling, you'll have to pay Social Security taxes on your SE income until your wages and SE income combined exceed the ceiling amount.

EXAMPLE: Bill earned $20,000 in employee wages and $70,000 in self-employment income in 2002. His wages were lower than the $84,900 Social Security tax ceiling for the year. His employer withheld a 7.65% FICA tax on his wages and he had to pay a 12.4% Social Security tax on $64,900 of his SE income. He stopped paying the Social Security tax after his wages and income combined equaled $84,900. This meant he didn't have to pay the Social Security tax on $5,100 of the $70,000 he earned as an IC. However, he had to pay the 2.9% Medicare tax on all his SE income. ■

Paying Estimated Tax

What many self-employed people like best about their employment status is that it allows freedom in planning and handling their own finances. Unlike employees, they don't have taxes withheld from their compensation by their clients or customers. As a result, many self-employed people have higher take-home pay than employees earning similar amounts.

Unfortunately, however, self-employed workers do not have the luxury of waiting until April 15 to pay all their taxes for the previous year. The IRS wants to get its money a lot faster than that, so the self-employed are required to pay taxes on their estimated annual incomes in four payments spread out over each year. These are called estimated taxes and are used to pay both income taxes (see Chapter 9) and self-employment taxes (see Chapter 10).

Because they have to pay estimated taxes, self-employed people need to carefully budget their money. If you fail to set aside enough of your earnings to pay your estimated taxes, you could face a huge tax bill on April 15—and have a tough time coming up with the money to cover it.

Most States Have Estimated Taxes, Too If your state has income taxes, it probably requires the self-employed to pay estimated taxes. The due dates are generally the same as for federal estimated tax. State income tax rates are lower than federal income taxes. The exact rate depends on the state in which you live. Contact your state tax office for information and the required forms. (See Appendix 3 for contact details.)

A. Who Must Pay

You must pay estimated taxes if you are a sole proprietor, partner in a partnership or member of a limited liability company and you expect to owe at least $1,000 in federal tax for the year. If you've formed a C corporation, it may also have to pay estimated taxes.

However, if you paid no taxes last year—for example, because your business made no profit or you weren't working—you don't have to pay any estimated tax this year no matter how much tax you expect to owe. But this is true only if you were a U.S. citizen or resident for the year and your tax return for the previous year covered the whole 12 months.

1. Sole Proprietors

Most self-employed people are sole proprietors. A sole proprietor and his or her business are one and the same for tax purposes, so you simply pay your estimated taxes out of your own pocket. You, not your business, pay the taxes.

2. Partners and Limited Liability Companies

Partnerships and limited liability companies, or LLCs, are similar to sole proprietorships. They don't pay any taxes; instead, all partnership and LLC income passes through to the partners or LLC members. (See Chapter 2, Sections C and D.) The partners or LLC members must pay individual estimated tax on their shares of partnership or LLC income. This is so whether it's actually paid to them or not. The partnership or LLC itself pays no tax. The only exception is if the owners of an LLC elect to be taxed as a C corporation, which is very unusual. (See Chapter 2, Section D.)

3. Corporations

A corporation is separate from you for tax purposes. Both you and your corporation might have to pay estimated taxes.

You will ordinarily be an employee of your corporation and receive a salary directly from it. Income and employment taxes must be withheld from your salary just as for any employee. (See Chapter 13.) You won't need to pay any estimated tax on your salary. But if you receive dividends or distributions from your corporation, you'll need to pay tax on them during the year—unless the total tax due on the amounts you received is less than $500. You can cover the taxes due either by paying estimated tax or by increasing the tax withheld from your salary; it doesn't make much practical difference which you choose.

If you've formed a C corporation, it must pay quarterly estimated taxes if it will owe $500 or more in corporate tax on its profits for the year. These taxes are deposited with a bank, not paid directly to the IRS. However, most small C corporations don't have to pay any income taxes or estimated taxes because all the profits are taken out of the corporation by the owners in the form of salaries, bonuses and benefits. (See Chapter 2.)

S corporations ordinarily don't have to pay estimated taxes because all profits are passed through to the shareholders, as in a partnership. (See Chapter 2.)

 For detailed guidance on C corporation estimated taxes, see IRS Publication 542, *Tax Information for Corporations.* You can obtain this and all other IRS publications by calling the IRS at 800-TAX-FORM, visiting your local IRS office or downloading them from the IRS Internet site at www.irs.gov.

B. How Much You Must Pay

You should determine how much estimated tax to pay after completing your tax return for the previous year. Most people want to pay as little estimated tax as possible during the year so they can earn interest on their money instead of handing it over to the IRS. However, the IRS imposes penalties if you don't pay enough estimated tax. (See Section E1.) There's no need to get excessively concerned about these penalties. They aren't terribly large in the first place and it's easy to avoid having to pay them. All you have to do is pay at least the smaller of:

- 90% of your total tax due for the current year, or
- 100% of the tax you paid the previous year—or more if you're a high-income taxpayer (see below).

You normally make four estimated tax payments each year. There are three different ways you can calculate your payments. You can use any one the three methods without paying a penalty as long as you pay the minimum total the IRS requires, as explained above. One of the methods—basing your payments on last year's tax—is extremely easy to use. The other two are more complex to figure out, but might permit you to make smaller payments.

1. Payments Based on Last Year's Tax

The easiest and safest way to calculate your estimated taxes is to simply pay 100% of the total federal taxes you paid last year, or more if you're a high-income taxpayer as described below. You can base your estimated tax on the amount you paid the prior year even if you weren't in business that year, but your return for the year must have been for a full 12-month period.

You should determine how much estimated tax to pay for the current year at the same time that you file your tax return for the previous year—no later than April 15. Take the total amount of tax you had to pay for the year and divide by four. If this comes out to an odd number, round up to get an even number. These are the amounts you'll have to pay in estimated tax. You'll make four equal payments throughout the year and the following year. (See the chart in Section C to learn when you must make your payments).

> **EXAMPLE:** Gary, a self-employed consultant, earned $50,000 last year. He figures his taxes for the prior year on April 1 of this year and determines he owed $9,989.32 for the year.

To determine his estimated tax for the current year he divides this amount by four: $9,989.32 divided by four equals $2497.33. He rounds this up to $2,500. He'll make four $2,500 estimated tax payments to the IRS. As long as he pays this much, Gary won't have to pay a penalty even if he ends up owing more than $10,000 in tax to the IRS for the year because his income goes up, his deductions go down or both.

a. High-income taxpayers must pay more

High-income taxpayers—those with adjusted gross incomes of more than $150,000 or $75,000 for married couples filing separate returns—must pay more than 100% of their prior year's tax.

Your adjusted gross income or AGI is your total income minus deductions for:

- IRA, Keogh and SEP-IRA contributions
- health insurance
- one-half of your self-employment tax, and
- alimony, deductible moving expenses and penalties you pay for early withdrawals from a savings account before maturity or early redemption of certificates of deposit.

To find out your AGI, look at line 33 on your last year's tax return, Form 1040.

The estimated tax amount you must pay is 112% of the prior year's income tax for returns filed in 2002 and 110% for returns filed in 2003 and after.

EXAMPLE: Mary, a self-employed consultant, earned $250,000 in gross income in 2003. Her adjusted gross income was $200,000 after subtracting the value of her Keogh Plan contributions, health insurance deduction and half her self-employment taxes. Mary paid $50,000 in income and self-employment taxes in 2003. In 2004, Mary must pay 110% of the tax she paid in 2003—$5,430 in estimated tax. As long as she pays this amount she won't have to pay a penalty to the IRS even if she earns more than she did in 2003.

b. Mid-course correction

Your third estimated tax payment is due on September 15. By this time you should have a pretty good idea of what your income for the year will be. If you're reasonably sure that your income for the year will be at least 25% less than what you earned last year, you can forgo the last estimated tax payment due on January 15 of next year. You have already paid enough estimated tax for the year.

If it looks as if your income will be greater than last year, you don't have to pay more estimated tax. The IRS cannot penalize you so long as you pay 100% of what you paid last year—or more if you're a high-income taxpayer.

c. You may owe tax on April 15

Basing your estimated tax on last year's income is generally the best method to use if you expect your income to be higher this year than last year. You'll be paying the minimum possible without incurring a penalty. However, if you do end up earning more than last year, using this method will cause you to underpay your taxes. You won't have to pay a penalty, but you'll have to make up the underpayment when you file your tax return for the year. This could present you with a big tax bill if your income rose substantially from last year. To make sure you have enough money for this, it's a good idea to sock away a portion of your income in a separate bank account just for taxes. (See Section C.)

2. Payments Based on Estimated Taxable Income

If you're absolutely certain your net income will be less this year than last year, you'll pay less estimated tax if you base your tax on your taxable income for the current year instead of basing it on last year's tax. This is not worth the time and trouble, however, unless you'll earn at least 30% less this year than last.

The problem with using this method is that you must estimate your total income and deductions for the year to figure out how much to pay. Obviously, this can be difficult or impossible to compute accurately. And there are no magic formulas to look to for guidance. The best way to proceed is to sit down with your tax return for the previous year.

Try to figure out whether your income this year will be less than you had last year. You'll find all your income for last year listed on lines 7 through 22 of your Form 1040. Also, determine whether your deductions will be greater than last year. You'll find these listed in the Adjusted Gross Income and Tax and Credits sections of your Form 1040, lines 23 through 52.

Pay special attention to your business income and expense figures in Parts I and II of your Schedule C, Profit or Loss From Business. Decide whether it's likely you'll earn less business income this year than last. You'll probably earn less, for example, if you plan to work fewer hours than last year, you've lost important clients or business conditions are generally poor. Also, determine whether your deductible business expenses will be greater this year than last—for example, because you plan to purchase expensive business equipment and deduct the cost. (See Chapter 9, Section B.)

Take comfort in knowing that you need not make an exact estimate of your taxable income. You won't have to pay a penalty if you pay at least 90% of your tax due for the year.

EXAMPLE: Larry, a self-employed consultant, earned $45,000 last year and paid $10,000 in income and self-employment taxes. Larry expects to earn much less this year because a key client has gone out of business. The lost client accounted for more than one-third of Larry's income last year, so Larry estimates he'll earn about $30,000 this year. The minimum estimated tax Larry must pay is 90% of the tax he will owe on his $30,000 income, which he estimates to be $6,000.

IRS Form 1040-ES contains a worksheet to use to calculate your estimated tax. You can obtain the form by calling the IRS at 800-TAX-FORM, visiting your local IRS office or downloading it from the IRS Internet site at www.irs.gov.

Or if you have a tax preparation computer program, it can help you with the calculations.

If you have your taxes prepared by an accountant, he or she should determine what estimated tax to pay. If your income changes greatly during the year, ask your accountant to help you prepare a revised estimated tax payment schedule.

3. Payments Based on Quarterly Income

A much more complicated way to calculate your estimated taxes is to use the annualized income installment method. It requires that you separately calculate your tax liability at four points during the year—March 31, May 31, August 31 and December 31—prorating your deductions and personal exemptions. You base your estimated tax payments on your actual tax liability for each quarter. (See the chart in Section C.)

This method is often the best choice for people who receive income very unevenly throughout the year—for example, those who work in seasonal businesses. Using this method, they can pay little or no estimated tax for the quarters in which they earned little or no income.

EXAMPLE: Ernie's income from his air conditioning repair business is much higher in the summer than it is during the rest of the year. By using the annualized income installment method, he makes one large estimated tax payment on September 15, after the quarter in which he earns most of his income. His other three annual payments are quite small.

If you use this method, you must file IRS Form 2210 with your tax return; this form shows your calculations.

 You'll Need Help With This Math
You really need a good grasp of tax law and mathematics to use the annualized income installment method. The IRS worksheet used to calculate your payments using this method contains 43 separate steps. If you want to use this method, give yourself a break and hire an accountant or at least use a tax preparation computer program to help with the calculations.

See IRS Publication 505, *Tax Withholding and Estimated Tax,* for a detailed explanation of the annualized income method. You can obtain the form by calling the IRS at: 800-TAX-FORM, visiting your local IRS office or downloading it from the IRS Internet site at www.irs.gov.

C. When to Pay Estimated Tax

Estimated tax must ordinarily be paid in four installments, with the first one due on April 15. However, you don't have to start making payments until you actually earn income. If you don't receive any income by March 31, you can skip the April 15 payment. In this event, you'd ordinarily make three payments for the year, starting on June 15. If you don't receive any income by May 31, you can skip the June 15 payment as well and so on.

The following chart shows the due dates and the periods each installment covers.

ESTIMATED TAX DUE

Income received for the period	Estimated tax due
January 1 through March 31	April 15
April 1 through May 31	June 15
June 1 through August 31	September 15
September 1 through December 31	January 15 of next year

SPECIAL RULE FOR FARMERS AND FISHERMEN

If at least two-thirds of your annual income comes from farming or fishing, you need make only one estimated tax payment on January 15. The first three payment periods in the chart above don't apply.

Also, you can skip the January 15 payment if you file your tax return and pay all taxes due for the previous year by January 31 of the current year. This is a little reward the IRS gives you for filing your tax return early.

However, it's rarely advantageous to file early because you'll have to pay any tax due on January 15 instead of waiting until April 15—meaning you'll lose three months of interest on your hard-earned money.

Your estimated tax payment must be postmarked by the dates noted above, but the IRS need not actually receive them then. If any of these days falls on a weekend or legal holiday, the due date is the next business day.

⚠ The Year May Not Begin in January

Don't get confused by the fact that the January 15 payment is the fourth estimated tax payment for the previous year, not the first payment for the current year. The April 15 payment is the first payment for the current year.

⚠ Beware the Ides of April

April 15 can be a financial killer for the self-employed because there are two separate financial obligations due on that date. By then, you not only have to pay any income and self-employment taxes that are due for the previous year, you also usually have to make your first estimated tax payment for the current year. If you've underpaid your estimated taxes by a substantial amount, you could have a whopping tax bill.

Many self-employed people establish separate bank accounts into which they deposit a portion of each payment they receive from their clients. This way they have some assurance that they'll have enough money to pay their taxes. The amount you should deposit depends on your federal and state income tax brackets and the amount of your tax deductions. Depending on your income, you'll probably need to deposit 25% to 50% of your pay. If you deposit too much, of course, you can always spend the money later on other things.

> **EXAMPLE:** Wilma, a self-employed worker who lives in Massachusetts, is in the 27% marginal federal income tax bracket and must pay a 6% state income tax. She must also pay a 15.3% self-employment tax. All these taxes amount to 48.3% of her pay. But she doesn't have to set aside this much because her deductions will reduce her actual tax liability. Using the amount of her deductions from last year as a guide, Wilma determines she needs to set aside 35% to 40% of her income for estimated taxes.

D. How to Pay

The IRS wants to make it easy for you to send in your money, so the mechanics of paying estimated taxes are very simple. You file federal estimated taxes using IRS Form 1040-ES. This form contains instructions and four numbered payment vouchers for you to send in with your payments. You must provide your name, address, Social Security number (or EIN if you have one) and amount of the payment on each voucher. You file only one payment voucher with each payment, no matter how many unincorporated businesses you have.

If you're married and file a joint return, the names on your estimated tax vouchers should be exactly the same as those on your income tax return. Even if your spouse isn't self-employed, he or she should be listed on the vouchers so that the money gets credited to the right account.

If you made estimated tax payments last year, you should receive a copy of the current year's Form 1040-ES in the mail. It will have payment vouchers preprinted with your name, address and Social Security number.

If you did not pay estimated taxes last year, get a copy of Form 1040-ES from the IRS. Do so by calling the IRS at 800-TAX-FORM, visiting your local IRS office or downloading it from the IRS Internet site at www.irs.gov. After you make your first payment, the IRS should mail you a Form 1040-ES package with the preprinted vouchers.

Use the addressed envelopes that come with your Form 1040-ES package. If you use your own envelopes, make sure you mail your payment vouchers to the address shown in the Form 1040-ES instructions for the place where you live. Do not mail your estimated tax payments to the same place you sent your Form 1040.

You may pay all or part of your estimated taxes by credit card (Visa, MasterCard, Discover Card or American Express Card). You must do this through one of two private companies providing this service. You'll have to pay the company a fee based on the amount of your payment (the fee does not go to the IRS). You can arrange to make your payment by phone or through the Internet. You may contact these companies at:

> PhoneCharge, Inc.
> 1–888–255–8299
> www.1888ALLTAXX.com

> Official Payments Corporation
> 1–800–272–982
> 1–877–754–4413 (Customer Service)
> www.officialpayments.com

Keep Your Canceled Checks

It's not unheard of for the IRS to make a bookkeeping error and then claim that you paid less estimated tax than you did or to apply your payment to the wrong year. If this happens, provide the IRS with a copy of the front and back of your canceled estimated tax checks. The agency encodes a series of tracking numbers on the endorsement side of any check that enable it to locate where payments were applied in its system. This points up the importance of keeping your canceled estimated tax checks.

Don't use money market checks to pay estimated taxes or checks from an account in which the bank doesn't return the original checks to you. Even if your bank promises to give you free copies of your checks, the copies may be so poor the IRS can't read them.

TELL THE IRS IF YOU MOVE

You're supposed to notify the IRS if you are making estimated tax payments and you change your address during the year. You can use IRS Form 8822, Change of Address, for this purpose. It's a simple change of address form. Or you may send a signed letter to the IRS Center where you filed your last return stating:

- your full name and your spouse's full name
- your old address and spouse's old address (if different)
- your new address, and
- Social Security numbers for you and your spouse.

E. Paying the Wrong Amount

If you pay too little estimated tax, the IRS will make you pay a penalty. If you pay too much, you can get the money refunded or apply it to your current year's estimated taxes.

1. Paying Too Little

The IRS imposes a monetary penalty if you underpay your estimated taxes. Fortunately, the penalty is not very onerous. You have to pay the taxes due plus a percentage penalty for each day your estimated tax payments were unpaid. The percentage is set by the IRS each year. The penalty was 6% in early 2002.

The penalty has ranged between 6% and 8% in recent years. This is the mildest of all IRS interest penalties. Even if you paid no estimated tax at all during the year, the underpayment penalty you'd have to pay would be no more than 5% to 6% of your total taxes due for the year.

You can find out what the current penalty is in the most recent version of IRS Publication 505, *Tax Withholding and Estimated Tax*. You can obtain the form by calling the IRS at 800-TAX-FORM, visiting your local IRS office or downloading it from the IRS Internet site at http://www.irs.gov.

The penalty is comparable to the interest you'd pay on borrowed money. Many self-employed people decide to pay the penalty at the end of the tax year rather than take money out of their businesses during the year to pay estimated taxes. If you do this, though, make sure you pay all the taxes you owe for the year by April 15 of the following year. If you don't, the IRS will tack on additional interest and penalties. The IRS usually adds a penalty of 1/2% to 1% per month to a tax bill that's not paid when due.

To avoid these charges, you can pay your estimated taxes by credit card. But if you don't pay off your balance quickly, the interest you pay on your credit card balance may exceed the IRS penalty.

Because the penalty is figured separately for each payment period, you can't avoid having to pay it by increasing the amount of a later payment. For example, you can't avoid a penalty by doubling your June 15 payment to make up for failing to make your April 15 payment. If you miss a payment, the IRS suggests that you divide the amount equally among your remaining payments for the year. But this won't avoid a penalty on payments you missed or underpaid.

Since the penalty must be paid for each day your estimated taxes remain unpaid, you'll have to pay more if you miss a payment early in the tax year rather than later. For this reason, you should try to pay your first three estimated tax payments on time. You can let the fourth payment (due on January 15) go. The penalty you'll have to pay for missing this payment will likely be very small.

The IRS will assume you've underpaid your estimated taxes if you file a tax return showing that you owe $500 or more in additional tax, and the amount due is more than 10% of your total tax bill for the year.

If you have underpaid, you can determine the amount of the underpayment penalty by completing IRS Form 2210, Underpayment of Estimated Tax by Individuals, and pay the penalty when you send in your return. Tax preparation programs can do this for you. However, it is not necessary for you to compute the penalty you owe. You can leave it to the IRS to determine the penalty and send you a bill. If you receive a bill, you may wish to complete Form 2210 anyway to make sure you aren't overcharged.

2. Paying Too Much

If you pay too much estimated tax, you have two options: You may have the IRS refund the overpayment to you, or you can credit all or part of the money to your current year's estimated taxes. Unfortunately, you can't get back the interest your overpayment earned while sitting in the IRS coffers; that belongs to the government.

To take the credit, write in the amount you want credited instead of refunded to you on line 68a of your Form 1040. The payment is considered to have been made on April 15. You can use all the credited amount toward your first payment, or you can spread it out in any way you choose among any or all of your payments. Be sure to take the amount you have credited into account when figuring your estimated tax payments.

It doesn't make much practical difference which option you choose. Most people take the credit so they don't have to wait for the IRS to send them a refund check. ■

Rules for Salespeople, Drivers and Clothing Producers

You need to read this chapter only if you work as a:

- business-to-business salesperson
- full-time life insurance salesperson
- clothing or needlecraft producer who works at home
- driver who distributes food products, beverages or laundry
- direct seller, or
- licensed real estate agent.

If you fall within the first four categories, you may be a statutory employee; read Section A, below. If you fall within the last two categories, you may be a statutory independent contractor (IC); skip directly to Section B.

A. Statutory Employees

If you are a business-to-business or life insurance salesperson, clothing producer who works at home or driver who distributes food products, beverages or laundry, and if you also meet several other primary requirements (see Section A1), you are a statutory employee. This label derives from the fact that your employment status for certain purposes is defined and explained by laws passed by Congress.

Practically speaking, being a statutory employee only has two consequences for you, but neither of them are particularly good. Fortunately, it's easy to avoid being classified as a statutory employee and continue being an independent contractor. (See Section A1.)

The first and worst consequence of statutory employee status is that the hiring firms for which you work must pay half of your Social Security and Medicare taxes themselves and withhold the other half from your pay and send it to the IRS, just as for any other employee. (See Chapter 13.) As a result, you'll receive less take-home pay. This is not only because a whopping 7.65% must be deducted from your paychecks, but also because hiring firms will probably insist on paying

you less compensation than they would if you were an IC for employment tax purposes, to make up for the fact that they have to pay a 7.65% Social Security and Medicare tax for you out of their own pockets. You won't need to include these Social Security and Medicare taxes in your estimated tax payments. (See Chapter 11.)

You'll also receive a Form W-2, Wage and Tax Statement, from the hiring firms for which you work instead of a Form 1099-MISC, the form used to report ICs' income to the IRS. (See Chapter 13, Section B1d.) The W-2 will show the Social Security and Medicare tax withheld from your pay and your Social Security and Medicare income. You'll have to file your W-2s with your tax returns, so the IRS will know exactly how much income you've earned as a statutory employee. The hiring firms will also file a copy with the Social Security Administration.

As a statutory employee, you report income and earnings on Schedule C, Profit or Loss From Business, the same form used by self-employed people who are sole proprietors. Unlike regular employees whose business deductions are strictly limited, you can deduct the full amount of your business expenses. (See Chapter 9.)

You are an IC for income tax purposes as long as you qualify as one under the regular IRS rules. (See Chapter 15.) If you qualify, no income tax need be withheld from your compensation and you'll have higher take-home pay as a result. But you will need to pay your income taxes four times during the year in the form of estimated taxes. (See Chapter 11.)

Most hiring firms would prefer that you be classified as an IC for employment tax purposes instead of as a statutory employee. That would allow them to avoid the burden of paying half your FICA taxes themselves and withholding your share from your pay. This chapter describes some simple ways you can avoid this status. Doing so may help you get work you might be denied as a statutory employee.

IF YOU HAVE MULTIPLE BUSINESSES

If you have another business in which you are not classified as a statutory employee, you must file a separate Schedule C for that business. You aren't allowed to use expenses from your statutory employment to offset earnings from your self-employment.

EXAMPLE: Margaret works as a business-to-business salesperson in which she qualifies as a statutory employee. She also works part time as a self-employed marketing consultant. This year she had $5,000 in travel expenses from her selling job. She can't deduct any of this expense from her earnings as a consultant. She can only deduct it from her income as a salesperson. When Margaret does her taxes, she must file a separate Schedule C for each of her occupations.

1. Requirements for Statutory Employee Status

You're a statutory employee only if you satisfy all of these requirements:

- you perform services personally for the hiring firm
- you make no substantial investment in the equipment or facilities you use to work, and
- you have a continuing relationship with the hiring firm.

a. Personal service

You're a statutory employee only if your oral or written agreement with the hiring firm requires you to do substantially all the work yourself. In other words, you can't hire helpers or subcontract the work out to others.

b. No substantial investment

Statutory employees must not have a substantial investment in equipment or premises used to perform their work—for example, office space, machinery and office furniture. An investment is substantial if it is more than an employee would be expected to provide—for example, paying office rent or expensive computer equipment. Vehicles you use on the job do not count as substantial investments.

c. Continuing relationship

A continuing relationship means you work for the hiring firm on a regular or recurring basis. A single job is not considered a continuing relationship. But regular part-time or regular seasonal employment qualifies.

AVOIDING STATUTORY EMPLOYEE STATUS

Even if you do the type of work normally performed by a statutory employee, you can avoid being classified as one. To do this, set up your work relationship so that it does not satisfy one or more of the three requirements discussed in Section 1. For example, you can:

- Sign a written agreement with the person or firm that hires you stating that you have the right to subcontract or delegate the work out to others. This way, you make clear that you don't have to do the work personally.
- Avoid having a continuing relationship with any one hiring firm by working on single projects, not ongoing tasks.
- Invest in outside facilities, such as your own office.

However, even if you do these things, some hiring firms may want to classify you as a statutory employee because they don't understand the law. You may have to educate the people or firms you work for about these rules.

2. Types of Statutory Employees

You won't be a statutory employee just because you satisfy the three threshold requirements explained above. You must also satisfy additional requirements for each type of statutory employee occupation. These rules present you with yet more ways to avoid statutory employee status. If the type of work you do and the way you do it don't fall squarely within the additional rules below, you won't be classified as a statutory employee.

a. Business-to-business salespeople

If you're a business-to-business salesperson, you're a statutory employee only if you satisfy the three threshold requirements discussed above (see Section A1) and you also:

- work at least 80% of the time for one person or company
- sell on behalf of, or turn your orders over to, the hiring firm
- sell merchandise for resale or supplies for use in the buyer's business operations, as opposed to goods purchased for personal consumption at home, and
- sell only to wholesalers, retailers, contractors or those who operate hotels, restaurants or similar establishments; this does not include manufacturers, schools, hospitals, churches, municipalities or state and federal governments.

EXAMPLE: Linda sells books to retail bookstores for Scrivener & Sons Publishing Company. Her territory covers the entire Midwest. She works only for Scrivener and is paid a commission based on the amount of each sale. She turns her orders over to Scrivener's, which ships the books to each bookstore customer. Linda is a Scrivener's statutory employee.

b. Life insurance salespeople

If your full-time occupation is soliciting life insurance applications or annuity contracts, you're a statutory employee only if you satisfy the threshold requirements explained in Section A1, and:

- you work primarily for one life insurance company, and
- the company provides you with work necessities such as office space, secretarial help, forms, rate books and advertising material.

EXAMPLE: Walter sells life insurance full time for the Old Reliable Life Insurance Company. He works out of Old Reliable's Omaha office where he is provided with a desk, clerical help and rate books and insurance applications. Walter is Old Reliable's statutory employee.

c. Clothing or needlecraft producers

If you make or sew buttons, quilts, gloves, bedspreads, clothing, needlecraft products or similar products, you're a statutory employee only if you satisfy the threshold requirements explained in Section A1, and you:

- work away from the hiring firm's place of business—usually in your own home or workshop or in another person's home
- work only on goods or materials the hiring firm furnishes
- work according to the hiring firm's specifications; generally, such specifications are simple and consist of patterns or samples, and
- are required to return the processed material to the hiring firm or person designated by it.

If your work set-up meets all these requirements, the hiring firm must pay the employer's share of FICA on your compensation and withhold your share of FICA taxes from your pay. However, no FICA tax is imposed if the hiring firm pays you less than $100 for a calendar year.

EXAMPLE: Rosa sews buttons on shirts and dresses. She works at home. She does work for various companies, including Upscale Fashions, Inc. Upscale provides Rosa with all the clothing and the buttons she must sew. The only equipment Rosa provides is a needle. Upscale gives Rosa a sample of each outfit showing where the buttons are supposed to go. When Rosa finishes each batch of clothing, she returns it to Upscale. Rosa is a statutory employee.

d. Food, beverage and laundry distributors

You're also a statutory employee if you work as a driver and distribute meat or meat products, vegetables or vegetable products, fruits or fruit products, bakery products, beverages other than milk, or laundry or dry cleaning to customers designated by the hiring firm as well as those you solicit. It makes no difference whether you operate from your own truck or trucks belonging to the person or firm that hired you.

EXAMPLE: Alder Laundry and Dry Cleaning enters into an agreement with Sharon to pick up and deliver clothing for its customers. Sharon is a statutory employee because she meets all three threshold requirements: her agreement with Alder acknowledges that she will do the work personally, she has no substantial investment in facilities (her truck doesn't count since it's used to deliver the product) and she has a continuing relationship with Alder.

B. Statutory Independent Contractors

If you're a direct seller or licensed real estate agent, you are automatically considered an independent contractor for Social Security, Medicare and federal unemployment tax purposes, provided that:

- your pay is based on sales commissions, not on the number of hours you work, and
- you have a written contract with the hiring firm providing that you will not be treated as an employee for federal tax purposes.

Consider yourself lucky and be thankful your industry lobbyists were able to get these special rules adopted by Congress. Since your worker status is automatically determined by law, hiring firms need not worry about the IRS. This should make it very easy for you to get work as an independent contractor in your chosen field.

You undoubtedly know whether or not you're a licensed real estate agent whom the IRS will automatically classify as a statutory independent contractor.

You're a direct seller for IRS purposes if you sell consumer products to people in their homes or at a place other than an established retail store—for example, at swap meets. Consumer products include tangible personal property that is used for personal, family or household purposes—for example, vacuum cleaners, cosmetics, encyclopedias and gardening equipment. It also includes intangible products such as cable services and home study educational courses.

EXAMPLE: Larry is a Mavon Guy. He sells men's toiletries door-to-door. He is paid a 20% commission on all his sales. This is his only remuneration from Mavon. He has a written contract with Mavon that provides that he will not be treated as an employee for federal tax purposes. Larry is a statutory non-employee—that is, an independent contractor, for federal employment tax purposes.

If they also satisfy the requirements outlined above, people who sell or distribute newspapers or shopping news are also considered to be direct sellers. This is true whether they are paid by the publisher based on the number of papers delivered, or they purchase newspapers from the publisher and then sell them and keep the money. ■

Taxes for Workers You Hire

If you do all the work in your unincorporated business yourself, you don't need to read this chapter. However, if, like many self-employed people, you hire others to assist you or you incorporate your business, it's wise to learn a little about federal and state tax requirements that apply to you and your workers.

A. Hiring People to Help You

Sooner or later, most self-employed people need to hire people to help them—for example:

- Agnes, a freelance graphic designer, hires a part-time assistant to help her meet a pressing deadline from her biggest client.
- Arthur, an architect, hires a computer consultant to help him choose and install a new computer system and show him how to use new design software.
- Amy sells books from several publishers to New England bookstores; she hires Bill to cover her sales territory while she's on vacation.

Whenever you hire a helper, you need to be concerned about obeying federal and state tax laws.

1. Different Tax Rules for Independent Contractors and Employees

The tax rules you have to follow when you hire helpers differ depending upon whether they qualify as employees or are self-employed—also called independent contractors (ICs) by the IRS and other government agencies.

If you hire an employee to help you in your business, you become subject to a wide array of state and federal tax requirements. You must withhold taxes from your employees' pay, and you must pay other taxes yourself. You must also comply with complex and burdensome bookkeeping and reporting requirements.

If you hire an IC, you need not comply with these requirements. All you have to do is report the amount you pay the IC to the IRS and your state tax department. However, hiring an IC is not necessarily cheaper than hiring an employee. Some ICs charge far more than what you'd pay an employee to do similar work. Nevertheless, many self-employed still prefer to hire ICs instead of employees because of the smaller tax and bookkeeping burdens.

2. Determining Worker Status

Initially, it's up to you to determine whether any person you hire is an employee or an IC. If you decide that a worker is an employee, you must comply with the federal and state tax requirements discussed in Section B. If you decide the worker is an IC, you need only comply with the income reporting and tax identification number requirements covered in Section C.

However, your decision about how to classify a worker is subject to review by various government agencies, including:

- the IRS
- your state's tax department
- your state's unemployment compensation insurance agency, and
- your state's workers' compensation insurance agency.

Any agency that determines that you misclassified an employee as an IC may impose back taxes, fines and penalties.

Scrutinizing agencies use various tests to determine whether a worker is an IC or an employee. The determining factor is usually whether you have the right to control the worker. If you have the right to direct and control the way a worker performs—both as to the final results and the details of when, where and how the work is done—then the worker is your employee. On the other hand, if your control is limited to accepting or rejecting the final results the worker achieves, he or she is an IC. (See Chapter 15 for a detailed discussion of how to determine whether a worker is an IC or an employee.)

A part of the Tax Code known as the IRS Safe Harbor or Section 530 enables firms that hire ICs to win IRS employment tax audits. If you're audited for employment tax purposes, the auditor must first determine whether you qualify for Safe Harbor protection. If you do, no assessments or penalties may be imposed. You may continue treating the workers involved as ICs for these purposes, and the IRS will not question their status.

This means you need not pay the employer's share of the workers' Social Security and Medicare taxes or withhold income or Social Security taxes from their pay. However, the workers could still be considered employees for other purposes, such as pension plan rules and state unemployment compensation taxes.

To qualify for Safe Harbor protection, you must satisfy three requirements. You must have:

- filed all required 1099 forms for the workers in question
- consistently treated the workers involved and others doing substantially similar work as ICs, and
- had a reasonable basis for treating the workers as ICs—for example, treating such workers as ICs is a common practice in your industry or an attorney or accountant told you they qualified as ICs.

Part Timers and Temps Can Be Employees

Don't think that a person you hire to work part time or for a short period must be an IC. People who work for you only temporarily or part time are your employees if you have the right to control the way they work.

For a detailed discussion of the practical and legal issues employers face when hiring ICs, see *Hiring Independent Contractors: The Employer's Legal Guide*, by Stephen Fishman (Nolo).

B. Tax Concerns When Hiring Employees

Whenever you hire an employee, you become an unpaid tax collector for the federal government. You are required to withhold and pay both federal and state taxes for the worker. These taxes are called payroll taxes or employment taxes.

You must also satisfy these requirements if you incorporate your business and continue to actively work in it. In this event, you will be an employee of your corporation.

1. Federal Payroll Taxes

The IRS regulates federal payroll taxes, which include:

- Social Security and Medicare taxes—also known as FICA
- unemployment taxes—also known as FUTA, and
- income taxes—also known as FITW.

Don't Forget Yourself

Remember: Your corporation—and not you personally—must pay these payroll taxes for you if you incorporate your business and work as an employee of your corporation. (See Chapter 2, Section B.)

PROS AND CONS OF HIRING EMPLOYEES AND ICs

There are advantages and disadvantages to hiring employees and ICs.

HIRING EMPLOYEES

Pros	Cons
You can closely supervise employees.	You must pay federal and state payroll taxes for them.
You can give employees extensive training.	You must usually provide them with workers' compensation coverage.
You automatically own any intellectual property employees create on the job.	You must provide them with office space and equipment.
You don't need to worry about government auditors claiming you misclassified employees	You ordinarily provide them with employee benefits such as vacations and sick leave.
Employees can't sue you for damages if they are injured on the job, provided you have workers' compensation insurance.	You're liable for their actions.
Employees can generally be fired at any time.	You can be sued for labor law violations.

HIRING ICS

Pros	Cons
You don't have to pay federal and state payroll taxes for ICs.	You risk exposure to audits by the IRS and other agencies.
You don't have to provide workers' compensation insurance for ICs.	You can't closely supervise or train them.
You don't have to provide office space or equipment for ICs.	ICs usually can't be terminated unless they violate their contract.
You don't have to provide employee benefits to ICs.	ICs can sue you for damages if they are injured on the job.
You're generally not liable for ICs' actions.	You may lose copyright ownership if you don't obtain an assignment of rights.
You face reduced exposure to lawsuits for labor law violations.	ICs may usually work for your competitors as well as you.

 IRS *Circular E, Employer's Tax Guide,* provides detailed information on federal payroll taxes. It is an outstanding resource that you should have if you hire employees. You can get a free copy by calling the IRS at 800-TAX-FORM, by calling or visiting your local IRS office or by downloading it from the IRS website at www.irs.gov.

a. FICA

FICA is an acronym for Federal Income Contributions Act, the law requiring employers and employees to pay Social Security and Medicare taxes. The IRS imposes FICA taxes on both employers and employees. If you hire an employee, you must collect and remit his or her part of the taxes by withholding it from paycheck amounts and sending it to the IRS. You must also pay a matching amount.

The amounts you must withhold and pay are listed in the current edition of IRS Circular E. For 2002, for example, employers and employees were each required to pay 7.65% on the first $84,900 of an employee's annual wages. The 7.65% figure is the sum of the 6.2% Social Security tax and the 1.45% Medicare tax.

There is no Social Security tax on the portion of an employee's annual wages that exceed the $84,900 ceiling. However, the Medicare tax marches on: Both you and the employee must pay the 1.45% Medicare tax on any wages over $84,900. The ceiling for the Social Security tax changes annually. You can find out the Social Security tax ceiling for the current year in IRS Circular E, *Employer's Tax Guide*; the amount is printed right on the first page.

b. FUTA

FUTA is an acronym for the Federal Unemployment Tax Act; the law establishes federal unemployment taxes. Most employers must pay both state and federal unemployment taxes. But even if you're exempt from the state tax, you may still have to pay the federal tax. Employers alone are responsible for FUTA. You may not collect or deduct it from employees' wages.

You must pay FUTA taxes if:

- You pay $1,500 or more to employees during any calendar quarter—that is, any three-month period beginning with January, April, July or October, or
- You had at least one employee for some part of a day in any 20 or more different weeks during the year. The weeks don't have to be consecutive, nor does it have to be the same employee each week.

Technically, the FUTA tax rate is 6.2%, but in practice, you rarely pay this much. You are given a credit of 5.4% if you pay the applicable state

unemployment tax in full and on time. This means that the actual FUTA tax rate is usually 0.8%. In 2002, the FUTA tax was assessed on the first $7,000 of an employee's annual wage—which means that the FUTA tax usually is $56 per year per employee.

c. FITW

FITW is an acronym for federal income tax withholding. When you hire an employee, you're not only a tax collector for the government, but you are also a manager of your employee's income. The IRS fears that employees will not save enough from their wages to pay their tax bill on April 15. It also wants, of course, to speed up tax collections. So the IRS tells you, the employer, not to pay your employees their entire wages but to send the money to the IRS—this is the employee version of the estimated taxes ICs must pay. (See Chapter 11.)

You must calculate and withhold federal income taxes from all your employees' paychecks. You normally deposit the funds in a bank, which transmits the money to the IRS. Employees are solely responsible for paying federal income taxes. Your only responsibility is to withhold the funds and remit them to the government.

You must ask each employee you hire to fill out IRS Form W-4, Employee's Withholding Allowance Certificate. The information on this form is used to help determine how much tax must be withheld from the employee's pay.

By January 31 of each year, you must give each employee you hired the previous year a copy of IRS Form W-2, Wage and Tax Statement, showing how much he or she was paid and how much tax was withheld for the year. You must also send copies to the Social Security Administration.

You can obtain copies of these forms by calling the IRS at 800-TAX-FORM, by visiting your local IRS office or by downloading them from the IRS Internet site at www.irs.gov.

For detailed information on FITW, see IRS Publication 505, *Tax Withholding and Estimated Tax.* You can obtain a copy by calling the IRS at 800-TAX-FORM, by visiting your local IRS office or from the IRS Internet site at www.irs.gov.

d. Paying payroll taxes

You pay FICA, FUTA and FITW either electronically or by making federal tax deposits at specified banks. The IRS will tell you how often you must make your payroll tax deposits. The frequency depends on the total taxes you pay. If you pay by mail, you must submit an IRS Federal Tax Deposit coupon (Form 8109-B) with each payroll tax payment. If you have employees, you must also report these payments to the IRS on Form 941, Employer's Quarterly Federal Tax Return, after each calendar quarter in which you have employees. Form 941 shows how many employees you had, how much they were paid and the amount of FICA and income tax withheld.

Once each year, you must also file IRS Form 940, Employer's Annual Federal Unemployment Tax Return (or the simpler Form 940-EZ). This form shows the IRS how much federal unemployment tax you owe.

Instead of depositing payroll tax payments by check with specified banks, you may pay them directly to the IRS electronically using the IRS's Electronic Federal Tax Payment System (EFTPS). Using EFTPS, you can make deposits by phone or by using your personal computer. If you pay more than $200,000 in payroll taxes each year, using EFTPS is mandatory. If you pay less than $200,000, using the electronic system is optional. For information on EFTPS or to get an enrollment form, call EFTPS Customer Service at 800-555-4477 or 800-945-8400.

Figuring out how much to withhold, doing the necessary recordkeeping and filling out the required forms can be complicated. If you have a computer, computer accounting programs such as QuickBooks can help with all the calculations and print out your employees' checks and IRS forms.

You can also hire a bookkeeper or payroll tax service to do the work. Payroll tax services are usually not expensive, especially if you only have one or two employees.

e. Penalties for failing to pay FICA and FITW

As far as the IRS is concerned, an employer's most important duty is to withhold and pay over Social Security and income taxes. Employee FICA and FITW are also known as trust fund taxes because the employer is deemed to hold the withheld funds in trust for the U.S. government.

If you fail to pay trust fund taxes, you can get into the worst tax trouble there is. The IRS can—and often does—seize a business's assets and force it to close down if it owes back payroll taxes. You can also get thrown in jail, but this rarely happens.

At the very least, you'll have to pay all the taxes due plus interest. The IRS may also impose a penalty known as the trust fund recovery penalty if it determines that you willfully failed to pay the taxes. The agency can claim you willfully failed to pay taxes if you knew the taxes were due and didn't pay them. If you paid such taxes in the past, then stopped paying them, that constitutes pretty good evidence that you knew the taxes were due.

The trust fund recovery penalty is also known as the 100% penalty because the amount of the penalty is equal to 100% of the total amount of employee FICA and FITW taxes the employer failed to withhold and pay to the IRS. This can be a staggering sum. As a business owner, you'll be personally liable for the 100% penalty—that is, you will have to pay it out of your own pocket, even if you've incorporated your business.

THEIR DOGS ATE THEIR HOMEWORK

You have to make sure these taxes are paid. The IRS does not take kindly to excuses. For example, the IRS assessed a $40,000 penalty against two brothers in the floor covering business when their company failed to pay FITW and FICA for its employees for over two years. The brothers had the money to pay the taxes and had entrusted the task to an office manager. The manager failed to make the payments. The brothers pleaded ignorance about it, claiming that the manager intercepted and screened the mail and altered check descriptions and quarterly reports.

Both the IRS and court were unmoved. Although the court stated it was not unreasonable for the brothers to entrust the payments to their office manager, the brothers were still ultimately responsible to make sure the taxes were paid, and were therefore liable for the penalty. (*Conklin Bros. v. United States*, 986 F.2d 315 (9th Cir. 1993).)

 For guidance on how to deal with the IRS if you are having trouble meeting your payroll tax obligations, see *Tax Savvy for Small Business*, by Fred Daily (Nolo).

f.   Rules for family members

Self-employed people often hire family members to help them. And a tax rule argues in favor of this family togetherness: if you hire your child, spouse or parent as an employee, you may not have to pay FICA and FUTA taxes.

Employing your child. You need not pay FUTA taxes for services performed by your child who is under 21 years old. You need not pay FICA taxes for your child under 18 who works in your trade or business, or your partnership if it's owned solely by you and your spouse.

> **EXAMPLE:**: Lisa, a 16-year-old, makes deliveries for her mother's mail order business, which is operated as a sole proprietorship. Although Lisa is her mother's employee, her mother need not pay FUTA until Lisa reaches 21 and need not pay FICA taxes until she reaches 18.

However, these rules do not apply—and you must pay both FICA and FUTA—if you hire your child to work for:

- your corporation, or
- your partnership, unless all the partners are parents of the child.

> **EXAMPLE:** Ron works in a computer repair business that is half owned by his mother and half owned by her partner, Ralph, who is no relation to the family. FICA and FUTA taxes must be paid for Ron because he is working for a partnership and not all the partners are his parents.

INCOME TAX BREAK FOR CHILD-EMPLOYEES

You must withhold income taxes from your child's pay only if it exceeds the standard deduction for the year. The standard deduction was $4,700 in 2002 and is adjusted every year for inflation. A child who is paid less than this amount need not pay any income taxes on his or her salary.

You might consider getting your child to do some work around the office instead of paying him or her an allowance for doing nothing. If your child's pay is below the standard deduction amount, it is not only tax-free, but you can also deduct the amount from your own taxes as a business expense if the child's work is business-related—for example, cleaning your office, answering the phone or making deliveries. However, you can only deduct your child's wages if they are reasonable—that is, if they are about what you'd pay a stranger for the same work. Don't try paying your child $100 per hour for office cleaning so you can get a big tax deduction.

If you pay your child $600 or more during the year, you must file Form W-2 reporting the earnings to the IRS. No matter how much you pay your child, each year you should fill out and have your child sign IRS Form W-4, Employee's Withholding Allowance Certificate. If you pay your child less than $200 per week, keep the form in your records. If you pay your child more than $200 per week, keep a copy of the form for your records and file a copy of the form with the IRS.

Employing your spouse. If you pay your spouse to work in your trade or business, the payments are subject to FICA taxes and federal income tax withholding, but not FUTA taxes.

EXAMPLE: Kay's husband, Simon, is a sole proprietor computer programmer. Kay works as his assistant and is paid $1,500 per month. Simon must pay the employer's share of FICA taxes for Kay and withhold employee FICA and federal income taxes from her pay.

But this rule does not apply—and FICA, FUTA and FITW must all be paid—if your spouse works for:

- a corporation, even if you control it, or
- a partnership, even if your spouse is a partner along with you.

EXAMPLE: Laura's husband, Rob, works as a draftsperson in Laura's architectural consulting firm, a corporation of which she is the sole owner. The corporation must pay FICA, FUTA and FITW for Rob.

Employing a parent. The wages of a parent you employ in your trade or business are subject to income tax withholding and FICA taxes.

EXAMPLE: Don owns and operates a graphic design firm and employs Art, his father, as a part-time designer. Since the firm is a business, Don must pay the employer's share of FICA taxes for Art and withhold employee FICA and federal income taxes from his pay.

2. State Payroll Taxes

Employers in all states are required to pay and withhold state payroll taxes for employees. These taxes include:

- state unemployment compensation taxes in all states
- state income tax withholding in most states, and
- state disability taxes in a few states.

a. Unemployment compensation

Federal law requires that all states provide most types of employees with unemployment compensation, also called UC or unemployment insurance.

Employers are required to contribute to a state unemployment insurance fund. Employees make no contributions, except in Alaska, New Jersey, Pennsylvania and Rhode Island, where employers must withhold small employee contributions from employees' paychecks. Employees who are laid off or fired for reasons other than serious misconduct are entitled to receive unemployment benefits from the state fund. You need not provide unemployment for ICs.

If your payroll is very small—below $1,500 per calendar quarter—you probably won't have to pay UC taxes. In most states, you must pay state UC taxes for employees if you're paying federal UC taxes, also called FUTA taxes. (See Section B1.) However, some states have more strict requirements. Contact your state labor department for details of your state's law.

b. State income tax withholding

All states except Alaska, Florida, Nevada, South Dakota, Texas, Washington and Wyoming have income taxation. New Hampshire and Tennessee impose income taxes on dividend and interest income only. If you do business in a state that imposes state income taxes, you must withhold the applicable tax from your employees' paychecks and pay it to the state taxing authority. No state income tax withholding is required for workers who qualify as ICs.

It's easy to determine whether you need to withhold state income taxes for a worker: If you are withholding federal income taxes, then you must withhold state income taxes as well. Each state has its own income tax withholding forms and procedures. Contact your state tax department for information. (See Appendix 3 for contact details.)

c. State disability insurance

Five states have state disability insurance that provides employees with coverage for injuries or illnesses that are not related to work. Injuries that are job-related are covered by workers' compensation. (See Section B3.) The states with disability insurance are: California, Hawaii, New Jersey, New York and Rhode Island. Puerto Rico also has a disability insurance program.

In these states, employees contribute to disability insurance in amounts their employers withhold from their paychecks. Employers must also make contributions in Hawaii, New Jersey, New York and Puerto Rico.

Except in New York, the disability insurance coverage requirements are the same as for UC insurance. If you pay UC for a worker, you must withhold and pay disability insurance premiums as well. You need not provide disability for ICs.

3. Workers' Compensation Insurance

Subject to some important exceptions, employers in all states must provide their employees with workers' compensation insurance to cover work-related injuries. Workers' compensation is not a payroll tax. You must purchase a workers' compensation policy from a private insurer or state workers' compensation fund. (See Chapter 6, Section F.)

C. Tax Reporting for Independent Contractors

If you hire an IC, you don't have to worry about withholding and paying state or federal payroll taxes or filling out lots of government forms. This is one reason ICs generally prefer hiring other ICs rather than employees.

However, if you pay an unincorporated IC $600 or more during the year for business-related services, you must:

- file IRS Form 1099-MISC telling the IRS how much you paid the worker, and
- obtain the IC's taxpayer identification number.

The IRS imposes these requirements because it is very concerned that many ICs don't report all the income they earn to avoid paying taxes. To help prevent this, the IRS wants to find out how much you pay ICs you hire and make sure it has their correct tax ID numbers.

The filing and ID requirements apply to all ICs you hire who are sole proprietors or partners in partnerships, which includes the vast majority of ICs. However, they don't apply to corporations, probably because large businesses have a strong legislative lobby. The IRS has attempted to change the law to include corporations, but so far it hasn't succeeded.

This means that if you hire an incorporated IC, you don't have to file anything with the IRS.

EXAMPLE: Bob, a self-employed consultant, pays $5,000 to Yvonne, a CPA, to perform accounting services. Yvonne has formed her own one-person corporation called Yvonne's Accounting Services, Inc. Bob pays the corporation, not Yvonne personally. Since Bob is paying a corporation, he need not report the payment on Form 1099-MISC or obtain Yvonne's tax ID number.

This is one of the main advantages of hiring incorporated ICs, because the IRS uses Form 1099 as a lead to find people and companies to audit.

However, it's wise to make sure you have the corporation's full legal name and federal employer identification number. Without this information, you may not be able to prove to the IRS that the payee was incorporated. An easy way to do this is to have the IC fill out IRS Form W-9, Request for Taxpayer Identification Number, and keep it in your files. This simple form merely requires the corporation to provide its name, address and EIN. (See Appendix 1 for a copy of the form.)

When in Doubt, File a Form 1099

The IRS may impose a $50 fine if you fail to file a Form 1099 when required. But, far more serious, you'll be subject to severe penalties if the IRS later audits you and determines you misclassified the worker.

If you're not sure whether you must file a Form 1099-MISC for a worker, go ahead and file one anyway. You lose nothing by doing so and will save yourself the severe consequences of not filing if you were legally required to do so.

 For a detailed discussion of the consequences of not filing a 1099 form, see *Hiring Independent Contractors: The Employer's Legal Guide*, by Stephen Fishman (Nolo).

There are two exceptions to the rule that you don't have to file 1099 forms for payments to corporations. You must report all payments of $600 or more you make to a doctor or lawyer who is incorporated. However, this is necessary only where the payments are for your business. You need not report payments you make to incorporated doctors or lawyers for personal services— for example, if you hire a doctor to take care of a personal health problem or hire a lawyer to write your will or handle your other personal legal matters.

1. $600 Threshold for IC Income Reporting

You need to obtain an unincorporated IC's taxpayer ID number and file a 1099 form with the IRS only if you pay the IC $600 or more during a year for business-related services. It makes no difference whether the sum was one payment for a single job or the total of many small payments for multiple jobs.

EXAMPLE: Andre, a computer consultant, hires Thomas, a self-employed programmer, to help create a computer program. Andre classifies Thomas as an IC and pays him $2,000 during the year. Thomas is a sole proprietor. Since Andre paid Thomas more than $599 for business-related services, Andre must obtain Thomas's taxpayer ID number and file Form 1099 with the IRS reporting the payment.

In calculating whether the payments made to an IC total $600 or more during a year, you must include payments for parts or materials the IC used in performing the services. For example, if you hire a painter to paint your home office, the cost of the paint would be included in the tally.

However, not all payments you make to ICs are counted towards the $600 threshold.

a. Payments for merchandise

You don't need to count payments solely for merchandise or inventory. This includes raw materials and supplies that will become a part of merchandise you intend to sell.

> **EXAMPLE:** Betty pays $5,000 to purchase 100 used widgets from Joe's Widgets, a sole proprietorship he owns. Betty intends to repair and resell the widgets. The payment need not be counted toward the $600 threshold because Betty is purchasing merchandise from Joe, not services.

b. Payments for personal services

You need only count payments you make to ICs for services they perform in the course of your trade or business. A trade or business is an activity carried on for gain or profit. You don't count payments for services that are not related to your business, including payments you make to ICs for personal or household services or repairs—for example, payments to babysitters, gardeners and housekeepers. Running your home is not a profit-making activity.

> **EXAMPLE:** Joe, a self-employed designer, pays Mary a total of $1,000 during the year for gardening services for his residence. None of the payments count toward the $600 threshold because they don't relate to Joe's design business. Joe need not obtain Mary's taxpayer ID number or file a 1099 form reporting the payments to the IRS.

2. Obtaining Taxpayer Identification Numbers

Some ICs work in the underground economy—that is, they're paid in cash and never pay any taxes or file tax returns. The IRS may not even know they exist. The IRS wants you to help it find these people by supplying the taxpayer ID numbers from all ICs who meet the requirements explained above.

If an IC won't give you his or her number or the IRS informs you that the number the IC gave you is incorrect, the IRS assumes the person isn't going to voluntarily pay taxes. So it requires you to withhold taxes from the compensation you pay the IC and remit them to the IRS. This is called backup withholding. If you fail to backup withhold, the IRS will impose an assessment against you equal to 30% of what you paid the IC.

a. Avoiding backup withholding

Backup withholding can be a bookkeeping burden for you. Fortunately, it's very easy to avoid it. Have the IC fill out and sign IRS Form W-9, Request for Taxpayer Identification Number, and retain it in your files. (See Appendix 1 for a copy of the form.) You don't have to file the W-9 with the IRS. This simple form merely requires the IC to list his or her name, address and taxpayer ID number. Partnerships and sole proprietors with employees must have a federal employer identification number (EIN), which they obtain from the IRS. In the case of sole proprietors without employees, the taxpayer ID number is the IC's Social Security number.

If the IC doesn't already have an EIN, but promises to obtain one, you don't have to backup withhold for 60 days after he or she applies for one. Have the IC fill out and sign the W-9 form, stating "Applied For" in the space where the ID number is supposed to be listed. If you don't receive the IC's ID number within 60 days, start backup withholding.

b. Backup withholding procedure

If you are unable to obtain an IC's taxpayer ID number or the IRS informs you that the number the IC gave you is incorrect, you'll have to do backup withholding. You must begin doing so after you pay an IC $600 or more during the year. You need not backup withhold on payments totaling less than $600.

To backup withhold, deposit with your bank 30% of the IC's compensation every quarter. You must make these deposits separately from the payroll tax deposits you make for employees. Report the amounts withheld on IRS Form 945, Annual Return of Withheld Federal Income Tax. This is an annual return you must file by January 31 of the following year. See the instructions to Form 945 for details. You can obtain a copy of the form by calling the IRS at 800-TAX-FORM, by contacting your local IRS office or by downloading it from the IRS Internet site at http://www.irs.gov.

3. Filling Out Your Form 1099

You must file a 1099-MISC form for each IC to whom you paid $600 or more during the year. You must obtain original 1099 forms from the IRS. You cannot photocopy this form because it contains several pressure-sensitive copies. Each 1099 form contains two parts and can be used for two different workers. All your 1099 forms must be submitted together along with one copy of Form 1096, which is a transmittal form—the IRS equivalent of a cover letter. You must obtain an original Form 1096 from the IRS; you cannot submit a photocopy. Obtain these forms by calling the IRS at 800-TAX-FORM or by contacting your local IRS office.

Filling out Form 1099-MISC is easy. Follow this step-by-step approach.

- List your name and address in the first box titled Payer's name.
- Enter your taxpayer identification number in the box entitled Payer's Federal identification number.

9595 ☐ VOID ☐ CORRECTED				
PAYER'S name, street address, city, state, ZIP code, and telephone no.	**1** Rents $	OMB No. 1545-0115	**2002** Form **1099-MISC**	**Miscellaneous Income**
	2 Royalties $			
	3 Other income $	**4** Federal income tax withheld $		**Copy A** **For Internal Revenue Service Center**
PAYER'S Federal identification number / RECIPIENT'S identification number	**5** Fishing boat proceeds $	**6** Medical and health care payments $		**File with Form 1096.**
RECIPIENT'S name	**7** Nonemployee compensation $	**8** Substitute payments in lieu of dividends or interest $		For Privacy Act and Paperwork Reduction Act Notice, see the **2002 General Instructions for Forms 1099, 1098, 5498, and W-2G.**
Street address (including apt. no.)	**9** Payer made direct sales of $5,000 or more of consumer products to a buyer (recipient) for resale ▶ ☐	**10** Crop insurance proceeds $		
City, state, and ZIP code	**11**	**12**		
Account number (optional) / 2nd TIN not. ☐	**13** Excess golden parachute payments $	**14** Gross proceeds paid to an attorney $		
15	**16** State tax withheld $ $	**17** State/Payer's state no.	**18** State income $ $	

Form **1099-MISC**   Cat. No. 14425J   Department of the Treasury - Internal Revenue Service

Do Not Cut or Separate Forms on This Page — Do Not Cut or Separate Forms on This Page

- The IC you have paid is called the "Recipient" on this form, meaning the person who received the money. You must provide the IC's taxpayer identification number, name and address in the boxes indicated. For sole proprietors, you must list the individual's name first, then you may list a different business name, though this is not required. You may not enter only a business name for a sole proprietor.

- Enter the amount of your payments to the IC in Box 7, entitled "Nonemployee compensation." Be sure to fill in the right box or the Form 1099-MISC will be deemed invalid by the IRS.

- If you've done backup withholding for an IC who has not provided you with a taxpayer ID number, enter the amount withheld in Box 4.

The Form 1099-MISC contains five copies. These must be filed as follows:

- Copy A, the top copy, must be filed with the IRS no later than February 28 of the year after payment was made to the IC. If you don't use the remaining two spaces for other ICs, leave those spaces blank. Don't cut the page.

- Copy 1 must be filed with your state taxing authority if your state has a state income tax. The filing deadline is February 28 for most states, but check with your state tax department to make sure. Your state may also have a specific transmittal form or cover letter you must obtain.

- Copy B and Copy 2 must be given to the worker no later than January 31 of the year after payment was made.

- Copy C is for you to retain for your files.

All the IRS copies of each 1099 form are filed together with Form 1096, the simple transmittal form. You must add up all the payments reported on all the 1099 forms and list the total in the box indicated on Form 1096. File the forms with the IRS Service Center listed on the reverse of Form 1096.

Do Not Staple   6969

Form **1096**	**Annual Summary and Transmittal of U.S. Information Returns**	OMB No. 1545-0108
Department of the Treasury Internal Revenue Service		**2002**

FILER'S name

Street address (including room or suite number)

City, state, and ZIP code

Name of person to contact	Telephone number ( )	**For Official Use Only**
Fax number ( )	E-mail address	

1 Employer identification number	2 Social security number	3 Total number of forms	4 Federal income tax withheld $	5 Total amount reported with this Form 1096 $

Enter an "X" in only one box below to indicate the type of form being filed.   If this is your **final return**, enter an "X" here . . . . ▶ ☐

W-2G 32	1098 81	1098-E 84	1098-T 83	1099-A 80	1099-B 79	1099-C 85	1099-DIV 91	1099-G 86	1099-INT 92	1099-LTC 93	1099-MISC 95	1099-MSA 94	1099-OID 96
☐	☐	☐	☐	☐	☐	☐	☐	☐	☐	☐	☐	☐	☐

1099-PATR 97	1099-Q 31	1099-R 98	1099-S 75	5498 28	5498-MSA 27
☐	☐	☐	☐	☐	☐

Please return this entire page to the Internal Revenue Service. Photocopies are not acceptable.

Under penalties of perjury, I declare that I have examined this return and accompanying documents, and, to the best of my knowledge and belief, they are true, correct, and complete.

FILING 1099s ELECTRONICALLY

FILING 1099s ELECTRONICALLY

If you wish, you may file your 1099s with the IRS electronically instead of by mail. You must get permission from the IRS to do this by filing IRS Form 4419, *Application for Filing Information Returns Magnetically/Electronically.* If you file electronically, the deadline for filing 1099s with the IRS is extended to March 31. For more information, you can visit the IRS website at www.irs.gov (click on "IRS e-file"), or call the IRS Information Reporting Program at 304-263-8700.

1099s may also be sent to independent contractors electronically—that is, by e-mail. But you may do this only if the contractor agrees. If he or she doesn't agree, you must deliver the 1099 by mail or in person.

D. Special Reporting Requirements for California

Beginning January 1, 2001, any person or business that hires an independent contractor in California must notify the California Employment Development Department (EDD) and let it know how much the IC is paid and some other basic information. This rule applies to any IC for whom you are required to file a Form 1099 with the IRS—in other words, to any IC to whom you pay $600 or more in the course of a year.

The EDD and other California state agencies will use this information to aid in the enforcement of child support orders issued against ICs. It is not supposed to be used for any other purpose—for example, as an audit lead.

1. When Report Must Be Filed

You do not file these EDD reports at the same time that you file your 1099 forms. Rather, you must file the EDD reports within 20 days after you do any of the following:

- enter into an oral or written contract or contracts with an IC in California in which you promise to pay the IC a total of $600 or more for his or her services, or
- actually pay an IC $600 or more. If you make multiple payments to the IC, you must file the EDD report within 20 days after the total reaches $600 or more.

Thus, if you use many ICs, you will most likely find yourself having to file EDD reports at various times throughout the year.

2. Contents of Report

On the EDD report, you must give the following information:

- the IC's full name and Social Security number
- your name, business name, address and telephone number
- your federal employer identification number, California state employer account number, Social Security number or other identifying number as required by the EDD
- the date you signed the contract with the IC or, if there is no contract, the date that your payments to the IC reached $600
- the total dollar amount of the contract, if any, and
- the contract expiration date.

The EDD will retain this information until November 1 following the tax year in which you and the IC entered into the contract. If you did not actually enter into the contract, the EDD will retain the information until November 1 following the tax year in which the payments reached $600.

The EDD has created a form hiring firms can use to comply with its reporting requirements—*Report of Independent Contractor(s),* Form DE 542. You can download a copy from the EDD website at www.edd.cahwnet.gov/txicr.htm. You can also obtain copies by calling the EDD at 888-745-3886 or by visiting your local employment tax office (it's listed in your local telephone directory in the State Government section under "Employment Development Department"). ■

Recordkeeping and Accounting Made Easy

You probably didn't become self-employed so you could turn into a bookkeeper or accountant. But even though it can be a bit of a pain, all self-employed people need to keep records of their income and expenses. Among other things, keeping good records will enable you to reap a rich harvest in tax deductions. So time spent on recordkeeping is usually time well spent.

A. Simple Bookkeeping

Except in a few cases, the IRS does not require any special kind of records. You may choose any system suited to your business that clearly shows your income and expenses. If you are in more than one business, keep a separate set of books for each business.

If, like most self-employed people, you run a one-person service business and are a sole proprietor, you don't need a fancy or complex set of books. You can get along very nicely with just a few items. They include:

- a business checking account
- income and expense journals
- files for supporting documents, such as receipts and canceled checks, and
- if you buy equipment such as computers or copiers to use in your business, an asset log to support your depreciation deductions.

Special Concerns If You Hire Employees
If you have employees, you must create and keep a number of records, including payroll tax records, withholding records and employment

---

BENEFITS OF KEEPING RECORDS

Keeping good records will help you in a number of ways.

Monitor the progress of your business. Without records, you'll never have an accurate idea of how your business is doing. You may think you're making money when you're really not. Records can show whether your business is improving or what changes you need to make to increase the likelihood of success.

Prepare financial statements. You need good records to prepare accurate financial statements. These include income (profit and loss) statements and balance sheets. These statements can be essential in dealing with your bank or creditors.

Keep track of deductible expenses. You may forget expenses when you prepare your tax return unless you record them when they occur. Every $100 in expenses you forget to

deduct will cost you about $45 in additional income and self-employment taxes if you earn a mid-level income, putting you in the 27% marginal tax bracket.

Prepare your tax returns. You need good records to prepare your tax return or to enable an accountant to prepare your return for you in a reasonable amount of time. These records should show the income, expenses and credits you report. Generally, these can be the same records you use to monitor your business and prepare your financial statements.

Win IRS audits. If you're audited by the IRS, it will be up to you to prove that you have accurately reported your income and expenses on your tax returns. An IRS auditor will not simply take your word that your return is accurate. You need accurate records and receipts to back up your returns.

tax returns. And you must keep these records for four years.

For detailed information, see IRS Circular E, *Employer's Tax Guide.* You can get a free copy by calling the IRS at 800-TAX-FORM, by calling or visiting your local IRS office or by downloading it from the IRS website at www.irs.gov.

Also, contact your state tax agency for your state's requirements. (See Appendix 3 for contact details.)

1. Business Checkbook

One of the first things you should do when you become self-employed is to set up a separate checking account for your business. Your business checkbook will serve as your basic source of information for recording your business expenses and income. Deposit all your self-employment compensation, such as the checks you receive from clients, into the account and make all business-related payments by writing checks from the account. Don't use your business account for personal expenses or your personal account for business.

Keeping a separate business account is not required by law if you're a sole proprietor, but it will provide many important benefits.

- It will be much easier for you to keep track of your business income and expenses if they're paid from a separate account.
- Your business account will also clearly separate your personal expenses and business income and expenses; this will prove very helpful if you're audited by the IRS.
- Your business account will help convince the IRS that you are running a business and not engaged in a hobby. Hobbyists don't generally have separate bank accounts for their hobbies. This is a huge benefit if you incur losses from your business because losses from hobbies are not fully deductible. (See Chapter 9.)

- Perhaps most important, having a separate business bank account will help to establish that you're an independent contractor, not an employee. Employees don't have separate business accounts. Your business account helps show that you're in business for yourself and are, therefore, an independent contractor.

a. Setting up your bank account

At a minimum, you'll need to open a separate checking account in which you will deposit all your self-employment income and from which you will pay all your business expenses.

There is no need to open your business checking account at the same bank where you have your personal checking account. Shop around and open your account with the bank that offers you the best services at the lowest price.

If you're doing business under your own name, consider opening up a second account in that name and using it solely for your business instead of a separate business account. You'll usually pay less for a personal account than for a business account.

If you do open a business account, make sure it is in your business name. If you're a sole proprietor, this can be your personal name. If you've formed a corporation or limited liability company, the account should be in your corporate or company name.

If you're a sole proprietor and doing business under an assumed name, you'll likely have to give your bank a copy of your fictitious business name statement. (See Chapter 3.)

Use a Separate Credit Card for Business

Use a separate credit card for business expenses instead of using one card for both personal and business items. Credit card interest for business purchases is 100% deductible; interest for personal purchases is not deductible at all. Using a separate card for business purchases will make it much easier for you to keep track of how much interest you've paid for business purchases. The card doesn't have to be in your business name. It can just be one of your personal credit cards.

If you've incorporated, call your bank and ask what documentation is required to open the account. You will probably need to show the bank a corporate resolution authorizing the opening of a bank account and showing the names of the people authorized to sign checks.

Typically, you will also have to fill out a separate bank account authorization form provided by your bank. You will also need to have a federal employer identification number. (See Chapter 5.)

Similarly, if you've established a limited liability company (see Chapter 2), you'll likely have to show the bank a company resolution authorizing the account.

You may also want to establish interest-bearing accounts for your business, in which you can deposit cash you don't immediately need. For example, you may want to set up a business savings account or a money market mutual fund in your business name.

b. Paying yourself

To pay yourself when you're a sole proprietor, write a business check to yourself and deposit the money in your personal account. This is known as a withdrawal or personal draw. Use your personal account to pay your non-business or personal expenses.

c. When you write checks

If you already keep an accurate, updated personal checkbook, simply do the same for your business checkbook. If, however, like many people, you tend to be lax in keeping up your checkbook, you're going to have to change your habits. Now that you're in business, you can't afford this kind of carelessness. Unless you write large numbers of business checks, maintaining your checkbook won't take much time.

When you write business checks, you may have to make some extra notations besides the date, number, amount of the check, and the name of the person or company to which the check is written. If it's not clear from the name of the payee what a check is for, describe the business reason for the check—for example, the equipment or service you purchased.

You can use the register that comes with your checkbook and write in all this information manually, or you can use a computerized register. (See Section B.)

Don't Write Checks for Cash

Avoid writing checks payable to cash, since it's unclear what specific business purpose such checks have. Writing cash checks might lead to questions from the IRS if you're audited. If you must write a check for cash to pay a business expense, be sure to include the receipt for the cash payment in your records.

d. Making deposits

When you make deposits into your business checking account, record in your check register:

- the date and amount of the deposit, and
- a description of the source of the funds—for example, the client's name.

2. Income and Expense Records

In addition to a business checkbook, you should maintain income and expense records.

These records, which should be updated at least monthly, will show you how much you're spending and for what, and will also clearly indicate how much money you're making. They will also make it much easier for you or a tax pro to prepare your tax returns. Instead of having to locate, categorize and add up the amount of each bill or canceled check at tax time, you can simply use the figures in your records.

You can track your expenses by creating what accountants call a chart of accounts—a listing by category of all your expenses and income. It's very easy to do this. You can do it manually on ledger sheets (blank sheets are provided in Appendix 1) or you can set up a computer spreadsheet program, such as Excel or Lotus, to do it. If you don't have a spreadsheet program, you can obtain a free copy of a version of Excel from the Sun Microsystems website at www.sun.com/staroffice/get.html. The program is called StarOffice. Many inexpensive shareware spreadsheet programs are also available.

If you already have or would prefer to use a financial computer program such as Quicken, you can do that instead of using the method described in this section. See Section A3 for more information about these programs.

a. Expense journal

Your expense journal will show what you buy for your business. You can easily create it by using ledger sheets you can get from any stationery or office supply store. Get ledger sheets with at least 12 or 14 columns. Devote a separate column to each major category of expenses you have. Alternatively, you can purchase accounting record books with the expense categories already printed on them. These cost more, however, and may not offer categories that meet your needs.

To decide what your expense categories should be, sit down with your first month's bills and receipts and divide them up into categorized piles. Some common expense categories many self-employed people have include:

- business meals and entertainment
- travel
- telephone
- supplies and postage
- office rent
- utilities for an outside office
- professional dues, publications and books
- business insurance
- payments to other self-employed people
- advertising costs
- equipment, and
- license fees.

You should always include a final category called Miscellaneous for various and sundry expenses that are not easily pigeon-holed.

Depending on the nature of your business, you may not need all these categories—or you might need additional or different headings. For example, a graphic designer might have categories for printing and typesetting expenses, or a writer might have a category for agent fees.

You can add or delete expense categories as you go along—for example, if you find your Misc. category contains many items for a particular type of expense, add it as an expense category.

You don't need a category for automobile expenses, since these expenses require a different kind of documentation for tax purposes.

In separate columns, list the check number for each payment, date and name of the person or company paid. If you pay by check, record its number in the check number column.

Once a month, go through your check register, credit card slips, receipts and other expense records and record the required information for each transaction. Also, total the amounts for each category when you come to the end of the page so you can keep a running total of what you've spent for each category for the year to date.

The following example shows a portion of an expense journal.

(See Appendix 1 for a sample of an expense journal that you can copy or adapt and use.)

EXPENSE JOURNAL

Date	Check No.	Transaction	Amount	Adver-tising	Outside Contrac-tors	Utilities	Supplies	Rent	Travel	Equip-ment	Meals & Entertain-ment	Misc.
5/1	123	ABC Properties	500					500				
5/1	124	Office Warehouse	150				150					
5/10	VISA	Computer World	1000							1000		
5/15	VISA	Cafe Ole'	50								50	
5/16	CASH	Sam's Stationery	50				50					
5/18	125	Electric Co.	50			50						
5/30	126	Bill Carter	500		500							
TOTAL This Page			2300		500	50	200	500		1000	50	
TOTAL Year to Date			7900	200	2000	250	400	2500	300	1500	250	500

b. Income journal

The income journal shows you how much money you're earning, and the source of each payment. At a minimum, your income ledger should have columns for the source of the funds—for example, the client's name—your invoice number if there is one, the amount of the payment and the date you received it. If you have lots of different sources of income, you can create different categories for each source and devote separate columns to them in your journal.

(See Appendix 1 for a sample of an income journal that you can copy or adapt and use.)

INCOME JOURNAL

Source	Invoice	Amount	Date Received
Joe Smith	123	$2,500	5/5
Acme Inc.	124	$1,250	5/15
Sue Jones	Personal Loan	$2,000	5/20
Total		$5,750	

c. Automobile mileage and expense records

If you use a car or other vehicle for business purposes other than just commuting to and from work, you're entitled to take a deduction for gas and other auto expenses. You can either deduct the actual cost of your gas and other expenses or take the standard rate deduction based on the number of business miles you drive. In 2002, the standard rate was 36.5 cents per mile. (See Chapter 9, Section E.)

Either way, you must keep a record of the total miles you drive during the year. And if you use your car for both business and personal use, you must record your business and personal mileage. Obtain a mileage log book from a stationery or office supply store; you can get one for a few dollars. Keep it in your car with a pen attached. Note your odometer reading in the logbook on the day you start using your car for business. Record your mileage every time you use your car for business and note the business purpose for the trip. Add up your business mileage when you get to the end of each page in the logbook. This way you'll only have to add the page totals at the end of the year instead of slogging through all the individual entries.

Here's an example of a portion of a page from a mileage logbook.

CAR MILEAGE AND EXPENSE LOGBOOK

Date	Destination	Business Purpose	Mileage at Beginning of Trip	Mileage at End of Trip	Business Miles	User's Name
5/1	Fresno	See Art Andrews— potential client	50,000	50,100	100	Jack S.
5/5	Stockton	Delivered documents to Bill James	50,500	50,550	50	Jack S.
5/15	Sacramento	Meeting at Acme Corp.	51,000	51,100	100	Jack S.
TOTAL Business Miles					250	

If you think you may want to take the deduction for your actual auto expenses instead of the standard rate, keep receipts for all your auto-related expenses including gasoline, oil, tires, repairs and insurance. You don't need to include these expenses in your ledger sheets; just keep them in a folder or envelope. At tax time, add them up to determine how big a deduction you'll get using the actual expense method. Also add in the amount you're entitled to deduct for depreciation of your auto. (See Chapter 9, Section D3.) Your total deduction using your actual auto expenses may or may not be larger than the deduction you'll get using the standard rate. You're generally allowed to use the method that gives you the largest deduction.

⚠ Use a Credit Card for Gas

If you use the actual expense method for car expenses, use a credit card when you buy gas. It's best that this be a separate card—either a gas company card or a separate bank card. The monthly statements you receive will serve as your gas receipts. If you pay cash for gas, you must either get a receipt or make a note of the amount in your mileage logbook.

Costs for business-related parking (other than at your office) and for tolls are separately deductible, whether you use the standard rate or the actual expense method. Get and keep receipts for these expenses.

3. Using Computer Financial Programs to Track Income and Expenses

There are a number of computer programs designed to help people keep track of their finances. The most popular are *Quicken* and *MS Money*. These programs work differently than the manual or spreadsheet system described in the preceding section, but they can do the job just fine.

Programs like *Quicken* work off a computerized check register. You enter your deposits (income) and withdrawals (expenses) from your business checking account into the register. You can also record cash and credit card expenses using separate accounts. You note the category of each income or expense item in the register. *Quicken* can then take this information and automatically create income and expense reports—that is, it will show you the amounts you've spent or earned for each category. It can also create profit and loss statements. You can even import these amounts into tax preparation software, such as *TurboTax*, when it's time to do your income taxes.

Quicken or *MS Money* provide all the tools most self-employed people will need to keep their books. But far more sophisticated accounting programs are available. Programs such as *QuickBooks, Mind Your Own Business* and *Peachtree Accounting* can accomplish more complex bookkeeping tasks, such as double entry bookkeeping. You may need one of these programs if you sell goods and maintain an inventory.

4. Supporting Documents

The IRS lives by the maxim that Figures Lie and Liars Figure. It knows very well that you can claim anything in your books, since you create them yourself. For this reason, the IRS requires that you have documents to support the entries in your books and on your tax returns. You don't have to file any of these documents with your tax returns, but you must have them available to back up your returns if you're audited.

a. Income documents

When the IRS audits a small business, it usually asks for both your business and personal bank statements. If you don't have them, the IRS may subpoena them from your bank. If your bank deposits are greater than the income you report on your tax return, the IRS auditor will assume you've underreported your income and impose additional tax, interest and penalties.

To avoid this, you need to be able to prove the source of all your income. Keep supporting documents showing the source and amounts of all the income you receive as an independent contractor. This includes bank deposit slips, invoices and the 1099-MISC forms your clients give you. Keep your bank statements as well.

b. Expense documents

You also need supporting documents for business expenses. In the absence of a supporting document, an IRS auditor will likely conclude that an item you claim as a business expense is really a personal expense and refuse to allow the deduction. If you're in the mid-level income, 27% marginal tax bracket, every $100 in disallowed deductions will cost you $27, plus interest and penalties. And your income subject to Social Security tax for the year will go up, costing you about $12 for every $100 in disallowed deductions.

The best supporting document for an expense is a paid receipt that shows who you paid, how much, the date and the item or service purchased.

If you don't have a receipt, keep your canceled check. A canceled check isn't as good as a receipt because it doesn't show what you bought. You can verify your purchases, however, by matching the check with your bill or invoice.

Here's an easy way to keep your travel expense records. When you go on a business trip, keep all your receipts in an envelope. When you get back from your trip, sort all your receipts by category—for example, airfare, hotel bills, meals and tips, entertainment, taxis and car rental.

Total your expenses for each category and write the totals on the outside of the envelope. Then list the total for all your travel expenses excluding meals and entertainment.

Note on the envelope the dates and place of your trip and the percentage of your time devoted to business. Also note the business reason for the trip. If you have correspondence or other records documenting the business purpose, keep them in the envelope as well. Keep a separate envelope for each trip you take.

To make things even more simple, you can avoid having to record the actual cost of your own meals and other incidentals while traveling on business if you use the IRS's standard allowance for these items. The standard allowance ranges between $30 to $46 per day based on your destination and the number of days you were away from home.

To determine the standard allowance for a trip, see IRS Publication 463, *Travel, Entertainment and Gift Expenses*. You can get a free copy by calling the IRS at 800-TAX-FORM, by calling or visiting your local IRS office or by downloading it from the IRS website at www.irs.gov.

Your final step is to transfer the figures from your envelope to your monthly expense journal. (See Section A2.) Enter in your journal the total for all your expenses excluding meals and entertainment under Travel, or Miscellaneous if you don't have a separate travel category.

If your trip was not exclusively for business, multiply your total expenses by the percentage of your trip that you spent on business, and enter that in your journal. For example, if you spent 75% of your time on business, multiply your expense total by that amount. If your trip was less than 50% for business, you can't deduct airfare or other transportation costs to your destination (see Chapter 9, Section F), so don't include this amount in your expense journal.

If your trip was entirely for business, list the total amount of your meals and entertainment separately in a Business Meals Entertainment category if you have one, or under Miscellaneous. If your trip was not solely for business, only list your meals and entertainment on days devoted to business. Make a note in your journal if you use the IRS standard allowance for meals.

If you pay by credit card, keep your credit card slips and save your monthly billing statements. The best approach is to set aside a separate credit card just for business expenses. If you pay an expense with an ATM card or another electronic funds transfer method, keep your receipt and bank statement.

The reason for saving supporting documents is to prove to the IRS that an expense was related to your business. Sometimes it will be clear from the face of a receipt, sales slip or the payee's name on your canceled check that the item you purchased was for your business. But if it's not clear, note what the purchase was for on the document.

c. Entertainment, meal and travel expense records

Deductions for business-related entertainment, meals and travel are a hot button item for the IRS because they have been greatly abused by many taxpayers. You need to have more records for these expenses than for almost any others, and they will be closely scrutinized if you're audited.

Whenever you incur an expense for business-related entertainment, meals or travel, you must document:

- the date the expense was incurred
- the amount
- the place
- the business purpose for the expense, and
- if entertainment or meals are involved, the business relationship of the people at the event—for example, their names and occupations and any other information needed to establish their business relation to you.

All this recordkeeping is not as hard as it sounds. Your receipts will ordinarily indicate the date, amount and place in which you incurred the expense. You just need to describe the business purpose and business relationship if entertainment or meals are involved. You can write this directly on your receipt.

EXAMPLE: Mary, a freelance computer programmer, has lunch with Harold, president of Acme Technologies, Inc., to discuss programming work. Her restaurant receipt shows the date, the name and location of the restaurant, the number of people served and the amount of the expense. Since Mary paid by credit card, the receipt even shows the amount of the tip. Mary just has to document the business purpose for the lunch. She writes on the receipt: "Lunch with Harold Lipshitz, President Acme Technologies, Inc. Discussed signing contract for programming services."

You must keep supporting documents for expenses (other than lodging) that tally more than $75. Keep your receipts or credit card slips for such expenses. Canceled checks alone are not sufficient; you must also have the bill for the expense.

d. Filing supporting documents

If you don't have a lot of receipts and other documents to save, you can simply keep them all in a single folder, shoebox or other safe place.

If you have a lot of supporting documents to save or are the type of person who likes to be extremely well organized, separate your documents by category—for example, income, travel expenses, equipment purchases. You can use a separate file folder for each category or get an accordion file with multiple pockets.

5. Asset Records

When you purchase property such as computers, office furniture, copiers or cellular telephones to use in your business, you must keep records to verify:

- when and how you acquired the asset
- purchase price
- cost of any improvements—for example, a major upgrade for your computer
- Section 179 deduction taken (see Chapter 9, Section D1)
- deductions taken for depreciation (see Chapter 6, Section D2)
- how you used the asset
- when and how you disposed of the asset
- selling price, and
- expenses of sale.

Set up an asset log showing this information for each item you purchase.

EXAMPLE: Patty purchases a $3,200 computer for her business on January 3. She uses it exclusively for business and decides to deduct the entire purchase price in a single year using Section 179. She prepares the following asset log for the computer.

ASSET LOG

Description of Property	Date Placed in Service	Cost or Other Basis	Business/ Investment Use %	Section 179 Deduction	Depreciation Prior Years	Basis for Depreciation	Method/ Convention	Recovery Period	Rate or Table %	Depreciation Deduction
Computer	1/3	3,200	100%	3,200	0	0	N/A	N/A	N/A	0
TOTAL				3,200						0

You can purchase asset logs from stationery or office supply stores, or set one up yourself using ledger paper or a spreadsheet program. (See Appendix 1 for a sample log you can copy and use.) You can also use a computer accounting program such as *Quicken Home & Business* to do so. If you have an accountant prepare your tax returns, he or she can create an asset log for you.

Be sure to keep your receipts for each asset purchase, since they'll usually verify what you purchased, when you bought the asset and how much you paid.

a. Listed property

Listed property is a term the IRS uses to refer to a certain type of business assets that can easily be used for personal as well as business purposes. Listed property includes:

- cars, boats, airplanes and other vehicles
- computers
- cellular phones, and
- any other property generally used for entertainment, recreation or amusement—for example, VCRs, cameras and camcorders.

Unless you use listed property exclusively for business and keep it at your business location, the IRS imposes special recordkeeping requirements to depreciate or take a Section 179 deduction for it.

EXAMPLE: Mary, a freelance writer, does all of her work in her home office, which is clearly her business location. She purchases a computer for her office which she uses 100% for writing. She doesn't need to keep a log of her business use.

If you use listed property both for business and personal uses, you must document your usage—both business and personal. Keep a log book, business diary or calendar showing the dates, times and reasons for which the property is used. (See Appendix 1 for a log sample you can copy and use.) You also can purchase log books at stationery or office supply stores.

EXAMPLE: Bill, an accountant, purchases a computer he uses 50% for business and 50% to play games. He must keep a log showing his business use of the computer. Following is a sample from one week in his log.

USAGE LOG FOR PERSONAL COMPUTER

Date	Time of Business Use	Reason for Business Use	Time of Personal Use
5/1	4.5 hours	Prepared client tax returns	1.5 hours
5/2			3 hours
5/3	2 hours	Prepared client tax returns	
5/4			2 hours

B. How Long to Keep Records

Keep all your supporting documents for at least three years after you file your tax returns. If you've failed to file tax returns, underreported your income or taken deductions to which you're not entitled, keep your supporting documents indefinitely. They may help you if you're audited.

Keep your asset records for three years after the depreciable life of the asset ends. For example, keep records for five-year property (such as computers) for eight years.

You should keep your ledger sheets for as long as you're in business, since a potential buyer of your business might want to see them.

C. Accounting Methods and Tax Years

To put it mildly, accounting methods and tax years are rather dry subjects, but it's essential that you understand the basics about them. The vast majority of self-employed people use the cash method and calendar tax year—the simplest of the methods available.

1. Methods of Accounting

There are two basic methods of accounting: cash basis and accrual basis. Using the cash basis method is like maintaining a checkbook. You record income only when the money is received, and expenses when they are actually paid.

EXAMPLE: You sign a contract to perform $25,000 worth of services for a client. Under the cash basis accounting method, you report as income only that portion of the promised $25,000 the client actually paid.

In contrast, in accrual basis accounting, you report income or expenses as they are earned or incurred rather than when they are actually collected or paid. Under this method, you report the money promised by a contract as income for the current year, even if the client has not yet paid you any of the money.

The cash method is by far the simplest and is used by most self-employed people who provide services and do not maintain inventory or offer credit. The accrual method can be difficult to use because there are complex rules to determine when income or expenses are accrued. The accrual method is used by businesses that provide for credit sales or maintain an inventory.

It's Not So Easy to Change Your Mind

You choose your accounting method by checking a box on your tax form when you file your tax return. Once you choose a method, you can't change it without getting permission from the IRS. You must file IRS Form 3115, Application for Change in Accounting Method, 180 days before the end of the year in which you want to make the change. Changing your accounting method can have serious consequences, so consult a tax pro before filing this form.

2. Tax Years

You are required to pay taxes for a 12-month period, also known as the tax year. Sole proprietors, partnerships, limited liability companies, S corporations and personal service corporations (see Chapter 2) are required to use the calendar year as their tax years—that is, January 1 through December 31.

However, there are exceptions that permit some small businesses to use a tax year that does not end in December, also known as a fiscal year. You need to get the IRS's permission to use a fiscal year. The IRS doesn't like businesses to use fiscal years, but it might grant you permission if you can show a good business reason for it.

One good reason to use a fiscal year is that your business is seasonal. For example, if you earn most of your income in the spring and incur most of your expenses in the fall, a tax year ending in July or August might be better than a calendar tax year ending in December because the income and expenses on each tax return will be more closely related. To get permission, you must file IRS Form 8716, Election to Have a Tax Year Other Than a Required Tax Year. ■

Safeguarding Your Self-Employed Status

The IRS and many other government agencies would prefer you to be an employee rather than a self-employed person. This chapter shows you how to avoid being viewed as an employee by the powers that be.

The term generally used to describe self-employed people for tax purposes is independent contractor. Independent contractor is therefore used to identify the self-employed throughout this chapter.

A. Who Decides Your Work Status?

Initially, it's up to you and each hiring firm you deal with to decide whether you should be classified as an independent contractor or employee. But the decision about how you should be classified is subject to review by various government agencies, including:

- the IRS
- your state's tax department
- your state's unemployment compensation insurance agency
- your state's workers' compensation insurance agency, and
- the United States Labor Department and National Labor Relations Board.

The IRS considers worker misclassification to be a serious problem costing the U.S. government billions of dollars in taxes that would otherwise be paid if the workers involved were classified as employees and taxes were automatically withheld from their paychecks. Most state agencies live by the same theory.

The IRS or your state tax department might question your status in a routine audit of your tax returns. More commonly, however, you'll come to the government's attention if it investigates the classification practices of a firm that hired you. Government auditors may question you and examine your records and the hiring firm's records, too. Because the rules for determining whether you're an independent contractor or employee are rather vague and subjective, it's often easy for the government to claim that you're an employee even though both you and the hiring firm sincerely believed you qualified as an independent contractor. (See Section D.)

B. If the Government Reclassifies You

If you're like most independent contractors, you probably think that a government agency determination that one or more of your clients should classify you as an employee is solely the client's problem. Unfortunately, this is not the case. What's bad for your clients can also be very bad for you.

If the IRS or another government agency audits you or a hiring firm you've worked for and determines that you should have been classified as an employee instead of an independent contractor, it can and probably will impose assessments and penalties on the firm. Some companies have gone bankrupt because of such assessments.

Rest assured that the government will not penalize or fine you if you've been misclassified as an independent contractor. However, this does not mean being reclassified as an employee won't adversely affect you. For example, the hiring firm may dispense with your services because it doesn't want to pay the additional expenses involved in treating you as an employee. It is not unusual for IRS settlement agreements with hiring firms to require that the firms terminate contracts with independent contractors—with no input from the independent contractors. Or the hiring firm may insist on reducing your compensation to make up for the extra employee expenses. But even if none of these things happen, it's likely you'll be treated very differently on the job. For example, the hiring firm—now your employer—will probably expect you to follow its orders and may attempt to restrict you from working for other companies.

WORKER GETS THE AX WHEN THE IRS CALLS

Dave, a financial analyst, was hired by a large New York bank and classified as an independent contractor for IRS purposes. He signed an independent contractor agreement and submitted invoices to the bank's accounting department to be paid. The bank withheld no taxes from his pay, paid no Social Security or Medicare taxes for him and provided him with no employee benefits.

However, Dave was otherwise treated largely as an employee. He worked on a team along with regular bank employees and shared their supervisor. He performed the same functions as the employees and worked the same core hours. Because the bank required him to work at its headquarters, he received an admittance card key, office equipment and supplies from the bank.

Dave's happy worklife changed abruptly when the IRS notified the bank that it wanted to examine its employment records to determine whether the company was complying with the tax laws. Fearing that it should have classified Dave as an employee instead of an independent contractor, the bank summarily fired him in the hope this would lessen potential problems with IRS auditors. It didn't work. The bank was required to reclassify Dave as an employee for the two years he had worked for it. Dave was entitled to a refund of half his Social Security and Medicare taxes for those years and was able to collect unemployment benefits, but he was still out of a job.

1. Tax Consequences

An IRS determination that you should be classified as an employee can also have adverse tax consequences for you. You will have to file amended tax returns for the years involved. On the plus side, you'll be entitled to claim a refund for half the self-employment taxes you paid on the compensation you received as a misclassified independent contractor.

But you might lose valuable business deductions because business expenses, such as home offices and health insurance premiums, are either not deductible or limited for employees. You'll end up owing more taxes if the value of these lost deductions exceeds the amount of your self-employment tax refund. Your employer will also have to start withholding your income and Social Security taxes from your pay.

From a tax perspective, however, by far the worst thing that can happen to you if you're reclassified as an employee by the IRS is that your Keogh retirement plan will lose its tax-qualified status. Of course, if you don't have a Keogh plan, you will not be affected by this threat.

Generally, in a Keogh plan, your contributions are tax deductible and you don't pay any tax on the interest your investment earns until you retire. (See Chapter 16.) But if your Keogh is disqualified, you'll have to pay tax on your contributions and on the interest you've earned from your investments. If you have a substantial amount invested in a Keogh plan, you could face a staggering tax bill.

2. Qualifying for Employee Benefits

One good thing that can happen if you're reclassified as an employee is that you may qualify for benefits your employer gives to its other employees, such as health insurance, pension benefits and unemployment insurance.

If you've incurred out-of-pocket expenses for medical care, you may be entitled to be reimbursed. However, these benefits may be short-lived if the hiring firm decides it can't afford to keep you on as an employee.

IRS AUDIT RUINS INDEPENDENT CONTRACTOR'S LIFE

John, a New Hampshire-based narrator of corporate videos and TV commercials, thought he was an independent contractor. He was characterized as one by hundreds of clients, for whom he usually worked for only a few hours or days.

However, when the IRS audited him, it determined that he was really his clients' temporary employee because he worked on the clients' premises and some of his clients paid his union dues. When John told his clients that they had to classify him as an employee, issue a W-2 and pay payroll taxes, some of them told him they couldn't afford to hire him any more because of the added expense.

In addition, John had to refile his tax returns for the years in question and recharacterize the compensation he received as wages instead of self-employment income. John was entitled to a refund for half of the self-employment taxes he paid on this compensation. But he lost some substantial business deductions—for example, a $10,000 deduction he took in one year for mileage and auto expenses. The loss of these deductions more than outweighed the refund of self-employment taxes. The net result of being an employee for John is that he lost work for future years and had to pay more taxes for past years.

C. Determining Worker Status

Various government agencies and courts use slightly different tests to determine how workers should be classified. Unfortunately, these tests are confusing, subjective and often don't lead to a conclusive answer about whether you're an independent contractor or employee. This is why some hiring firms are afraid to hire independent contractors.

This section provides an overview of the most important test for independent contractor status. However, it's practically impossible for anyone to learn and follow all the different tests various government agencies use to determine worker status. You'll be better off simply following the guidelines for preserving your independent contractor status. (See Section E.)

Most, but not all, government agencies use the right of control test to determine whether you're an employee or independent contractor. You're an employee under this test if a hiring firm has the right to direct and control how you work—both as to the final results and as to the details of when, where and how you perform the work.

The employer may not always exercise this right—for example, if you're experienced and well trained, your employer may not feel the need to closely supervise you. But if the employer has the right to do so, you're still considered an employee.

> **EXAMPLE:** Mary takes a job as a hamburger cook at the local AcmeBurger. AcmeBurger personnel carefully train her in how to make an AcmeBurger hamburger—including the type and amount of ingredients to use, the temperature at which the hamburger should be cooked and so forth.

Once Mary starts work, AcmeBurger managers closely supervise how she does her job. Virtually every aspect of Mary's behavior on the job is under AcmeBurger control—including what time she arrives at and leaves work, when she takes her lunch break, what she wears and the sequence of the tasks she must perform. If Mary proves to be an able and conscientious worker, her supervisors may not look over her shoulder very often. But they have the right to do so at any time. Mary is AcmeBurger's employee.

In contrast, you're an independent contractor if the hiring firm does not have the right to control how you do the job. Because you're an independent businessperson not solely dependent on the firm for your livelihood, its control is limited to accepting or rejecting the final results you achieve. Or if a project is broken down into stages or phases, the firm's input is limited to approving the work you perform at each stage. Unlike an employee, you are not supervised daily.

> **EXAMPLE:** AcmeBurger develops a serious plumbing problem. AcmeBurger does not have any plumbers on its staff, so it hires Plumbing by Jake, an independent plumbing repair business owned by Jake. Jake looks at the problem and gives an estimate of how much it will cost to fix. The manager agrees to hire him, and Jake and his assistant commence work.
>
> Because Jake is clearly running his own business, it's virtually certain that AcmeBurger does not have the right to control the way Jake performs his plumbing services. Its control is limited to accepting or rejecting the final result. If AcmeBurger doesn't like the work Jake has done, it can refuse to pay him. Jake is an independent contractor.

It can be difficult to figure out whether a hiring firm has the right to control you. Government auditors can't look into your mind to see if you are controlled by a hiring firm. They have to rely instead on indirect or circumstantial evidence indicating control or lack of it—for example, whether a hiring firm provides you with tools and equipment, where you do the work, how you're paid and whether you can be fired.

The factors each agency relies upon to measure control vary. Some agencies look at 14 factors to see if you're an employee or independent contractor; some look at 11; some consider only three. Which of these factors is of the greatest or least importance is anyone's guess. This can make it very difficult to know whether you pass muster as an independent contractor.

D. IRS Approach to Worker Status

The IRS uses the right of control test to determine whether you're an independent contractor or employee for tax purposes. The agency developed a list of 20 factors its auditors were supposed to use to measure how much control a hiring firm had over you. This test has become very well known—discussed in countless magazine and journal articles, posted all over the Internet and practically memorized by many independent contractors. Many of your prospective clients will be aware of the test and may even ask you about it.

Special IRS Rules for Some Workers
If you're a licensed real estate agent, direct seller, business-to-business salesperson, home worker who makes clothing items, full-time life insurance salesperson or driver who distributes food products, beverages or laundry, your status may be predetermined for IRS purposes under special rules. (See Chapter 12.)

It's important to understand, however, that the 20 Factor Test is only an analytical tool IRS auditors use to measure control. It is not the legal test the IRS uses for determining worker status. IRS auditors have never been restricted to considering only the 20 factors on the test, nor are they required to consider them all.

Unfortunately, the 20 Factor Test left much to be desired as an analytical tool. It proved to be so subjective and complex that trying to apply it was often a waste of time. Even the IRS found it difficult to apply the test consistently. People performing the same services have been found to be employees in some IRS districts and independent contractors in others. In one case, for example, a Methodist minister was found to be an employee of his church; a Pentecostal pastor was found to be an independent contractor in another case the same year. (*Weber vs. Commissioner*, 103 TC 378 (1994); *Shelley v. Commissioner*, TCM 1994-432 (1994).)

Hiring firms, independent contractors, attorneys and tax experts complained bitterly for years that it was impossible to know who was and was not an independent contractor under the 20 Factor Test, and that aggressive IRS auditors took advantage of this confusion by classifying every worker as an employee. Legislation was introduced in Congress to clarify the issue by establishing a simple test for determining worker status—a test that would probably have led to far more workers qualifying as independent contractors than under current law.

In an obvious attempt to block such legislation and to set the rules itself, the IRS issued a training manual for its auditors in 1996, setting forth a somewhat simpler approach to measure control. It should be easier for you to qualify as an independent contractor for IRS purposes under this manual than under the 20 Factor Test. Although the manual doesn't have the force of law, IRS auditors are supposed to follow it.

The manual provides the best guidance the IRS has ever made public on how to classify workers. Even more important, it evinces a much kinder, gentler attitude by the IRS on worker classification issues. Declaring that classifying a worker as an independent contractor instead of an employee "can be a valid and appropriate business choice," the manual admonishes IRS auditors to "approach the issue of worker classification in a fair and impartial manner."

 You can download a free copy of the IRS manual from the IRS website at www.irs.gov/pub/irs-utl/emporind.pdf. Or you can request a copy by calling the IRS at 800-TAX-FORM.

1. How the IRS Measures Control

IRS auditors look at three areas to determine whether a hiring firm has the right to control a worker. These are:

- your behavior on the job
- your finances, and
- your relationship with the hiring firm.

The following chart shows the primary factors the IRS looks at for each area.

The IRS test is not a model of clarity. There is no guidance on how important each factor is and how many factors must weigh in favor of independent contractor status for you to be classified as an independent contractor. The IRS says there is no magic number of factors. Rather, the factors showing lack of control must outweigh those that indicate control. No one factor alone is enough to make you an employee or an independent contractor.

To make your life easier, this chapter offers you a list of eight guidelines for you to follow during your worklife. If you do, it's likely that you will be viewed as an independent contractor by the IRS and any other government agency.

IRS TEST FOR WORKER STATUS

Behavioral Control Factors showing whether a hiring firm has the right to control how you perform the specific tasks you've been hired to do.	**You will more likely be considered self-employed if you:** • are not given instructions by the hiring firm • provide your own training	**You will more likely be considered an employee if you:** • receive instructions you must follow about how to do your work • receive detailed training from the hiring firm
Financial Control Factors showing whether a hiring firm has a right to control your financial life.	**You will more likely be considered self-employed if you:** • have a significant investment in equipment and facilities • pay business or travel expenses yourself • make your services available to the public • are paid by the job • have opportunity for profit or loss	**You will more likely be considered an employee if you:** • have equipment and facilities provide by the hiring firm free of charge • have your business or traveling expenses reimbursed • make no effort to market your services to the public • are paid by the hour or other unit of time • have no opportunity for profit or loss—for example, because you're paid by the hour and have all expenses reimbursed
Relationship Between Worker and Hiring Firm Factors showing whether you and the hiring firm believe you're self-employed or an employee	**You will more likely be considered self-employed if you:** • don't receive employee benefits such as health insurance • sign a client agreement with the hiring firm • can't quit or be fired at will • are performing services that are not a regular part of the hiring firm's regular business activities	**You will more likely be considered an employee if you:** • receive employee benefits • have no written client agreement • can quit at any time without incurring any liability to the hiring firm • can be fired at any time • are performing services that are part of the hiring firm's core business

a. Payment by the hour

If you want to be classified as an independent contractor, it's better not to be paid an hourly wage unless it's a common practice in your line of business. The IRS recognizes that some ICs—lawyers, for example—are usually paid by the hour.

b. Expenses

Paying business expenses yourself rather than getting reimbursed by your client will help establish your IC status. It really makes no difference what the expense is, as long as it's for your business. It can be office rent, equipment, salaries, travel expenses, telephone bills, photocopying charges or anything else.

Although not fatal, any expense that your client reimburses you for will not help establish your IC status—and it could actually impair your effort (and your client's efforts) to prove that you are not an employee of the client.

c. Advertising

Failure to offer your services to the public is a sign of employee status. In the past, the IRS usually only considered advertising in telephone books and newspapers as evidence that an independent contractor offered services to the public. Of course, many independent contractors don't get business this way; they rely primarily on word of mouth. The IRS now recognizes this fact of life and doesn't consider advertising essential for proving independent contractor status.

d. Form of direction

The IRS makes a distinction between receiving instructions on how to work—a very strong indicator of employee status—and being given suggestions. A suggestion about how work is to be performed does not constitute the right to control. However, if you must comply with suggestions or you would suffer adverse consequences if you didn't comply, (such as being fired or not assigned more work), then the suggestions are, in fact, instructions.

e. Training

Periodic or ongoing training about how to do your work is strong evidence of an employment relationship. However, a client may provide you with a short orientation or information session about the company's policies, new product line or new government regulations without jeopardizing your independent contractor status. Training programs that are voluntary and that you attend without receiving pay do not disqualify you from being classified as an independent contractor.

f. Investment

A significant investment in equipment and facilities is not necessary for independent contractor status. The manual notes that some types of work simply do not require expensive equipment—for example, writing and certain types of consulting. But even if expensive equipment is needed to do a particular type of work, an independent contractor can always rent it.

g. Performing key services

One of the most important factors IRS auditors look at is whether the services performed by a worker are key to the hiring firm's regular business. The IRS figures that if the services you perform are vital to a company's regular business, the company will be more likely to control how you perform. For example, a law firm is less likely to supervise and control a painter it hires to paint its offices than a paralegal it hires to work on its regular legal business.

However, IRS auditors are required to examine all the facts and circumstances. For example, a paralegal hired by a law firm could very well be an independent contractor if he or she was a specialist hired to help with especially difficult or unusual legal work.

Written Agreements Are More Important Than Ever

A written independent contractor agreement can never make you an independent contractor by itself. However, if the evidence is so evenly balanced that it is difficult or impossible for an IRS auditor to decide whether you're an independent contractor or employee, the existence of a written independent contractor agreement can tip the balance in favor of independent contractor status. This makes using written independent contractor agreements more important than ever before. (See Chapter 18.)

h. Full-time work

Working full time for a single client should not by itself make you an employee in the eyes of the IRS. Nevertheless, it is never helpful to your IC status to work for just one client at a time. There may be many situations where it can't be avoided; for example, if you can't get any other work at the time or if the nature of the work you are doing for the client demands your full time and attention. Still, you should attempt to keep the period of exclusivity down to a minimum—no more than six months to a year. Performing the same services full-time for the same client year after year inevitably makes you look like an employee of that client.

i. Long-term work for a single client

Performing services for the same client year after year used to be seen as a sign you were an employee. No longer. The IRS now recognizes that independent contractors may work for a client on a long-term basis, either because they sign long-term contracts or because their contracts are regularly renewed by the client because they do a good job or price their services reasonably, or because no one else is readily available to do the work.

j. Time and place of work

It is not important to the IRS where or when you work. For example, the fact that you work at a client's offices during regular business hours is not considered evidence of employee status. On the other hand, the fact that you work at home at hours of your own choosing is not strong evidence that you're an independent contractor either, since many employees now work at home as well.

2. Rules for Technical Services Workers

If you're a computer programmer, systems analyst, engineer or provide similar technical services and obtain work through brokers, special tax rules may make it very difficult for you to work as an independent contractor even if you may qualify as one under the IRS test.

Most hiring firms can rely on a defense, found in Section 530 of the Tax Code, if the IRS claims they misclassified workers. By using Section 530, an employer who misclassifies a worker as an independent contractor can avoid paying any fines or penalties for failing to pay employment taxes if it can show it had a reasonable basis for treating the worker as an independent contractor. Section 530 has made hiring firms' lives a little easier by giving them an additional defense against the IRS.

However, another part of the tax code (Section 1706) provides that the Section 530 defense may not be used by brokers that contract to provide their clients with:

- engineers
- designers
- drafters
- computer programmers
- systems analysts, or
- other skilled workers in similar technical occupations.

Section 1706 doesn't make anyone an employee. But it does make it harder for brokers to avoid paying assessments and penalties if the IRS claims they've misclassified a technical services worker as an independent contractor. Because of Section 1706, brokers who contract to provide companies with technical services workers usually classify the workers as their employees and issue them W-2s. One result of this is that you'll likely receive less pay from the broker than if you were classified an independent contractor because it has to pay payroll taxes for you and provide workers' compensation.

Some brokers may make an exception and treat you as an independent contractor if you are clearly running an independent business—for example, you deal directly with many clients and are incorporated. For example, one Silicon Valley software tester occasionally obtains work through brokers and is never classified as an employee of the broker. Brokers feel safe treating her as an independent contractor because she has incorporated her business, has employees and has many clients, including several Fortune 500 companies. The brokers sign a contract with the tester's corporation, not with her personally.

Section 1706 has no application at all if you contract directly with a client instead of going through a broker. But many high tech firms are still wary of hiring independent contractors.

E. Preserving Your Status

If you consistently follow the guidelines discussed below, it's likely that any government agency or court would determine that you qualify as an independent contractor. However, there are no guarantees.

Some of these guidelines may be a bit more strict than those now followed by the IRS. This is because not all government agencies follow the IRS standards. Various state agencies, such as state tax departments and unemployment compensation and workers' compensation agencies, may have

tougher classification standards than the IRS. This means you can't rely solely on the IRS rules.

EXAMPLE: Debbi, an independent contractor accountant based in Rhode Island, clearly qualifies as an independent contractor under the IRS test. However, very restrictive Rhode Island employment laws require that she be classified as an employee for state purposes if she performs services for other accounting firms. This means they must withhold state income taxes from her pay, pay unemployment taxes and provide her with workers' compensation insurance. In addition, if Debbi has employees of her own, they may become the firm's employees as well under Rhode Island law.

Some hiring firms are terrified of government audits and are very nervous about hiring independent contractors. Companies that have had problems with government audits in the past or are in industries that are targeted by government auditors are likely to be especially skittish. Recent targets include trucking firms, courier services, securities dealers, high technology firms, nurse registries, building contractors and manufacturer representatives. Such hiring firms may be more willing to hire you as an independent contractor if you can show that you follow the guidelines. Document your efforts and be ready to show the documentation to nervous clients.

Many other companies don't give government audits a second thought and are more than happy to classify you as an independent contractor and save the money and headaches involved in treating you as an employee. These companies may not worry whether you qualify as an independent contractor, but you should. You could still end up getting fired, taking a pay cut or having to pay extra taxes if some government bureaucrat decides you're really an employee. So even though your client may not appreciate your efforts, continue to follow the guidelines discussed here; both you and your client will be glad you did if the government comes calling.

1. Retain Control of Your Work

The most fundamental difference between employees and independent contractors is that employers have the right to tell their employees what to do. (See Section D.) Never permit a hiring firm to supervise or control you as it does its employees. It's perfectly all right for the hiring firm to give you detailed guidelines or specifications for the results you're to achieve. But how you go about achieving those results should be entirely up to you.

A few guidelines will help emphasize that you are the one who is responsible.

- Do not ask for or accept instructions or orders from the hiring firm about how to do your job. For example, you should decide what equipment or tools to use, where to purchase supplies or services, who will perform what tasks and what routines or work patterns must be used. It's fine for a hiring firm to give you suggestions about these things, but you must always preserve your right to accept or reject such suggestions.
- Do not ask for or receive training on how to do your work from a hiring firm. If you need additional training, seek it elsewhere.
- A hiring firm may give you a deadline for when your work should be completed, but you should generally establish your own working hours. For example, if you want, you could work 20 hours two days a week and take the rest of the week off. In some cases, however, it may be necessary to coordinate your working hours with the client's schedule—for example, where you must perform work on the client's premises or work with its employees.
- Decide on your own where to perform the work—that is, a client should not require you to work at a particular location. Of course, some services must be performed at a client's premises or other particular place.
- Decide whether to hire assistants to help you and, if you do, pay and supervise them

yourself. Only you should have the right to fire your assistants.
- Do not attend regular employee meetings or functions such as employee picnics.
- Avoid providing frequent formal written reports about the progress of your work—for example, daily phone calls to the client. It is permissible, however, to give reports when you complete various stages of a project.
- Do not obtain, read or pay any attention to a hiring firm's employee manuals or other rules for employees. The rules governing your relationship with the hiring firm are contained solely in your independent contractor agreement, whether written or oral. (See Chapter 18.)

If you work outside the client's premises, it's usually not difficult to avoid being controlled. Neither the client nor its employees will have much opportunity to try to supervise you. For example, Katherine, a freelance legal writer, never has any problems being controlled by a large legal publisher for whom she performs freelance assignments. She says anonymity on the job helps with this: "I get my freelance assignments by phone, do all the work at home and in the local law library and then transmit the project from my computer to the publisher by modem. I've hardly ever been in the publisher's office."

On the other hand, you could have problems if you work in a client's workplace. The client's supervisors or managers may try to treat you as if you were an employee. Before you start work, make clear to the client that you do not fall within its regular personnel hierarchy; you are an outsider. You might ask the client to designate one person with whom you will deal. If anyone in the company gives you problems, you can explain that you deal only with your contact person and refer the person to your contact.

Note, however, that it's fine for a client to require you to comply with government regulations about how to perform your services. For example, a client may require a construction contractor to comply with municipal building codes that impose detailed rules on how a building is constructed. The IRS and other government agencies would not likely consider this to be an exercise of control over the contractor by the client.

2. Show Opportunities for Profit or Loss

Because they are in business for themselves, independent contractors have the opportunity to earn profits or suffer losses. If you have absolutely no risk of loss, you're probably not an independent contractor.

a. Business expenses

The best way to show an opportunity to realize profit or loss is to have recurring business expenses. If receipts do not match expenses, you lose money and may go into debt. If receipts exceed expenses, you earn a profit.

Good examples of independent contractor expenses include:

- salaries for assistants
- travel and other similar expenses incurred in performing your services
- substantial investment in equipment and materials
- rent for an office or workplace
- training and educational expenses
- advertising
- licensing, certification and professional dues
- insurance
- leasing of equipment
- supplies, and
- repairs and maintenance of business equipment.

Don't go out and buy things you don't really need. But if you've been thinking about buying equipment or supplies to use in your business, go ahead and take the plunge. You'll not only solidify your independent contractor status, but you'll get a tax deduction as well. (See Chapter 9.)

In addition, it's best that you don't ask clients to reimburse you for expenses such as travel, photocopying and postage. It's a better practice to bill clients enough for your services to pay for these items yourself. Setting your compensation at a level that covers your expenses also frees you from having to keep records of your expenses. Keeping track of the cost of every phone call or photocopy you make for a client can be a real chore and may be more trouble than it's worth.

b. Get paid by the project

Another excellent way to show opportunity for profit or loss is to be paid an agreed price for a specific project, rather than to bill by unit of time, such as by the hour. If the project price is higher than the expenses, you'll make money; if not, you'll lose money. However, this form of billing is too risky for many independent contractors.

Many independent contractors—for example, attorneys and accountants—are typically paid by the hour. If hourly payment is customary in your field, this factor should not affect your independent contractor status.

3. Look Like an Independent Business

Take steps to make yourself look like an independent business person. There are several things you can do to cultivate this image.

- Don't obtain employee-type benefits from your clients, such as health insurance, paid vacation, sick days, pension benefits or life or disability insurance; instead, charge your clients enough to purchase these items yourself.
- Incorporate your business or form an LLC instead of operating as a sole proprietor. (See Chapter 2.)
- Obtain a fictitious business name instead of using your own name for your business. (See Chapter 3.)
- Obtain all necessary business licenses and permits. (See Chapter 5.)

- Obtain business insurance. (See Chapter 6.)
- Maintain a separate bank account for your business. (See Chapter 14.)

You may have an easier time getting work if you do these things. For example, a large corporation that regularly used the services of one independent contractor asked her to incorporate or at least obtain a business license because it was worried she might otherwise be viewed as the company's employee.

4. Work Outside Hiring Firms' Premises

The IRS no longer considers working at a hiring firm's place of business to be an important factor in determining whether a worker is an independent contractor or employee, but many state agencies still do. For example, in half the states you may be considered an employee for unemployment compensation purposes if you work at the hiring firm's place of business or another place it designates.

Working at a location specified by a hiring firm implies that the firm has control, especially if the work could be done elsewhere. If you work at a hiring firm's place of business, you're physically within the firm's direction and supervision. If you can choose to work off the premises, the firm obviously has less control.

Unless the nature of the services you're performing requires it, don't work at the hiring firm's office or other business premises. An independent contractor hired to lay a carpet or paint an office must obviously work at the hiring firm's premises. But if your work can be done anywhere, do it outside the client's premises.

Working at a home office will not show you're an independent contractor as far as the IRS is concerned since many employees are now doing so. Renting an office outside your home definitely will show independent contractor status. This really shows you're operating your own business and gives you a recurring business expense to help establish risk of loss.

5. Make Your Services Widely Available

Independent contractors normally offer their services to the general public, not just to one person or entity. The IRS recognizes that many independent contractors rely on word of mouth to get clients and don't do any active marketing. (See Section E1.) However, nervous clients and other government auditors will be impressed if you market your services to the public.

There are many relatively inexpensive ways you can do so—for example:

- obtain a business card and stationery
- hang out a shingle in front of your home or office, advertising your services
- maintain listings in business and telephone directories
- attend trade shows and similar events
- join professional organizations
- advertise in newspapers, trade journals and magazines
- mail brochures or other promotional materials to prospective clients, and
- phone potential clients to drum up business.

Keep copies of advertisements, promotional materials and similar items to show prospective clients and government auditors.

6. Have Multiple Clients

IRS guidelines provide that you can work full time for a single client on a long-term basis and still be an independent contractor. (See Section D.) Nevertheless, having multiple clients shows that you're running an independent business because you are not dependent on any one firm for your livelihood. Some potential clients may be afraid to hire you as an independent contractor unless you perform services for others besides them.

It's best to have more than one client at a time. Government auditors will rarely question the status of an independent contractor who works for three or four clients simultaneously. However, the nature of your work may require that you work full time for one client at a time. In this event, at least try to work for more than one client over the course of a year—for example, work full time for one client for six months and full time for another client for the other six months.

Having multiple clients also gives you increased economic security. One independent contractor thinks of herself as an eight-legged spider, with each client a separate leg. If she loses one client, things are still economically stable because she has her other legs to stand on.

If you seem to be locked into having just one client, you may be able to drum up new business by offering special rates for small jobs you would otherwise lose.

⚠ Don't Sign Noncompetition Agreements
Some clients may ask or require you to sign noncompetition agreements restricting your ability to work for the client's competitors while working for the client, afterwards or both. You should avoid such restrictions. Not only will they make you look like an employee, they may also make it impossible for you to earn a living.

7. Use Written Agreements

Use written independent contractor agreements for all but the briefest, smallest projects. Among other things, the agreement should make clear that you are an independent contractor and the hiring firm does not have the right to control the way you work. A written agreement won't make you an independent contractor by itself, but it is helpful—particularly if you draft it yourself.

Also, don't accept new projects after the original project is completed without signing a new independent contractor agreement. You can easily be converted from an independent contractor to an employee if you perform assignment after assignment for a client without negotiating new contracts. (See Chapters 18 and 19 for more about written agreements.)

8. Avoid Accepting Employee Status

Some clients will refuse to hire you as an independent contractor and insist on classifying you as an employee. This is a particularly common problem for independent contractors who work for high technology companies. Because the government closely scrutinizes such firms' hiring practices and because of special IRS rules, high tech companies are often wary of using independent contractors. (See Section D2.)

Some companies may hire you themselves as an employee. Others may insist that you contract with a broker or employment agency who treats you as its employee. The firm then hires you through the broker.

It's best to avoid performing the exact same services as an independent contractor and employee because:

- being classified as both an independent contractor and employee on your tax returns may make an IRS audit more likely
- it could lead government auditors to conclude you're an employee for all purposes
- you'll generally be paid less than if you were an independent contractor because the hiring firm or broker will have to provide you with workers' compensation and unemployment insurance; on the plus side, however, you may be able to collect unemployment when your services end
- you may not be able to deduct unreimbursed expenses incurred while you were an employee or the deductions may be limited (see Chapter 9), and
- you can't apply your employee income to your independent contractor business to help it show a profit; if your business keeps showing losses, the IRS might conclude it's a hobby and disallow your business deductions. (See Chapter 9.) ■

Retirement Options for the Self-Employed

When you're self-employed, you don't have an employer to provide you with a pension. It's up to you to establish and fund your own pension plan to supplement any Social Security benefits you'll receive. This chapter provides an overview of the main retirement options for the self-employed.

This chapter is not a guide about where to invest your money. There are hundreds of investment choices—including stocks, bonds, mutual funds, money market accounts and certificates of deposit. And there are a seemingly equal number of books, magazines, websites and other resources devoted to investment strategy.

Deciding how to invest your money is not the first decision you must make when planning for your retirement. Rather, you must first decide what type of retirement account or accounts to establish. There are several types of accounts specifically designed for the self-employed that provide terrific tax benefits. These will help you save for retirement and may reduce your tax burden when you do retire.

Choosing what type of account to establish is just as important as deciding what to invest in once you open your account, if not more so. Once you establish your account, you can always change your investments with little or no difficulty. But changing the type of accounts you have may prove difficult and costly.

The purpose of this chapter is to give you a very general understanding of the retirement options that you have as a self-employed person. For a thorough discussion of retirement planning for self-employed people, including information on how to choose, establish and administer a retirement plan or plans on your own, see *Creating Your Own Retirement Plan: IRAs and Keoghs for the Self-Employed*, by Twila Slesnick and John Suttle (Nolo). Two easy-to-understand guides on retirement investing are:

- *Get a Life: You Don't Need a Million to Retire Well*, by Ralph Warner (Nolo), and
- *Investing for Dummies*, by Eric Tyson (IDG Books)

For additional information on the tax aspects of retirement, see:
- IRS Publication 560, *Retirement Plans for the Small Business*, and
- IRS Publication 590, *Individual Retirement Accounts*.

You can obtain these and all other IRS publications by calling the IRS at 800-TAX-FORM, visiting your local IRS office or downloading the publications from the IRS Internet site at: www.irs.gov.

A. Reasons to Have a Retirement Plan(s)

In all likelihood, you will receive Social Security benefits when you retire. However, Social Security will probably provide you with no more than half of your needs when you retire, possibly less depending upon your retirement lifestyle. You'll need to make up the shortfall with your own retirement investments.

Luckily, when it comes to saving for retirement, the self-employed are actually better off than most employees. This is because the federal government allows you to set up retirement accounts specifically designed for small business people that provide some terrific income tax benefits. These include SIMPLE IRAs, SEP-IRAs and Keogh Plans.

You can establish such accounts through a bank, savings and loan, credit union, insurance company, brokerage house, mutual fund company or other financial institution.

Retirement accounts are simply shells that protect you from being taxed by the government. After deciding what type of account you want you must then decide what to invest in. You can invest in almost anything—for example, stocks, bonds, mutual funds, money market funds or certificates of deposit. You can transfer your money from one type of investment to another within your account as market conditions change.

These accounts provide you with two enormous tax benefits:

- you pay no taxes on the income your retirement investments earn until you withdraw the funds upon retirement, and
- you can deduct the amount you contribute to your retirement account from your income taxes for the year, subject to certain limits.

1. Tax Deferral

The money you earn on an investment is ordinarily taxed in the year you earn it. For example, you must pay taxes on the interest you earn on a savings account or certificate of deposit when that interest accrues. When you sell an investment at a profit, you must pay income tax on this amount as well—for example, you must pay tax on the profit you earn from selling stock.

But this is not the case when you invest in a tax-qualified retirement account such as an IRA, SEP-IRA or Keogh plan. The money your investment earns is not taxable to you until you withdraw the funds when you retire—when you will usually be in a lower income tax bracket than you were during your working years.

You're not supposed to make withdrawals until you reach age 59-1/2, subject to certain exceptions. If you make early withdrawals, you must ordinarily pay regular income tax on the amount you take out, plus a 10% federal tax penalty.

2. Tax Deduction

Avoiding income tax on your retirement investments until you retire is a good deal in and of itself. But there is an additional outstanding tax benefit to retirement accounts: You can usually deduct the amount you contribute to your retirement account from your income taxes for the year. This can give you a substantial income tax saving.

EXAMPLE: Art, a self-employed sole proprietor, establishes a retirement account at his local bank and contributes $10,000 this year. He can deduct the entire amount from his income taxes. Since Art is in the 27% tax bracket, he saves $2,700 in income taxes for the year (27% x $10,000) and has saved $10,000 toward his retirement.

How much you can contribute each year depends on what type of account you establish and how much money you earn. However, you usually won't be able to make any contributions if you have a loss from your business. You must have self-employment income to fund these retirement accounts.

The combination of tax deferral and a current tax deduction makes a huge difference in how much you'll save for retirement. The following chart shows the difference in growth between a tax-deferred and a taxable account over 30 years.

HOW MUCH MONEY WILL YOU NEED WHEN YOU RETIRE?

How much money you'll need when you retire depends on many factors, including your lifestyle. You could need anywhere from 50% to 100% of the amount you earned while employed. The average is about 70% to 80% of pre-retirement earnings. But this is only an average—your own needs and habits will determine how much you should sock away.

GROWTH OF A TAXABLE VS. TAX-DEFERRED ACCOUNT

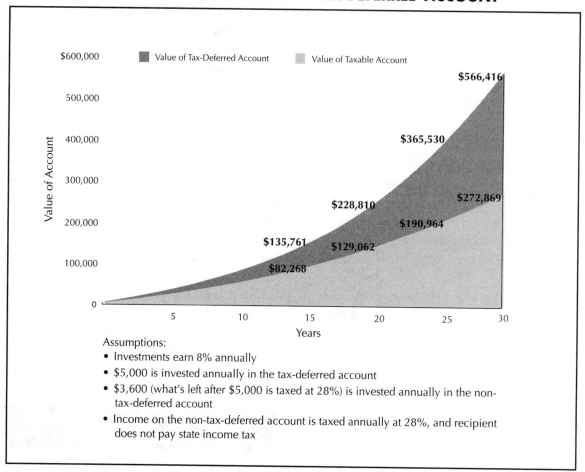

Assumptions:
- Investments earn 8% annually
- $5,000 is invested annually in the tax-deferred account
- $3,600 (what's left after $5,000 is taxed at 28%) is invested annually in the non-tax-deferred account
- Income on the non-tax-deferred account is taxed annually at 28%, and recipient does not pay state income tax

From *Get a Life: You Don't Need a Million to Retire Well,* By Ralph Warner (Nolo).

B. Individual IRAs

The simplest type of tax-deferred retirement account is the individual retirement account or IRA. If you can afford to invest no more than a few thousand dollars per year in a retirement plan, an IRA is a good choice. If you can contribute more than the IRA limit, you can establish an IRA *and* one or more of the employer IRAs or Keogh plans discussed below.

An IRA is a trust or custodial account set up for the benefit of an individual or his or her beneficiaries. The trustee or custodian administers the account. The trustee can be a bank, mutual fund, brokerage firm or other financial institution, such as an insurance company, which has been approved by the IRS. The custodian must meet strict IRS requirements regarding the safekeeping of your account.

IRAs are extremely easy to set up and administer. You need not file any special tax forms with the IRS. The financial institution you use to set up your account will ordinarily request that you complete IRS Form 5305, Individual Retirement Trust Account, which serves as a preapproved IRA agreement. Keep the form in your records.

Most financial institutions offer an array of IRA accounts that provide for different types of investments. You can invest your IRA money in just about anything—stocks, bonds, mutual funds, Treasury bills and notes and bank certificates of deposit. However, you can't invest in collectibles such as art, antiques, stamps or other personal property.

You have two different types of IRAs to choose from:

- traditional IRAs, and
- Roth IRAs.

You can have as many IRA accounts as you want. But there is a maximum amount you may contribute to all of your IRA accounts each year. This amount will keep going up every year as shown in the following chart:

ANNUAL IRA CONTRIBUTION LIMITS

Tax Year	Under Age 50	Aged 50 or Over
2002–2004	$3000	$3500
2005	$4000	$4500
2006–2007	$4000	$5000
2008 and later	$5000	$6000

After 2008, the limit will be adjusted each year for inflation in $500 increments.

In addition to these contribution limits, workers who are at least 50 years old at the end of the year may make increased annual contributions of $500 per year during 2002 through 2005, and $1,000 per year thereafter. This is intended to allow these older people catch up with younger folks who will have many more years to make contributions at the higher levels.

These contribution limits may be doubled if you're married—for example, a married couple in 2002–2004 could contribute up to $3,000 per spouse into their IRAs, for a total of $6,000.

This is so even if one spouse isn't working. But you must file a joint return, and the working spouse's earnings must be at least as much as the IRA contribution.

1. Traditional IRAs

Traditional IRAs have been around since 1974. The principal feature of these IRAs is that you can receive an income tax deduction for the amounts you contribute each year to your account, as long as you don't earn more than a set yearly limit. Thereafter, your earnings accumulate in the account tax free until you withdraw them.

The money in an IRA is not supposed to be withdrawn until you reach age 59-1/2, unless you die or become disabled. The amounts you withdraw are then included in your regular income for income tax purposes. You must begin withdrawing your money from your IRA by April 1 of the year after you turn 70.

As a general rule, if you make early withdrawals, you must pay regular income tax on the amount you take out plus a 10% federal tax penalty. There are some exceptions to this early withdrawal penalty, including when you withdraw money to purchase a first home or pay education expenses. To learn about these and other exceptions in detail, see *Creating Your Own Retirement Plan: IRAs and Keoghs for the Self-Employed*, by Twila Slesnick and John Suttle (Nolo).

2. Roth IRAs

Like traditional IRAs, Roth IRAs allow your retirement savings to grow tax free. The two prime ways in which a Roth is different from a contributory IRA are:

- contributions to Roths aren't tax deductible, and
- the distributions (money you take from the account) are tax free in most circumstances.

Unlike a traditional IRA, you can only establish a Roth IRA if your income is below a certain level. If you are single, your ability to make a contribution starts to phase out when your income reaches $95,000 and you are totally out of luck when your income reaches $110,000. If you are married and filing a joint return with your spouse, your ability to make a contribution starts to phase out at $150,000, and you are prohibited from making a contribution at $160,000. If you are married and filing a separate return from your spouse, the income limit is a low $10,000.

C. Employer IRAs

The two IRAs described above—traditional IRAs and Roth IRAs—are retirement accounts that you can set up for yourself as an individual. In addition to those accounts, you can also set up something called an employer IRA.

You don't have to have employees to establish these IRAs. You can have an employer IRA as long as you're in business and earn a profit—you don't need to have any employees working for you. It makes no difference how you organize your business: you can be a sole proprietor, partner in a partnership, member of a limited liability company or owner of a regular or S corporation. There are two kinds of employer IRAs: SEP-IRAs and SIMPLE IRAs. The great advantage of employer IRAs is that you can contribute more than the individual IRA contribution limits. And you can have them in addition to an individual IRA.

1. SEP-IRAs

SEP-IRAs are specifically designed for the self-employed. Any person who receives any self-employment income from providing a service can establish a SEP-IRA. It doesn't matter whether you work full-time or part-time. You can even have a SEP-IRA if you a covered by a retirement plan at a full-time employee job.

A SEP-IRA is a simplified employee pension. It's very similar to an IRA except that you can contribute much more money each year. Instead of being limited to a $3,000–$5,000 annual contribution (see the chart above), you can invest up to 13.04% of your net profit from self-employment every year—up to a maximum of $30,000 a year

(in 2002).You don't have to make contributions every year, and your contributions can vary from year to year. As with IRAs, the range of investments available is nearly limitless.

You can deduct your contributions to SEP-IRAs from your income taxes up to these limits. The interest on your SEP-IRA investments then accrues tax free until you withdraw the money upon retirement.

Withdrawals from SEP-IRAs are subject to the same rules that apply to IRAs. This means that if you withdraw your money from your SEP-IRA before you reach age 59½, you'll have to pay a 10% tax penalty plus regular income taxes on your withdrawal, unless an exception applies.

2. SIMPLE IRAs

Self-employed people and companies with fewer than 100 employees can set up SIMPLE IRAs. However, you are not allowed to have any other retirement plans for your business (although you may still have an individual IRA).

The money in a SIMPLE IRA can be invested like any other IRA. SIMPLE IRA contributions are divided into two parts. The first part is a salary reduction contribution. You can contribute up to a set amount each year—the contribution limit is $7,000 for 2002 and rises in $1,000 increments annually through 2005. Thereafter, it will be indexed to inflation and rise in $500 increments. You can add to this a matching contribution equal to 3% of your net income—but in no event more than your salary reduction contribution. Once the net income from your business exceeds about $30,000 you'll be able to make larger contributions to a SEP IRA or Keogh plan than to a SIMPLE IRA.

Withdrawals from SIMPLE IRAs are subject to the same rules as for individual IRAs with one big exception: Early withdrawals from SIMPLE IRAs are subject to a 25% tax penalty during the first two years if you are under 59½, and a 10% penalty after two years if you are still under 59½.

D. Keogh Plans

Keogh plans—named after the congressman who sponsored the legislation that created them—are just for self-employed people. Keoghs allow the self-employed to set aside more money for retirement than any other type of plan.

You can't have a Keogh if you incorporate your business. Keoghs require more paperwork to set up than employer IRAs, but they also offer more options: You can contribute more to them and still take an income tax deduction.

1. Types of Keogh Plans

There are two basic types of Keogh plans:
- defined contribution plans, in which benefits are based on the amount contributed to and accumulated in the plan, and
- defined benefit plans, which provide for a set benefit upon retirement.

There are two types of defined contribution plans: profit-sharing plans and money purchase plans. These plans can be used separately or in tandem with each other.

a. Profit-sharing plans

You may contribute up to 20% of your net self-employment income to a profit-sharing Keogh plan, up to a maximum of $40,000 per year. You can contribute any amount up to the limit each year, or not contribute at all.

b. Money purchase plans

In a money purchase plan, you contribute a fixed percentage of your net self-employment earnings every year. You decide how much to contribute each year. Make sure you will be able to afford the contributions each year because you can't skip them, even if your business earns no profit for the year. In return for giving up flexibility, you can contribute more to a money purchase plan—

25% of your net self-employment earnings, up to a maximum of $40,000 per year.

2. Setting Up a Keogh Plan

You must establish your Keogh plan by the end of your tax year—but you can wait until your tax return is due the following year to make contributions. Ordinarily, your return is due by April 15, but you may file a request for an extension until August 15. By doing so, you'll have three extra months to contribute to your plan.

If you wish, you can deposit a small advance to set up your account and then wait until you file your tax return to make your full contribution for the year.

As with individual IRAs and employer IRAs, you can set up a Keogh plan at most banks, brokerage houses, mutual funds and other financial institutions and trade or professional organizations. You'll have a huge array of investments to choose from.

To set up your plan, you must adopt a written Keogh plan and set up a trust or custodial account with your plan provider to invest your funds. Your plan provider will ordinarily have an IRS-approved master or prototype Keogh plan for you to sign. You can also have a special plan drawn up for you, but this is expensive and unnecessary for most self-employed people.

3. Withdrawing Your Money

You may begin to withdraw your money from your Keogh plan after you reach age 59½. If you have a profit-sharing plan, early withdrawals are permitted without penalty in cases of financial hardship, if you become disabled or to pay health expenses in excess of 7.5% of your adjusted gross income. If you have a money purchase plan, early withdrawals are permitted if you become disabled, leave your business after age 55 or make child-support or alimony payments from the plan under a court order. Otherwise, early withdrawals from profit-sharing and money purchase Keogh plans are subject to a 10% penalty.

E. If You Have Employees

If you work for yourself and have no employees, you can probably choose, establish and administer your own retirement plan with little or no assistance. The instant you add employees to the mix, however, virtually every aspect of your plan becomes more complex due primarily to nondiscrimination rules. These rules are designed to ensure that your retirement plan benefits all employees and not just you. In general, the laws prohibit you from doing the following:

- making disproportionately large contributions for some plan participants like yourself) and not for others,
- unfairly excluding certain employees from participating in the plan, and
- unfairly withholding benefits from former employees or their beneficiaries.

If the IRS finds your plan to be discriminatory at any time (usually during an audit), the plan could be disqualified. If this happens. you and your employees would owe income tax, and probably penalties as well.

Having employees also increases the plan's reporting requirements. You must provide employees with a summary of the terms of the plan, notification of any changes you make and an annual report of contributions. And you must file an annual tax return.

Because of this complexity, any self-employed person who has employees should turn to professional consultants for help in choosing, establishing and administering a retirement plan.

⚠ **Beware of Retirement Account Deadlines**
If you want to establish any of the retirement accounts discussed in this chapter and take a tax deduction for the year, you must meet specific deadlines. The deadlines vary according to the type of account you set up, as shown in the following chart. Once you establish your account, you have until the due date of your tax return for the year (April 15 of the following year, plus any filing extensions) to contribute to your account and take a deduction.

Plan Type	Deadline for Establishing Plan
Traditional IRA	Due date of tax return (April 15 plus extensions)
Roth IRA	Due date of tax return (April 15 plus extensions)
SEP-IRA	Due date of tax return (April 15 plus extensions)
Simple IRA	October 1
Keogh Profit-Sharing Plan	December 31
Keogh Money Purchase Plan	December 31
Keogh Defined Benefit Plan	December 31

■

Copyrights, Patents and Trade Secrets

Self-employed people are often hired to create or contribute to the creation of copyrights, patents or trade secrets—for example, writings, photos, graphics, music, software programs, designs or inventions. This chapter explains the legalities surrounding these creative works—who owns them and how those who create them can protect their rights.

A. Intellectual Property

Products of the human intellect that have economic value—that is, ideas or creations that are worth money—are tagged with the lofty name of intellectual property. This includes work of which you are the author, such as writings, computer software, films, music and inventions, as well as techniques, processes or other information not generally known.

A body of federal and state law has been created giving the owners of intellectual property ownership rights similar to those enjoyed by owners of tangible personal property, such as automobiles. Intellectual property may be owned, bought and sold just like other property.

There are four separate bodies of law that protect intellectual property: copyrights and patents, which are governed solely by federal law, and trademarks and trade secrets, which are protected under state and federal laws.

1. Copyrights

The federal copyright law (17 U.S.C. §§101 and following) protects all original works of authorship. A work of authorship is any work created by a person that other people can understand or perceive, either by themselves or with the help of a machine such as a computer or television. Authorship can include all kinds of written works, plays, music, artwork, graphics, photos, films and videos, computer software, architectural blue-prints and designs, choreography and pantomimes.

The owner of a copyright has a bundle of rights that enable him or her to control how the work may be used. These include the exclusive right to copy and distribute the protected work, to create works derived from it—updated editions of a book, for example—and to display and perform it. These rights come into existence automatically the moment a work of authorship is created. The owner need not take any additional steps or file legal documents to secure a copyright.

Copyright owners typically profit from their works by selling or licensing all or some of these rights to others—publishers, for example. (See Section B for more on establishing and transferring copyrights.)

Many self-employed people earn their livings by creating works of authorship for their clients—for example, freelance writers and graphic artists, self-employed computer programmers and photographers.

 For a detailed discussion of copyright, see *The Copyright Handbook: How to Protect and Use Written Works,* by Stephen Fishman and *Copyright Your Software,* by Stephen Fishman (both published by Nolo).

2. Patents

The federal patent law (35 U.S.C. §§100 and following) protects inventions that are new, useful and not obvious to someone versed in the relevant technology. To obtain a patent, an inventor must file an application with the U.S. Patent and Trademark Office in Washington, DC, and pay a fee. If the Patent Office determines that the invention is sufficiently new, useful and unobvious, it will issue the inventor a patent.

A patent gives an inventor a monopoly on the use and commercial exploitation of the invention. A patent lasts 20 years from the application date.

Anyone who wants to use or sell a patented invention during a patent's term must obtain the patent owner's permission. A patent may protect articles—for example, machines, chemicals, manufactures and biological creations—and processes—that is, methods of accomplishing things.

Self-employed workers with technical expertise are often called on by their clients to help develop new inventions that may end up being patentable. These people need to understand the rules governing who will own the patent. (See Section C.)

 For a detailed discussion of patents, see *Patent It Yourself*, by David Pressman (Nolo).

3. Trade Secrets

A trade secret is information that other people do not generally know and that provides its owner with a competitive advantage in the marketplace. The information can be an idea, writing, formula, process or procedure, technical design, customer list, marketing plan or any other secret that gives the owner an economic advantage.

To establish a trade secret, you must take reasonable steps to keep the confidential information or know-how secret—for example, by not publishing it or otherwise making it freely available to the public. The laws of most states will protect the owner from disclosures of the secret by:

- the owner's employees
- people who agree not to disclose it, such as ICs the owner hires
- industrial spies, and
- competitors who wrongfully acquire the information.

In the course of your work, you may be exposed to your client's most valuable trade secrets—for example, highly confidential marketing plans, new products under development, manufacturing techniques or customer lists. Understandably, your client probably doesn't want you

blabbing its trade secrets to others, particularly to its competitors.

To make sure you'll keep such information confidential, many clients will ask you to sign a nondisclosure agreement stating that you may not reveal the client's trade secrets to others without permission. A nondisclosure provision can be included in a client agreement or can be a separate document. Carefully review any nondisclosure provision a client asks you to sign. (See Chapter 20, Section B.)

On the other hand, you may have your own trade secrets you don't want others you deal with to disclose. In this event, you should ask them to sign your own nondisclosure agreement. (See Section E for a detailed discussion of nondisclosure agreements and a sample form.)

 For more information on trade secrets, see *Nondisclosure Agreements: Protect Your Trade Secrets & More*, by Richard Stim and Stephen Fishman (Nolo).

4. Trademarks

The state and federal trademark laws protect the right to exclusively use a name, logo or other device that identifies and distinguishes a product or service. In addition to names and logos, trademark law can be used to protect product packaging designs and the shape or design of a product—for example, a Coca-Cola bottle. If a competitor uses a protected trademark, the trademark holder can obtain a court injunction and monetary damages

 For additional information on trademarks, see *Trademark: Legal Care for Your Business and Product Name*, by Stephen Elias (Nolo).

Types of Intellectual Property			
	What Is Protected?	**Examples**	**Length of Protection**
Trade Secret	Formula, method, device, machine, compilation of facts or any information that is confidential and gives a business an advantage.	*Coca-Cola* formula; special method for assembling a patented invention; new invention for which patent application has not been filed.	As long as information remains confidential and functions as a trade secret.
Utility Patent	Machines, compositions, plants, processes, articles of manufacture.	Cellular telephone, the drug known as Vicodan, a hybrid daffodil, the Amazon 1-click process, a rake.	17 years from date of issue for patents filed before or on June 17, 1995; 20 years from the date of filing for patent applications filed after June 17,1995.
Copyright	Books, photos, music, recordings, fine art, graphics, videos, film, architecture, computer programs.	*The Firm* (book and movie), Andy Warhol prints, Roy Orbison's *Greatest Hits* (music recording, compact disc artwork and video), architectural plans for design of apartment building, Macromedia *Dreamweaver* program.	Life of the author plus 70 years for works created by a single author. Other works such as works made for hire, 120 years from date of creation or 95 years from first publication.
Trademark	Word, symbol, logo, design, slogan, trade dress or product configuration.	*Nike* name and distinctive swoosh logo, "What Do You Want To Do Today" slogan, *Mr. Clean* character, *Absolut* vodka bottle.	As long as business continuously uses trademark in connection with goods. Federal registrations must be renewed every 10 years.

B. Copyright Ownership

Any work of authorship you produce for a client is automatically protected by copyright the moment it is created. At that same moment, somebody becomes the owner of the copyright. Who owns the copyright in a work you create is important because the owner alone has the right to copy, distribute or otherwise commercially exploit the work—that is, to earn money from it. Unfortunately, self-employed people and hiring firms can get into disputes about who owns the copyright in the work product.

To avoid disputes over ownership, you need to understand some of the basics of copyright law.

You Don't Need a C in a Circle to Have a Copyright

Many self-employed people don't know that a work need not contain a copyright notice—the familiar © symbol followed by the publication date and copyright owner's name—to be protected by copyright laws. Likewise, you are not required to register your copyright.

Giving others notice of the copyright and registering it are both optional. However, both are highly desirable if the work is published. They enable the copyright owner to receive the maximum damages possible if someone copies and uses the work without permission and the owner files and wins a copyright infringement suit.

You can register your copyright by filling out a short registration form and sending it to the Copyright Office in Washington, DC, along with one or two copies of the work and a fee.

For more information on copyrights, see *The Copyright Handbook: How to Protect and Use Written Works*, by Stephen Fishman (Nolo).

1. Works Created by Independent Contractors

Self-employed workers ordinarily qualify as independent contractors for copyright purposes. The fundamental rule is that independent contractors own the copyright in works of authorship they create for a client unless they sign a piece of paper transferring those rights to the client. Without your signature on such a document, the client—the person who paid you to create the work—may have no copyright rights at all or at most may share copyright ownership with you.

As the owner of the copyright, you have the right to resell your work to others or to copy, distribute and create new works based on the work.

EXAMPLE: Tom hires Jane, an independent contractor computer programmer, to create a computer program. Tom and Jane have an oral work agreement. Jane creates the program. Since Jane never signed an agreement transferring any of her copyright rights to Tom, Jane still owns all the copyright rights in the program. Jane has the exclusive right to sell the program to others or permit them to use it. Even though Tom paid Jane to create the program, he doesn't own it and can't sell or license it to others.

In the real world, copyrights are rarely left to fate. Independent contractors are normally asked to sign written agreements transferring all or some of their copyright rights to the client who hires them. But if you find yourself working with an inexperienced client who doesn't understand the ownership rules, be sure to take the initiative and set forth in writing who will own the copyright in your work. (See Chapter 19, Section B8.)

Copyright transfers can take one of three forms. You can:

- transfer some of your rights
- transfer all of your rights, or
- sign a work made for hire agreement, which transfers all your copyright rights and then some.

Which rights you transfer to clients and which you keep for yourself is a matter for negotiation. After you and the client reach an agreement on copyright ownership, one of you must write a copyright transfer agreement and you must sign it to make it legally valid. You may include the understanding as a clause in a client agreement or negotiate it as a separate freestanding agreement.

⚠ Beware of Conflicting Copyright Transfers

If you're performing similar work for two or more clients simultaneously and agree to assign the intellectual property rights in your work to both clients, you could end up transferring the same rights twice. Before you agree to sell a client anything you create, review your existing agreements to make sure you haven't already sold it.

PHOTOGRAPHER WINS PYRRHIC VICTORY AGAINST MAGAZINE

Resolving copyright ownership disputes can take a great deal of time, angst and money if you have to go to court. Even if you eventually win your case, you may feel like a loser. Consider the case of Marco, a professional photographer who took photographs for several issues of *Accent Magazine,* a trade journal for the jewelry industry, over a six-month period. Marco had an oral agreement with the magazine and was paid a fee of about $150 per photograph. *Accent,* claiming it owned the copyright in the photos, wanted to re-use them without paying Marco an additional fee. Marco claimed that he owned the photos and that *Accent* had to pay him for permission to use them again. Marco and the magazine were never able to reach an accord on who owned the photos.

When the magazine tried to use the photos without Marco's permission, he asked a court to block publication. The court refused and Marco filed an appeal with the federal appeals court in Philadelphia. After about two years, Marco won his appeal. But he probably ended up spending far more on attorney fees than the photos were worth. (*Marco v. Accent Publishing Co., Inc.,* 969 F.2d 1547 (3d Cir. 1992).)

2. Transferring Some Rights

You are not legally required to give a client all your copyright rights. You can transfer some rights and retain others. When you do this, you may sell the rights you retain to people other than the client.

As discussed above, a copyright is really a bundle of rights, including the exclusive rights to copy, distribute, perform, display and create derivative works, such as adaptations or new editions from a work. Each of these rights can be transferred together or separately. They can also be divided and subdivided by media, geography, time, market segment or any other way you and a client can think up. You can often make more money by dividing up your copyright rights and selling them piecemeal to several different purchasers than you could selling them all to a single client.

The bundle of copyright rights in any work of authorship can be divided and sold separately. Exactly how you can most profitably divide your copyright rights depends on the nature of the work and the market for it. For example, the copyright in a computer program is often divided by geography or type of computer system.

> **EXAMPLE:** Bill, a famous freelance videogame designer, is hired by Fun & Sun Gameware to create a new videogame. He signs an agreement transferring to Gameware only the right to distribute the game for the Nintendo videogame system in the United States. Bill retains all his other copyright rights. He sells the right to publish the game in Japan to Nippon Games and sells the right to create a film based on the game to Repulsive Pictures.

The copyright in a magazine article may be divided by priority of publication—that is, a writer may grant a magazine the right to publish an article for the first time and retain the rights to sell it to others later. Freelance writers often earn substantial income by selling reprint rights to their work. Similarly, graphic artists often grant a client only the right to use an image or design in a certain publishing category and keep the right to resell their work for use in other categories.

> **EXAMPLE:** Sally, a self-employed graphic designer, creates and sells 25 spot illustrations for use in a school textbook. She grants the

textbook publisher the exclusive right to use the images in textbooks, but retains the right to sell them to others to use for different purposes—for example, in magazine articles.

When you divide up your copyright rights this way, the transfer is often called a license. Licenses fall into two broad categories: exclusive and nonexclusive.

DIVIDING UP YOUR COPYRIGHT BUNDLE

It's often wise to keep as many rights for yourself as possible since you may be able to sell them to others and make additional money from your work.

However, you may not be able to keep many copyright rights. Many clients want to have all the copyright rights in works they pay self-employed people to create. Other clients will pay you substantially less for some rights than they would for all your rights. If the market for your work is limited, it may make more economic sense to sell all your rights and get as much money as possible from the client instead of taking less and then trying to sell your work to others.

The normal practices in your particular field will usually have a big impact on the negotiations. These traditions and the terminology used to describe various types of copyright transfers vary widely. If you're not familiar with them, ask others in your field or contact professional organizations or trade groups for information.

a. Exclusive licenses

When a copyright owner grants someone an exclusive license, he or she gives that person, called the licensee, the exclusive right to one or more, but not all, of the copyright rights. An exclusive license is a transfer of copyright ownership. It must be in writing to be valid.

> **EXAMPLE:** Jane writes an article on economics and grants *The Economist's Journal* the exclusive right to publish it for the first time in the United States and Canada. Jane has granted the *Journal* an exclusive license. Only the *Journal* may publish the article for the first time in the U.S. and Canada. The magazine owns this right. But Jane retains all her other copyright rights. This means she has the right to republish her article after it appears in the *Journal* and to include it in a book. She also retains the right to create derivative works from it—for example, to expand it into a book-length work.

b. Nonexclusive licenses

In contrast, a nonexclusive license gives a person the right to exercise one or more of a copyright owner's rights, but does not prevent the copyright owner from giving other people permission to exercise the same right or rights at the same time. A nonexclusive license is the most limited form of rights transfer you can grant a client.

As with exclusive licenses, nonexclusive licenses may be limited as to time, geography, media or in any other way. They can be granted orally or in writing. The much better practice, however, is to use some sort of writing; this can avoid possible misunderstandings.

> **EXAMPLE:** Bill, a freelance computer programmer, agrees to create an accounting program for AcmePool, a swimming pool company. Bill thinks other swimming pool companies might be interested in buying the program as well, so he grants AcmePool only a nonexclusive right to use the program. This means he can sell it to others, not just Acme-Pool. AcmePool has no right to sell the pro-

gram. AcmePool agreed to the deal because Bill charged it much less than he would have charged had AcmePool acquired ownership of the program.

3. Transferring All Rights

When people transfer all the copyright rights they own in a work of authorship, the transaction is called an assignment or an all rights transfer. When such a transaction is completed, the original copyright owner no longer has any ownership rights at all. The new owner—the assignee—has all the copyright rights the transferor formerly held. The new owner is then free to sell licenses or to assign the copyright to someone else.

An assignment can be made either before or after a work is created, but it must be in writing to be valid. An assignment can be a separate document or it can be included in a client agreement.

> **EXAMPLE:** Tom hires Jane, a self-employed programmer, to create a computer program. Before Jane starts work, Tom has her sign an independent contractor agreement providing, among other things, that she transfers all her copyright rights in the program to Tom. Jane completes her work and delivers the program, and Tom pays her. Tom owns all the copyright rights in the program.

4. Works Made for Hire

When employees create works of authorship as part of their jobs, their employers automatically own all the copyright rights in the work. Works created on the job are called works made for hire. Certain types of works created by independent contractors can also qualify as works made for hire. When a work is made for hire, the person who ordered or commissioned it and paid for it is considered to be the author for copyright purposes, not the person who created it. This commissioning party—not the actual creator—automatically owns all the copyright rights.

a. Types of works made for hire

Nine categories of works created by independent contractors can be works made for hire:

- a contribution to a collective work—for example, a work created by more than one author, such as a newspaper magazine, anthology or encyclopedia
- a part of an audiovisual work—for example, a motion picture screenplay
- a translation
- supplementary works—for example, forewords, afterwords, supplemental pictorial illustrations, maps, charts, editorial notes, bibliographies, appendixes and indexes
- a compilation—for example, an electronic database
- an instructional text
- a test
- answer material for a test, and
- an atlas.

b. Written agreement requirement

It's not enough that your work falls into one of these categories. You and the client must sign a written agreement stating that the work you create shall be a work made for hire. The agreement must be signed before you begin work to be effective. The client cannot wait until after your work is completed and delivered and then decide that it should be a work made for hire.

Think of a work for hire agreement as the hydrogen bomb of copyright transfers. When you sign such an agreement, you not only give up all your ownership rights in the work until the end of time, you're not even considered the work's author. You won't be legally entitled to any credit for your work, such as having your name attached if the work is published, unless your agreement with the client requires it.

EXAMPLE: The editor of *The Egoist Magazine* asks Gloria, a freelance writer, if she would be interested in writing an article for the magazine on night life in Palm Beach. Gloria agrees and the editor sends her a letter agreement to sign setting forth such terms as compensation, the deadline for the article and its length. The letter also specifies that the article "shall be a work made for hire."

Gloria signs the agreement, writes the article and is paid by the magazine. Since the article qualifies as a work made for hire, the magazine is the initial owner of all the copyright rights in the article. Gloria owns no copyright rights. As the copyright owner, the magazine is free to sell reprint rights in the article, film and TV rights, translation rights and any other rights anyone wants to buy. Gloria is not entitled to license or sell any rights in the article because she doesn't own any. She gave up all her copyright rights by signing the work for hire agreement.

Many writer and artist organizations strongly advise their members to refuse to sign work for hire agreements. However, an increasing number of clients insist on such agreements. In some cases, signing a work for hire agreement is a take it or leave it proposition: If you don't agree to

sign, the client will find someone else who will. For example, *The New York Times* now requires freelance contributors to sign work for hire agreements; the paper will simply refuse to publish a freelance article unless the author signs on the dotted line.

On the other hand, you can often get a client to agree to something less than a work for hire agreement if you ask. If the client refuses, you can still sign the work for hire agreement, but you lose nothing by asking.

5. Sharing Ownership With Clients

If a client does not obtain a copyright transfer from you, you will own the work you create for him or her. However, a client who qualifies as a co-author might be considered a co-owner of the work along with you. For this to occur, the client must actually help you create the work. Giving suggestions or supervision is not enough.

A client who qualifies as a co-author will jointly share copyright ownership in the work with you. As co-authors, you're each entitled to use or let other people use the work without obtaining approval of the other co-author. But any profits you make must be shared with the other co-authors. This could cause problems—for example, if co-authors sold the same work to competing publishers, the value of the work could be diluted. It's usually in co-authors' interests to work together to avoid this.

EXAMPLE: Marlon, a legendary actor, hires Tom, a freelance writer, to ghostwrite his autobiography. Tom is an IC, not Marlon's employee. Marlon fails to have Tom sign a written agreement transferring to Marlon his copyright rights in his work. However, Marlon worked closely with Tom in writing the autobiography, contributing not only ideas, but also writing portions of the book.

As a result, Marlon and Tom would probably be considered co-authors and joint owners of the autobiography. Both would have the right to sell the autobiography to a publisher, serialize it in magazines, sell it to movie producers or otherwise commercially exploit the work. However, Marlon and Tom would have to share any profits earned.

If a client doesn't qualify as a co-author, at most it will have a nonexclusive right to use the work. But it wouldn't be allowed to sell or license any copyright rights in the work because it wouldn't own any. The independent contractor would own all the rights and be able to sell or license them without the client's permission, and without sharing the profits with the client.

EXAMPLE: Mark pays Sally, a freelance photographer, to take some pictures of toxic waste dumps to supplement his treatise on toxic waste management. Sally didn't sign an agreement transferring her copyright rights in the photos to Mark. Mark does not qualify as a co-author of the photos because he didn't help take them. As a result, Sally owns the copyright in the photos. Mark has a nonexclusive license to use the photos in his treatise, but this doesn't prevent Sally from selling the photos to others or otherwise exploiting her copyright rights.

C. Patent Ownership

Patent rights initially belong to the person who develops an invention. However, patent rights can be assigned—that is, transferred—to others just as copyrights can. Firms that hire independent contractors to help create new technology or anything else that might qualify for a patent normally have the independent contractors assign to them in advance all patent rights in the work.

Such an assignment may be included in an independent contractor agreement or in a separate document.

If you have no signed assignment, it's far from clear who will own inventions you develop. Unlike copyrights, where silence indicates independent contractor ownership, there is no such presumption in the world of patents. The law regarding ownership of inventions by employees is very clear—an employer owns any inventions an employee was hired to create. But courts have barely addressed who owns inventions made by independent contractors in the absence of a written ownership agreement.

You can assert ownership over your invention or other work, but be prepared for a costly legal dispute if you do. The client could claim you had a duty to assign your patent rights to it even though there was no written assignment agreement. You would probably have a good chance of winning such a case, but it would be no sure thing. It's best to avoid such disputes in advance by clearly defining in writing who will own the work.

D. Trade Secret Ownership

Trade secret ownership rules are similar to those for patents. You are the initial owner of any trade secrets you develop while working for a client. But ownership rights in trade secrets can be assigned to others just as patents can be. Hiring firms typically require independent contractors to sign written agreements assigning their trade secret ownership rights to the client in advance.

In the absence of such an agreement, you probably own your trade secrets and can sell them to others, including the client's competitors. However, if you used the client's resources to develop the trade secret information, the client might have a nonexclusive license to use it without your permission. This is called a shop right.

E. Using Nondisclosure Agreements

It is relatively simple to protect tangible valuables, like jewelry, computers and luxury cars. You lock them up in vaults, drawers or a garage. But it is not so easy to protect knowledge and ideas, even though this intellectual property may be the key to building your creative dream. Many self-employed entrepreneurs are fearful of sharing their intellectual property with others, something you almost always have to do to gain financial backing, development deals or other essential partnerships. Fortunately, the informed and consistent use of well-drafted nondisclosure agreements can help you protect these assets if you have to disclose them to potential backers, partners, clients and others.

1. What Is a Nondisclosure Agreement?

Nondisclosure agreements—also known as NDAs or confidentiality agreements—are frequently used in the business world before confidential information is disclosed. Nondisclosure agreements have just one purpose: to protect your trade secrets. Trade secrets include any information that is not generally known that has economic value or gives you a competitive edge. It includes—but is not limited to—such things as:

- Unpublished computer code
- Product development agreements and other related agreements
- Business plans
- Financial projections
- Marketing plans
- Sales data
- Cost and pricing information
- Customer lists, and
- Patent pending applications.

See Section A3 above for a general discussion of trade secrets.

By using a nondisclosure agreement, you agree to share such information only after the other party agrees, in writing, to keep the information secret.

Using a nondisclosure agreement accomplishes several basic purposes:

- It conclusively establishes that the person to whom you disclose the information has a legal duty not to disclose your trade secrets without your permission.
- It makes clear to the person who receives a trade secret that it must be kept in confidence. This will impress on him or her that you are serious about maintaining your trade secrets.
- If it's ever necessary to file a lawsuit, a signed nondisclosure agreement will help you prove that you treated the information you disclosed as a trade secret, and that the person to whom you disclosed it knew that it should be kept confidential.

2. When to Use Nondisclosure Agreements

Before you give any person access to information that gives you a competitive advantage, you should have him or her sign a nondisclosure agreement. You may need to ask any or all of the following people to sign:

- Clients and potential clients
- Employees and potential employees
- Consultants (independent contractors)
- Business partners and investors
- Licensees or customers, and
- Suppliers.

a. Clients

It will often be necessary for you to disclose your trade secrets to people and companies for whom you perform your services or sell your ideas. For example, a self-employed computer programmer may have to make trade secret computer code available to a client, or an inventor may have to disclose the idea for a new invention to a manufacturer. Always try to have the client sign an NDA before you disclose such information. (Some clients may refuse to do so—see below.)

b. Employees

It is advisable to have all employees who may come into contact with your trade secrets sign NDAs. Employees should sign nondisclosure agreements before they begin work or on their very first day of work. If you have employees who have not signed nondisclosure agreements, you should ask them to do so before they are given access to any trade secrets.

If your business is a partnership, all partners should sign a partnership agreement containing a nondisclosure provision.

c. Independent contractors (consultants)

The consultant you hire today may end up working for a competitor tomorrow. Never expose a consultant to trade secrets without having a signed nondisclosure agreement on file. It's best for such an agreement to be included within an overall consulting or independent contractor agreement that covers all aspects of the parties' relationship, including the services to be performed, who will own the consultant's or independent contractor's work product and payment. Several consultant and independent contractor agreements are included in *Hiring Independent Contractors: The Employer's Legal Guide*, by Stephen Fishman (Nolo).

d. Business partners and investors

Trade secrets must frequently be disclosed during negotiations with prospective business partners, investors, licensees, suppliers or customers. It's advisable to have the other party sign an NDA before you disclose any trade secrets. This way, you will be protected if the negotiations do not result in a final agreement.

NDAs CAN BE A TOUCHY ISSUE

In high-tech industries, NDAs are as common as diamonds at weddings. However, many people refuse to sign them. It is common for venture capitalists, securities analysts and top consultants to refuse to sign NDAs. The reason is that these people review lots of ideas, many of which are similar. They think that signing NDAs will make it impossible for them to do business—and may expose them to the potential for expensive lawsuits. Instead, such people preach the honor system.

Refusal to sign NDAs is also common in publishing and in Hollywood, where editors and executives review large numbers of ideas for books and scripts that are often similar in content or focus. Occasionally, companies outside the United States, where business is sometimes less legalistic, may also balk at signing nondisclosure agreements.

Possibly the best way to deal with this problem is to take the time to develop a relationship of trust with the people with whom you are considering working, before telling them all your best ideas. This might involve dealing with lower-level information and ideas to see how they are treated before revealing your most important information.

However, some people and companies will never sign an NDA. In that event, you must decide whether to go ahead and disclose the information or walk away. If the person or company has an impeccable reputation for integrity, you may conclude it is worthwhile to go ahead and make the disclosure.

Keep in mind that you may be able to successfully sue such people for trade secret violations even if they haven't signed an NDA. You'll need to consult with a lawyer if you find yourself in this situation.

3. Other Means of Protecting Trade Secrets

Using NDAs is the single most important thing you can do to protect your trade secrets. But it's not your only strategy. You don't have to turn your office into an armed camp to protect your trade secrets, but you must take reasonable precautions to keep them confidential.

Such precautions may include:

- marking documents containing trade secrets "Confidential"
- locking trade secret materials away after business hours
- maintaining computer security
- limiting the number of people who know about your confidential information, and
- destroying documents containing trade secrets as soon as the documents are no longer needed.

4. Drafting a Nondisclosure Agreement

The Nondisclosure Agreement below can be used with any outside individual or company to whom you grant access to your trade secrets. The agreement is included in Appendix 2.

1. Introductory Paragraph

Fill in the date the agreement will take effect. This can be the date it is signed or a date in the future. Next, fill in your name—this should be the name you use for your business. You are referred to as "Discloser" in the rest of the agreement. Finally, fill in the name of the individual or company being granted access to your trade secrets (the "Recipient").

> **SUGGESTED LANGUAGE:**
>
> This is an agreement, effective _____, between _____ (the "Discloser") and _____ (the "Recipient"), in which Discloser agrees to disclose, and Recipient agrees to receive, certain trade secrets of Discloser on the following terms and conditions:

2. Trade Secrets

Select either Alternative 1 or 2, and delete the alternative you are not using. Here's how to choose:

Alternative 1. It's best to specifically identify the trade secrets covered by the agreement; use this clause if you can individually list the material being provided. However, be careful that your description is not so narrowly worded that it may leave out important information you wish to have covered by the agreement. If you later discover that you want to disclose confidential information not included in the agreement, you and the other person or company can complete and sign an addendum identifying the information. Alternatively, you could complete a whole new NDA. Do whichever is most convenient.

> **SUGGESTED LANGUAGE:**
>
> Recipient understands and acknowledges that the following information constitutes trade secrets belonging to Discloser:
>
> _____

Alternative 2. Use this clause if it's not possible to specifically identify the trade secrets—for example, if the information to be disclosed does not exist when the agreement is signed, you're not sure what will be disclosed or it's simply too much trouble to identify everything that could be disclosed. This clause contains a general description of the types of information covered. It includes virtually everything that could be a trade secret.

3. Purpose of Disclosure

Describe the reason for disclosing trade secrets. For example, this may be for you to perform consulting services for the recipient or to further the parties' business relationship.

4. Nondisclosure

This provision is the heart of the agreement. The Recipient promises to treat the Discloser's trade secrets with a reasonable degree of care and not to disclose them to third parties without the Discloser's consent. Recipient also promises not to make commercial use of the information without Discloser's permission.

Finally, the Recipient may not disclose the information to its employees or consultants unless they have signed confidentiality agreements protecting the trade secret rights of third parties, such as the Discloser. If an employee or consultant has signed such an agreement, it's not necessary for him or her to sign a separate agreement promising to keep the Discloser's information confidential.

If the Recipient breaks these promises, the Discloser can sue in court to obtain monetary damages and possibly a court order to prevent the Recipient from using the information.

5. Return of Materials

In this clause, the Recipient promises to return original materials you've provided, as well as copies, notes and documents pertaining to the trade secrets. The form gives Recipient 30 days to return the materials, but you can change this time period if you wish.

SUGGESTED LANGUAGE:

Upon Discloser's request, Recipient shall promptly (within 30 days) return all original materials provided by Discloser and any copies, notes or other documents in Recipient's possession pertaining to Discloser's trade secrets.

---

6. Exclusions

This provision describes all the types of information that are not covered by the agreement. These exclusions are based on court decisions and state trade secret laws that say these types of information do not qualify for trade secret protection.

SUGGESTED LANGUAGE:

This agreement does not apply to any information which:

(a) was in Recipient's possession or was known to Recipient, without an obligation to keep it confidential, before such information was disclosed to Recipient by Discloser;

(b) is or becomes public knowledge through a source other than Recipient and through no fault of Recipient;

(c) is or becomes lawfully available to Recipient from a source other than Discloser; or

(d) is disclosed by Recipient with Discloser's prior written approval.

---

7. Term of Agreement

There are two alternative provisions dealing with the agreement's term, which is the length of time the agreement remains in effect. Select the clause that best suits your needs and delete the other:

Alternative 1. This provision has no definite time limit—in other words, the Recipient's obligation of confidentiality lasts until the trade secret information ceases to be a trade secret. This may occur when the information becomes generally known, is disclosed to the public by the discloser or ceases being a trade secret for some other reason. This gives the discloser the broadest protection possible. Disclosers ordinarily prefer to use this provision.

SUGGESTED LANGUAGE:

This Agreement and Recipient's duty to hold Discloser's trade secrets in confidence shall remain in effect until the above-described trade secrets are no longer trade secrets or until Discloser sends Recipient written notice releasing Recipient from this Agreement, whichever occurs first.

Alternative 2. Some recipients don't want to be subject to open-ended confidentiality obligations. Use this clause if the Recipient requires that the agreement state a definite date by which the agreement, and the Recipient's confidentiality obligations, expires. Five years is a common time period, but the time limit can be much shorter, even as little as six months. In Internet and technology businesses, the time period may need to be shorter because of the fast pace of innovation. But the Discloser should attempt to make sure the time period lasts as long as the confidential information is likely to remain valuable.

> **SUGGESTED LANGUAGE:**
>
> This Agreement and Recipient's duty to hold Discloser's trade secrets in confidence shall remain in effect until _____ or until whichever of the following occurs first:
>
> - Discloser sends Recipient written notice releasing Recipient from this Agreement, or
>
> - The above-described trade secrets are no longer trade secrets.

8. No Rights Granted

This provision makes clear that the Recipient is acquiring absolutely no ownership rights in or to the information. This means the Recipient can't sell or license the information to others.

> **SUGGESTED LANGUAGE:**
>
> Recipient understands and agrees that this Agreement does not constitute a grant or an intention or commitment to grant any right, title or interest in Discloser's trade secrets to Recipient.

9. Warranty

A warranty is a promise. In this provision, the Discloser promises to the Recipient that it has the right to disclose the information. This is intended to assure the Recipient that it won't be sued by some third party who claims the trade secrets belonged to it and the Discloser had no right to reveal them to the Recipient.

> **SUGGESTED LANGUAGE:**
>
> Discloser warrants that it has the right to make the disclosures under this Agreement.

10. Injunctive Relief

If the Recipient violates a nondisclosure agreement, one of the most important legal remedies a trade secret owner can obtain is a court order preventing the violator from using or profiting from the Discloser's trade secrets.

This provision is intended to make such a court order—called an injunction—easier for the Discloser to obtain. Some Recipients may object to inclusion of this provision because they want to make it as hard as possible for the Discloser to obtain an injunction.

> **SUGGESTED LANGUAGE:**
>
> Recipient acknowledges and agrees that in the event of a breach or threatened breach of this Agreement, money damages would be an inadequate remedy and extremely difficult to measure. Recipient agrees, therefore, that Discloser shall be entitled to an injunction to restrain Recipient from such breach or threatened breach. Nothing in this Agreement shall be construed as preventing Discloser from pursuing any remedy at law or in equity for any breach or threatened breach.

11. Attorney Fees

This agreement says that if a lawsuit is brought to enforce the agreement, the loser pays the winner's attorney fees. Without such a provision, attorney fees are usually not recoverable.

> **SUGGESTED LANGUAGE:**
>
> If any legal action arises relating to this Agreement, the prevailing party shall be entitled to recover all court costs, expenses and reasonable attorney fees.

12. Modifications

This provision requires that any changes to the agreement be made in writing and signed by both parties to be legally effective. This means, for example, that a change agreed to over the telephone won't be legally enforceable; one of the parties must write down the change and both must sign it.

SUGGESTED LANGUAGE:

This Agreement represents the entire agreement between the parties regarding the subject matter and supersedes all prior agreements or understandings between them. All additions or modifications to this Agreement must be made in writing and must be signed by both parties to be effective.

---

13. No Agency

This clause is intended to make clear to both parties that the nondisclosure agreement does not make the two parties partners or allow either party to act as an agent for the other. This prevents either party from entering into contracts or incurring debts on behalf of the other party.

SUGGESTED LANGUAGE:

This Agreement does not create any agency or partnership relationship between the parties.

---

14. Applicable Law

Every state has its own laws regarding contract interpretation. These laws differ from state to state. The parties can choose any state's laws to govern the agreement, regardless of where they are located or where the agreement is signed. It's usually advantageous to have the law of your home state govern the agreement, since this is the law both you and your attorney are probably most familiar with. However, state laws on trade secrecy don't differ enough to make this a make-or-break issue.

SUGGESTED LANGUAGE:

This Agreement is made under, and shall be construed according to, the laws of the State of _____.

---

15. Signatures

The parties don't have to be in the same room when they sign the agreement. It's even fine if the dates are a few days apart. But the NDA is not valid until both parties have signed it. So don't start revealing your secrets until then. Each party should sign at least two copies, and keep at least one. This way, both parties have an original signed agreement. (See Chapter 18, Section D for detailed information on how to sign a legal agreement.) ∎

Using Written Client Agreements

A contract—also called an agreement—is a legally binding promise. Whenever you agree to perform services for a client, you enter into a contract; you promise to do work and the client promises to pay you for it.

The word contract often intimidates people who conjure up visions of voluminous legal documents laden with legalese. However, a contract need not be long or complex. Many contracts consist of only a few simple paragraphs. Indeed, most contracts don't even have to be in writing. Even so, it's never a good idea to rely on an oral agreement with a client.

CLIENT AGREEMENTS DON'T HAVE TO BE INTIMIDATING

Some self-employed workers shy away from using written agreements. You might be afraid of intimidating your clients or making them think you don't trust them. This could happen if you're not careful. For example, a prospective client might think twice about hiring you if you present a 20-page contract for a simple one-day project. The client might conclude that you're either paranoid, hard to deal with or both.

You can avoid this problem, however, if you calibrate your agreements to your assignments. Use simple contracts or short letter agreements for simple projects and save the longer, more complex agreements for bigger jobs.

A. Reasons to Use Written Agreements

Most contracts don't have to be in writing to be legally binding. For example, you and a client can enter into a contract over the phone or during a lunch meeting at a restaurant. No magic words need be spoken. You just have to agree to perform services for the client in exchange for some-

thing of value—usually money. Theoretically, an oral agreement is as valid as a 50-page contract drafted by a high-powered law firm.

EXAMPLE: Gary, a freelance translator, receives a phone call from a vice-president of Acme Oil Co. The VP asks Gary to translate some Russian oil industry documents for $2,000. Gary says he'll do the work for the price. Gary and Acme have a valid oral contract.

SOME AGREEMENTS MUST BE IN WRITING

Some types of agreements must be in writing to be legally enforceable. Each state has a law, usually called the Statute of Frauds, listing the types of contracts that must be in writing to be valid.

A typical list includes:

- any contract that cannot possibly be performed in less than one year. Example: John agrees to perform consulting services for Acme Corp. for the next two years for $2,000 per month. Since the agreement cannot be performed in less than one year, it must be in writing to be legally enforceable.
- contracts for the sales of goods—that is, tangible personal property such as a computer or car—worth $500 or more.
- a promise to pay someone else's debt. Example: The president of a corporation personally guarantees to pay for the services you sell to the corporation. The guarantee must be in writing to be legally enforceable.
- contracts involving the sale of real estate, or real estate leases lasting more than one year.

Any transfer of copyright ownership must also be in writing to be valid. (See Chapter 17, Section B.)

In the real world, however, using oral agreements is like driving without a seatbelt. Things will work out fine as long as you don't have an accident; but if you do have an accident, you'll wish you had buckled up. An oral agreement can work if you and your client agree completely about its terms and obey them. Unfortunately, things don't always work so perfectly.

Here are some of the most important reasons why you should always sign a written agreement with a client before starting work.

1. Avoiding Misunderstandings

Courts are crowded with lawsuits filed by people who enter into oral agreements with one another and later disagree over what was said. Costly misunderstandings can develop if you perform services for a client without a writing clearly stating what you're supposed to do. Such misunderstandings may be innocent; you and the client may have simply misinterpreted one another. Or they may be purposeful; without a writing to contradict him or her, a client can claim that you orally agreed to anything.

Consider a good written client agreement to be your legal lifeline. If disputes develop, the agreement will provide ways to solve them. If you and the client end up in court, a written agreement will establish your legal duties to each other.

For these same reasons, your clients should be happy to sign a well-drafted contract. Be wary of any client who refuses to put your agreement in writing. Such a client might be a bad credit risk. If a prospective client balks at signing an agreement, you may wish to obtain a credit report on him or her, or talk with others who have worked for that client to see if they had problems. If you think you might have payment problems, ask for a substantial down payment upfront and for progress payments if the project is lengthy. (See Chapter 7, Section B.)

WRITTEN AGREEMENTS PREEMPT CHEAP TALK

When you put your agreement in writing, it is usually treated as the final word on the areas covered. That is, it takes precedence over anything you and the client said to each other but did not include in your written agreement.

However, if you and the client end up in court or arbitration because you disagree over the terms or meaning of your contract, things you and the client said to each other during the negotiating process but didn't write down can be used to explain unclear terms in the written contract or to prove additional terms where the writing is incomplete. Since you and the client may disagree about what was said during negotiations, it's best to make the written contract as clear and complete as possible.

2. Assuring That You Get Paid

A written agreement clearly setting out your fees will help ward off disputes about how much the client agreed to pay you. If a client fails to pay and you have to negotiate or eventually even sue for your money, the written agreement will be proof of how much you're owed. Relying on an oral agreement with a client can make it very difficult for you to get paid in full or to get paid at all.

ORAL AGREEMENT COSTS IC $600

One self-employed worker recently learned the hard way that an oral agreement isn't worth the paper on which it is not printed. Jane, a commercial illustrator who works as a freelancer for a variety of ad agencies and other clients, orally agreed to do a series of drawings for a dress designer. Jane did the drawings and submitted her bill for $2,000. The designer refused to pay, alternately claiming that payment was conditional on the drawings being published in a fashion magazine and that Jane was charging too much.

Jane filed a lawsuit against the designer in small claims court to collect her $2,000. The judge had no trouble finding that Jane had an enforceable oral contract with the designer who admitted that he had asked Jane to do the work. However, the judge awarded Jane only $1,400 because she could not document her claim that she was to be paid $100 per hour and the designer made a convincing presentation that designers usually charge no more than $70 per hour.

3. Defining Projects

The process of deciding what to include in an agreement helps both you and the client. It forces you both to think carefully, perhaps for the first time, about exactly what you're supposed to do. Hazy and ill-defined ideas get reduced to a concrete contract specification or description of the work that you will perform. This gives you and the client a yardstick by which to measure your performance, the best way to avoid later disputes that you haven't performed adequately.

4. Establishing IC Status

A well-drafted client agreement will also help establish that you are an independent contractor, not the client's employee. You can suffer severe consequences if the IRS or another government agency decides you're an employee instead of an independent contractor. (See Chapter 15.)

B. Reviewing a Client's Agreement

Many clients have their own agreements they'll ask you to sign. This may be a copy of an agreement they've used in the past with other people they've hired, a standard agreement prepared by an attorney or a letter summarizing the terms to which you've agreed. You'll almost always be better off if you use your own agreement, not one provided by your client, because it gives you the greatest control over the contract terms. Take the initiative and send the client an agreement to sign immediately after you accept an assignment. Don't wait for the client to provide you with an agreement of its own.

If a client insists on using its own agreement, read that document carefully. It may contain provisions that are unfair to you—for example, provisions requiring you to repay the client if an IRS auditor determines you're an employee and imposes fines and penalties against the client. Pay special attention to noncompetition provisions restricting your right to work for other companies and nondisclosure provisions that prevent you from using information you learn while working for the client.

Remember that any contract can be rewritten, even if the client claims it's a standard agreement that all outside workers sign. This is a matter for negotiation. Seek to delete or rewrite unfair provisions. There may also be provisions you want to add. (See Chapter 20, Section D.)

For practical guidance on how to conduct contract negotiations, see:

- *Getting to Yes: Negotiating Agreement Without Giving In,* by Roger Fisher and William Ury (Penguin Books)
- *Negotiating Rationally,* by Max H. Bazerman and Margaret A. Neale (Free Press), and
- *Win-Win Negotiating,* by Fred E. Jandt (John Wiley & Sons).

C. Creating Your Own Client Agreements

You don't need to hire a lawyer to draft an independent contractor agreement. All you need is a brain and a little common sense. This book contains a number of sample forms you can use and copious guidance on how to custom tailor them to fit your particular needs. This may take a little work, but when you're done, you'll have an agreement you can use over and over again with minor alterations.

1. Types of Agreements

There are two main types of client agreements. Use the type of agreement that best suits your own needs and the needs of your clients.

a. Letter agreements

A letter agreement is usually a short contract written in the form of a letter. After you and the client reach a tentative agreement—over the phone, in a meeting, by fax or electronic mail—you set forth the contract terms in a letter written on your stationery, sign two copies and send them to the client. If the client agrees to the terms in the letter, he or she signs both copies at the bottom and returns one signed copy to you. At that point, you and the client have a fully enforceable, valid contract. Many self-employed people use letter agreements because they seem less intimidating to clients than more formal-looking contracts. Others use them because of business custom. (See Chapter 19, Section D.)

b. Standard contracts

A standard contract usually contains a number of paragraphs and captions. It is usually longer and more comprehensive than a letter agreement. It's a good idea to use a standard contract if:

- the project is long and complex or involves a substantial amount of money, or
- you're dealing with a client you don't trust, either because it's a new client or because your past dealings indicate the client is untrustworthy. (See Chapter 19.)

PROPOSALS ARE NOT CLIENT AGREEMENTS

Clients often choose the outside workers they hire through a competitive bidding process. They ask a number of people to submit written proposals describing how they'll perform the work and the price they'll charge. The client chooses the IC who submits the best proposal.

Some self-employed people write quite lengthy and detailed proposals and depend on them instead of standard contracts. This is a mistake. Proposals normally do not address many important issues that should be covered in a contract, such as the term of the agreement, how it can be terminated and how disputes will be resolved. If a problem arises that is not covered by the proposal, you and the client will have to negotiate a solution in the middle of the project. If you can't reach a solution, either you or the client may end up taking the other to court to resolve the battle.

The best course is to have a signed contract in hand before starting work. If you submit a proposal to a client, it should state that if the client agrees to proceed, you will forward a contract for signature within a specific number of days.

2. The Drafting Process

Draft contract forms you can use over and over again with various clients. You can use the forms as the basis for your agreement and make alterations you need to suit the particular situation. If you perform the same type of work for every client, you might need just one or two form agreements. This might include a brief letter agreement for small jobs and a longer standard contract for larger projects. However, if your work varies, you may need several different agreements. If you hire self-employed people to work for you, you'll need an agreement for them as well. (See Chapter 19.)

EXAMPLE: Ellen, a freelance publicist, usually uses a letter agreement with her clients. However, when she is hired to do a particularly long project, she prefers to use a longer standard contract because it affords her added protection if something goes wrong. She also occasionally hires other freelance publicists to work for her as ICs when she gets very busy. Ellen uses a lengthy subcontractor agreement with them because it helps to establish that they're ICs instead of her employees and makes their duties as clear as possible.

Ellen uses the forms in this book to draft three different IC agreements she keeps on her computer and uses over and over again: a letter agreement, a standard IC agreement and a subcontractor agreement.

3. Using the Forms in This Book

This book contains a sample client agreement that almost any self-employed person who sells services can adapt to meet his or her needs. Each of the clauses in the agreement is discussed in detail. A sample brief letter agreement is also provided. (See Chapter 19.)

There are two ways to use these clauses. You can retype the language suggested in this book to assemble your own final agreement. This will allow you to tailor your document to your specific needs. Alternatively, you can complete and use the tear-out sample agreement in Appendix 2. This is easier than creating your own agreement, but gives you less flexibility regarding the content of your agreement.

Your IC agreement will make the best impression on IRS and other government auditors if it looks like a custom-made agreement you've drafted specifically for the client, not a standard form you've torn out of a book. And making a good impression is important if you want to keep your self-employed status and not be viewed as an employee of the client.

For this reason, it is advisable to retype the form provided here—whether on a computer or typewriter—and use that instead of the pre-printed form in Appendix 2.

D. Putting Your Agreement Together

Whether you use a simple letter agreement or formal standard contract, make sure it's properly signed and put together. This is not difficult if you know what to do. And this section provides all the instruction you should need to get it right.

1. Signatures

It's best for both you and the client to sign the agreement in ink. You need not be together when you sign, nor do you have to sign at the same time. There's no legal requirement that the signatures be located in any specific place in a business contract, but they are customarily placed at the end of the agreement; that helps signify that you both have read and agreed to the entire document.

It's very important that both you and the client sign the agreement properly. Failure to do so can have drastic consequences. How to sign depends on the legal form of your business and the client's business.

a. Sole proprietors

If you or the client are sole proprietors, you can simply sign your own names because a sole proprietorship is not a separate legal entity.

However, if you use a fictitious business name (see Chapter 2), it's best for you to sign on behalf of your business. This will help show you're an IC, not an employee.

EXAMPLE: Chris Kraft is a sole proprietor who runs a marketing research business. Instead of using his own name for the business, he calls it AAA Marketing Research. He should sign his contracts like this:

AAA Marketing Research

By: _____
　　　Chris Kraft

b. Partnerships

If either you or the client is a partnership, a general partner should sign on the partnership's behalf. Only one partner needs to sign. The signature block for the partnership should state the partnership's name and the name and title of the person signing on the partnership's behalf. If a partner signs only his or her name without mentioning the partnership, the partnership is not bound by the agreement.

EXAMPLE: Chris, a self-employed marketing consultant, contracts to perform marketing research for a Michigan partnership called The Argus Partnership. Randy Argus is one of the general partners. He signs the contract on the partnership's behalf like this:

The Argus Partnership
A Michigan Partnership

By: _____
　　　Randy Argus, a General Partner

If the client is a partnership and the person who signs the agreement is not a partner, the signature should be accompanied by a partnership resolution stating that the person signing the agreement has the authority to do so. The partnership resolution is a document signed by one or more of the general partners stating that the person named has the authority to sign contracts on the partnership's behalf.

c.   Corporations

If either you or the client is a corporation, the agreement must be signed by someone who has authority to sign contracts on the corporation's behalf. The corporation's president or chief executive officer (CEO) is presumed to have this authority.

If someone other than the president of an incorporated client signs—for example, the vice-president, treasurer or other corporate officer—ask to see a board of directors resolution or corporate bylaws authorizing him or her to sign. If the person signing doesn't have authority, the corporation won't be legally bound by the contract.

Keep in mind that if you sign personally instead of on your corporation's behalf, you'll be personally liable for the contract.

The signature block for a corporation should state the name of the corporation and indicate by name and title the person signing on the corporation's behalf.

EXAMPLE: Chris, a self-employed marketing consultant, contracts to perform marketing research with a corporation called Kiddie Krafts, Inc. The contract is signed by Susan Ericson. Because she is the president of the corporation, Chris doesn't need a corporate resolution showing she has authority to bind the corporation. The signature block should appear in the contract like this:

Kiddie Krafts, Inc.
A California Corporation

By: _____
            Susan Ericson, President

d.   Limited liability companies

The owners of a limited liability company (LLC) are called "members." Members may hire others to run their LLC for them. These people are called "managers." If either you or your client is an LLC, the agreement should be signed by a member or manager on the LLC's behalf.

EXAMPLE: Amy Smart, a California-based self-employed graphic artist, has formed an LLC to run her business called Great Graphics, LLC. She should sign all her agreements like this:

Great Graphics, LLC
A California Limited Liability Company

By: _____
            Amy Smart, Member

2. Dates

When you sign an agreement, include the date and make sure the client does, too. You can simply put a date line next to the place where each person signs—for example:

Date: _____, 20XX

You and the client don't have to sign on the same day. Indeed, you can sign weeks apart.

3. Attachments or Exhibits

An easy way to keep a letter agreement or standard contract as short as possible is to use attachments, also called exhibits. You can use them to list lengthy details such as performance specifications. This makes the main body of the agreement shorter and easier to read.

If you have more than one attachment or exhibit, they should be numbered or lettered—for example, Attachment 1 or Exhibit A. Be sure that the main body of the agreement mentions that the attachments or exhibits are included as part of the contract.

4. Altering the Contract

Sometimes it's necessary to make last-minute changes to a contract just before it's signed. If you use a computer to prepare the agreement, it's usually easy to make the changes and print out a new agreement.

However, it's not necessary to prepare a new contract. Instead, the changes may be handwritten or typed onto all existing copies of the agreement. If you use this approach, be sure that all those signing the agreement also sign their initials as close as possible to the place where the change is made. If both people who sign don't initial each change, questions might arise as to whether the change was part of the agreement.

5. Copies of the Contract

Prepare at least two copies of your letter agreement or standard contract. Make sure that each copy contains all the needed exhibits and attachments. Both you and the client should sign both copies—and both of you should keep one signed copy of the agreement.

6. Faxing Contracts

It has become very common for self-employed people and their clients to communicate by fax machine. People often send drafts of their proposed agreement back and forth to each other by fax. When a final agreement is reached, one signs a copy of the contract and faxes it to the other, who signs it and faxes it back.

A faxed signature is probably legally sufficient if neither you nor the client dispute that it is a fax of an original signature. However, if a client claims that a faxed signature was forged, it could be difficult or impossible to prove it's genuine, since it is very easy to forge a faxed signature with modern computer technology. Forgery claims are rare, however, so this is usually not a problem. Even so, it's a good practice for you and the client to follow up the fax with signed originals exchanged by mail or air express.

E. Changing the Agreement After It's Signed

No contract is engraved in stone. You and the client can always modify or amend your contract if circumstances change. You can even agree to call the whole thing off and cancel your agreement.

> **EXAMPLE:** Barbara, a self-employed well digger, agrees to dig a 50-foot-deep well on property owned by Kate for $2,000. After digging 10 feet, Barbara hits solid rock that no one knew was there. To complete the well, she'll have to lease expensive heavy equipment. To defray the added expense, she asks Kate to pay her $4,000 instead of $2,000 for the work. Kate agrees. Barbara and Kate have amended their original agreement.

Neither you nor the client is ever obligated to accept a proposed modification to your contract. Either of you can always say no and accept the consequences. At its most dire, this may mean a court battle over breaking the original contract. However, you're usually better off reaching some sort of accommodation with the client, unless he or she is totally unreasonable.

Unless your contract is one that must be in writing to be legally valid—for example, an agreement that can't be performed in less than one year (see Section A), it can usually be modified by an oral agreement. In other words, you need not write down the changes.

EXAMPLE: Art signs a contract with Zeno to build an addition to his house. Halfway through the project, Art decides that he wants Zeno to do some extra work not covered by their original agreement. Art and Zeno have a telephone conversation in which Zeno agrees to do the extra work for extra money. Although nothing is put in writing, their change to their original agreement is legally enforceable.

Self-employed workers and their clients change their contracts all the time and never write down the changes. The flexibility afforded by such an informal approach to contract amendments might be just what you want. However, misunderstandings and disputes can arise from this approach. It's always best to have some sort of writing showing what you've agreed to do. You can do this informally. For example, you can simply send a confirming letter following a telephone call with the client summarizing the changes you both agreed to make. Be sure to keep a copy for your files.

However, if the amendment involves a contract provision that is very important—your payment, for example—insist on a written amendment and insist that you and the client sign it. The amendment should set forth all the changes and state that the amendment takes precedence over the original contract. (See Appendix 2 for an Amendment form.) ■

Drafting Your Own Client Agreement

This chapter guides you in creating a client agreement that you can use for almost any type of service you provide your clients. This is a full-blown formal contract. It covers nearly all concerns you would want covered in an agreement. (See Appendix 2 for a tear-out version.)

Some self-employed people prefer not to use formal contracts because they're afraid they will intimidate clients. If you prefer something a little less formal, this book also provides a short, simple letter agreement that will meet your needs. (See Section D.)

However, it's a good idea to use a more comprehensive formal contract if:

- you are hired to do a project that is long and complex or involves a substantial amount of money, or

- you're dealing with a new client or a client who has been untrustworthy in the past.

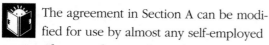 The agreement in Section A can be modified for use by almost any self-employed person. If you prefer a ready-made contract, you can find several client agreements tailored to specific occupations in *Consultant and Independent Contractor Agreements,* by Stephen Fishman (Nolo), including agreements for use by consultants, household service providers, salespeople, accountants and bookkeepers, artists, writers and construction contractors. These agreements are included in both tear-out versions and on CD-ROM.

A. Essential Provisions

There are a number of provisions that should be included in most client agreements. All of these sample clauses are included in the Client Agreement. (Section C shows how an entire agreement might look when assembled.)

These provisions may be all you need for a basic agreement. Or you may need to combine them with some of your own clauses or one or more of the optional clauses discussed below. (See Section B.)

Title of agreement. You don't need a title for a client agreement, but if you want one, call it Independent Contractor Agreement, Client Agreement, Agreement for Professional Services or Consulting Agreement. Consulting Agreement may sound a little more high-toned than Independent Contractor Agreement; it is most often used by highly skilled professionals. Since you are not your client's employee, do not use Employment Agreement as a title.

SUGGESTED LANGUAGE:

INDEPENDENT CONTRACTOR AGREEMENT

Names of parties. Here at the beginning of your contract, it's best to refer to yourself by your full business name. Later on in the contract, you can use an obvious abbreviation.

If you're a sole proprietor, use the full name you use for your business. This can be your own name or a fictitious business name or assumed name you use to identify your business. (See Chapter 2.) For example, if consultant Al Brodsky calls his one-person marketing research business "ABC Marketing Research," he would use that name on the contract. Using a fictitious business name helps show that you're a business, not an employee.

If your business is incorporated, use your corporate name, not your own name—for example: "John Smith, Incorporated" instead of "John Smith."

Similarly, if you've formed a limited liability company (see Chapter 2), use the name of the LLC, not your personal name—for example: "Jane Brown, a Limited Liability Corporation" instead of "Jane Brown."

Do not refer to yourself as an employee or to the client as an employer.

For the sake of brevity, it is usual to identify yourself and the client by shorter names in the rest of the agreement. You can use an abbreviated version of your full name—for example, ABC for ABC Marketing Research. Or you can refer to yourself simply as Contractor or Consultant.

Refer to the client initially by its company name and subsequently by a short version of the name or as Client or Firm.

Include the addresses of the principal place of businesses of both the client and yourself. If you or the client have more than one office or workplace, the principal place of business is the main office or workplace.

SUGGESTED LANGUAGE:

This Agreement is made between [Client's name] (Client) with a principal place of business at [Client's business address] and [Your name] (Contractor), with a principal place of business at [Your business address].

---

1. Services to Be Performed

The agreement should describe in as much detail as possible what you are expected to accomplish. Word the description carefully to emphasize the results you're expected to achieve. Don't describe the method by which you will achieve the results. As an independent contractor, it should be up to you to decide how to do the work. The client's control should be limited to accepting or rejecting your final results. The more control the client exercises over how you work, the more you'll look like an employee. (See Chapter 15.)

EXAMPLE: Jack hires Jill to prepare an index for his multi-volume history of ancient Sparta. Jill should describe the results she is expected to achieve like this: Contractor agrees to prepare an index of Client's History of Sparta of at least 100 single-spaced pages. Contractor will provide Client with a printout of the finished index and a 3.5 inch computer disk version in ASCII format.

The agreement should not tell Jill how to create the index: "Contractor will prepare an alphabetical three-level index of Client's History of Sparta. Contractor will first prepare 3 by 5 inch index cards list-

ing every index entry beginning with Chapter One. After each chapter is completed, Contractor will deliver the index cards to Client for Client's approval. When index cards have been created for all 50 chapters, Contractor will create a computer version of the index using Complex Software Version 7.6. Contractor will then print out and edit the index and deliver it to Client for approval."

It's perfectly okay for the agreement to establish very detailed specifications for your finished work product. But the specs should only describe the end results you must achieve, not how to obtain those results. You can include the description in the main body of the Agreement. Or if it's a lengthy explanation, put it on a separate document and attach it to the agreement. (See Chapter 18, Section D3.)

SUGGESTED LANGUAGE—ALTERNATIVE A— IF SERVICES LISTED:

Contractor agrees to perform the following services: [Describe services you will perform.]

SUGGESTED LANGUAGE—ALTERNATIVE B— IF EXHIBIT ATTACHED:

Contractor agrees to perform the services described in Exhibit A, which is attached to this Agreement.

Choose Alternative B if the explanation of the services is attached to the main contract.

2. Payment

Self-employed people who provide services to others can be paid in many different ways. (See Chapter 7, Section A.) The two most common payment methods are:

- a fixed fee, or
- payment by unit of time.

a. Fixed fee

In a fixed fee agreement, you charge an agreed amount for the entire project. (See Chapter 7, Section A1.)

**SUGGESTED LANGUAGE—
ALTERNATIVE A—FIXED FEE:**

In consideration for the services to be performed by Contractor, Client agrees to pay Contractor $[State amount].

---

b. Unit of time

Many self-employed people—for example, lawyers, accountants and plumbers—customarily charge by the hour, day or other unit of time. (See Chapter 7, Section A1.) Charging by the hour does not support your independent contractor status, but you can get away with it if it's a common practice in the field in which you work.

**SUGGESTED LANGUAGE—
ALTERNATIVE B—UNIT OF TIME:**

In consideration for the services to be performed by Contractor, Client agrees to pay Contractor at the rate of $[State amount] per [hour, day, week or other unit of time].

---

c. Capping your payment

Clients often wish to place a cap on the total amount they'll spend on the project when you're paid by the hour because they're afraid you might work slowly to earn a larger fee. If the client insists on a cap, make sure it allows you to work enough hours to get the project done.

OPTIONAL LANGUAGE—CAPPING PAYMENT

[OPTIONAL: Contractor's total compensation shall not exceed $____ without Client's written consent.]

---

3. Terms of Payment

Terms of payment means how you will bill the client and be paid. Generally, you will have to submit an invoice to the client setting out the amount due before you can get paid. An invoice doesn't have to be fancy or filled with legalese. It should include an invoice number, the dates covered by the invoice, the hours expended if you're being paid by the hour and a summary of the work performed. (See Chapter 7, Section B2, for a detailed discussion and sample invoice form.)

a. Payment upon completing work

The following provision requires you to send an invoice after you complete work. The client is required to pay your fixed or hourly fee within a set number of days after you send the invoice. The time period of 30 days is a typical payment term, but it can be shorter or longer if you wish. Note that the time for payment starts to run as soon as you send your invoice, not when the client receives it. This will help you get paid more quickly.

**SUGGESTED LANGUAGE—ALTERNATIVE A—
PAYMENT ON COMPLETION:**

Upon completing Contractor's services under this Agreement, Contractor shall submit an invoice. Client shall pay Contractor within ____ [10, 15, 30, 45, 60] days from the date of Contractor's invoice.

---

b. Divided payments

You can also opt to be paid part of a fixed or hourly fee when the agreement is signed and the remainder when the work is finished. The amount of the upfront payment is subject to negotiation. Many self-employed people like to receive at least one-third to one-half of a fee before they start work. If the client is new or might have problems paying you, it's wise to get as much money in advance as you can.

The following provision requires that you be paid a specific amount when the client signs the agreement and the rest when the work is finished.

SUGGESTED LANGUAGE—ALTERNATIVE B— DIVIDED PAYMENTS:

Contractor shall be paid $[State amount] upon signing this Agreement and the remaining amount due when Contractor completes the services and submits an invoice. Client shall pay Contractor within ____ [10, 15, 30, 45, 60] days from the date of Contractor's invoice.

---

c. Fixed fee installment payments

If the project is long and complex, you may prefer to be paid in installments rather than waiting until the project is finished to receive the bulk of your payment. One way to do this is to break the job into phases or milestones and be paid a fixed fee when each phase is completed. Clients often like this pay-as-you-go arrangement, too.

To do this, draw up a schedule of installment payments, tying each payment to your completion of specific services. It's usually easier to set forth the schedule in a separate document and attach it to the agreement as an exhibit. The main body of the agreement should simply refer to the attached payment schedule.

SUGGESTED LANGUAGE—ALTERNATIVE C— INSTALLMENT PAYMENTS:

Contractor shall be paid according to the Schedule of Payments set forth in Exhibit __ [A or B] attached to and made part of this agreement.

Following is a form of a schedule of payments you can complete and attach to your agreement. This schedule requires four payments: a down payment when the contract is signed and three installment payments. However, you and the client can have as many payments as you want.

SUGGESTED LANGUAGE— PAYMENT SCHEDULE EXHIBIT— SCHEDULE OF PAYMENTS

Client shall pay Contractor according to the following schedule of payments:

1) $[State sum] when this Agreement is signed.

2) $[State sum] when an invoice is submitted and the following services are completed:

[Describe first stage of services]

3) $[State sum] when an invoice is submitted and the following services are completed:

[Describe second stage of services]

4) $[State sum] when an invoice is submitted and the following services are completed:

[Describe third stage of services]

[ADD ANY ADDITIONAL PAYMENTS]

All payments shall be due within ____ [10, 15, 30, 45, 60] days from the date of Contractor's invoice.

---

d. Hourly payment for lengthy projects

Use the following clause if you're being paid by the hour or other unit of time and the project will last more than one month. Under this provision, you submit an invoice to the client each month setting forth how many hours you've worked and the client is required to pay you within a specific number of days from the date of each invoice.

SUGGESTED LANGUAGE—ALTERNATIVE D— PAYMENTS AFTER INVOICE:

Contractor shall send Client an invoice monthly. Client shall pay Contractor within [10, 15, 30, 45, 60] days from the date of each invoice.

---

4. Expenses

Expenses are the costs you incur that you can attribute directly to your work for a client. They include, for example, the cost of phone calls or traveling done on the client's behalf. Expenses do not include your normal fixed overhead costs, such as your office rent or the cost of commuting to and from your office. They also do not include materials the client provides you to do your work. (See Section A5.)

In the recent past, the IRS viewed the payment of a worker's expenses by a client as a sign of employee status. However, the agency now downgrades the importance of this factor. IRS auditors will focus instead on whether a worker has any expenses that were not reimbursed, particularly fixed ongoing costs such as office rent or employee salaries. (See Chapter 15.)

Even though the IRS has changed its stance, other government agencies may consider payment of a worker's business or traveling expenses to be a strong indication of employment relationship. For this reason, it is usually best that your compensation be high enough to cover your expenses; you should not be separately reimbursed for them.

Setting your compensation at a level high enough to cover your expenses has another advantage: It frees you from having to keep records of your expenses. Keeping track of the cost of every phone call or photocopy you make for a client can be a real chore and may be more trouble than it's worth.

However, if a project will involve expensive traveling, you may wish to separately bill the client for the cost. The following provision contains an optional clause for this.

**SUGGESTED LANGUAGE—ALTERNATIVE A—
IF IC RESPONSIBLE FOR EXPENSES:**

Contractor shall be responsible for all expenses incurred while performing services under this Agreement.

OPTIONAL: However, Client shall reimburse Contractor for all reasonable travel and living expenses necessarily incurred by Contractor while away from Contractor's regular place of business to perform services under this Agreement. Contractor shall submit an itemized statement of such expenses. Client shall pay Contractor within 30 days from the date of each statement.

However, some self-employed people customarily have expenses paid by their clients. For example, attorneys, accountants and many self-employed consultants typically charge their clients separately for photocopying charges, deposition fees and travel. Where there is an otherwise clear independent contractor relationship and payment of expenses is customary in your trade or business, you can probably get away with doing it.

**SUGGESTED LANGUAGE—ALTERNATIVE B—
IF CLIENT RESPONSIBLE FOR EXPENSES:**

Client shall reimburse Contractor for the following expenses that are directly attributable to work performed under this Agreement:

- travel expenses other than normal commuting, including airfares, rental vehicles, and highway mileage in company or personal vehicles at __[state amount] cents per mile
- telephone, fax, online and telegraph charges
- postage and courier services
- printing and reproduction
- computer services, and
- other expenses resulting from the work performed under this Agreement.

Contractor shall submit an itemized statement of Contractor's expenses. Client shall pay Contractor within 30 days from the date of each statement.

---

5. Materials

Generally, you should provide all the materials and equipment necessary to complete a project. However, this might not always be possible. For example:

- a computer consultant may have to perform work on the client's computers
- a marketing consultant may need research materials from the client, or
- a freelance copywriter may need copies of the client's old sales literature.

Specify any materials you need from the client in your agreement.

a. You provide all materials

If you furnish all the materials and equipment, use the following clause.

SUGGESTED LANGUAGE—ALTERNATIVE A— IF IC PROVIDES MATERIALS:

Contractor will furnish all materials and equipment used to provide the services required by this Agreement.

---

b. Client provides materials or equipment

List the materials or equipment the client will provide. If you need these items by a specific date, specify the deadline as well.

SUGGESTED LANGUAGE—ALTERNATIVE B— IF CLIENT PROVIDES MATERIALS:

Client shall make available to Contractor, at Client's expense, the following materials, facilities and equipment:

[List]_____.

These items will be provided to Contractor by [Date] _____.

---

6. Term of Agreement

The term of the agreement refers to when it begins and ends. Unless the agreement provides a specific starting date, it begins on the date it's signed. If you and the client sign on different dates, the agreement begins on the date the last person signed. You normally shouldn't begin work until the client signs the agreement, so it's usually best that the agreement not provide a specific start date that might be before the client signs.

The agreement should have a definite ending date. This ordinarily will mark the final deadline for you to complete your services. However, even if the project is lengthy, the end date should not be too far in the future. A good outside time limit is 12 months. A longer term makes the agreement look like an employment agreement, not an independent contractor agreement. If the work is not completed at the end of 12 months, you can negotiate and sign a new agreement.

SUGGESTED LANGUAGE:

This Agreement will become effective when signed by both parties and will end no later than

_____, 20__.

---

7. Terminating the Agreement

Signing a contract doesn't make you bound by it forever no matter what happens. You and the client can agree to call off your agreement at any time. In addition, contracts typically contain provisions allowing either person to terminate the agreement under certain circumstances. Termination means either party can end the contract without the other side's agreement.

When a contract is terminated, both you and the client stop performing—that is, you discontinue your work and the client has no obligation to pay you for any work you may do after the effective date of termination. However, the client is legally obligated to pay you for any work you did prior to the termination date.

EXAMPLE: Murray, a self-employed programmer, agrees to design an Internet site for Mary and signs a client agreement. About half-way through the project, Murray decides to terminate the agreement because Mary refuses to pay him the advance required by the contract. When the termination becomes effective, Murray has no obligation to do any further work for Mary, but he is still entitled to be compensated for the work he already did.

On the down side, however, you remain liable to the client for any damages it may have suffered due to your failure to perform as agreed before the termination date.

EXAMPLE: Jill, a self-employed graphic artist, contracts with Bill to design the cover for a book Bill plans to publish. Bill terminates the agreement when Jill fails to deliver the cover by the contract deadline. Jill has no duty to create the cover. Nor is Bill required to pay Jill even if she does produce a cover. However, Jill is liable for any damages Bill suffered by her failure to live up to the agreement. It turned out that the delay in providing a cover cost Bill an extra $1,000 in printing bills. Jill is liable for this amount.

It's important to clearly define the circumstances under which you or the client may end the agreement.

In the past, the IRS viewed a termination provision giving either you, the client or both of you the right to terminate the agreement at any time to be strong evidence of an employment relationship. However, the agency no longer considers this to be such an important factor.

Even so, it's wise to place some limits on the client's right to terminate the contract. It's usually not in your best interest to give a client the right to terminate you for any reason or no reason at all, since the client may abuse that right.

Instead, both you and the client should be able to terminate the agreement without legal repercussions only if there is reasonable cause to do so; or, at most, only by giving written notice to the other.

a. Termination with reasonable cause

Termination with reasonable cause means either you or the client must have a good reason to end the agreement. A serious violation of the agreement is reasonable cause to terminate the agreement—but what is considered serious depends on the particular facts and circumstances.

A minor or technical contract violation is not serious enough to justify ending the contract for cause. For example, if a client promised to let you use office space a few hours a week, but failed to do so, the transgression would normally be viewed as minor and wouldn't justify terminating the agreement. However, if a self-employed programmer agreed to perform programming services for an especially low price because the client promised to let her use its mainframe computer, and the client then reneged and told the programmer to lease her own mainframe, the programmer likely would be justified in terminating the agreement.

Unless your contract provides otherwise, a client's failure to pay you on time may not necessarily constitute reasonable cause for you to terminate the agreement. You may add a clause to your contract providing that late payments are always reasonable cause for terminating the contract. The following clause provides that you may terminate the agreement if the client doesn't pay you what you're owed within 20 days after you make a written demand for payment. For example, if you send a client an invoice due within 30 days and the client fails to pay within that time, you may terminate the agreement 20 days after you send the client a written demand to be paid what you're owed. This may give clients an incentive to pay you.

The clause also makes clear that the client must pay you for the services you performed before the contract was terminated.

SUGGESTED LANGUAGE—ALTERNATIVE A—REASONABLE CAUSE:

With reasonable cause, either party may terminate this Agreement effective immediately by giving written notice of termination for cause. Reasonable cause includes:

- a material violation of this agreement, or
- nonpayment of Contractor's compensation 20 days after written demand for payment.

Contractor shall be entitled to full payment for services performed prior to the effective date of termination.

---

b. Termination without cause

Sometimes you or the client just can't live with a limited termination right. Instead, you want to be able to get out of the agreement at any time without incurring liability. For example, a client's business plans may change so that it no longer needs your services. Or you may have too much work and need to lighten your load.

If you want a broader right to end the work relationship, add a provision to the contract that gives either of you the right to terminate the agreement for any reason upon written notice. You need to provide at least a few days notice—being able to terminate without notice tends to make you look like an employee. A period of 30 days is a common notice period, but shorter notice may be appropriate if the project is of short duration.

SUGGESTED LANGUAGE—ALTERNATIVE B—WITHOUT CAUSE:

Either party may terminate this Agreement at any time by giving _____ [5, 10, 15, 30, 45, 60] days written notice of termination. Contractor shall be entitled to full payment for services performed prior to the date of termination.

---

8. Independent Contractor Status

One of the most important functions of an independent contractor agreement is to help establish that you are an independent contractor, not your client's employee. The key to doing this is to make clear that you, not the client, have the right to control how the work will be performed.

You will need to emphasize the factors the IRS and other agencies consider in determining whether a client controls how the work is done. Of course, if you merely recite what you think the IRS wants to hear but fail to adhere to these understandings, agency auditors won't be fooled. Think of this clause as a reminder to you and your client about how to conduct your business relationship. (See Chapter 15.)

SUGGESTED LANGUAGE:

Contractor is an independent contractor, not Client's employee. Contractor's employees or subcontractors are not Client's employees. Contractor and Client agree to the following rights consistent with an independent contractor relationship.

- Contractor has the right to perform services for others during the term of this Agreement.
- Contractor has the sole right to control and direct the means, manner and method by which the services required by this Agreement will be performed.
- Contractor has the right to hire assistants as subcontractors, or to use employees to provide the services required by this Agreement.
- The Contractor or Contractor's employees or subcontractors shall perform the services required by this Agreement; Client shall not hire, supervise or pay any assistants to help Contractor.
- Neither Contractor nor Contractor's employees or subcontractors shall receive any training from Client in the skills necessary to perform the services required by this Agreement.
- Client shall not require Contractor or Contractor's employees or subcontractors to devote full time to performing the services required by this Agreement.

- Neither Contractor nor Contractor's employees or subcontractors are eligible to participate in any employee pension, health, vacation pay, sick pay or other fringe benefit plan of Client.

---

9. Local, State and Federal Taxes

The agreement should address federal and state income taxes, Social Security taxes and sales taxes.

a. Income taxes

Your client should not pay or withhold any income or Social Security taxes on your behalf. Doing so is a very strong indicator that you are an employee, not an independent contractor. Indeed, some courts have classified workers as employees based upon this factor alone. Keep in mind that one of the best things about being self-employed is that you don't have taxes withheld from your paychecks. (See Chapter 8.)

Include a straightforward provision, such as the one suggested below, to help make sure the client understands that you'll pay all applicable taxes due on your compensation and the client should therefore not withhold taxes from your payments.

SUGGESTED LANGUAGE:

Contractor shall pay all income taxes, and FICA (Social Security and Medicare taxes) incurred while performing services under this Agreement. Client will not:

- withhold FICA from Contractor's payments or make FICA payments on Contractor's behalf
- make state or federal unemployment compensation contributions on Contractor's behalf, or
- withhold state or federal income tax from Contractor's payments.

---

b. Sales taxes

A few states require self-employed people to pay sales taxes, even if they only provide their clients with services. These states include Hawaii, New Mexico and South Dakota. Many other states require sales taxes to be paid for certain specified services. (See Chapter 8, Section A2c.)

Whether or not you're required to collect sales taxes, include the following provision in your agreement making it clear that the client will have to pay these and similar taxes. States constantly change sales tax laws and more are beginning to look at services as a good source of sales tax revenue. So this provision could come in handy in the future even if you don't really need it now.

SUGGESTED LANGUAGE:

The charges included here do not include taxes. If Contractor is required to pay any federal, state or local sales, use, property or value added taxes based on the services provided under this Agreement, the taxes shall be separately billed to Client. Contractor shall not pay any interest or penalties incurred due to late payment or nonpayment of any taxes by Client.

---

10. Notices

When you want to do something important involving the agreement, you need to tell the client about it. This is called giving notice. For example, you need to give the client notice if you want to modify the agreement or terminate it.

The following provision gives you several options for providing the client with notice: by personal delivery, by mail, or by fax or telex followed by a confirming letter.

If you give notice by mail, it is not effective until three days after it's sent. For example, if you want to end the agreement on 30 days notice and mail your notice of termination to the client, the agreement will not end until 33 days after you mailed the notice.

SUGGESTED LANGUAGE:

All notices and other communications in connection with this Agreement shall be in writing and shall be considered given as follows:

- when delivered personally to the recipient's address as stated on this Agreement
- three days after being deposited in the United States mail, with postage prepaid to the recipient's address as stated on this Agreement, or
- when sent by fax or telex to the last fax or telex number of the recipient known to the person giving notice. Notice is effective upon receipt, provided that a duplicate copy of the notice is promptly given by first class mail, or the recipient delivers a written confirmation of receipt.

---

11.   No Partnership

You want to make sure that you and the client are separate legal entities, not partners. If a client is viewed as your partner, you'll be liable for its debts and the client will have the power to make contracts that obligate you to others without your consent.

SUGGESTED LANGUAGE:

This Agreement does not create a partnership relationship. Neither party has authority to enter into contracts on the other's behalf.

---

12.   Applicable Law

It's a good idea for your agreement to indicate which state's law will govern if you have a dispute with the client. This is particularly helpful if you and the client are in different states. There is some advantage to having the law of your own state control, since local attorneys will likely be more familiar with that law.

SUGGESTED LANGUAGE:

This Agreement will be governed by the laws of the state of [Indicate state in which you have your main office] _____.

---

13.   Exclusive Agreement

When you put your agreement in writing, it is treated as the last word on the areas it covers, if you and the client intend it to be the final and complete expression of your agreement. The written agreement takes precedence over any written or oral agreements or promises previously made. This means neither you nor the client can bring up side letters, oral statements or other material not covered by the contract.

Business contracts normally contain a provision stating that the written agreement is the complete and exclusive agreement between those involved. This is to help make it clear to a court or a mediator or arbitrator that the parties intended the contract to be their final agreement. A clause such as this helps avoid claims that promises not contained in the written contract were made and broken.

Make sure that all documents containing any of the client's representations upon which you are relying are attached to the agreement as exhibits. (See Chapter 18, Section D3.) If they aren't attached, they likely won't be considered to be part of the agreement.

SUGGESTED LANGUAGE:

This is the entire Agreement between Contractor and Client.

---

14.   Signatures

The end of the main body of the agreement should contain spaces for you to sign, write in your title and date. Make sure the person signing the agreement has the authority to do so. (See Chapter 18, Section D1.)

SUGGESTED LANGUAGE:

Client:

[NAME OF CLIENT]

By: _____

(Signature)

_____

(Typed or Printed Name)

Title: _____

Date: _____

Contractor:

[NAME OF CONTRACTOR]

By: _____

(Signature)

_____

(Typed or Printed Name)

Taxpayer ID Number: _____

Date: _____

Signing by fax. It is increasingly common to use faxed signatures to finalize contracts. If you use faxed signatures, include a specific provision authorizing them at the end of the agreement.

OPTIONAL LANGUAGE—SIGNATURES BY FAX

Contractor and Client agree that this Agreement will be considered signed when the signature of a party is delivered by facsimile transmission. Signatures transmitted by facsimile shall have the same effect as original signatures.

B. Optional Provisions

There are several optional provisions you may wish to include in your agreement. They are not absolutely necessary for every client agreement, but they can be extremely helpful. You should carefully consider including them in your con-

tracts. Pay especially close attention to the provisions regarding:

- resolving disputes
- contract changes, and
- attorney fees.

It's usually to your advantage to include all of these provisions in your agreement.

1. Resolving Disputes

As you probably know, court litigation can be very expensive. To avoid this cost, alternative forms of dispute resolution have been developed that don't involve going to court. These include mediation and arbitration.

The following clause requires you and the client to take advantage of these alternate forms of dispute resolution. You're first required to submit the dispute to mediation. You agree on a neutral third person to serve as mediator and try to help you settle your dispute. The mediator has no power to impose a decision, only to try to help you arrive at one. (See Chapter 21, Section A.)

If mediation doesn't work, you must submit the dispute to binding arbitration. Arbitration is usually like an informal court trial without a jury, but arbitrators make the decisions instead of judges. It is usually much faster and cheaper than courts. You may be represented by a lawyer, but it's not required. (See Chapter 21, Section B.)

You should indicate where the mediation or arbitration would occur. You'll usually want it in the city or county where your office is located. You don't want to have to travel a long distance to attend a mediation or arbitration.

However, every state has an alternative to mediation or arbitration that can be even cheaper and quicker than either of these approaches: small claims court. Small claims courts are designed to help resolve disputes involving a relatively small amount of money. The amount ranges from $2,000 to $7,500, depending on the state in which you live. If your dispute involves more money than the small claims limit, you can waive the excess (that is, give up your right to sue for anything over the limit) and still bring a small claims suit. You don't need a lawyer to sue in small claims court; indeed, lawyers are barred from small claims court in several states. Small claims court is particularly useful where a client owes you a relatively small amount of money. (See Chapter 7, Section B4.)

The following clause provides that you or the client can elect to skip mediation and arbitration—and take your dispute to small claims court.

SUGGESTED LANGUAGE:

If a dispute arises under this Agreement, the parties agree to first try to resolve the dispute with the help of a mutually agreed-upon mediator in

_____ [State city or county where mediation will occur]. Any costs and fees other than attorney fees associated with the mediation shall be shared equally by the parties.

If it proves impossible to arrive at a mutually satisfactory solution through mediation, the parties agree to submit the dispute to binding arbitration in

_____ [Note the city or county where arbitration will occur] under the rules of the American Arbitration Association. Judgment upon the award rendered by the arbitrator may be entered in any court having jurisdiction to do so.

However, the complaining party may refuse to submit the dispute to mediation or arbitration and instead bring an action in an appropriate Small Claims Court.

---

2. Modifying the Agreement

It's very common for both you and your client to want to change the terms of an agreement after work has started. For example, the client might want to make a change in the contract specifications which could require you to do more work. Or you might discover that you underestimated how much time the project will take and need to be paid more to complete it.

When you modify your agreement in this way, you should write down the changes on a separate document, have it signed and attach it to your original agreement. (See the Appendix for a form for a contract amendment.)

The following provision recognizes that the original agreement you enter with the client may have to be changed. Although oral changes to contracts are enforceable, it's a better idea to write them down. This provision states that you and the client must write down your changes and both sign the writing. Such a contract provision requiring modifications to be in writing is probably a bit of overkill—that is, both you and the client can still make changes without writing them down. However, making this requirement explicit does stress the importance of documenting changes in writing.

Neither you nor the client must accept a proposed change to a contract. But because you are obligated to deal with each other fairly and in good faith, you can't simply refuse all modifications without attempting to reach a resolution.

⚠ Resolving Disputes Over Modification. If you use this clause, check to be sure you have also included the optional provision on resolving disputes. (See Section B1.) That way, if you and the client can't agree on the changes, the agreement will require that you submit your dispute to mediation; and, if that doesn't work, to binding arbitration. This avoids expensive court litigation. (See Chapter 21, Section A.)

SUGGESTED LANGUAGE:

Client and Contractor recognize that:

- Contractor's original cost and time estimates may be too low due to unforeseen events, or to factors unknown to Contractor when this Agreement was made
- Client may desire a mid-project change in Contractor's services that would add time and cost to the project and possibly inconvenience Contractor, or
- Other provisions of this Agreement may be difficult to carry out due to unforeseen circumstances.

If any intended changes or any other events beyond the parties' control require adjustments to this Agreement, the parties shall make a good faith effort to agree on all necessary particulars. Such agreements shall be put in writing, signed by the parties and added to this Agreement.

---

3. Attorney Fees

If you have to sue the client in court to enforce the agreement and you win, you normally will not be awarded the amount of your attorney fees unless your agreement requires it. Including an attorney fees provision in the agreement can be in your interest. It can help make filing a lawsuit economically feasible; you might even be able to convince a lawyer to file a case against your client without providing an upfront cash retainer. It will also give the client a strong incentive to negotiate with you if you have a good case.

Sometimes, however, an attorney fees provision can work against you. It may help your client find an attorney to sue you and make you more anxious to settle. If you think it's more likely you'll violate the agreement than the client will, an attorney fees provision is probably not a good idea.

Under the following provision, if either person has to sue the other in court to enforce the agreement and wins—that is, becomes the prevailing party—the loser is required to pay the other person's attorney fees and expenses.

SUGGESTED LANGUAGE:

If any legal action is necessary to enforce this Agreement, the prevailing party shall be entitled to reasonable attorney fees, costs and expenses in addition to any other relief to which he or she may be entitled.

---

4. Late Fees

Many self-employed people charge a late fee if the client doesn't pay within the time specified in the IC agreement or invoice. Charging late fees for overdue payments can get clients to pay on time. The late fee is normally expressed as a monthly interest charge. (See Chapter 7, Section B2.)

If you wish to charge a late fee, make sure it's mentioned in your agreement. You should also clearly state what your late fee is on all your invoices.

State Restrictions on Late Fees
Your state might restrict how much you can charge as a late fee. You'll have to investigate your state laws to find out. Check the index to the annotated statutes for your state—sometimes called a code—available in any law library. (See Chapter 7, Section B2.) Look under the terms interest, usury or finance charges. Also, a professional or trade organization may have helpful information on late fee restrictions.

You can safely charge as a late fee at least as much as banks charge businesses to borrow money. Find out the current bank interest rate by calling your bank or looking in the business section of your local newspaper.

The math requires two steps. First, divide the annual interest rate by 12 to determine your monthly interest rate.

EXAMPLE: Sam, a self-employed consultant, decides to start charging clients a late fee for overdue payments. He knows banks are charging 12% interest per year on borrowed money and decides to charge the same. He divides this rate by 12 to determine his monthly interest rate: 1%.

Then, multiply the monthly rate by the amount due to determine the amount of the monthly late fee.

EXAMPLE: Acme Corp. is 30 days late paying Sam a $10,000 fee. Sam multiples this amount by his 1% finance charge to determine his late fee: $100 (.01 x $10,000). He adds this amount to Acme's account balance. He does this every month for which the payment is late.

SUGGESTED LANGUAGE:

Late payments by Client shall be subject to late penalty fees of _____% per month from the due date until the amount is paid.

---

5. Liability to the Client

If something goes wrong with your work, you might end up getting sued by the client and having to pay damages.

EXAMPLE: Julie, a self-employed computer programmer, designs an inventory accounting program for a cosmetics company. A bug in the program causes the program to crash and the company is unable to conduct normal business for several days, losing tens of thousands of dollars. The company sues Julie, claiming that her program design was deficient.

Such lawsuits could easily cost more than you were paid for your work and could even bankrupt you. To avoid this, many self-employed people include provisions in their agreements limiting their liability. This is particularly wise if problems with your work or services could cause the client substantial injuries or economic losses.

a. Liability cap

The following optional clause limits your total liability for any damages to the client to a set dollar amount or to no more than you were paid, whichever is less. It also relieves you of liability for lost profits or other special damages to the client.

Such damages are also called incidental or consequential damages. These are damages that can far exceed the amount the client actually paid you for your work. They arise out of circumstances you knew about or should have foreseen when the contract was made. This type of damages often involves lost profits that logically result from your failure to live up to your agreement. For example, if you knew that your failure to deliver your work on time could cost the client a valuable business opportunity, you could be required to make up the lost profits the client would have earned had you delivered the work on time. The optional clause below states that you will not be responsible for these types of damages.

SUGGESTED LANGUAGE—ALTERNATIVE A— CAP ON LIABILITY:

Contractor's total liability to Client under this Agreement for damages, costs and expenses, regardless of cause, shall not exceed $_____ or the compensation received by Contractor under this Agreement, whichever is less. Contractor shall not be liable for Client's lost profits, or special, incidental or consequential damages.

---

b. No liability to client

The following provision limits your liability to the client to the maximum extent possible. It provides that you are not liable to the client for any losses or damages arising from your work.

> **SUGGESTED LANGUAGE—ALTERNATIVE B—NO LIABILITY:**
>
> Contractor shall not be liable to Client for any loss, damages or expenses resulting from Contractor's services under this Agreement.

6. Liability to Others

The work that you do can affect people other than the client. Such people are called third parties.

Third parties—people you don't know and have never dealt with yourself—typically enter the picture when they are directly or indirectly injured by the work you've performed for a client. The injuries can be physical, economic or both. For example, if an elevator crashed due to faulty software a self-employed programmer designed for the elevator manufacturer, the injured elevator passengers would be third parties. Even though the programmer never met or contracted with them, the programmer might be legally responsible for their injuries.

You need to be particularly concerned about your liability to third parties if you're engaged in a hazardous or risky project that could result in injuries to others if something goes wrong.

If third parties are damaged as a result of the work you perform for a client, they'll likely sue everyone involved—including you. Both you and the client may be liable for the full amount of such claims. Legal clauses called indemnification provisions are used to require one person to pay the other's attorney fees and damages arising from such claims. Such provisions don't affect third parties who sue you or absolve you from liability to them for your actions. The clause can only make the client pay any amounts due as a result of such liability.

EXAMPLE: Bart, a self-employed software engineer, creates an experimental software program designed to automate a chemical factory for BigCorp. The program fails and a chemical spill takes place, damaging nearby landowners.

The property owners affected by the chemical spill would undoubtedly sue not only BigCorp, but Bart as well, claiming that he negligently designed the software. Bart will likely be forced to defend himself against lawsuits filed by total strangers.

You may wish to include the following provision in your agreement requiring the client to indemnify you against third party claims. This means the client will be responsible for defending any lawsuits and for all damages and injuries that third parties suffer if something goes wrong with your work.

To accomplish this, the provision uses a standard legal phrase that is a bit convoluted. It states that the client shall "indemnify, defend, and hold harmless" the contractor against third party claims. This means the client is required to assume responsibility for dealing with third party claims and must repay you if they end up costing you anything.

Many clients will balk at including an indemnification provision in your agreement. Moreover, as a practical matter, such a provision is useless if the client doesn't have the money or insurance to pay the amount due. You may be better off charging the client enough to obtain your own liability insurance protecting you against third party claims. (See Chapter 6, Section D.)

> **SUGGESTED LANGUAGE:**
>
> Client will indemnify, defend and hold harmless Contractor against all liabilities, damages and expenses, including reasonable attorney fees, resulting from any third party claim or lawsuit arising from Contractor's performance under this Agreement.

7. Intellectual Property Ownership

If you're hired to create or contribute to the creation of intellectual property—for example, important business documents, marketing plans, software programs, graphics, designs, photos, music, inventions or trademarks—the agreement should specify who owns your work.

There are many options regarding ownership of intellectual property that self-employed people create. Typically, your client will want to own all the intellectual property rights in your work, but this doesn't have to be the case. For example, you could retain sole ownership and grant the client a license to use your work. The only limit on how you deal with ownership of your work is your own imagination. (See Chapter 17.)

a. You retain ownership

Under the following clause, you keep ownership of your work and merely give the client a nonexclusive license to use it. This means that the client may use your work, but does not own it and may not sell it to others. The license is royalty-free—meaning that the sole payment you receive for it is the sum the client paid you for your services. The client will make no additional payments for the license. (See Chapter 17, Section B2.)

**SUGGESTED LANGUAGE—ALTERNATIVE A—
NONEXCLUSIVE TRANSFER:**

Contractor grants to Client a royalty-free nonexclusive license to use anything created or developed by Contractor for Client under this Agreement (Contract Property). The license shall have a perpetual term and the Client may not transfer it. Contractor shall retain all copyrights, patent rights and other intellectual property rights to the Contract Property.

---

b. You transfer ownership to client

Under the following clause you transfer all your ownership rights to the client. But you must first get all your compensation from the client.

You also agree to help prepare any documents necessary to help the client obtain any copyright, patent or other intellectual property rights at no charge to the client. This would probably amount to no more than signing a patent or copyright registration application. However, the client is required to reimburse you for the expense of getting and assigning the rights.

**SUGGESTED LANGUAGE—ALTERNATIVE B—
TRANSFER ALL RIGHTS:**

Contractor assigns to Client all patent, copyright and trade secret rights in anything created or developed by Contractor for Client under this Agreement. This assignment is conditioned upon full payment of the compensation due Contractor under this Agreement.

Contractor shall help prepare any documents Client considers necessary to secure any copyright, patent or other intellectual property rights at no charge to Client. However, Client shall reimburse Contractor for reasonable out of pocket expenses.

---

c. Reusable materials

Many self-employed people who create intellectual property for clients have certain materials they use over and over again for different clients. For example, computer programmers may have certain utilities or program tools they incorporate into the software they create for many different clients.

You may lose the legal right to reuse such materials if you transfer all your ownership rights in your work to the client. To avoid this, include the following provision in your agreement. It provides that you retain ownership of such materials and only gives the client a nonexclusive license to use them. The license is royalty-free—meaning that the sole payment you receive for it is the sum the client paid you for your services. The client will make no additional payments for the license. The license also has a perpetual term, meaning it will last as long as your copyright, patent or other intellectual property rights do.

If you know what such materials consist of in advance, it's a good idea to list them in an exhibit attached to the agreement. This isn't absolutely necessary, however.

OPTIONAL LANGUAGE—RIGHT TO REUSE:

Contractor owns or holds a license to use and sublicense various materials in existence before the start date of this Agreement (Contractor's Materials).

[OPTIONAL: Contractor's Materials include, but are not limited to, those items identified in Exhibit __, attached to and made part of this Agreement.]

Contractor may, at its option, include Contractor's Materials in the work performed under this Agreement. Contractor retains all right, title and interest, including all copyrights, patent rights and trade secret rights in Contractor's Materials. Contractor grants Client a royalty-free nonexclusive license to use any Contractor's Materials incorporated into the work performed by Contractor under this Agreement. The license shall have a perpetual term and may not be transferred by Client.

---

8. Assignment and Delegation

An assignment is the process by which rights or benefits under a contract are transferred to someone else. For example, a client might assign the right to receive the benefit of your services to someone else. Such a person is called an assignee. When this occurs, the assignee steps into the original client's shoes. You must now work for the assignee, not the client with whom you contracted. If you fail to perform, the assignee may sue you for breach of contract.

> **EXAMPLE:** Terri, a self-employed designer, agrees to design a cover and chapter headings for several books published by Scrivener & Sons. Scrivener assigns this right to Pop's Books. This means that Terri must perform the work for Pop's instead of Scrivener. If Terri fails to do so, Pop's can sue her for breach of contract.

You may also assign the benefits you receive under an IC agreement to someone else.

> **EXAMPLE:** Jimmy agrees to provide Fastsoft 20 hours of computer programming services in exchange for being able to use its computer for 100 hours. Jimmy assigns, or transfers, the right to the computer time to his friend Kate. This means Fastsoft must let Kate use its computer.

Delegation is the flipside of assignment. Instead of transferring benefits under a contract, you transfer the duties. As long as the new person does the job correctly, all will be well. However, the person delegating duties under a contract usually remains responsible if the person to whom the delegation was made fails to perform.

> **EXAMPLE:** Jimmy delegates to Mindy his duty to perform 20 hours of programming services for Fastsoft. This means that Mindy, not Jimmy, will now do the work. But Jimmy remains liable if Mindy doesn't perform adequately.

a. Legal restrictions

Unless a contract provides otherwise, you can ordinarily freely assign and delegate it subject to some important legal limitations. For example, a client can't assign the benefit of your services to someone else without your consent if it would increase the work you must do or otherwise magnify your burden under the contract. Similarly, you can't delegate your duties without the client's consent if it would decrease the benefits the client would receive.

One of the most important limitations for self-employed people is that contracts for personal services are ordinarily not assignable or delegable without the client's consent. This type of contract involves services that are personal in nature. Examples include contracts for the services of lawyers, physicians, architects, writers and artists. Courts consider it unfair for either a client or self-employed person to change horses in midstream in these cases.

EXAMPLE: Arthur contracts with Betty, a freelance artist, to paint his portrait. He later attempts to assign his rights to his wife Carla—that is, require Betty to paint Carla's portrait instead of his. Neither Arthur nor Carla can force Betty to paint Carla's portrait because Betty's contract with Arthur was a personal services contract.

b. Contract restrictions

Your contract may also place limits on assignment and delegation. Contractual limits on your right to delegate your duties to others are not supportive of your independent contractor status since they allow the client to control who will do the work. Moreover, it is often advantageous for you to have the right to delegate your contractual obligations to others. This gives you flexibility, for example, to hire someone else to do the work if you don't have time to do it.

However, some clients may balk at allowing you to delegate your contractual duties without the client's consent. This is usually where the client has hired you because of your special expertise, reputation for performance or financial stability and the client doesn't want some other person performing the services.

Also, there may be cases where you really don't want the client to have the right to assign the benefit of your services to someone else, who may turn out to be incompetent.

In this event, you may include the following provision in your agreement. It bars both you and the client from assigning your rights or delegating your duties without the other party's consent.

SUGGESTED LANGUAGE:

Neither party may assign any rights or delegate any duties under this Agreement without the other party's prior written approval.

C. Sample Client Agreement

The following sample agreement is a fixed fee agreement calling for mediation and arbitration of disputes and payment of attorney fees. Note that the headings in the sample agreement include a citation in parentheses that coincides with the discussion earlier in the chapter.

SAMPLE GENERAL IC AGREEMENT

Independent Contractor Agreement (See Section A)

This Agreement is made between Acme Widget Co. (Client) with a principal place of business at 123 Main Street, Marred Vista, CA 90000 and ABC Consulting, Inc. (Contractor), with a principal place of business at 456 Grub Street, Santa Longo, CA 90001.

Services to Be Performed (A1)

Contractor agrees to perform the following services: Install and test Client's DX9-105 widget manufacturing press so that it performs according to the manufacturer's specifications.

Payment (A2)

In consideration for the services to be performed by Contractor, Client agrees to pay Contractor $20,000.

Terms of Payment (A3)

Upon completing Contractor's services under this Agreement, Contractor shall submit an invoice. Client shall pay Contractor within 30 days from the date of Contractor's invoice.

Expenses (A4)

Contractor shall be responsible for all expenses incurred while performing services under this Agreement.

Materials (A5)

Contractor will furnish all materials and equipment used to provide the services required by this Agreement.

Term of Agreement (A6)

This Agreement will become effective when signed by both parties and will end no later than May 1, 20XX.

Terminating the Agreement (A7)

With reasonable cause, either party may terminate this Agreement effective immediately by giving written notice of termination for cause. Reasonable cause includes:

- a material violation of this agreement, or
- nonpayment of Contractor's compensation 20 days after written demand for payment.

Contractor shall be entitled to full payment for services performed prior to the effective date of termination.

Independent Contractor Status (A8)

Contractor is an independent contractor, not Client's employee. Contractor's employees or subcontractors are not Client's employees. Contractor and Client agree to the following rights consistent with an independent contractor relationship.

- Contractor has the right to perform services for others during the term of this Agreement.
- Contractor has the sole right to control and direct the means, manner and method by which the services required by this Agreement will be performed.
- Contractor has the right to hire assistants as subcontractors, or to use employees to provide the services required by this Agreement.
- The Contractor or Contractor's employees or subcontractors shall perform the services required by this Agreement; Client shall not hire, supervise or pay any assistants to help Contractor.
- Neither Contractor nor Contractor's employees or subcontractors shall receive any training from Client in the skills necessary to perform the services required by this Agreement.
- Client shall not require Contractor or Contractor's employees or subcontractors to devote full time to performing the services required by this Agreement.
- Neither Contractor nor Contractor's employees or subcontractors are eligible to participate in any employee pension, health, vacation pay, sick pay or other fringe benefit plan of Client.

Local, State and Federal Taxes (A9a)

Contractor shall pay all income taxes, and FICA (Social Security and Medicare taxes) incurred while performing services under this Agreement. Client will not:

- withhold FICA from Contractor's payments or make FICA payments on Contractor's behalf
- make state or federal unemployment compensation contributions on Contractor's behalf, or
- withhold state or federal income tax from Contractor's payments.

Sales Taxes (A9b)

The charges included here do not include taxes. If Contractor is required to pay any federal, state or local sales, use, property or value added taxes based on the services provided under this Agreement, the taxes shall be separately billed to Client. Contractor shall not pay any interest or penalties incurred due to late payment or nonpayment of any taxes by Client.

Notices (A10)

All notices and other communications in connection with this Agreement shall be in writing and shall be considered given as follows:

- when delivered personally to the recipient's address as stated on this Agreement
- three days after being deposited in the United States mail, with postage prepaid to the recipient's address as stated on this Agreement, or
- when sent by fax or telex to the last fax or telex number of the recipient known to the person giving notice. Notice is effective upon receipt provided that a duplicate copy of the notice is promptly given by first class mail, or the recipient delivers a written confirmation of receipt.

No Partnership (A11)

This Agreement does not create a partnership relationship. Neither party has authority to enter into contracts on the other's behalf.

Applicable Law (A12)

This Agreement will be governed by the laws of the state of California.

Exclusive Agreement (A13)

This is the entire Agreement between Contractor and Client.

Resolving Disputes (B1)

If a dispute arises under this Agreement, the parties agree to first try to resolve the dispute with the help of a mutually agreed-upon mediator in Mariposa County. Any costs and fees other than attorney fees associated with the mediation shall be shared equally by the parties.

If it proves impossible to arrive at a mutually satisfactory solution through mediation, the parties agree to submit the dispute to binding arbitration in Mariposa County under the rules of the American Arbitration Association. Judgment upon the award rendered by the arbitrator may be entered in any court having jurisdiction to do so.

However, the complaining party may refuse to submit the dispute to mediation or arbitration and instead bring an action in an appropriate Small Claims Court.

Modifying the Agreement (B2)

Client and Contractor recognize that:

- Contractor's original cost and time estimates may be too low due to unforeseen events, or to factors unknown to Contractor when this Agreement was made
- Client may desire a mid-project change in Contractor's services that would add time and cost to the project and possibly inconvenience Contractor, or
- Other provisions of this Agreement may be difficult to carry out due to unforeseen circumstances.

If any intended changes or any other events beyond the parties' control require adjustments to this Agreement, the parties shall make a good faith effort to agree on all necessary particulars. Such agreements shall be put in writing, signed by the parties and added to this Agreement.

Attorneys' Fees (B3)

If any legal action is necessary to enforce this Agreement, the prevailing party shall be entitled to reasonable attorney fees, costs and expenses in addition to any other relief to which he or she may be entitled.

Signatures (A14)

Client:

Acme Widget Co.

By: _____
                              (Signature)
_____ BASILIO CHEW _____
                        (Typed or Printed Name)

Title: _____ President _____

Date: _____ April 30, 20XX _____

Contractor: _____ ABC Consulting, Inc. _____

By: _____
                              (Signature)
_____ GEORGE BAILEY _____
                        (Typed or Printed Name)

Title: _____ President _____

Taxpayer ID Number: 123-45-6789 _____

Date: _____ April 30, 20XX _____

D. Using Letter Agreements

Many self-employed people and their clients commonly use letter agreements instead of more formal standard contracts. A letter agreement is usually a short contract written in the form of a letter. Although letter agreements may lack the gravitas of standard agreements, they are perfectly valid, binding contracts.

In a typical arrangement where a letter agreement is used, you and a client will reach a tentative agreement on an assignment in a meeting, over the phone, by fax, electronic mail or a combination of all four. After the agreement is reached, one of you drafts a letter documenting the important terms, signs it and sends it to the other person to sign.

Some clients have their own form letter agreements they use with all self-employed people they hire and will insist on using them. Review the letter carefully to make sure it meshes with the client's and your own oral statements and does not contain unfair provisions. (See Chapter 20.)

However, many clients will be happy for you to take on the work of drafting the agreement. You'll almost always be better off if you draft the agreement yourself because you can:

- avoid including any terms that are unduly favorable to the client, and
- make sure the agreement is completed and sent out quickly.

Take the initiative and offer to draw up the letter agreement. Explain that this is part of your service and that using an agreement you've drafted helps establish that you're not the client's employee.

Use the information in this chapter to draft one or more appropriate form letters you can use over and over again with minor alterations. This will be particularly easy to do if you use a word processor and keep the forms on disk.

 ### Don't Begin Work Until the Client Signs on Bottom Line

No matter who drafts a letter agreement, don't begin work until you have a copy signed by the client. You don't want to begin work only to discover that the client wants to cancel the project or make major changes in your agreement.

1. Pros and Cons of Letter Agreements

Letter agreements are usually shorter and easier to draft than regular contracts. They are also less formal looking. As a result, they often seem less intimidating to clients. Many clients who are fearful of signing a formal contract without having a lawyer review it will sign a letter agreement with no hesitation.

And in some fields, using letter agreements is the commonly accepted practice for doing business. For example, letter agreements are commonly used when freelance writers accept short assignments from magazines or other publications. If this is the case in your field of work, you may have to use letter agreements as a matter of course.

Because letter agreements are usually much shorter than standard client agreements, they are particularly useful for brief projects where relatively little money is involved. A potential client could well think you're crazy if you insist on a lengthy formal contract for a simple one-day

project. Clients don't want to spend a lot of time on legal documentation for minor projects—and you probably don't either.

However, in the interests of brevity, letter agreements typically make no mention of many provisions contained in longer standard agreements that could prove very useful if a problem arises—for example, provisions concerning dispute resolution, how the agreement may be terminated and provisions cementing your status as an independent contractor.

Both you and your client may be better off using a standard client agreement if:

- the project is a large and complex one that involves a substantial amount of money
- you're dealing with a new client you're not sure you can trust, or
- you are otherwise worried that problems or disputes may occur. (See Chapter 18, Section A.)

2. What to Include

A letter agreement can be as short as one-half page. At a minimum, however, it should contain:

- a description of the services you will perform
- the deadline by which you must complete your services
- the fees you will charge, and
- when you will be paid.

Your agreement doesn't have to end here, however. Depending on the nature of your services and the client, there may be several other provisions you'll want to include. (See Section B5.)

a. Services to be performed

The single most important part of the agreement is the description of the services you'll perform for the client. This description will set out the specifics of the work you're required to do and will serve as the yardstick to measure whether your performance was satisfactory.

Describe in as much detail as possible the work you're expected to accomplish. However, word the description carefully to emphasize the results you're expected to achieve. Don't describe the method by which you will achieve the results. It should be up to you to decide how to do the work. The client's control should be limited to accepting or rejecting your final results.

It's fine for the agreement to establish very detailed specifications for your finished work product. But the specs should only describe the end results you must achieve, not how to obtain those results.

You can include the description in the main body of the agreement. Or if it's a lengthy explanation, put it on a separate document and attach it to the agreement. (See Chapter 18, Section D3.)

**SUGGESTED LANGUAGE—ALTERNATIVE A—
DESCRIPTION IN AGREEMENT:**

I will perform the following services on your behalf: [Describe services you will perform.]

**SUGGESTED LANGUAGE—ALTERNATIVE B—
DESCRIPTION ATTACHED:**

I will perform the services described in the Exhibit attached to this Agreement.

Choose Alternative B if the explanation of the services is attached to the agreement.

b. Deadlines

The agreement should also make clear when your work will be completed and delivered to the client. Make sure you give yourself enough time to complete the job. It's better to err on the side of caution and give yourself more time than you think you'll need.

SUGGESTED LANGUAGE:

I agree to complete these services on or before _____ [date].

---

c. Payment

Self-employed people can be paid in many different ways. (See Chapter 7, Section A.)

The two most common payment methods are:
- a fixed fee, and
- payment by unit of time.

Fixed fee

In a fixed fee agreement, you charge an agreed amount for the entire project. (See Chapter 7, Section A1a.)

**SUGGESTED LANGUAGE—ALTERNATIVE A—
FIXED FEE:**

In consideration of my performance of these services, you agree to pay me $[State amount].

Unit of time

Many self-employed people charge by the hour, day or other unit of time—for example, lawyers, accountants and plumbers. (See Chapter 7, Section A1b.) Charging by the hour does not support the idea that you are an independent contractor, but you can get away with it if it's a common practice in your field.

**SUGGESTED LANGUAGE—ALTERNATIVE B—
UNIT OF TIME:**

In consideration of my performance of these services, you agree to pay me at the rate of $[State amount] per [Hour, day, week or other unit of time].

Clients often wish to place a cap on the total amount they'll spend on the project when you're paid by the hour because they're afraid you might work slowly just to earn a larger fee. If the client insists on a cap, make sure it allows you to work enough hours to get the project done.

OPTIONAL LANGUAGE—CAP ON PAYMENT:

My total compensation shall not exceed $____[State amount] without your written consent.

---

d. Terms of payment

Terms of payment means how you will bill the client and be paid. The client will not likely pay you for your work until you submit an invoice setting out the amount due. An invoice doesn't have to be fancy. It should include an invoice number, the dates covered by the invoice, the hours expended if you're being paid by the hour and a summary of the work performed. (See Chapter 7, Section B, for a detailed discussion and sample invoice form.) A blank invoice form is included in Appendix 1.

Full payment upon completing work

The following provision requires you to send an invoice after you complete work. The client is required to pay your fixed or hourly fee within a set number of days after you send the invoice. Thirty days is a typical payment term, but it can be shorter or longer if you wish. Note that the time for payment starts to run as soon as you send your invoice, not when the client receives it. This will help you get paid more quickly.

SUGGESTED LANGUAGE—ALTERNATIVE A—PAYMENT ON COMPLETION:

I will submit an invoice after my services are completed. You shall pay me within ____ [10, 15, 30, 45, 60] days from the date of the invoice.

Divided payments

You can also opt to be paid part of your fee when the agreement is signed and the remainder when the work is finished. When you're paid by the hour, such an upfront payment is often called a retainer. The amount of the upfront payment is subject to negotiation. Many self-employed people like to receive at least one-third to one-half of their fees before they start work. If the client is new or might have problems paying you, it's wise to get as much money in advance as you can.

The following provision requires that you be paid a specific amount when the client signs the agreement and the rest when the work is finished.

SUGGESTED LANGUAGE—ALTERNATIVE B—DIVIDED PAYMENTS:

I will be paid in two installments. The first installment shall be $[state amount] and is payable by [due date]. The remaining $____ [state amount] will be due within [10, 15, 30, 45, 60] days after I complete my services and submit an invoice.

---

e. Optional provisions

There are a number of other provisions you can add to a letter agreement. These aren't absolutely necessary, but they can benefit you. They are all discussed in detail in sections A and B of this chapter. They include provisions:

- requiring the client to reimburse you for expenses you incur in performing the work (see Section A4)
- requiring the client to provide you with materials, equipment or facilities (see Section A5)
- requiring mediation and arbitration of disputes (see Section B1)
- allowing you to obtain attorney fees if you sue the client and win (see Section B3)
- requiring the client to pay a late fee for late payments (see Section B4)

- limiting your liability to the client if something goes wrong (see Section B5), and
- restricting the client's ability to assign its benefits or delegate its duties under the agreement (see Section B8).

In addition, if your work involves the creation of intellectual property—for example, any type of work of authorship, such as an article or other written work—you should include a provision in your agreement stating who will own your work. (See Section B7.)

3. Putting the Agreement Together

There are two ways to handle a letter agreement. The old-fashioned way is to prepare and sign two copies and mail or deliver them to the client to sign. The client signs both copies, then returns one signed copy to you by mail or messenger and retains one copy for its records. Both copies are original, binding contracts.

Today, however, it's very common for an IC to draft a letter agreement, sign it and then fax a copy to the client. The client signs the letter and faxes a copy back to you. This has the advantage of speed, but you don't have the client's original signature on the letter, only a copy.

A faxed signature is probably legally sufficient if you and the client don't dispute that it is a fax of an original signature. However, if a client claims that a faxed signature was forged, it could be difficult or impossible to prove it's genuine since it is very easy to forge a faxed signature with modern computer technology. Forgery claims are rare, however, so this is usually not a problem. Even so, it's a good practice for you and the client to follow up the fax with signed originals exchanged by mail or air express.

4. Sample Letter Agreement

The following letter agreement is between a self-employed public relations consultant and an oil company. The consultant agrees to create a marketing plan for the company's new oil additive called Zotz. The work will be performed for a fixed fee paid in two installments.

MALONEY & ASSOCIATES
1000 GRUB STREET
MARRED VISTA, CA 90000

February 1, 20XX

Jerry Wellhead
Vice President
Acme Oil Co.
1000 Greasy Way
Tulsa, OK 10000

Dear Jerry:

I am pleased to have the opportunity to provide my services. This letter will serve as our agreement.

I will perform the following services on your behalf: I will create a marketing plan for the rollout of Acme's new oil additive called Zotz. The plan will include guidelines for magazine, radio and television advertising.

I agree to complete these services on or before March 1, 20XX.

In consideration of my performance of these services, you agree to pay me $5,000.

I will be paid in two installments. The first installment shall be $2,500 and is payable by February 5, 20XX. The remaining $2,500 will be paid within 30 days after I complete my services and submit an invoice.

If this Agreement meets with your approval, please sign below to make this a binding contract between us. Please sign both copies and return one to me. The other signed copy is for your records.

Sincerely,

Susan Maloney

Agreed to:

Acme Oil Co.

By: _____
   (Signature)

Jerry Wellhead

Title: Vice President

Date: _____

Reviewing a Client's Agreement

Many clients have their own agreements they will want to use. This is particularly likely if you work for firms that often use third parties to perform services or for large companies that have their own legal departments.

A client may present you with a lengthy, complex agreement, hand you a pen and tell you to sign. You may be told that the agreement is only a standard form that all non-employees who work for the client sign. However, signing a client agreement is never a mere technical formality. A client agreement is not simply a bunch of words on a piece of paper. It's a binding, legal document that will have important consequences for you in the real world.

Since client-drafted agreements are usually written with the client's best interests in mind, not yours, you'll almost always be better off if you use your own agreement. A client will be more willing to do this if you:

- provide a well-drafted agreement of your own (see Chapter 19), and
- point out that if the client is audited, an IRS or other government auditor will be far more impressed by an agreement you drafted than a standard form prepared by the client; using your agreement helps establish that you're an independent contractor, not the client's employee, and may help the client avoid assessments and penalties in the event of an audit.

If the client insists on using its own agreement, be sure to review the document before you accept the assignment. Read the agreement carefully and make sure you understand it and are comfortable with it before signing. If there are any provisions you don't understand, ask the client to explain them to you and rewrite them so that you do understand them.

No matter what the client may say, no agreement is engraved in stone, even if it's a "standard" agreement the client claims everybody signs. You can always request that an unfair or unduly burdensome provision be deleted or changed. If the client refuses, you have the option of turning down the assignment or going ahead anyway, but you lose nothing by asking.

When you review a client's agreement, make sure it:

- jibes with the client's statement and your own oral statement (see Section A)
- contains all necessary provisions (see Section B), and
- does not contain unfair provisions (see Section C).

There may also be provisions you want to add. (See Section D.)

CARELESS DOCTOR DONE IN BY AN AGREEMENT

One emergency room physician learned the hard way that it's always necessary to carefully read and understand an agreement before signing it. The doctor, who worked on the East Coast, received an offer to work as an independent contractor for a hospital in Hawaii. The doctor agreed to take the job and signed a lengthy independent contractor agreement prepared by the hospital without reading it carefully. The agreement provided a two-year term. She thought this meant she had guaranteed work for two years and this would justify the expense of moving to Hawaii.

The doctor moved to Hawaii and started work. But within three months, she had serious disagreements with hospital officials over various clinical and administrative issues. The hospital notified her that she was being terminated. She protested, pointing out that her contract was for two years. When she took a closer look, however, she discovered that the agreement included a provision allowing the hospital to terminate her if it concluded it was necessary for the emergency department to operate efficiently.

A. Agreement Consistent With Promises

Unfortunately, some clients are in the habit of telling people they hire one thing to get them to accept an assignment, then writing something very different in the agreements they prepare.

The language in your written agreement will be an important map in your relationship with the client. If a client says one thing to you in person and the agreement says something else, the agreement ordinarily will control. For example, if the client tells you that your work must be completed in two months, but the agreement imposes a one-month deadline, the work will have to be done in one month.

For this reason, make absolutely sure the agreement meshes with what the client has told you and what you have told the client. If there are differences, point them out. And if they're important differences, change the document to reflect your true agreement.

HOW TO CHANGE AN AGREEMENT

If you want to delete all or part of a provision, you can simply cross it out. Minor wording changes can be written in by hand or typed. Both you and the client should sign your initials as near the deletions or additions as possible.

If you wish to add an extensive amount of new wording, it's best to retype the entire agreement to prevent it from becoming illegible or downright confusing. This is easy to do if the agreement is written on a word processor.

Another approach is to write the changes on a separate piece of paper, called an attachment, that you and the client sign. If you use an attachment, state that if there is a conflict between the attachment and the main contract, the attachment will prevail. (See Chapter 18, Section D3.)

B. Reviewing the Contract

You should also make sure that the agreement contains all necessary provisions. At a bare minimum, it should include:

- your name and address
- the client's name and address
- the dates the contract begins and ends
- a description of the services you'll perform
- how much you'll be paid, and
- how you'll be paid.

These and other standard provisions are normally included in client agreements. If the client's agreement lacks any of these provisions, you should add them. (See Chapter 19, Section A.)

If you're creating or helping to create intellectual property—for example, writings, photos, graphics, music, software programs, designs or inventions—the agreement should also contain a clause making it clear who will own your work. (See Chapter 19, Section B7.)

C. Provisions to Avoid

Clients' agreements sometimes contain provisions that are patently unfair to you. You should seek to delete these entirely or at least replace them with provisions that are more equitable. Examine the agreement carefully for provisions such as the following.

1. Indemnifying the Client

Indemnification is a fancy legal word that means a promise to repay someone for their losses or damages if a specified event occurs. Some contracts may contain indemnification provisions that require you to indemnify the client if various problems occur—for example, if a problem with your work injures a third party who sues the client. In effect, these provisions require you to act as the client's insurer.

When it comes to indemnifying the client, your rule should be to just say no. Examine the client's agreement carefully to see if it contains such a provision. If you find one, try to delete it. Indemnification clauses can be hard to spot and even harder to understand. They'll usually contain the words indemnification or hold harmless, but not always. Any provision that requires you to defend or repay the client is an indemnification provision.

a. Problems with the IRS and other agencies

If the IRS or another government agency determines that the client has misclassified you as an independent contractor, the client may have to pay back taxes, fines and penalties. (See Chapter 15.) Some hiring firms try to shift the risk of IRS or other penalties to the independent contractor's shoulders by including an indemnification clause in their agreements. Such provisions typically require you to repay the hiring firm for any losses suffered if you are reclassified as an employee. Here's an example of such a provision.

> If Contractor is determined to be Client's employee, Contractor shall indemnify and hold Client harmless from any and all liabilities, costs and expenses Client may incur, including attorney fees and penalties.

Do not sign an agreement that contains such a provision. The cost of fighting an IRS or other government audit and paying the possible penalties for worker misclassification can be enormous. This provision makes you responsible for paying all of these costs. If you are presented with an agreement containing such a provision, strike it out or refuse to sign the contract.

b. Injuries and damages arising from your services

Your work or services on the client's behalf may damage or injure third parties—that is, people other than you and the client. For example, a passerby might be injured by a dropped hammer while walking by a construction project undertaken by a self-employed building contractor. Or a software program written by an outside programmer designed to run an elevator might fail and cause injuries. It's likely that the people injured in these situations—the passerby and the elevator passengers—would sue the client to pay for the costs of their medical care and other expenses related to their injuries.

Clients often include indemnification provisions in their contracts making the people they hire responsible for all damages and injuries that other people suffer if something goes wrong with their work. Many of these provisions are so broadly written they require you to indemnify the client even if the claim is frivolous, mainly the client's fault or already covered by the client's insurance.

EXAMPLE: Art, a self-employed engineer, designs and installs a new type of widget in BigCorp's factory. Art signed an agreement prepared by BigCorp's lawyers containing the following indemnification provision:

Contractor shall indemnify and hold Client harmless from any and all claims, losses, actions, damages, interest, penalties, and reasonable attorney fees and costs arising by reason of Contractor's performance under this Agreement.

One of BigCorp's employees alters the widget's setting without Art's permission. As a result, the widget explodes and injures a visitor at the factory who sues BigCorp. Art has to pay all of BigCorp's costs of defending the lawsuit and any damages the injured person recovers even though the explosion wasn't his fault. This is because the indemnification clause requires Art to repay BigCorp for any claim brought by anyone that could be said to "arise" from Art's services for BigCorp.

Most indemnification clauses are even more convoluted and harder to read than the one in the example above. The wisest course is to strike out any such provision from the client's agreement.

If the client insists on keeping such a provision, you should seek to add a provision to the agreement limiting your total liability to the client to a specified dollar amount or no more than the client pays you. This will prevent you from losing everything you own or going bankrupt. (See Chapter 19, Section B5.)

Also, make sure you have enough liability insurance to cover any potential claims. Feel free to charge the client more to cover your increased insurance costs. (See Chapter 7.)

c. Intellectual property infringement

If you create or help create intellectual property for a client, the client may seek to have you indemnify it for the costs involved if other people claim that your work infringes their copyright, patent, trade secret or other intellectual property rights.

EXAMPLE: Jennifer, a self-employed computer programmer, creates a program for Acme Corp. A few months later, BigCorp, Jennifer's former employer, claims that she stole substantial portions of the program from software it owned and sues Jennifer and Acme for copyright infringement. Since Jennifer's contract with Acme contained an indemnification provision, she is legally obligated to pay Acme's attorney fees for defending the lawsuit and any money Acme may have to pay BigCorp as damages or to settle the claim.

Intellectual property indemnity clauses are routinely included in publishing contracts, software consulting agreements and almost any other type of agreement involving the creation of intellectual property. You'd be better off without such a clause—that is, less of your own money will be at risk on the job—but it's often hard to get clients to remove them. After all, the clauses are mainly aimed at ensuring proper behavior. You shouldn't commit intellectual property infringement and clients do not to want to pay any damages if you do.

Instead of deleting the clause, your best approach may be to add a provision limiting your total liability to the client to a specified dollar amount or no more than the client pays you. (See Chapter 19, Section B5a.)

2. Insurance Requirements

Look carefully to see if the client's agreement contains a provision requiring you to maintain insurance coverage. Many clients want all self-employed people they hire to have extensive insurance coverage because it helps eliminate an injured person's motivation to attempt to recover from the client for fear you won't be able to pay. It's not unreasonable for a client to require you to have liability insurance. (See Chapter 6, Section B.)

However, some clients go overboard and require you to obtain an excessive amount of insurance or obtain unusual and expensive policies. For example, one self-employed courier recently contracted with a courier firm to make document deliveries using his own car. The contract included an insurance clause requiring him to obtain cargo insurance. His insurance agent told him this type of coverage was usually obtained only by trucking firms and would cost several thousand dollars per year. It was ridiculous for a document courier to be required to obtain such coverage, since it provided far more coverage than the client needed and cost far more than the courier could afford to pay. The courier simply ignored the contract and never obtained the cargo insurance.

The better practice is to delete provisions requiring excessive insurance from your contract or demand substantially more compensation to pay for the extra insurance. Make it clear to the client that you have to charge more than you usually do because it's requiring you to carry so much insurance coverage.

Following is a very reasonable provision requiring you to carry liability insurance you can add to a client's agreement in place of an unreasonable insurance clause.

SUGGESTED LANGUAGE:

Client shall not provide any insurance coverage for Contractor or Contractor's employees or contract personnel. Contractor agrees to maintain an insurance policy to cover any negligent acts committed by Contractor or Contractor's employees or agents while performing services under this Agreement.

---

3. Noncompetition Restrictions

Businesses that hire self-employed people sometimes want to restrict them from performing similar services for their competitors. To do this, they include a noncompetition clause in a client agreement barring them from working for competitors. Try to eliminate such provisions since they limit your ability to earn a living.

At most, you might agree to the following provision barring you from performing the same services for named competitors of the client while you're performing them for the client.

SUGGESTED LANGUAGE:

Contractor agrees that, while performing services required by this Agreement, Contractor will not perform the exact same services for the following competitors of Client: [LIST COMPETITORS].

---

4. Confidentiality Provisions

Many clients routinely include confidentiality provisions in their agreements. These provisions bar you from disclosing to others the client's trade secrets—for example, marketing plans, information on products under development, manufacturing techniques or customer lists. It's not unreasonable for a client to want you to keep its secrets away from the eyes and ears of competitors.

Unfortunately, however, many of these provisions are worded so broadly that they can make it difficult for you to work for other clients without fear of violating your duty of confidentiality. If, like most self-employed people, you make your living by performing similar services for many firms in the same industry, insist on a confidentiality provision that is reasonable in scope and defines precisely what information you must keep confidential. Such a provision should last for only a limited time—five years at the most.

a. Unreasonable provision

A general provision barring you from making any unauthorized disclosure or using any technical, financial or business information you obtain directly or indirectly from the client is unreasonable. Such broad restrictions can make it very difficult for you to do similar work for other clients without violating the confidentiality clause. Here's an example of an overbroad provision.

Contractor may be given access to Client's proprietary or confidential information while working for Client. Contractor agrees not to use or disclose such information except as directed by Client.

Such a provision doesn't make clear what information is and is not the client's confidential trade secrets, so you never know for sure what information you must keep confidential and what you can disclose when working for others.

Also, since this provision bars you from later using any of the client's confidential information to which you have access, it could prevent you from using information you already knew before working with the client. It could also bar you from using information that becomes available to the public. You would then be in the absurd position of not being allowed to use information that the whole world knows about. Always attempt to delete or rewrite such a provision.

Specifically, do not sign a contract requiring you to keep confidential any information:

- you knew about before working with the client
- you learn from a third person who has no duty to keep it confidential
- you develop independently even though the client later provides you with similar or identical information, or
- that becomes publicly known though no fault of your own—for example, you wouldn't have to keep a client's manufac-

turing technique confidential after it is disclosed to the public in an article in a trade journal written by someone other than you.

b. Reasonable provision

A reasonable nondisclosure provision makes clear that, while you may not use confidential information the client provides, you have the right to freely use information you obtain from other sources or that the public learns later.

The following nondisclosure provision enables you to know for sure what material is, and is not, confidential by requiring the client to mark confidential any document you get in the course of that work. A client who tells you confidential information must later write it down and deliver it to you within 15 days.

SUGGESTED LANGUAGE:

During the term of this Agreement and for _____ [6 months to 5 years] afterward, Contractor will use reasonable care to prevent the unauthorized use or dissemination of Client's confidential information. Reasonable care means at least the same degree of care Contractor uses to protect its own confidential information from unauthorized disclosure.

Confidential information is limited to information clearly marked as confidential, or disclosed orally and summarized and identified as confidential in a writing delivered to Contractor within 15 days of disclosure.

Confidential information does not include information that:

- the Contractor knew before Client disclosed it
- is or becomes public knowledge through no fault of Contractor
- Contractor obtains from sources other than Client who owe no duty of confidentiality to Client, or
- Contractor independently develops.

---

5. Unfair Termination Provisions

Your agreement can always be terminated if you or the client breaches one of its major terms—for example, you seriously fail to satisfy the project specifications. Ordinarily, however, neither you nor the client can terminate the agreement just because you feel like it. Some clients add termination provisions to their contracts allowing them to terminate the agreements at will—that is, for any reason or no reason at all. For example, the agreement may provide that the client has the right to terminate the agreement on ten days written notice.

If you sign an agreement with such a provision, you lose the security of knowing the client must allow you to complete your assignment and pay you for it provided you live up to the terms of your agreement. Instead, you can be fired at any time, just like an employee.

If the client insists on such a provision, fairness dictates that it be mutual—that is, you should have the same termination rights as the client. The client should also be required to give you reasonable notice of the termination. How long the notice should be depends on the length of the project. For lengthy projects, 30 days notice may be appropriate. For short projects, it may make sense to require just a few days notice. Finally, the agreement should make clear that the client must pay you for all the work you performed prior to termination. (See Chapter 19, Section A7a.)

6. Time of the Essence

Examine the client's agreement carefully to see if it contains the phrase "time is of the essence." You'll often find such clauses in the portion of the contract dealing with the project deadlines.

These simple words can have a big legal impact. Ordinarily, a delay in performance of your contractual obligations is not considered important enough to constitute a material breach of the agreement. This means the client can sue you for any damages sustained due to your lateness, but is not entitled to terminate the contract.

> **EXAMPLE:** Barney, a construction contractor, contracts to build a new wing on the AAA Motel. The contract provides that the wing is to be completed by April 1. Barney completes the new wing four weeks late. AAA may sue him for any damages caused by the delay. But since the contract lacks a time is of the essence clause, it may not terminate the contract and is legally obligated to pay Barney the contract price.

However, if the contract includes a time is of the essence provision, most courts hold that even a slight delay in performance will constitute a material breach. The client cannot only sue you for damages, but can terminate the contract. This means the client need not perform its contractual obligations—for example, the client need not pay you.

> **EXAMPLE:** Assume that Barney's contract in the above example included a time is of the essence clause. This would mean that the AAA Motel was legally entitled to terminate the contract when Barney missed the completion deadline and sue Barney for breach of contract.

If you want to be able to have a little slippage in your deadlines, delete any time is of the essence clause from the client's agreement.

D. Provisions You May Wish to Add

There are a number of provisions that benefit you that you may wish to add to the client's agreement. These provisions are all discussed in detail in Chapter 19 and include:

- requiring mediation and arbitration of disputes (see Chapter 19, Section B1)
- recognizing that the contract may have to be modified in the future and providing a mechanism to do so (see Chapter 19, Section B2)
- allowing you to obtain attorney fees if you sue the client and win (see Chapter 19, Section B3)
- requiring the client to pay a late fee for late payments (see Chapter 19, Section B4)
- limiting your liability to the client if something goes wrong (see Chapter 19, Section B5), and
- restricting the client's ability to assign its benefits or delegate its duties under the agreement (see Chapter 19, Section B8).

E. Client Purchase Orders

Not all clients use standard contracts. Instead, you may be handed a preprinted form that looks very different from the contracts in this book. Such a form is usually called a purchase order. Some clients use purchase orders instead of, or in addition to, standard contracts.

A purchase order is an internal form developed by a client authorizing you to perform work and bill for it. Typically, purchase orders are used by larger companies that have separate accounting departments. Accounting departments often don't want to have to deal with lengthy or confusing client agreements.

Purchase orders are designed to provide the minimum information a company needs to document the services you'll perform and how much you'll be paid. They typically contain much the same information as a letter agreement: a description of the services you'll perform, payment terms and deadlines. (See Chapter 18.) The order should be signed by the client. You should include the purchase order number on your invoices and all correspondence with the client.

Some companies use purchase orders in conjunction with standard contracts or letter agreements. That is, either you or the client will prepare a contract or letter agreement and the client will also prepare a purchase order. In this event, make sure the terms of the purchase order are consistent with your client agreement.

Other companies use purchase orders alone for small projects because they don't want to go to the trouble of drafting a client agreement. Make certain the purchase order is properly filled out. This should include an accurate description of the services you'll perform, the due date and the terms of payment.

Some companies' accounting departments will not pay you unless you have a signed purchase order, even if you have a signed letter agreement or standard client agreement.

Before you start work for a client, find out if it uses purchase orders. If it does, insist on being provided a signed order before you start work.

Following is an example of a typical purchase order for services.

PURCHASE ORDER

Acme, Inc.

P.O. #: 123

Vendor: Gerard & Associates
          123 Solano Avenue
          Berkeley, CA 99999
          510-555-5555

Date: 8/1/20XX

Delivery Date: 9/1/20XX

Terms: 18¢ per word translated. Total price not to exceed $6,084.

Description of Services: Contractor will translate Acme instruction manual from the English language into idiomatic Russian using the Cyrillic alphabet. The translated material will be provided in Word Perfect format. Contractor will provide one disk copy and one printed copy of all translated material.

Authorized by: _____

               Joe Jones

Help Beyond This Book

If a client claims that your work doesn't meet the contract specifications, insists that you've missed a deadline or fails to pay you for any reason, you've got a potential legal dispute on your hands. The way you handle such disputes will have a big impact on your self-employment success. The best way to handle them is usually through informal negotiations. Call or meet with the client and talk out your differences. If you reach a settlement, promptly write it down and have all involved sign it.

> **EXAMPLE:** Gwen, a self-employed computer programmer, is hired by Acme Corp. to create a custom software program for $10,000. Gwen delivers the program on time. However, Acme refuses to pay Gwen because it claims the program doesn't fully live up to the contract specifications. Gwen meets with Acme's president and admits that the program doesn't do everything it's supposed to do.
>
> However, she demonstrates that the program fulfills at least 80% of Acme's requirements. Gwen offers, therefore, to accept $8,000 as full payment instead of the $10,000 stated as full payment in the original contract. Acme's president agrees. Gwen drafts a short agreement stating that Acme will pay her $8,000 in full settlement of their dispute.

A. Help Resolving Disputes

If informal negotiations don't work, you have a number of options:

- alternative dispute resolution, which includes mediation and arbitration, and
- filing a lawsuit in court.

This chapter discusses those options in detail. It also provides guidance on how to find and use more specific legal resources, including lawyers and other knowledgeable experts. And finally, it explains the basics of doing your own legal research.

1. Mediation and Arbitration

Mediation and arbitration—often lumped together under the term alternative dispute resolution, or ADR—are two methods for settling disputes without resorting to expensive court litigation. People often confuse the two, but they are in fact very different. Mediation is never binding on the participants, whereas arbitration usually is binding and often takes the place of a court action.

a. Mediation

In mediation, a neutral third person called a mediator meets with the people involved in the dispute and makes suggestions as to how to resolve their controversy. Typically, the mediator either sits both sides down together and tries to provide an objective view of their dispute, or shuttles between them as a hopefully cool conduit for what may be hot opinions.

Where the underlying problem is actually a personality conflict or simple lack of communication, a good mediator can often help those involved in the dispute find their own compromise settlement. Where the argument is more serious, a mediator may at least be able to lead them to a mutually satisfactory ending of both the dispute and their relationship that will obviate time-consuming and expensive litigation.

If you've ever had a dispute with a friend or relative that another friend or relative helped resolve by meeting with you both and helping you talk things over, you've already been through a process very like mediation.

Mediation is nonbinding. That means that if either person involved in the dispute doesn't like the outcome of the mediation, he or she can ask for binding arbitration or go to court.

b. Arbitration

If those involved in a dispute cannot resolve it by mediation, they often submit it to arbitration. The arbitrator—again, a neutral third person—is either selected directly by those involved in the dispute or is designated by an arbitration agency.

An arbitrator's role is very different from that of a mediator. Unlike a mediator who seeks to help the parties resolve their dispute themselves, an arbitrator personally imposes a solution.

The arbitrator normally hears both sides at an informal hearing. You can be represented by a lawyer at the hearing, but it's not required. The arbitrator acts as both judge and jury: After the hearing, he or she issues a decision called an award. The arbitrator follows the same legal rules a judge or jury would follow in deciding whether you or the other side has a valid legal claim and should be awarded money.

Arbitration can be either binding or nonbinding. If arbitration is nonbinding, either person named in the award can take the matter to court if he or she doesn't like the outcome. Binding arbitration is usually final. You can't go to court and try the dispute again if you don't like the arbitrator's decision—except in unusual cases where you can show the arbitrator was guilty of fraud, misconduct or bias. In effect, binding arbitration takes the place of a court trial.

If the losing party to a binding arbitration doesn't pay the money required by an arbitration award, the winner can easily convert the award into a court judgment which can be enforced just like any other court judgment—in other words, a binding arbitration award is just as good as a judgment you could get from a court.

FINDING A MEDIATOR OR ARBITRATOR

It is usually up to you and the client to decide who should serve as a mediator or arbitrator. You can normally choose anyone you want unless your contract restricts your choice.

It can be a professional mediator or arbitrator or just someone you both respect. A professional organization may be able to refer you to a good mediator or arbitrator. Businesses often use private dispute resolution services that maintain a roster of mediators and arbitrators—often retired judges, attorneys or business people with expertise in a particular field. Two of the best known of these services are:

- **The American Arbitration Association.** This is the oldest and largest private dispute resolution service, with offices in most major cities. It handles both mediations and arbitrations. The main office is in New York City: 800-778-7879. The American Arbitration Association also has a very informative site on the Internet at www.adr.org.

- **Judicate.** This Philadelphia-based firm emphasizes mediation and handles disputes in all 50 states. It can be reached at 800-488-8805.

c. Agreeing to mediation and arbitration

No one can be forced into arbitration or mediation; you must agree to it, either in the contract or later when a dispute arises. Business contracts today commonly include an arbitration provision and many also require mediation. This is primarily because of two truths: speed and cost.

Mediation and arbitration are usually much faster than court litigation. Most arbitrations and mediations are concluded in less than six months. Court litigation often takes years.

No one can ever tell how much a court case will cost, but it's usually a lot. Business lawyers typically charge from $150 to $250 per hour. Unless the amount of money involved is small and the case can be tried in small claims court (see Section A2c), arbitration and mediation are usually far cheaper than a lawsuit. A private dispute resolution company will typically charge about $500 to $1,000 for a half-day of arbitration or mediation.

 For detailed guidance on mediation and arbitration, see *How to Mediate Your Dispute*, by Peter Lovenheim (Nolo).

2. Filing a Lawsuit

If your attempts to settle the dispute through informal negotiations or mediation fail and the client won't agree to binding arbitration, your remaining alternative is to sue the client in court. Or you or the client may choose to skip informal negotiations or arbitration altogether and immediately go to court.

Most legal disputes between self-employed people and clients involve a breach of contract. A person who fails to live up to the terms of a contract is said to have breached it. In a typical breach of contract case, the person who sues—called the plaintiff—asks the judge to issue a judgment against the person being sued—called the defendant. Usually, the plaintiff wants money, also known as damages.

a. What you need to prove

Proving a breach of contract case is not complicated. You must first show that the contract existed. If it is written, the document itself should be presented to the court. If the contract is oral, you'll have to testify as to its terms. You must also show that you did everything you were required to do under the contract.

You must then make clear how the client breached the contract and show the amount of damages you have suffered as a result. In many situations, this amounts to no more than showing that the client committed itself to buy certain services from you, that you provided those services, and that the client has not paid a legitimate bill for a stated number of dollars.

> **EXAMPLE:** Ted, a self-employed graphic designer, contracted with the Acme Sandblasting Company to redesign its logo and newsletter. Ted completed the work, but Acme refused to pay him. After informal negotiations failed, Ted sued Acme in court. To win his case, Ted should produce the written contract with Acme, a decent-looking sample of the redesigned newsletter and a letter from someone with expertise in the field stating that the work met or exceeded industry standards. Ted would also be wise to try to rebut the likely points the client might make. For example, if the design work was a few weeks late, Ted would want to present a good excuse, such as the fact that Acme asked for time-consuming changes.

b. What you can sue for

If you sue a client for breach of contract, forget about collecting the huge awards you hear about people getting when they're injured in accidents and sue for personal injuries. Damages for breach of contract are strictly limited by law. As a general rule, you'll get just enough to compensate you for your direct economic loss—that is, the amount of money you lost because the client failed to live up to its promises. For example, if a client promised to pay you $1,000 for your services, but failed to pay after you performed them, you'd be entitled to $1,000 in damages.

You can't get punitive damages—special damages designed to punish wrongdoers—or damages to compensate you for your emotional pain or suffering, even though clients who breach their contracts can really be a pain. On the bright side, however, if a client sues you for breach of contract, damages are limited in the same way.

c. Small claims court

Most business contract suits are filed in state court. All states have a special court especially designed to handle disputes where only a small amount of money is involved. These are called small claims courts. The amount for which you can sue in small claims court varies from state to state—but usually ranges between $2,500 to $5,000.

Small claims court has the same advantages as arbitration: it's usually fast and inexpensive. You don't need a lawyer to go to small claims court. Indeed, some states don't allow lawyers to represent people in small claims court.

Small claims court is particularly well suited to help you collect against clients who fail to pay you, provided the amount is relatively small. (See Chapter 7, Section B4.)

 For detailed guidance on how to represent yourself in small claims court, see *Everybody's Guide to Small Claims Court*, by Ralph Warner, National and California editions (Nolo).

d. Suing in other courts

If your claim exceeds the small claims court limit for your state, you'll need to file your lawsuit in another court. Most business lawsuits are handled in state courts. Every state has its own trial court system with one or more courts that deal with legal disputes between people and businesses. These courts are more formal than small claims courts and the process usually takes longer. You may be represented by a lawyer, but you don't have to be. Many people have successfully handled their own cases in state trial courts.

For detailed guidance on how to represent yourself, see: *Represent Yourself in Court: How to Prepare and Try a Winning Case*, by Paul Bergman and Sara Berman-Barrett (Nolo). This book explains how to handle a civil case yourself, without a lawyer, from start to finish.

B. Finding and Using a Lawyer

An experienced attorney may help answer your questions and allay your fears about setting up and running your business. Many different areas of law may be involved when you're self-employed, including:

- federal tax law
- state tax law
- contract law, and
- general business law.

Fortunately, there are attorneys who specialize in advising small businesses. These lawyers are a bit like general practitioner doctors: they know a little about a lot of different areas of law. A lawyer with plenty of experience working with businesses like yours should be able to answer your questions.

Such a lawyer can help you:
- start your business—review incorporation documents, for example
- analyze zoning ordinances, land use regulations and private title documents that may restrict your ability to work at home
- review client agreements
- coach or represent you in lawsuits or arbitrations where the stakes are high or the legal issues complex
- deal with intellectual property issues—copyrights, trademarks, patents, trade secrets and business names, or
- look over a proposed office lease.

1. Finding a Lawyer

When you begin looking for a lawyer, try to find someone with experience representing businesses similar to yours. It's usually not wise to start your search by consulting phone books, legal directories or advertisements. Lawyer referral services operated by bar associations are usually equally unhelpful. Often, they simply supply the names of lawyers who have signed onto the service, accepting the lawyer's own word for what types of skills he or she has.

The best way to locate a lawyer is through referrals from other self-employed people in your community. Industry associations and trade groups are also excellent sources of referrals. If you already have or know a lawyer, he or she might also be able to refer you to an experienced person who has the qualifications you need. Other people, such as your banker, accountant or insurance agent, may know of good business lawyers.

2. Paying a Lawyer

Whenever you hire a lawyer, insist upon a written explanation of how the fees and costs will be paid.

Most business lawyers charge by the hour. Hourly rates vary, but in most parts of the United States, you can get competent services for your business for $150 to $250 an hour. Comparison shopping among lawyers will help you avoid overpaying. But the cheapest hourly rate isn't necessarily the best. A novice who charges only $80 an hour may take three hours to review a consulting contract. A more experienced lawyer who charges $200 an hour may do the same job in half an hour and make better suggestions. If a lawyer will be delegating some of the work on your case to a less experienced associate, paralegal or secretary, that work should be billed at a lower hourly rate. Be sure to get this information recorded in your initial written fee agreement.

Sometimes, a lawyer may quote you a flat fee for a specific job. For example, a lawyer may offer to incorporate your business for a flat fee of $2,000. You pay the same amount regardless of how much time the lawyer spends. This can be cheaper than paying an hourly fee, but not always.

Alternatively, some self-employed people hire lawyers on retainer—that is, they pay a flat annual fee in return for the lawyer handling all their routine legal business. However, few small businesses can afford to keep a lawyer on retainer.

L. R. STEIN
ATTORNEY AT LAW

USING A LAWYER AS A LEGAL COACH

One way to keep your legal costs down is to do as much work as possible yourself and simply use the lawyer as your coach. For example, you can draft your own agreements, giving your lawyer the relatively quick and inexpensive task of reviewing them.

But get a clear understanding about who's going to do what. You don't want to do the work and get billed for it because the lawyer duplicated your efforts. And you certainly don't want any crucial elements to fall through cracks because you each thought the other person was attending to the work.

C. Help From Other Experts

Lawyers aren't the only ones who can help you deal with the legal issues involved in being self-employed. Tax professionals, members of trade groups and the Small Business Administration can also be very helpful.

1. Tax Professionals

Tax professionals include tax attorneys, certified public accountants and enrolled agents. Tax pros can answer your tax questions and help you with tax planning, preparing your tax returns and dealing with IRS audits. (See Chapter 8, Section B2.)

2. Industry and Trade Associations

Business or industry trade associations or similar organizations can be useful sources of information and services. Many such groups track federal and state laws, lobby Congress and state legislatures and even help members deal with the IRS and other federal and state agencies. Many also offer their members insurance and other benefits and have useful publications.

There are hundreds of such organizations representing every conceivable occupation—for example, the American Society of Home Inspectors, the Association of Independent Video and Filmmakers and the Graphic Artists Guild. There are also national membership organizations that allow all types of self-employed people to join—for example, the National Association of the Self Employed and the Home Office Association of America.

If you don't know the name and address of an organization you may be eligible to join, ask other self-employed people. Or check out the *Encyclopedia of Associations* (Gale Research); it should be available in your public library. Also, many of these organizations have websites on the Internet, so you may be able to find the one you want by doing an Internet search. (See Section E.)

3. Small Business Administration

The U.S. Small Business Administration, or SBA, is an independent federal agency that helps small businesses. The SBA is best known for providing loan guarantees to bolster small businesses that want to start or expand, but it provides several other useful services for small businesses, including:

- **SBA Answer Desk.** The Answer Desk is a nationwide, toll-free information center that helps callers with questions and problems about starting and running businesses. Service is provided through a computerized telephone message system augmented by staff counselors. It is available 24 hours a day, seven days a week, with counselors available Monday through Friday, 9 am to 5 pm Eastern Time. The Answer Desk can be reached at 800-8-ASK-SBA.

- **Publications.** The SBA also produces and maintains a library of publications, videos and computer programs. These are available by mail to SBA customers for a nominal fee. A complete listing of these products is in the *Resource Directory for Small Business Management*. SBA field offices also offer free publications that describe SBA programs and services.

- **SBA Internet site.** You can download SBA publications from the SBA Internet site and obtain information about SBA programs and services, points of contact and calendars of local events. The Internet address is www.sba.gov.

- **SCORE program.** The Service Corps of Retired Executives, or SCORE, is a group of retired business people who volunteer to help others in business. To find a SCORE chapter in your area, visit the SCORE website at www.score.org, or call the national SCORE office at 800-634-0245.

The SBA has offices in all major cities. Look in the phone book under U.S. Government for the office nearest you.

D. Doing Your Own Legal Research

If you decide to investigate the law on your own, your first step should be to obtain a good guide to help you understand legal citations, use the law library and understand what you find there. There are a number of sources that provide a good introduction to legal research, including *Legal Research: How to Find and Understand the Law*, by Stephen Elias and Susan Levinkind (Nolo). This book simply explains how to use all major legal research tools and helps you frame your research questions

Next, you need to find a law library that's open to the public. Your county should have a public law library, often at the county courthouse. Public law schools often contain especially good collections and generally permit the public to use

them. Some private law schools grant access to their libraries—sometimes for a modest fee. The reference department of a major public or university library may have a fairly decent legal research collection. Finally, don't overlook the law library in your own lawyer's office. Many lawyers will agree to share their books with their clients.

1. Researching Federal Tax Law

Many resources are available to augment and explain the tax information in this book. Some are free and others are reasonably priced. Tax publications for professionals are expensive, but are often available at public libraries or law libraries.

a. IRS website

Somewhat surprisingly, the IRS has perhaps the most useful and colorful Internet site of any government agency. It contains virtually every IRS publication and tax form, IRS announcements and a copy of the *IRS Audit Manual on Independent Contractors*. It's almost worth getting on the Internet just to use this site. The Internet address is www.irs.gov.

b. IRS booklets

The IRS also publishes over 350 free booklets explaining the tax code, and many are clearly written and useful. These IRS publications range from several pages to several hundred pages in length. Many of the most useful IRS publications are cited in the tax chapters in this book.

The following IRS publications cover basic tax information that every self-employed person should know about:

- Publication 334, *Tax Guide for Small Businesses*
- Publication 505, *Tax Withholding and Estimated Tax*

- Publication 937, *Employment Taxes and Information Returns,* and
- Publication 15, *Circular E, Employer's Tax Guide.*

IRS publications are available in IRS offices, by calling 800-TAX-FORM or by sending in an order form. They can also be downloaded from the IRS's Internet site at www.irs.gov.

Don't Rely Exclusively on the IRS

IRS publications are useful to obtain information on IRS procedures and to get the agency's view of the tax law. But keep in mind that these publications only present the IRS's interpretation of the law, which may be very one-sided and even contrary to court rulings. Don't rely exclusively on IRS publications for information.

c. IRS telephone information

The IRS offers a series of prerecorded tapes of information on various tax topics on a toll-free telephone service called TELETAX. Call 800-829-4477. See IRS Publication 910 for a list of topics.

You can talk to an IRS representative at 800-829-1040, but expect difficulty getting though from January through May. Doublecheck anything an IRS representative tells you over the phone; the IRS is notorious for giving misleading or outright wrong answers to taxpayers' questions. The IRS does not stand behind oral advice that turns out to be incorrect.

d. Directories of IRS rulings

The IRS has issued thousands of rulings on how workers in every conceivable occupation should be classified for tax purposes. Tax experts have collected and categorized these rulings by occupation. By using these publications, you can find citations to IRS rulings involving workers similar to you. Several such publications are available:

- *Employment Status—Employee v. Independent Contractor,* 391-2nd T.M., by Helen Marmoll, summarizes and provides citations to IRS rulings on classification of workers in 374 different occupations—everything from accountants to yacht sales agents. Unfortunately, this guide is out of print. But you may be able to find it in a law library with a good tax collection.
- An online database of hundreds of cases involving ICs categorized by occupation can be found at the website http://WorkerStatus.Com/. Unfortunately, you must pay a membership fee to access the database.
- Many state Chambers of Commerce publish guides that list IRS rulings for various occupations. For example, the California Chamber of Commerce publishes a guide called *Independent Contractors: A Manager's Guide and Audit Reference.* It categorizes thousands of IRS rulings by occupation and also covers rulings by California state agencies. Call your state Chamber of Commerce to see if it publishes such a guide for your state; it probably has an office in your state capital.

An industry trade group or association may also be aware, or even have copies, of helpful IRS rulings and court decisions.

e. Tax guides

Dozens of privately published self-help tax guides are available. The most detailed and authoritative are:

- *Master Tax Guide* (Commerce Clearing House)
- *Master Federal Tax Manual* (Research Institute of America), and
- *Federal Tax Guide* (Prentice-Hall).

You can find these in many public libraries.

2. Researching Other Areas of Law

Many fields of law other than federal tax law are involved when you're self-employed. For example, your state laws may control how you form a sole proprietorship or corporation, protect trade names, form contracts and resolve disputes.

If you have questions about your state workers' compensation, tax law or employment laws, first contact the appropriate state agency for more information. Many of these agencies publish informative pamphlets. See Appendix 3 of this book for lists of state workers' compensation agencies and sales and income tax departments.

In-depth research into your state law will require you to review:

- legislation, also called statutes, passed by your state legislature
- administrative rules and regulations issued by state administrative agencies such as your state tax department and unemployment compensation agency, and
- published decisions of your state courts.

Many states, particularly larger ones, have legal encyclopedias or treatises that organize summaries of state case law and some statutes alphabetically by subject. Through citation footnotes, you can locate the full text of the cases and statutes. These works are a good starting point for in-depth state law research.

It's also helpful if you can find a treatise on the subject you're researching. A treatise is a book that covers a specific area of law. The West Publishing Company publishes a series of short paperback treatises called the Nutshell Series. If you are facing a possible contract dispute, you may want to look at *Contracts in a Nutshell*, by Gordon A. Schaber and Claude D. Rohwer, and *Corporations in a Nutshell*, by Robert Hamilton.

A relatively unknown resource for quickly locating state business laws is the United States Law Digest volume of the *Martindale-Hubbel Law Directory*. It contains a handy summary of laws for each state. Dozens of business law topics are covered, including Corporations, Insurance,

Leases, Statute of Frauds and Trademarks, Trade Names and Service Marks. The *Martindale-Hubbel Law Directory* is in most public libraries.

E. Online Resources

The online world includes the Internet, commercial online services such as America Online and CompuServe and specialized computer databases such as Westlaw and Lexis. All contain useful information for the computer-savvy self-employed.

1. Internet Resources

A vast array of information for small business owners is available on the Internet. To get access to the Internet, you need a computer and modem, appropriate software and an account with an Internet access provider. You can get Internet access free in many university and some public libraries.

There are hundreds of Internet sites dealing with small business issues, such as starting a small business, marketing and business opportunities. Beware, however, that no one checks these sites for accuracy. A good way to find these sites is through an Internet directory such as Yahoo. You can access Yahoo at www.yahoo.com. Click on

How to Read a Case Citation

To locate a published court decision, you must understand how to read a case citation. A citation provides the names of the people or companies involved on each side of the case, the volume of the legal publication—called a reporter—in which the case can be found, the page number on which it begins and the year in which the case was decided. Here is an example of what a legal citation looks like: *Smith v. Jones Int'l,* 123 F.3d 456 (1995). Smith and Jones are the names of the people having the legal dispute. The case is reported in volume 123 of the Federal Reporter, Third Series, beginning on page 456; the court issued the decision in 1995.

Federal court decisions. There are several different federal courts and the decisions of each are published in a different reporter. Opinions by the federal district courts are in a series called the Federal Supplement, or F.Supp.

Any case decided by a federal court of appeals is found in a series of books called the Federal Reporter. Older cases are contained in the first series of the Federal Reporter, or F. More recent cases are contained in the second or third series of the Federal Reporter, F.2d or F.3d.

Cases decided by the U.S. Supreme Court are found in three publications: United States Reports (identified as U.S.), the Supreme Court Reporter identified as S.Ct.) and the Supreme Court Reports, Lawyer's Edition (identified as L.Ed.). Supreme Court case citations often refer to all three publications.

There are also federal courts that specialize in handling tax disputes, including the United States Tax Court and United States Claims Court—formerly Court of Claims. Published decisions of the United States Tax Court can be found in the Tax Court Reports, or TC, published by the U.S. Government Printing Office. Tax Court decisions can also be found in a reporter called Tax Court Memorandum Decisions, or TCM, published by Commerce Clearing House, Inc.

Decisions from all federal courts involving taxation can be found in a reporter called U.S. Tax Cases, or USTC, published by Commerce Clearing House, Inc.

State court decisions. Most states publish their own official state reports. All published state courts' decisions are also included in the West Reporter System. West has divided the country into seven regions—and publishes all the decisions of the supreme and appellate state courts in the region together. These reporters are:

A. and A.2d. Atlantic Reporter (First and Second Series), which includes decisions from Connecticut, Delaware, the District of Columbia, Maine, Maryland, New Hampshire, New Jersey, Pennsylvania, Rhode Island and Vermont.

N.E. and N.E.2d. Northeastern Reporter (First and Second Series), which includes decisions from New York, Illinois, Indiana, Massachusetts and Ohio.

N.W. and N.W.2d. Northwestern Reporter (First and Second Series), which includes decisions from Iowa, Michigan, Minnesota, Nebraska, North Dakota, South Dakota and Wisconsin.

P. and P.2d. Pacific Reporter (First and Second Series), which includes decisions from Alaska, Arizona, California, Colorado, Hawaii, Idaho, Kansas, Montana, Nevada, New Mexico, Oklahoma, Oregon, Utah, Washington and Wyoming.

S.E. and S.E.2d. Southeastern Reporter (First and Second Series), which includes decisions from Georgia, North Carolina, South Carolina, Virginia and West Virginia.

So. and So.2d. Southern Reporter (First and Second Series), which includes decisions from Alabama, Florida, Louisiana and Mississippi.

S.W. and S.W.2d. Southwestern Reporter (First and Second Series), which includes decisions from Arkansas, Kentucky, Missouri, Tennessee and Texas.

All California appellate decisions are published in a separate volume, the California Reporter (Cal. Rptr.) and all decisions from New York appellate courts are published in a separate volume, New York Supplement (N.Y.S.).

the Business and Economy category and then on the Small Business Information listing.

A few particularly useful websites for self-employed people include:

- the CCH Business Owner's Toolkit at www.toolkit.cch.com/
- the Quicken small business website at www.quicken.com/small_business/
- the Yahoo Small Business Center at http://smallbusiness.yahoo.com/
- the Small Business Taxes & Management website at www.smbiz.com/

A growing number of court decisions are also available on the Internet for free or at nominal cost. You can find a comprehensive set of links to free case law websites at www.findlaw.com. You can also obtain legal decisions from the subscription websites www.westlaw.com and www.lexis.com.

NOLO INTERNET SITE

Nolo maintains an Internet site that is useful for the self-employed. The site contains helpful articles, information about new legislation, book excerpts and the Nolo catalog. The site also includes a legal encyclopedia with specific information for people who are self-employed, as well as a legal research center you can use to find state and federal statutes. The Internet address is www.nolo.com.

Yet another part of the Internet are Usenet newsgroups. These are collections of electronic-mail messages on specific topics, called postings, that can be read by anybody with access to the Internet. Most newsgroups are completely open—meaning anybody can just jump into the discussion by posting anything they want—although users are usually encouraged to keep to the topic of the newsgroup. Other newsgroups are moderated, meaning that there is a moderator who reviews postings before allowing them to appear in that newsgroup. Moderated newsgroups almost always contain more focused discussion since the moderators want to keep the conversation on the track.

You can use newsgroups to network with other self-employed people, ask specific questions and even find work. Some of the many newsgroups of interest to the self-employed include:

- misc.taxes.moderated
- misc.jobs.contract
- misc.entrepreneurs
- misc.business.consulting
- alt.computer.consultants, and
- alt.computer.consultants.moderated.

If you don't know how to access Internet newsgroups, review the instructions for your Web browser for guidance.

2. Commercial Online Services

Some of the best known parts of the online world are commercial online services such as CompuServe and America Online. To access these systems, a person must become a subscriber and pay a monthly (and sometimes hourly) fee. These systems typically offer online chats with other users logged onto the system, posting of public messages on various topics and vast collections of electronic databases. All of these services have special areas devoted to small business people and consultants. For example, CompuServe has a Working at Home Forum and America Online has a Small Business area. You can also obtain information on taxes and download copies of IRS tax forms.

■

Forms and Documents

Documents

Asset Log

Expense Journal

Income Journal

Invoice Form

Application for Employer Identification Number—Form SS4

Request for Taxpayer Identification Number and Certification—Form W-9

ASSET LOG

Description of Property	Date Placed in Service	Cost or Other Basis	Business/ Investment Use %	Section 179 Deduction	Depreciation Prior Years	Basis for Depreciation	Method/ Convention	Recovery Period	Rate or Table%	Depreciation on Deduction
TOTAL										

Asset Log

EXPENSE JOURNAL

EXPENSE JOURNAL

Date	Check No.	Transaction	Amount	1 Advertising	2 Supplies, Postage, Etc.	3 Outside Contractors
	TOTAL THIS PAGE					
	TOTAL YEAR TO DATE					

4	5	6	7	8	9	10	11
Travel	Equipment	Rent	Utilities	Meals and Entertainment			Misc.

www.nolo.com

INCOME JOURNAL

Source	Invoice	Date	Amount
		TOTAL	

NOLO www.nolo.com

INVOICE

_____

_____

_____

_____

Date: _____

Invoice Number: _____

Your Order Number: _____

Terms: _____

Time period of: _____

To: _____

_____

_____

_____

Services: _____

_____

_____

Material Costs: _____

Expenses: _____

TOTAL AMOUNT OF THIS INVOICE: _____

Signed by: _____

Form **SS-4**

(Rev. December 2001)

Department of the Treasury
Internal Revenue Service

Application for Employer Identification Number

(For use by employers, corporations, partnerships, trusts, estates, churches, government agencies, Indian tribal entities, certain individuals, and others.)

▶ See separate instructions for each line.   ▶ Keep a copy for your records.

EIN

OMB No. 1545-0003

Type or print clearly.

1 Legal name of entity (or individual) for whom the EIN is being requested

2 Trade name of business (if different from name on line 1)

3 Executor, trustee, "care of" name

4a Mailing address (room, apt., suite no. and street, or P.O. box)

5a Street address (if different) (Do not enter a P.O. box.)

4b City, state, and ZIP code

5b City, state, and ZIP code

6 County and state where principal business is located

7a Name of principal officer, general partner, grantor, owner, or trustor

7b SSN, ITIN, or EIN

8a **Type of entity** (check only one box)

☐ Sole proprietor (SSN) _____
☐ Partnership
☐ Corporation (enter form number to be filed) ▶ _____
☐ Personal service corp.
☐ Church or church-controlled organization
☐ Other nonprofit organization (specify) ▶ _____
☐ Other (specify) ▶

☐ Estate (SSN of decedent) _____
☐ Plan administrator (SSN) _____
☐ Trust (SSN of grantor) _____
☐ National Guard   ☐ State/local government
☐ Farmers' cooperative   ☐ Federal government/military
☐ REMIC   ☐ Indian tribal governments/enterprises
Group Exemption Number (GEN) ▶ _____

8b If a corporation, name the state or foreign country (if applicable) where incorporated

State

Foreign country

9 **Reason for applying** (check only one box)

☐ Started new business (specify type) ▶ _____

☐ Hired employees (Check the box and see line 12.)
☐ Compliance with IRS withholding regulations
☐ Other (specify) ▶

☐ Banking purpose (specify purpose) ▶ _____
☐ Changed type of organization (specify new type) ▶ _____
☐ Purchased going business
☐ Created a trust (specify type) ▶ _____
☐ Created a pension plan (specify type) ▶ _____

10 Date business started or acquired (month, day, year)

11 Closing month of accounting year

12 First date wages or annuities were paid or will be paid (month, day, year). **Note:** *If applicant is a withholding agent, enter date income will first be paid to nonresident alien. (month, day, year)* . . . . ▶

13 Highest number of employees expected in the next 12 months. **Note:** *If the applicant does not expect to have any employees during the period, enter "-0-."* . . . . ▶

Agricultural	Household	Other

14 Check **one** box that best describes the principal activity of your business.   ☐ Health care & social assistance   ☐ Wholesale–agent/broker

☐ Construction ☐ Rental & leasing ☐ Transportation & warehousing ☐ Accommodation & food service ☐ Wholesale–other ☐ Retail

☐ Real estate ☐ Manufacturing ☐ Finance & insurance ☐ Other (specify)

15 Indicate principal line of merchandise sold; specific construction work done; products produced; or services provided.

16a Has the applicant ever applied for an employer identification number for this or any other business? . . . . . ☐ Yes   ☐ No

Note: *If "Yes," please complete lines 16b and 16c.*

16b If you checked "Yes" on line 16a, give applicant's legal name and trade name shown on prior application if different from line 1 or 2 above.

Legal name ▶   Trade name ▶

16c Approximate date when, and city and state where, the application was filed. Enter previous employer identification number if known.

Approximate date when filed (mo., day, year) | City and state where filed | Previous EIN

Third Party Designee

Complete this section **only** if you want to authorize the named individual to receive the entity's EIN and answer questions about the completion of this form.

Designee's name

Address and ZIP code

Designee's telephone number (include area code)
(   )

Designee's fax number (include area code)
(   )

Under penalties of perjury, I declare that I have examined this application, and to the best of my knowledge and belief, it is true, correct, and complete.

Applicant's telephone number (include area code)
(   )

Name and title (type or print clearly) ▶

Applicant's fax number (include area code)
(   )

Signature ▶   Date ▶

For Privacy Act and Paperwork Reduction Act Notice, see separate instructions.   Cat. No. 16055N   Form **SS-4** (Rev. 12-2001)

Do I Need an EIN?

File Form SS-4 if the applicant entity does not already have an EIN but is required to show an EIN on any return, statement, or other document.[1] **See also the separate instructions for each line on Form SS-4.**

IF the applicant...	AND...	THEN...
Started a new business	Does not currently have (nor expect to have) employees	Complete lines 1, 2, 4a- 6, 8a, and 9- 16c.
Hired (or will hire) employees, including household employees	Does not already have an EIN	Complete lines 1, 2, 4a- 6, 7a- b (if applicable), 8a, 8b (if applicable), and 9- 16c.
Opened a bank account	Needs an EIN for banking purposes only	Complete lines 1- 5b, 7a- b (if applicable), 8a, 9, and 16a- c.
Changed type of organization	Either the legal character of the organization or its ownership changed (e.g., you incorporate a sole proprietorship or form a partnership)[2]	Complete lines 1- 16c (as applicable).
Purchased a going business[3]	Does not already have an EIN	Complete lines 1- 16c (as applicable).
Created a trust	The trust is other than a grantor trust or an IRA trust[4]	Complete lines 1- 16c (as applicable).
Created a pension plan as a plan administrator[5]	Needs an EIN for reporting purposes	Complete lines 1, 2, 4a- 6, 8a, 9, and 16a- c.
Is a foreign person needing an EIN to comply with IRS withholding regulations	Needs an EIN to complete a Form W-8 (other than Form W-8ECI), avoid withholding on portfolio assets, or claim tax treaty benefits[6]	Complete lines 1- 5b, 7a- b (SSN or ITIN optional), 8a- 9, and 16a- c.
Is administering an estate	Needs an EIN to report estate income on Form 1041	Complete lines 1, 3, 4a- b, 8a, 9, and 16a- c.
Is a withholding agent for taxes on non-wage income paid to an alien (i.e., individual, corporation, or partnership, etc.)	Is an agent, broker, fiduciary, manager, tenant, or spouse who is required to file **Form 1042,** Annual Withholding Tax Return for U.S. Source Income of Foreign Persons	Complete lines 1, 2, 3 (if applicable), 4a- 5b, 7a- b (if applicable), 8a, 9, and 16a- c.
Is a state or local agency	Serves as a tax reporting agent for public assistance recipients under Rev. Proc. 80-4, 1980-1 C.B. 581[7]	Complete lines 1, 2, 4a- 5b, 8a, 9, and 16a- c.
Is a single-member LLC	Needs an EIN to file **Form 8832,** Classification Election, for filing employment tax returns, **or** for state reporting purposes[8]	Complete lines 1- 16c (as applicable).
Is an S corporation	Needs an EIN to file **Form 2553,** Election by a Small Business Corporation[9]	Complete lines 1- 16c (as applicable).

[1] For example, a sole proprietorship or self-employed farmer who establishes a qualified retirement plan, or is required to file excise, employment, alcohol, tobacco, or firearms returns, must have an EIN. **A partnership, corporation, REMIC (real estate mortgage investment conduit), nonprofit organization (church, club, etc.), or farmers' cooperative must use an EIN for any tax-related purpose even if the entity does not have employees.**

[2] However, **do not** apply for a new EIN if the existing entity only **(a)** changed its business name, **(b)** elected on Form 8832 to change the way it is taxed (or is covered by the default rules), or **(c)** terminated its partnership status because at least 50% of the total interests in partnership capital and profits were sold or exchanged within a 12-month period. (The EIN of the terminated partnership should continue to be used. See Regulations section 301.6109-1(d)(2)(iii).)

[3] Do not use the EIN of the prior business unless you became the "owner" of a corporation by acquiring its stock.

[4] However, IRA trusts that are required to file **Form 990-T,** Exempt Organization Business Income Tax Return, must have an EIN.

[5] A plan administrator is the person or group of persons specified as the administrator by the instrument under which the plan is operated.

[6] Entities applying to be a Qualified Intermediary (QI) need a QI-EIN even if they already have an EIN. **See Rev. Proc. 2000-12.**

[7] See also *Household employer* on page 4. (**Note:** State or local agencies may need an EIN for other reasons, e.g., hired employees.)

[8] Most LLCs **do not** need to file Form 8832. See **Limited liability company (LLC)** on page 4 for details on completing Form SS-4 for an LLC.

[9] An existing corporation that is electing or revoking S corporation status should use its previously-assigned EIN.

♲

Instructions for Form SS-4

**Department of the Treasury
Internal Revenue Service**

(Rev. December 2001)

Application for Employer Identification Number

Section references are to the Internal Revenue Code unless otherwise noted.

General Instructions

Use these instructions to complete **Form SS-4,** Application for Employer Identification Number. Also see **Do I Need an EIN?** on page 2 of Form SS-4.

Purpose of Form

Use Form SS-4 to apply for an employer identification number (EIN). An EIN is a nine-digit number (for example, 12-3456789) assigned to sole proprietors, corporations, partnerships, estates, trusts, and other entities for tax filing and reporting purposes. The information you provide on this form will establish your business tax account.

 *An EIN is for use in connection with your business activities only. Do **not** use your EIN in place of your social security number (SSN).*

File only one Form SS-4. Generally, a sole proprietor should file only one Form SS-4 and needs only one EIN, regardless of the number of businesses operated as a sole proprietorship or trade names under which a business operates. However, if the proprietorship incorporates or enters into a partnership, a new EIN is required. Also, each corporation in an affiliated group must have its own EIN.

EIN applied for, but not received. If you do not have an EIN by the time a **return** is due, write "Applied For" and the date you applied in the space shown for the number. **Do not** show your social security number (SSN) as an EIN on returns.

If you do not have an EIN by the time a **tax deposit** is due, send your payment to the Internal Revenue Service Center for your filing area as shown in the instructions for the form that you are are filing. Make your check or money order payable to the **"United States Treasury"** and show your name (as shown on Form SS-4), address, type of tax, period covered, and date you applied for an EIN.

Related Forms and Publications

The following **forms** and **instructions** may be useful to filers of Form SS-4:
- **Form 990-T,** Exempt Organization Business Income Tax Return
- **Instructions for Form 990-T**
- **Schedule C (Form 1040),** Profit or Loss From Business
- **Schedule F (Form 1040),** Profit or Loss From Farming
- **Instructions for Form 1041 and Schedules A, B, D, G, I, J, and K-1,** U.S. Income Tax Return for Estates and Trusts

- **Form 1042,** Annual Withholding Tax Return for U.S. Source Income of Foreign Persons
- **Instructions for Form 1065,** U.S. Return of Partnership Income
- **Instructions for Form 1066,** U.S. Real Estate Mortgage Investment Conduit (REMIC) Income Tax Return
- **Instructions for Forms 1120 and 1120-A**
- **Form 2553,** Election by a Small Business Corporation
- **Form 2848,** Power of Attorney and Declaration of Representative
- **Form 8821,** Tax Information Authorization
- **Form 8832,** Entity Classification Election

For more **information** about filing Form SS-4 and related issues, see:
- **Circular A,** Agricultural Employer's Tax Guide (Pub. 51)
- **Circular E,** Employer's Tax Guide (Pub. 15)
- **Pub. 538,** Accounting Periods and Methods
- **Pub. 542,** Corporations
- **Pub. 557,** Exempt Status for Your Organization
- **Pub. 583,** Starting a Business and Keeping Records
- **Pub. 966,** EFTPS: Now a Full Range of Electronic Choices to Pay All Your Federal Taxes
- **Pub. 1635,** Understanding Your EIN
- **Package 1023,** Application for Recognition of Exemption
- **Package 1024,** Application for Recognition of Exemption Under Section 501(a)

How To Get Forms and Publications

Phone. You can order forms, instructions, and publications by phone 24 hours a day, 7 days a week. Just call 1-800-TAX-FORM (1-800-829-3676). You should receive your order or notification of its status within 10 workdays.

Personal computer. With your personal computer and modem, you can get the forms and information you need using the IRS Web Site at **www.irs.gov** or File Transfer Protocol at **ftp.irs.gov.**

CD-ROM. For small businesses, return preparers, or others who may frequently need tax forms or publications, a CD-ROM containing over 2,000 tax products (including many prior year forms) can be purchased from the National Technical Information Service (NTIS).

To order **Pub. 1796,** Federal Tax Products on CD-ROM, call **1-877-CDFORMS** (1-877-233-6767) toll free or connect to **www.irs.gov/cdorders.**

Cat. No. 62736F

Tax Help for Your Business

IRS-sponsored Small Business Workshops provide information about your Federal and state tax obligations. For information about workshops in your area, call 1-800-829-1040 and ask for your Taxpayer Education Coordinator.

How To Apply

You can apply for an EIN by telephone, fax, or mail depending on how soon you need to use the EIN.

Application by Tele-TIN. Under the Tele-TIN program, you can receive your EIN by telephone and use it immediately to file a return or make a payment. To receive an EIN by telephone, IRS suggests that you complete Form SS-4 so that you will have all relevant information available. Then call the Tele-TIN number at 1-866-816-2065. (International applicants must call 215-516-6999.) Tele-TIN hours of operation are 7:30 a.m. to 5:30 p.m. The person making the call must be authorized to sign the form or be an authorized designee. See **Signature** and **Third Party Designee** on page 6. Also see the **TIP** below.

An IRS representative will use the information from the Form SS-4 to establish your account and assign you an EIN. Write the number you are given on the upper right corner of the form and sign and date it. Keep this copy for your records.

If requested by an IRS representative, mail or fax (facsimile) the signed Form SS-4 (including any Third Party Designee authorization) **within 24 hours** to the Tele-TIN Unit at the service center address provided by the IRS representative.

 *Taxpayer representatives can use Tele-TIN to apply for an EIN on behalf of their client and request that the EIN be faxed to their **client** on the same day. (**Note:** By utilizing this procedure, you are authorizing the IRS to fax the EIN without a cover sheet.)*

Application by Fax-TIN. Under the Fax-TIN program, you can receive your EIN by fax within 4 business days. Complete and fax Form SS-4 to the IRS using the Fax-TIN number listed below for your state. A long-distance charge to callers outside of the local calling area will apply. Fax-TIN numbers can only be used to apply for an EIN. **The numbers may change without notice.** Fax-TIN is available 24 hours a day, 7 days a week.

Be sure to provide your fax number so that IRS can fax the EIN back to you. (**Note:** By utilizing this procedure, you are authorizing the IRS to fax the EIN without a cover sheet.)

Do not call Tele-TIN for the same entity because duplicate EINs may be issued. See **Third Party Designee** on page 6.

Application by mail. Complete Form SS-4 at least 4 to 5 weeks before you will need an EIN. Sign and date the application and mail it to the service center address for your state. You will receive your EIN in the mail in approximately 4 weeks. See also **Third Party Designee** on page 6.

Call 1-800-829-1040 to verify a number or to ask about the status of an application by mail.

If your principal business, office or agency, or legal residence in the case of an individual, is located in:	Call the Tele-TIN or Fax-TIN number shown or file with the "Internal Revenue Service Center" at:
Connecticut, Delaware, District of Columbia, Florida, Georgia, Maine, Maryland, Massachusetts, New Hampshire, New Jersey, New York, North Carolina, Ohio, Pennsylvania, Rhode Island, South Carolina, Vermont, Virginia, West Virginia	Attn: EIN Operation Holtsville, NY 00501 Tele-TIN 866-816-2065 Fax-TIN 631-447-8960
Illinois, Indiana, Kentucky, Michigan	Attn: EIN Operation Cincinnati, OH 45999 Tele-TIN 866-816-2065 Fax-TIN 859-669-5760
Alabama, Alaska, Arizona, Arkansas, California, Colorado, Hawaii, Idaho, Iowa, Kansas, Louisiana, Minnesota, Mississippi, Missouri, Montana, Nebraska, Nevada, New Mexico, North Dakota, Oklahoma, Oregon, Puerto Rico, South Dakota, Tennessee, Texas, Utah, Washington, Wisconsin, Wyoming	Attn: EIN Operation Philadelphia, PA 19255 Tele-TIN 866-816-2065 Fax-TIN 215-516-3990
If you have no legal residence, principal place of business, or principal office or agency in any state:	Attn: EIN Operation Philadelphia, PA 19255 Tele-TIN 215-516-6999 Fax-TIN 215-516-3990

Specific Instructions

Print or type all entries on Form SS-4. Follow the instructions for each line to expedite processing and to avoid unnecessary IRS requests for additional information. Enter "N/A" (nonapplicable) on the lines that do not apply.

Line 1—Legal name of entity (or individual) for whom the EIN is being requested. Enter the legal name of the entity (or individual) applying for the EIN exactly as it appears on the social security card, charter, or other applicable legal document.

Individuals. Enter your first name, middle initial, and last name. If you are a sole proprietor, enter your individual name, not your business name. Enter your business name on line 2. Do not use abbreviations or nicknames on line 1.

Trusts. Enter the name of the trust.

Estate of a decedent. Enter the name of the estate.

Partnerships. Enter the legal name of the partnership as it appears in the partnership agreement.

Corporations. Enter the corporate name as it appears in the corporation charter or other legal document creating it.

Plan administrators. Enter the name of the plan administrator. A plan administrator who already has an EIN should use that number.

Line 2—Trade name of business. Enter the trade name of the business if different from the legal name. The trade name is the "doing business as " (DBA) name.

 Use the full legal name shown on line 1 on all tax returns filed for the entity. (However, if you enter a trade name on line 2 and choose to use the trade name instead of the legal name, enter the trade name on all returns you file.) To prevent processing delays and errors, always use the legal name only (or the trade name only) on all tax returns.

Line 3—Executor, trustee, "care of" name. Trusts enter the name of the trustee. Estates enter the name of the executor, administrator, or other fiduciary. If the entity applying has a designated person to receive tax information, enter that person's name as the "care of" person. Enter the individual's first name, middle initial, and last name.

Lines 4a-b—Mailing address. Enter the mailing address for the entity's correspondence. If line 3 is completed, enter the address for the executor, trustee or "care of" person. Generally, this address will be used on all tax returns.

 *File **Form 8822**, Change of Address, to report any subsequent changes to the entity's mailing address.*

Lines 5a-b—Street address. Provide the entity's physical address **only** if different from its mailing address shown in lines 4a-b. **Do not** enter a P.O. box number here.

Line 6—County and state where principal business is located. Enter the entity's primary **physical** location.

Lines 7a-b—Name of principal officer, general partner, grantor, owner, or trustor. Enter the first name, middle initial, last name, and SSN of **(a)** the principal officer if the business is a corporation, **(b)** a general partner if a partnership, **(c)** the owner of an entity that is disregarded as separate from its owner (disregarded entities owned by a corporation enter the corporation's name and EIN), or **(d)** a grantor, owner, or trustor if a trust.

If the person in question is an **alien individual** with a previously assigned individual taxpayer identification number (ITIN), enter the ITIN in the space provided and submit a copy of an official identifying document. If necessary, complete **Form W-7**, Application for IRS Individual Taxpayer Identification Number, to obtain an ITIN.

You are **required** to enter an SSN, ITIN, or EIN unless the only reason you are applying for an EIN is to make an entity classification election (see Regulations section 301.7701-1 through 301.7701-3) and you are a nonresident alien with no effectively connected income from sources within the United States.

Line 8a—Type of entity. Check the box that best describes the type of entity applying for the EIN. If you are an alien individual with an ITIN previously assigned to you, enter the ITIN in place of a requested SSN.

 *This is not an election for a tax classification of an entity. See **"Limited liability company (LLC)"** on page 4.*

Other. If not specifically mentioned, check the "Other" box, enter the type of entity and the type of return, if any, that will be filed (for example, "Common Trust Fund, Form 1065" or "Created a Pension Plan"). Do not enter "N/A." If you are an alien individual applying for an EIN, see the **Lines 7a-b** instructions above.

● **Household employer.** If you are an individual, check the "Other" box and enter "Household Employer" and your SSN. If you are a state or local agency serving as a tax reporting agent for public assistance recipients who become household employers, check the "Other" box and enter "Household Employer Agent." If you are a trust that qualifies as a household employer, you do not need a separate EIN for reporting tax information relating to household employees; use the EIN of the trust.

● **QSub.** For a qualified subchapter S subsidiary (QSub) check the "Other" box and specify "QSub."

● **Withholding agent.** If you are a withholding agent required to file Form 1042, check the "Other" box and enter "Withholding Agent."

Sole proprietor. Check this box if you file Schedule C, C-EZ, or F (Form 1040) and have a qualified plan, or are required to file excise, employment, or alcohol, tobacco, or firearms returns, or are a payer of gambling winnings. Enter your SSN (or ITIN) in the space provided. If you are a nonresident alien with no effectively connected income from sources within the United States, you do not need to enter an SSN or ITIN.

Corporation. This box is for any corporation **other than a personal service corporation.** If you check this box, enter the income tax form number to be filed by the entity in the space provided.

 *If you entered **"1120S"** after the "Corporation" checkbox, the corporation **must** file Form 2553 **no later than the 15th day of the 3rd month of the tax year the election is to take effect.** Until Form 2553 has been received and approved, you will be considered a Form 1120 filer. See the Instructions for Form 2553.*

Personal service corp. Check this box if the entity is a personal service corporation. An entity is a personal service corporation for a tax year only if:

● The principal activity of the entity during the testing period (prior tax year) for the tax year is the performance of personal services substantially by employee-owners, and

● The employee-owners own at least 10% of the fair market value of the outstanding stock in the entity on the last day of the testing period.

Personal services include performance of services in such fields as health, law, accounting, or consulting. For more information about personal service corporations, see the Instructions for Forms 1120 and 1120-A and Pub. 542.

Other nonprofit organization. Check this box if the nonprofit organization is other than a church or church-controlled organization and specify the type of nonprofit organization (for example, an educational organization).

 *If the organization also seeks tax-exempt status, you **must** file either Package 1023 or Package 1024. See Pub. 557 for more information.*

If the organization is covered by a group exemption letter, enter the four-digit **group exemption number (GEN).** (Do not confuse the GEN with the nine-digit EIN.) If you do not know the GEN, contact the parent organization. Get Pub. 557 for more information about group exemption numbers.

Plan administrator. If the plan administrator is an individual, enter the plan administrator's SSN in the space provided.

REMIC. Check this box if the entity has elected to be treated as a real estate mortgage investment conduit (REMIC). See the Instructions for Form 1066 for more information.

Limited liability company (LLC). An LLC is an entity organized under the laws of a state or foreign country as a limited liability company. For Federal tax purposes, an LLC may be treated as a partnership or corporation or be disregarded as an entity separate from its owner.

By **default,** a domestic LLC with only one member is **disregarded** as an entity separate from its owner and must include all of its income and expenses on the owner's tax return (e.g., **Schedule C (Form 1040)**). Also by default, a domestic LLC with two or more members is treated as a partnership. A domestic LLC may file Form 8832 to avoid either default classification and elect to be classified as an association taxable as a corporation. For more information on entity classifications (including the rules for foreign entities), see the instructions for Form 8832.

 *Do not file Form 8832 if the LLC accepts the default classifications above. **However, if the LLC will be electing S Corporation status, it must timely file both Form 8832 and Form 2553.***

Complete Form SS-4 for LLCs as follows:
• A single-member, domestic LLC that accepts the default classification (above) does not need an EIN and generally should not file Form SS-4. Generally, the LLC should use the name and EIN of its **owner** for all Federal tax purposes. However, the reporting and payment of employment taxes for employees of the LLC may be made using the name and EIN of **either** the owner or the LLC as explained in Notice 99-6, 1999-1 C.B. 321. You can find Notice 99-6 on page 12 of Internal Revenue Bulletin 1999-3 at **www.irs.gov. (Note:** If the LLC-applicant indicates in box 13 that it has employees or expects to have employees, the owner (whether an individual or other entity) of a single-member domestic LLC will also be assigned its own EIN (if it does not

already have one) even if the LLC will be filing the employment tax returns.)
• A single-member, domestic LLC that accepts the default classification (above) and wants an EIN for filing employment tax returns (see above) or non-Federal purposes, such as a state requirement, must check the "Other" box and write "Disregarded Entity" or, when applicable, "Disregarded Entity—Sole Proprietorship" in the space provided.
• A multi-member, domestic LLC that accepts the default classification (above) must check the "Partnership" box.
• A domestic LLC that will be filing Form 8832 to elect corporate status must check the "Corporation" box and write in "Single-Member" or "Multi-Member" immediately below the "form number" entry line.

Line 9—Reason for applying. Check only **one** box. Do not enter "N/A."

Started new business. Check this box if you are starting a new business that requires an EIN. If you check this box, enter the type of business being started. **Do not** apply if you already have an EIN and are only adding another place of business.

Hired employees. Check this box if the existing business is requesting an EIN because it has hired or is hiring employees and is therefore required to file employment tax returns. **Do not** apply if you already have an EIN and are only hiring employees. For information on employment taxes (e.g., for family members), see Circular E.

 You may be required to make electronic deposits of all depository taxes (such as employment tax, excise tax, and corporate income tax) using the Electronic Federal Tax Payment System (EFTPS). See section 11, Depositing Taxes, of Circular E and Pub. 966.

Created a pension plan. Check this box if you have created a pension plan and need an EIN for reporting purposes. Also, enter the type of plan in the space provided.

 Check this box if you are applying for a trust EIN when a new pension plan is established. In addition, check the "Other" box in line 8a and write "Created a Pension Plan" in the space provided.

Banking purpose. Check this box if you are requesting an EIN for banking purposes only, and enter the banking purpose (for example, a bowling league for depositing dues or an investment club for dividend and interest reporting).

Changed type of organization. Check this box if the business is changing its type of organization. For example, the business was a sole proprietorship and has been incorporated or has become a partnership. If you check this box, specify in the space provided (including available space immediately below) the type of change made. For example, "From Sole Proprietorship to Partnership."

Purchased going business. Check this box if you purchased an existing business. **Do not** use the former owner's EIN unless you became the "owner" of a corporation by acquiring its stock.

-4-

Created a trust. Check this box if you created a trust, and enter the type of trust created. For example, indicate if the trust is a nonexempt charitable trust or a split-interest trust.

Exception. Do **not** file this form for certain grantor-type trusts. The trustee does not need an EIN for the trust if the trustee furnishes the name and TIN of the grantor/owner and the address of the trust to all payors. See the Instructions for Form 1041 for more information.

 Do not check this box if you are applying for a trust EIN when a new pension plan is established. Check "Created a pension plan."

Other. Check this box if you are requesting an EIN for any other reason; and enter the reason. For example, a newly-formed state government entity should enter "Newly-Formed State Government Entity" in the space provided.

Line 10—Date business started or acquired. If you are starting a new business, enter the starting date of the business. If the business you acquired is already operating, enter the date you acquired the business. Trusts should enter the date the trust was legally created. Estates should enter the date of death of the decedent whose name appears on line 1 or the date when the estate was legally funded.

Line 11—Closing month of accounting year. Enter the last month of your accounting year or tax year. An accounting or tax year is usually 12 consecutive months, either a calendar year or a fiscal year (including a period of 52 or 53 weeks). A calendar year is 12 consecutive months ending on December 31. A fiscal year is either 12 consecutive months ending on the last day of any month other than December or a 52-53 week year. For more information on accounting periods, see Pub. 538.

Individuals. Your tax year generally will be a calendar year.

Partnerships. Partnerships must adopt one of the following tax years:
- The tax year of the majority of its partners,
- The tax year common to all of its principal partners,
- The tax year that results in the least aggregate deferral of income, or
- In certain cases, some other tax year.
  See the Instructions for Form 1065 for more information.

REMICs. REMICs must have a calendar year as their tax year.

Personal service corporations. A personal service corporation generally must adopt a calendar year unless:
- It can establish a business purpose for having a different tax year, or
- It elects under section 444 to have a tax year other than a calendar year.

Trusts. Generally, a trust must adopt a calendar year except for the following:
- Tax-exempt trusts,
- Charitable trusts, and
- Grantor-owned trusts.

Line 12—First date wages or annuities were paid or will be paid. If the business has or will have employees, enter the date on which the business began or will begin to pay wages. If the business does not plan to have employees, enter "N/A."

Withholding agent. Enter the date you began or will begin to pay income (including annuities) to a nonresident alien. This also applies to individuals who are required to file Form 1042 to report alimony paid to a nonresident alien.

Line 13—Highest number of employees expected in the next 12 months. Complete each box by entering the number (including zero ("-0-")) of "Agricultural," "Household," or "Other" employees expected by the applicant in the next 12 months. For a definition of agricultural labor (farmwork), see Circular A.

Lines 14 and 15. Check the **one** box in line 14 that best describes the principal activity of the applicant's business. Check the "Other" box (and specify the applicant's principal activity) if none of the listed boxes applies.

Use line 15 to describe the applicant's principal line of business in more detail. For example, if you checked the "Construction" box in line 14, enter additional detail such as "General contractor for residential buildings" in line 15.

 Do not complete lines 14 and 15 if you entered zero "(-0-)" in line 13.

Construction. Check this box if the applicant is engaged in erecting buildings or other structures, (e.g., streets, highways, bridges, tunnels). The term "Construction" also includes special trade contractors, (e.g., plumbing, HVAC, electrical, carpentry, concrete, excavation, etc. contractors).

Real estate. Check this box if the applicant is engaged in renting or leasing real estate to others; managing, selling, buying or renting real estate for others; or providing related real estate services (e.g., appraisal services).

Rental and leasing. Check this box if the applicant is engaged in providing tangible goods such as autos, computers, consumer goods, or industrial machinery and equipment to customers in return for a periodic rental or lease payment.

Manufacturing. Check this box if the applicant is engaged in the mechanical, physical, or chemical transformation of materials, substances, or components into new products. The assembling of component parts of manufactured products is also considered to be manufacturing.

Transportation & warehousing. Check this box if the applicant provides transportation of passengers or cargo; warehousing or storage of goods; scenic or sight-seeing transportation; or support activities related to these modes of transportation.

Finance & insurance. Check this box if the applicant is engaged in transactions involving the creation, liquidation, or change of ownership of financial assets and/or facilitating such financial transactions;

underwriting annuities/insurance policies; facilitating such underwriting by selling insurance policies; or by providing other insurance or employee-benefit related services.

Health care and social assistance. Check this box if the applicant is engaged in providing physical, medical, or psychiatric care using licensed health care professionals or providing social assistance activities such as youth centers, adoption agencies, individual/family services, temporary shelters, etc.

Accommodation & food services. Check this box if the applicant is engaged in providing customers with lodging, meal preparation, snacks, or beverages for immediate consumption.

Wholesale–agent/broker. Check this box if the applicant is engaged in arranging for the purchase or sale of goods owned by others or purchasing goods on a commission basis for goods traded in the wholesale market, usually between businesses.

Wholesale–other. Check this box if the applicant is engaged in selling goods in the wholesale market generally to other businesses for resale on their own account.

Retail. Check this box if the applicant is engaged in selling merchandise to the general public from a fixed store; by direct, mail-order, or electronic sales; or by using vending machines.

Other. Check this box if the applicant is engaged in an activity not described above. Describe the applicant's principal business activity in the space provided.

Lines 16a-c. Check the applicable box in line 16a to indicate whether or not the entity (or individual) applying for an EIN was issued one previously. Complete lines 16b and 16c **only** if the "Yes" box in line 16a is checked. If the applicant previously applied for **more than one** EIN, write "See Attached" in the empty space in line 16a and attach a separate sheet providing the line 16b and 16c information for each EIN previously requested.

Third Party Designee. Complete this section **only** if you want to authorize the named individual to receive the entity's EIN and answer questions about the completion of Form SS-4. The designee's authority terminates at the time the EIN is assigned and released to the designee. **You must complete the signature area for the authorization to be valid.**

Signature. When required, the application must be signed by **(a)** the individual, if the applicant is an individual, **(b)** the president, vice president, or other principal officer, if the applicant is a corporation, **(c)** a responsible and duly authorized member or officer having knowledge of its affairs, if the applicant is a partnership, government entity, or other unincorporated organization, or **(d)** the fiduciary, if the applicant is a trust or an estate. Foreign applicants may have any duly-authorized person, (e.g., division manager), sign Form SS-4.

Privacy Act and Paperwork Reduction Act Notice. We ask for the information on this form to carry out the Internal Revenue laws of the United States. We need it to comply with section 6109 and the regulations thereunder which generally require the inclusion of an employer identification number (EIN) on certain returns, statements, or other documents filed with the Internal Revenue Service. If your entity is required to obtain an EIN, you are required to provide all of the information requested on this form. Information on this form may be used to determine which Federal tax returns you are required to file and to provide you with related forms and publications.

We disclose this form to the Social Security Administration for their use in determining compliance with applicable laws. We may give this information to the Department of Justice for use in civil and criminal litigation, and to the cities, states, and the District of Columbia for use in administering their tax laws. We may also disclose this information to Federal, state, or local agencies that investigate or respond to acts or threats of terrorism or participate in intelligence or counterintelligence activities concerning terrorism.

We will be unable to issue an EIN to you unless you provide all of the requested information which applies to your entity. Providing false information could subject you to penalties.

You are not required to provide the information requested on a form that is subject to the Paperwork Reduction Act unless the form displays a valid OMB control number. Books or records relating to a form or its instructions must be retained as long as their contents may become material in the administration of any Internal Revenue law. Generally, tax returns and return information are confidential, as required by section 6103.

The time needed to complete and file this form will vary depending on individual circumstances. The estimated average time is:

Recordkeeping	6 min.
Learning about the law or the form	22 min.
Preparing the form	46 min.
Copying, assembling, and sending the form to the IRS	20 min.

If you have comments concerning the accuracy of these time estimates or suggestions for making this form simpler, we would be happy to hear from you. You can write to the Tax Forms Committee, Western Area Distribution Center, Rancho Cordova, CA 95743-0001. **Do not** send the form to this address. Instead, see **How To Apply** on page 2.

Form **W-9**
(Rev. January 2002)
Department of the Treasury
Internal Revenue Service

Request for Taxpayer Identification Number and Certification

Give form to the requester. Do not send to the IRS.

Print or type
See Specific Instructions on page 2.

Name

Business name, if different from above

Check appropriate box: ☐ Individual/Sole proprietor ☐ Corporation ☐ Partnership ☐ Other ▶ .... ☐ Exempt from backup withholding

Address (number, street, and apt. or suite no.)

City, state, and ZIP code

List account number(s) here (optional)

Requester's name and address (optional)

Part I Taxpayer Identification Number (TIN)

Enter your TIN in the appropriate box. For individuals, this is your social security number (SSN). **However, for a resident alien, sole proprietor, or disregarded entity, see the Part I instructions on page 2.** For other entities, it is your employer identification number (EIN). If you do not have a number, see **How to get a TIN** on page 2.

Note: *If the account is in more than one name, see the chart on page 2 for guidelines on whose number to enter.*

Social security number

or

Employer identification number

Part II Certification

Under penalties of perjury, I certify that:

1. The number shown on this form is my correct taxpayer identification number (or I am waiting for a number to be issued to me), **and**

2. I am not subject to backup withholding because: **(a)** I am exempt from backup withholding, or **(b)** I have not been notified by the Internal Revenue Service (IRS) that I am subject to backup withholding as a result of a failure to report all interest or dividends, or **(c)** the IRS has notified me that I am no longer subject to backup withholding, **and**

3. I am a U.S. person (including a U.S. resident alien).

Certification instructions. You must cross out item **2** above if you have been notified by the IRS that you are currently subject to backup withholding because you have failed to report all interest and dividends on your tax return. For real estate transactions, item **2** does not apply. For mortgage interest paid, acquisition or abandonment of secured property, cancellation of debt, contributions to an individual retirement arrangement (IRA), and generally, payments other than interest and dividends, you are not required to sign the Certification, but you must provide your correct TIN. (See the instructions on page 2.)

Sign Here | Signature of U.S. person ▶ | Date ▶

Purpose of Form

A person who is required to file an information return with the IRS must get your correct taxpayer identification number (TIN) to report, for example, income paid to you, real estate transactions, mortgage interest you paid, acquisition or abandonment of secured property, cancellation of debt, or contributions you made to an IRA.

Use Form W-9 only if you are a U.S. person (including a resident alien), to give your correct TIN to the person requesting it (the requester) and, when applicable, to:

1. Certify the TIN you are giving is correct (or you are waiting for a number to be issued),

2. Certify you are not subject to backup withholding, or

3. Claim exemption from backup withholding if you are a U.S. exempt payee.

If you are a foreign person, use the appropriate Form W-8. See **Pub. 515,** Withholding of Tax on Nonresident Aliens and Foreign Entities.

Note: *If a requester gives you a form other than Form W-9 to request your TIN, you must use the requester's form if it is substantially similar to this Form W-9.*

What is backup withholding? Persons making certain payments to you must under certain conditions withhold and pay to the IRS 30% of such payments **after** December 31, 2001 (29% **after** December 31, 2003). This is called "backup withholding." Payments that may be subject to backup withholding include interest, dividends, broker and barter exchange transactions, rents, royalties, nonemployee pay, and certain payments from fishing boat operators. Real estate transactions are not subject to backup withholding.

You will **not** be subject to backup withholding on payments you receive if you give the requester your correct TIN, make the proper certifications, and report all your taxable interest and dividends on your tax return.

Payments you receive will be subject to backup withholding if:

1. You do not furnish your TIN to the requester, or

2. You do not certify your TIN when required (see the Part II instructions on page 2 for details), or

3. The IRS tells the requester that you furnished an incorrect TIN, or

4. The IRS tells you that you are subject to backup withholding because you did not report all your interest and dividends on your tax return (for reportable interest and dividends only), or

5. You do not certify to the requester that you are not subject to backup withholding under 4 above (for reportable interest and dividend accounts opened after 1983 only).

Certain payees and payments are exempt from backup withholding. See the instructions on page 2 and the separate **Instructions for the Requester of Form W-9.**

Penalties

Failure to furnish TIN. If you fail to furnish your correct TIN to a requester, you are subject to a penalty of $50 for each such failure unless your failure is due to reasonable cause and not to willful neglect.

Civil penalty for false information with respect to withholding. If you make a false statement with no reasonable basis that results in no backup withholding, you are subject to a $500 penalty.

Criminal penalty for falsifying information. Willfully falsifying certifications or affirmations may subject you to criminal penalties including fines and/or imprisonment.

Misuse of TINs. If the requester discloses or uses TINs in violation of Federal law, the requester may be subject to civil and criminal penalties.

Cat. No. 10231X

Form **W-9** (Rev. 1-2002)

Specific Instructions

Name. If you are an individual, you must generally enter the name shown on your social security card. However, if you have changed your last name, for instance, due to marriage without informing the Social Security Administration of the name change, enter your first name, the last name shown on your social security card, and your new last name.

If the account is in joint names, list first and then circle the name of the person or entity whose number you enter in Part I of the form.

Sole proprietor. Enter your **individual** name as shown on your social security card on the "Name" line. You may enter your business, trade, or "doing business as (DBA)" name on the "Business name" line.

Limited liability company (LLC). If you are a single-member LLC (including a foreign LLC with a domestic owner) that is disregarded as an entity separate from its owner under Treasury regulations section 301.7701-3, **enter the owner's name on the "Name" line.** Enter the LLC's name on the "Business name" line.

Other entities. Enter your business name as shown on required Federal tax documents on the "Name" line. This name should match the name shown on the charter or other legal document creating the entity. You may enter any business, trade, or DBA name on the "Business name" line.

Exempt from backup withholding. If you are exempt, enter your name as described above, then check the "Exempt from backup withholding" box in the line following the business name, sign and date the form.

Individuals (including sole proprietors) are not exempt from backup withholding. Corporations are exempt from backup withholding for certain payments, such as interest and dividends. For more information on exempt payees, see the Instructions for the Requester of Form W-9.

If you are a nonresident alien or a foreign entity not subject to backup withholding, give the requester the appropriate completed Form W-8.

Note: *If you are exempt from backup withholding, you should still complete this form to avoid possible erroneous backup withholding.*

Part I- Taxpayer Identification Number (TIN)

Enter your TIN in the appropriate box.

If you are a **resident alien** and you do not have and are not eligible to get an SSN, your TIN is your IRS individual taxpayer identification number (ITIN). Enter it in the social security number box. If you do not have an ITIN, see **How to get a TIN** below.

If you are a **sole proprietor** and you have an EIN, you may enter either your SSN or EIN. However, the IRS prefers that you use your SSN.

If you are an **LLC** that is **disregarded as an entity** separate from its owner (see *Limited liability company (LLC)* above), and are owned by an individual, enter your SSN (or "pre-LLC" EIN, if desired). If the owner of a disregarded LLC is a corporation, partnership, etc., enter the owner's EIN.

Note: *See the chart on this page for further clarification of name and TIN combinations.*

How to get a TIN. If you do not have a TIN, apply for one immediately. To apply for an SSN, get **Form SS-5**, Application for a Social Security Card, from your local Social Security Administration office. Get **Form W-7**,

Application for IRS Individual Taxpayer Identification Number, to apply for an ITIN, or **Form SS-4**, Application for Employer Identification Number, to apply for an EIN. You can get Forms W-7 and SS-4 from the IRS by calling 1-800-TAX-FORM (1-800-829-3676) or from the IRS Web Site at **www.irs.gov.**

If you are asked to complete Form W-9 but do not have a TIN, write "Applied For" in the space for the TIN, sign and date the form, and give it to the requester. For interest and dividend payments, and certain payments made with respect to readily tradable instruments, generally you will have 60 days to get a TIN and give it to the requester before you are subject to backup withholding on payments. The 60-day rule does not apply to other types of payments. You will be subject to backup withholding on all such payments until you provide your TIN to the requester.

Note: *Writing "Applied For" means that you have already applied for a TIN* **or** *that you intend to apply for one soon.*

Caution: *A disregarded domestic entity that has a foreign owner must use the appropriate Form W-8.*

Part II- Certification

To establish to the withholding agent that you are a U.S. person, or resident alien, sign Form W-9. You may be requested to sign by the withholding agent even if items 1, 3, and 5 below indicate otherwise.

For a joint account, only the person whose TIN is shown in Part I should sign (when required). Exempt recipients, see *Exempt from backup withholding* above.

Signature requirements. Complete the certification as indicated in **1** through **5** below.

1. Interest, dividend, and barter exchange accounts opened before 1984 and broker accounts considered active during 1983. You must give your correct TIN, but you do not have to sign the certification.

2. Interest, dividend, broker, and barter exchange accounts opened after 1983 and broker accounts considered inactive during 1983. You must sign the certification or backup withholding will apply. If you are subject to backup withholding and you are merely providing your correct TIN to the requester, you must cross out item **2** in the certification before signing the form.

3. Real estate transactions. You must sign the certification. You may cross out item **2** of the certification.

4. Other payments. You must give your correct TIN, but you do not have to sign the certification unless you have been notified that you have previously given an incorrect TIN. "Other payments" include payments made in the course of the requester's trade or business for rents, royalties, goods (other than bills for merchandise), medical and health care services (including payments to corporations), payments to a nonemployee for services, payments to certain fishing boat crew members and fishermen, and gross proceeds paid to attorneys (including payments to corporations).

5. Mortgage interest paid by you, acquisition or abandonment of secured property, cancellation of debt, qualified tuition program payments (under section 529), IRA or Archer MSA contributions or distributions, and pension distributions. You must give your correct TIN, but you do not have to sign the certification.

Privacy Act Notice

Section 6109 of the Internal Revenue Code requires you to give your correct TIN to persons who must file information returns with the IRS to report interest, dividends, and certain other income paid to you, mortgage interest you paid, the acquisition or abandonment of secured property, cancellation of debt, or contributions you made to an IRA or Archer MSA. The IRS uses the numbers for identification purposes and to help verify the accuracy of your tax return. The IRS may also provide this information to the Department of Justice for civil and criminal litigation, and to cities, states, and the District of Columbia to carry out their tax laws.

You must provide your TIN whether or not you are required to file a tax return. Payers must generally withhold 30% of taxable interest, dividend, and certain other payments to a payee who does not give a TIN to a payer. Certain penalties may also apply.

What Name and Number To Give the Requester

For this type of account:	Give name and SSN of:
1. Individual	The individual
2. Two or more individuals (joint account)	The actual owner of the account or, if combined funds, the first individual on the account [1]
3. Custodian account of a minor (Uniform Gift to Minors Act)	The minor [2]
4. a. The usual revocable savings trust (grantor is also trustee)	The grantor-trustee [1]
b. So-called trust account that is not a legal or valid trust under state law	The actual owner [1]
5. Sole proprietorship	The owner [3]

For this type of account:	Give name and EIN of:
6. Sole proprietorship	The owner [3]
7. A valid trust, estate, or pension trust	Legal entity [4]
8. Corporate	The corporation
9. Association, club, religious, charitable, educational, or other tax-exempt organization	The organization
10. Partnership	The partnership
11. A broker or registered nominee	The broker or nominee
12. Account with the Department of Agriculture in the name of a public entity (such as a state or local government, school district, or prison) that receives agricultural program payments	The public entity

[1] List first and circle the name of the person whose number you furnish. If only one person on a joint account has an SSN, that person's number must be furnished.

[2] Circle the minor's name and furnish the minor's SSN.

[3] **You must show your individual name,** but you may also enter your business or "DBA" name. You may use either your SSN or EIN (if you have one).

[4] List first and circle the name of the legal trust, estate, or pension trust. (Do not furnish the TIN of the personal representative or trustee unless the legal entity itself is not designated in the account title.)

Note: *If no name is circled when more than one name is listed, the number will be considered to be that of the first name listed.*

Instructions for the Requester of Form W-9

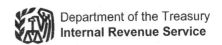

Department of the Treasury
Internal Revenue Service

(Rev. January 2002)

Request for Taxpayer Identification Number and Certification

Section references are to the Internal Revenue Code unless otherwise noted.

Changes To Note

- The backup withholding rate is reduced to 30% for reportable payments made in 2002 and 2003 (29% in 2004 and 2005).
- Payers with an electronic system may receive a Form W-9 electronically from an investment advisor or introducing broker who is authorized as the payee's agent. See **Electronic Submission of Forms W-9** below.

How Do I Know When To Use Form W-9?

Use Form W-9 to request the taxpayer identification number (TIN) of a **U.S. person** (including a resident alien) and to request certain certifications and claims for exemption. (See **Purpose of Form** on the Form W-9.) Withholding agents may require signed Forms W-9 from U.S. exempt recipients to overcome any presumptions of foreign status.

Advise foreign persons to use the appropriate Form W-8. See **Pub. 515,** Withholding of Tax on Nonresident Aliens and Foreign Entities, for more information and a list of the W-8 forms.

Also, a nonresident alien individual may, under certain circumstances, claim treaty benefits on scholarships and fellowship grant income. See Pub. 515 or **Pub. 519,** U.S. Tax Guide for Aliens, for more information.

Electronic Submission of Forms W-9

Requesters may establish a system for payees and payee's agents to submit Forms W-9 electronically, including by fax. A requester is anyone required to file an information return. A payee is anyone required to provide a taxpayer identification number (TIN) to the requester.

Payee's agent. A payee's agent can be an investment advisor (corporation, partnership, or individual) or an introducing broker. An investment advisor must be registered with the Securities Exchange Commission (SEC) under the Investment Advisers Act of 1940. The introducing broker is a broker-dealer that is regulated by the SEC and the National Association of Securities Dealers, Inc., and that is not a payer. Except for a broker who acts as a payee's agent for "readily tradable instruments," the advisor or broker must show in writing to the payer that the payee authorized the advisor or broker to transmit the Form W-9 to the payer.

Electronic system. Generally, the electronic system must:

- Ensure the information received is the information sent, and document all occasions of user access that result in the submission;
- Make reasonably certain that the person accessing the system and submitting the form is the person identified on Form W-9, the investment advisor, or the introducing broker;
- Provide the same information as the paper Form W-9;
- Be able to supply a hard copy of the electronic Form W-9 if the Internal Revenue Service requests it; and
- Require as the final entry in the submission an electronic signature by the payee whose name is on Form W-9 that authenticates and verifies the submission. The electronic signature must be under penalties of perjury and the perjury statement must contain the language of the paper Form W-9.

 For Forms W-9 that are not required to be signed, the electronic system need not provide for an electronic signature or a perjury statement.

For more details, see the following at **www.irs.gov:**
- Announcement 98-27, 1998-1 C.B. 865. You can find Announcement 98-27 on page 30 of Internal Revenue Bulletin (I.R.B.) 1998-15.
- Announcement 2001-91. You can find Announcement 2001-91 on page 221 of I.R.B. 2001-36.

Individual Taxpayer Identification Number (ITIN)

Form W-9 (or an acceptable substitute) is used by persons required to file information returns with the IRS to get the payee's (or other person's) correct TIN. For individuals, the TIN is generally a social security number (SSN).

However, in some cases, individuals who become U.S. resident aliens for tax purposes are not eligible to obtain an SSN. This includes certain resident aliens who must receive information returns but who cannot obtain an SSN.

These individuals must apply for an ITIN on **Form W-7,** Application for IRS Individual Taxpayer Identification Number, unless they have an application pending for an SSN. Individuals who have an ITIN must provide it on Form W-9.

Substitute Form W-9

You may develop and use your own Form W-9 (a substitute Form W-9) if its content is substantially similar to the official IRS Form W-9 and it satisfies certain certification requirements.

You may incorporate a substitute Form W-9 into other business forms you customarily use, such as account signature cards. However, the certifications on the substitute Form W-9 must clearly set forth (as shown on the official Form W-9) that:

1. The payee's TIN is correct,

2. The payee is not subject to backup withholding due to failure to report interest and dividend income, and

3. The payee is a U.S. person.

You may not:

1. Use a substitute Form W-9 that requires the payee, by signing, to agree to provisions unrelated to the required certifications or

2. Imply that a payee may be subject to backup withholding unless the payee agrees to provisions on the substitute form that are unrelated to the required certifications.

A substitute Form W-9 that contains a **separate signature line** just for the certifications satisfies the requirement that the certifications be clearly set forth.

If a **single signature line** is used for the required certifications and other provisions, the certifications must be highlighted, boxed, printed in bold-face type, or presented in some other manner that causes the language to stand out from all other information contained on the substitute form. Additionally, the following statement must be presented to stand out in the same manner as described above and must appear immediately above the single signature line:

"The Internal Revenue Service does not require your consent to any provision of this document other than the certifications required to avoid backup withholding."

If you use a substitute form, you are encouraged (but not required) to provide Form W-9 instructions to the payee. However, if the IRS has notified the payee that backup withholding applies, then you must instruct the payee to strike out the language in the certification that relates to underreporting. This instruction can be given orally or in writing. See item 2 of the **Certification** on Form W-9.

TIN Applied for

For interest and dividend payments and certain payments with respect to readily tradable instruments, the payee may return a properly completed, signed Form W-9 to you with "Applied For" written in Part I. This is an "awaiting- TIN" certificate. The payee has 60 calendar days, from the date you receive this certificate, to provide a TIN. If you do not receive the payee's TIN at that time, you must begin backup withholding on payments.

Reserve rule. You must backup withhold on any reportable payments made during the 60-day period if a payee withdraws more than $500 at one time, unless the payee reserves 30 percent of all reportable payments made to the account during 2002 (29% after 2003).

Alternative rule. You may also elect to backup withhold during this 60-day period, after a 7-day grace period, under one of the two alternative rules discussed below.

Option 1. Backup withhold on any reportable payments if the payee makes a withdrawal from the account after the close of 7 business days after you receive the awaiting-TIN certificate. Treat as reportable payments all cash withdrawals in an amount up to the reportable payments made from the day after you receive the awaiting-TIN certificate to the day of withdrawal.

Option 2. Backup withhold on any reportable payments made to the payee's account, regardless of whether the payee makes any withdrawals, beginning no later than 7 business days after you receive the awaiting-TIN certificate.

The 60-day exemption from backup withholding does not apply to any payment other than interest, dividends, and certain payments relating to readily tradable instruments. Any other reportable payment, such as nonemployee compensation, is subject to backup withholding immediately, even if the payee has applied for and is awaiting a TIN.

Even if the payee gives you an awaiting-TIN certificate, you must backup withhold on reportable interest and dividend payments if the payee does not certify, under penalties of perjury, that the payee is not subject to backup withholding.

Payees Exempt From Backup Withholding

Even if the payee does not provide a TIN in the manner required, you are **not required** to backup withhold on any payments you make if the payee is:

1. An organization exempt from tax under section 501(a), any IRA, or a custodial account under section 403(b)(7) if the account satisfies the requirements of section 401(f)(2);

2. The United States or any of its agencies or instrumentalities;

3. A state, the District of Columbia, a possession of the United States, or any of their political subdivisions or instrumentalities;

4. A foreign government or any of its political subdivisions, agencies, or instrumentalities; or

5. An international organization or any of its agencies or instrumentalities.

Other payees that **may be exempt** from backup withholding include:

6. A corporation;

7. A foreign central bank of issue;

8. A dealer in securities or commodities required to register in the United States, the District of Columbia, or a possession of the United States;

9. A futures commission merchant registered with the Commodity Futures Trading Commission;

10. A real estate investment trust;

11. An entity registered at all times during the tax year under the Investment Company Act of 1940;

12. A common trust fund operated by a bank under section 584(a);

13. A financial institution;

14. A middleman known in the investment community as a nominee or custodian; or

15. A trust exempt from tax under section 664 or described in section 4947.

The following types of payments are exempt from backup withholding as indicated for items **1** through **15** above.

Interest and dividend payments. All listed payees are exempt except the payee in item **9.**

Broker transactions. All payees listed in items **1** through **13** are exempt. A person registered under the Investment Advisers Act of 1940 who regularly acts as a broker is also exempt.

Barter exchange transactions and patronage dividends. Only payees listed in items **1** through **5** are exempt.

Payments reportable under sections 6041 and 6041A. Only payees listed in items **1** through **7** are generally exempt.

However, the following payments made to a corporation (including gross proceeds paid to an attorney under section 6045(f), even if the attorney is a corporation) and reportable on **Form 1099-MISC,** Miscellaneous Income, are **not exempt** from backup withholding.

- Medical and health care payments.
- Attorneys' fees.
- Payments for services paid by a Federal executive agency.

Payments Exempt From Backup Withholding

Payments that are not subject to information reporting also are not subject to backup withholding. For details, see sections 6041, 6041A, 6042, 6044, 6045, 6049, 6050A, and 6050N, and their regulations. The following payments are generally exempt from backup withholding.

Dividends and patronage dividends
- Payments to nonresident aliens subject to withholding under section 1441.
- Payments to partnerships not engaged in a trade or business in the United States and that have at least one nonresident alien partner.
- Payments of patronage dividends not paid in money.
- Payments made by certain foreign organizations.
- Section 404(k) distributions made by an ESOP.

Interest payments
- Payments of interest on obligations issued by individuals. However, if you pay $600 or more of interest in the course of your trade or business to a payee, you must report the payment. Backup withholding applies to the reportable payment if the payee has not provided a TIN or has provided an incorrect TIN.

- Payments of tax-exempt interest (including exempt-interest dividends under section 852).
- Payments described in section 6049(b)(5) to nonresident aliens.
- Payments on tax-free covenant bonds under section 1451.
- Payments made by certain foreign organizations.
- Mortgage or student loan interest paid to you.

Other types of payment
- Wages.
- Distributions from a pension, annuity, profit-sharing or stock bonus plan, any IRA, or an owner-employee plan.
- Certain surrenders of life insurance contracts.
- Gambling winnings if withholding is required under section 3402(q). However, if withholding is not required under section 3402(q), backup withholding applies if the payee fails to furnish a TIN.
- Real estate transactions reportable under section 6045(e).
- Cancelled debts reportable under section 6050P.
- Distributions from a medical savings account and long-term care benefits.
- Fish purchases for cash reportable under section 6050R.

Joint Foreign Payees

If the first payee listed on an account gives you a Form W-8 or a similar statement signed under penalties of perjury, backup withholding applies unless:

1. Every joint payee provides the statement regarding foreign status or

2. Any one of the joint payees who has not established foreign status gives you a TIN.

If any one of the joint payees who has not established foreign status gives you a TIN, use that number for purposes of backup withholding and information reporting.

For more information on foreign payees, see the **Instructions for the Requester of Forms W-8BEN, W-8ECI, W-8EXP, and W-8IMY.**

Names and TINs To Use for Information Reporting

Show the full name and address as provided on Form W-9 on the information return filed with the IRS and on the copy furnished to the payee. If you made payments to more than one payee or the account is in more than one name, enter on the first name line **only** the name of the payee whose TIN is shown on the information return. You may show the names of any other individual payees in the area below the first name line.

Sole proprietor. Enter the individual's name on the first name line. On the second name line, enter the business name or "doing business as (DBA)" if provided. **You may not enter only the business name.** For the TIN, you may enter either the individual's SSN or the employer identification number (EIN) of the business. However, the IRS prefers that you show the SSN.

LLC. For an LLC that is disregarded as an entity separate from its owner, you must show the owner's name on the first name line. On the second name line, you may enter the LLC's name. Use the **owner's** TIN.

Additional Information

For more information on backup withholding, see:
- **Pub. 1679,** A Guide to Backup Withholding or
- **Pub. 1281,** Backup Withholding on Missing and Incorrect Name/TINs.

Notices From the IRS

The IRS will send you a notice if the payee's name and TIN on the information return you filed do not match the IRS's records. You may have to send a "B" notice to the payee to solicit another TIN. Pubs. 1679 and 1281 contain copies of the two types of "B" notices.

2

Sample Agreements

General Independent Contractor Agreement

Contract Amendment Form

Nondisclosure Agreement

INDEPENDENT CONTRACTOR AGREEMENT

This Agreement is made between _____ (Client)

with a principal place of business at _____

and _____ (Contractor), with a

principal place of business at _____.

Services to Be Performed

(Check and complete applicable provision.)

☐ Contractor agrees to perform the following services:

_____

_____

OR

☐ Contractor agrees to perform the services described in Exhibit A, which is attached to and made part of this Agreement.

_____

_____

Payment

(Check and complete applicable provision.)

☐ In consideration for the services to be performed by Contractor, Client agrees to pay Contractor

$_____

OR

☐ In consideration for the services to be performed by Contractor, Client agrees to pay Contractor at the rate of

$_____ per _____.

(Check if applicable.)

☐ Contractor's total compensation shall not exceed $_____ without Client's written consent.

Terms of Payment

(Check and complete applicable provision.)

☐ Upon completing Contractor's services under this Agreement, Contractor shall submit an invoice. Client shall pay Contractor within _____ [10, 15, 30, 45, 60] days from the date of Contractor's invoice.

OR

☐ Contractor shall be paid $_____ [State amount] upon signing this Agreement and the remaining amount due when Contractor completes the services and submits an invoice. Client shall pay Contractor within _____ [10, 15, 30, 45, 60] days from the date of Contractor's invoice.

OR

☐ Contractor shall be paid according to the Schedule of Payments set forth in Exhibit _____ [A or B] attached to and made part of this Agreement.

OR

☐ Contractor shall send Client an invoice monthly. Client shall pay Contractor within [10, 15, 30, 45, 60] days from the date of each invoice.

Late Fees

(Check and complete if applicable.)

☐ Late payments by Client shall be subject to late penalty fees of _____% per month from the due date until the amount is paid.

Expenses

(Check applicable provision.)

☐ Contractor shall be responsible for all expenses incurred while performing services under this Agreement.

☐ However, Client shall reimburse Contractor for all reasonable travel and living expenses necessarily incurred by Contractor while away from Contractor's regular place of business to perform services under this Agreement. Contractor shall submit an itemized statement of such expenses. Client shall pay Contractor within 30 days from the date of each statement.

OR

☐ Client shall reimburse Contractor for the following expenses that are directly attributable to work performed under this Agreement:

- travel expenses other than normal commuting, including airfares, rental vehicles, and highway mileage in company or personal vehicles at _____ cents per mile
- telephone, facsimile (fax), online and telegraph charges
- postage and courier services
- printing and reproduction
- computer services, and
- other expenses resulting from the work performed under this Agreement.

Contractor shall submit an itemized statement of Contractor's expenses. Client shall pay Contractor within 30 days from the date of each statement.

Materials

(Check and complete if applicable.)

☐ Contractor will furnish all materials and equipment used to provide the services required by this Agreement.

☐ Client shall make available to Contractor, at Client's expense, the following materials, facilities and equipment: _____ [List]. These items will be provided to Contractor by _____ [Date].

Term of Agreement

This Agreement will become effective when signed by both parties and will end no later than _____, 20___.

Terminating the Agreement

(Check applicable provision.)

☐ With reasonable cause, either party may terminate this Agreement effective immediately by giving written notice of termination for cause. Reasonable cause includes:

- a material violation of this agreement, or
- nonpayment of Contractor's compensation 20 days after written demand for payment.

Contractor shall be entitled to full payment for services performed prior to the effective date of termination

OR

☐ Either party may terminate this Agreement at any time by giving _____ [5, 10, 15, 30, 45, 60] days written notice of termination without cause. Contractor shall be entitled to full payment for services performed prior to the effective date of termination.

Independent Contractor Status

Contractor is an independent contractor, not Client's employee. Contractor's employees or subcontractors are not Client's employees. Contractor and Client agree to the following rights consistent with an independent contractor relationship.

- Contractor has the right to perform services for others during the term of this Agreement.
- Contractor has the sole right to control and direct the means, manner and method by which the services required by this Agreement will be performed.
- Contractor has the right to hire assistants as subcontractors, or to use employees to provide the services required by this Agreement.
- The Contractor or Contractor's employees or subcontractors shall perform the services required by this Agreement; Client shall not hire, supervise or pay any assistants to help Contractor.
- Neither Contractor nor Contractor's employees or subcontractors shall receive any training from Client in the skills necessary to perform the services required by this Agreement.
- Client shall not require Contractor or Contractor's employees or subcontractors to devote full time to performing the services required by this Agreement.
- Neither Contractor nor Contractor's employees or subcontractors are eligible to participate in any employee pension, health, vacation pay, sick pay or other fringe benefit plan of Client.

Local, State and Federal Taxes

Contractor shall pay all income taxes, and FICA (Social Security and Medicare taxes) incurred while performing services under this Agreement. Client will not:

- withhold FICA (Social Security and Medicare taxes) from Contractor's payments or make FICA payments on Contractor's behalf
- make state or federal unemployment compensation contributions on Contractor's behalf, or
- withhold state or federal income tax from Contractor's payments.

The charges included here do not include taxes. If Contractor is required to pay any federal, state or local sales, use, property or value added taxes based on the services provided under this Agreement, the taxes shall be separately billed to Client. Contractor shall not pay any interest or penalties incurred due to late payment or nonpayment of such taxes by Client.

Notices

All notices and other communications in connection with this Agreement shall be in writing and shall be considered given as follows:

- when delivered personally to the recipient's address as stated on this Agreement
- three days after being deposited in the United States mail, with postage prepaid to the recipient's address as stated on this Agreement, or
- when sent by fax or telex to the last fax or telex number of the recipient known to the person giving notice. Notice is effective upon receipt, provided that a duplicate copy of the notice is promptly given by first class mail, or the recipient delivers a written confirmation of receipt.

No Partnership

This Agreement does not create a partnership relationship. Neither party has authority to enter into contracts on the other's behalf.

Applicable Law

This Agreement will be governed by the laws of the state of _____.

Exclusive Agreement

This is the entire Agreement between Contractor and Client.

Dispute Resolution

(Check if applicable)

☐ If a dispute arises under this Agreement, the parties agree to first try to resolve the dispute with the help of a mutually agreed-upon mediator in the following location _____ [List city or county where mediation will occur]. Any costs and fees other than attorney fees associated with the mediation shall be shared equally by the parties.

If it proves impossible to arrive at a mutually satisfactory solution through mediation, the parties agree to submit the dispute to binding arbitration in the following location _____ [List city or county where arbitration will occur] under the rules of the American Arbitration Association. Judgment upon the award rendered by the arbitrator may be entered in any court having jurisdiction to do so.

However, the complaining party may refuse to submit the dispute to mediation or arbitration and instead bring an action in an appropriate Small Claims Court.

Contract Changes

(Check if applicable)

☐ Client and Contractor recognize that:

- Contractor's original cost and time estimates may be too low due to unforeseen events, or to factors unknown to Contractor when this Agreement was made
- Client may desire a mid-project change in Contractor's services that would add time and cost to the project and possibly inconvenience Contractor, or
- Other provisions of this Agreement may be difficult to carry out due to unforeseen circumstances.

If any intended changes or any other events beyond the parties' control require adjustments to this Agreement, the parties shall make a good faith effort to agree on all necessary particulars. Such agreements shall be put in writing, signed by the parties and added to this Agreement.

Attorneys' Fees

If any legal action is necessary to enforce this Agreement, the prevailing party shall be entitled to reasonable attorney fees, costs and expenses in addition to any other relief to which he or she may be entitled.

Signatures

Client:

[Name of Client]

_____
Name of Client

By: _____
Signature

_____
Typed or Printed Name

Title: _____

Date: _____

Contractor

[Name of Contractor]

_____
Name of Contractor

By: _____
Signature

_____
Typed or Printed Name

Title: _____

Taxpayer ID Number: _____

Date: _____

If Agreement Is Faxed:

Contractor and Client agree that this Agreement will be considered signed when the signature of a party is delivered by facsimile transmission. Signatures transmitted by facsimile shall have the same effect as original signatures.

CONTRACT AMENDMENT FORM

AMENDMENT

This Amendment is made between _____ and

_____ to amend the the Original Agreement titled

_____ signed by them on

_____ .

The Original Agreement is amended as follows:

All provisions of the Original Agreement, except as modified by this Amendment, remain in full force and effect and are reaffirmed. If there is any conflict between this Amendment and any provision of the Original Agreement, the provisions of this Amendment shall control.

Client:

_____

By: _____
(Signature)

_____
Typed or Printed Name

Title: _____

Date: _____

Contractor:

_____

By: _____
(Signature)

_____
Typed or Printed Name

Title: _____

Date: _____

NOLO www.nolo.com

NONDISCLOSURE AGREEMENT

1. Introduction

This is an agreement, effective _____, between _____ (the "Discloser") and _____ (the "Recipient"), in which Discloser agrees to disclose, and Recipient agrees to receive, certain trade secrets of Discloser on the following terms and conditions:

2. Trade Secrets

[ALTERNATIVE 1]

Recipient understands and acknowledges that the following information constitutes trade secrets belonging to Discloser: _____

[ALTERNATIVE 2]

Recipient understands and acknowledges that Discloser's trade secrets consist of information and materials that are valuable and not generally known by Discloser's competitors. Discloser's trade secrets include:

    (a) Any and all information concerning Discloser's current, future or proposed products, including, but not limited to, formulas, designs, devices, computer code, drawings, specifications, notebook entries, technical notes and graphs, computer printouts, technical memoranda and correspondence, product development agreements and related agreements.

    (b) Information and materials relating to Discloser's purchasing, accounting and marketing, including, but not limited to, marketing plans, sales data, business methods, unpublished promotional material, cost and pricing information and customer lists.

    (c) Information of the type described above which Discloser obtained from another party and which Discloser treats as confidential, whether or not owned or developed by Discloser.

    (d) Other: _____

3. Purpose of Disclosure

Recipient shall make use of Discloser's trade secrets only for the purpose of:

_____

4. Nondisclosure

In consideration of Discloser's disclosure of its trade secrets to Recipient, Recipient agrees that it will treat Discloser's trade secrets with the same degree of care and safeguards that it takes with its own trade secrets, but in no event less than a reasonable degree of care. Recipient agrees that, without Discloser's prior written consent, Recipient will not:

    (a) disclose Discloser's trade secrets to any third party;

    (b) make or permit to be made copies or other reproductions of Discloser's trade secrets; or

    (c) make any commercial use of the trade secrets.

Recipient represents that it has, and agrees to maintain, an appropriate agreement with each of its employees and independent contractors who may have access to any of Discloser's trade secrets sufficient to enable Recipient to comply with all the terms of this Agreement.

5. Return of Materials

Upon Discloser's request, Recipient shall promptly (within 30 days) return all original materials provided by Discloser and any copies, notes or other documents in Recipient's possession pertaining to Discloser's trade secrets.

6. Exclusions

This agreement does not apply to any information which:

(a) was in Recipient's possession or was known to Recipient, without an obligation to keep it confidential, before such information was disclosed to Recipient by Discloser;

(b) is or becomes public knowledge through a source other than Recipient and through no fault of Recipient;

(c) is or becomes lawfully available to Recipient from a source other than Discloser; or

(d) is disclosed by Recipient with Discloser's prior written approval.

7. Term

[ALTERNATIVE 1]

This Agreement and Recipient's duty to hold Discloser's trade secrets in confidence shall remain in effect until the above-described trade secrets are no longer trade secrets or until Discloser sends Recipient written notice releasing Recipient from this Agreement, whichever occurs first.

[ALTERNATIVE 2]

This Agreement and Recipient's duty to hold Discloser's trade secrets in confidence shall remain in effect until _____ or until whichever of the following occurs first:

- Discloser sends Recipient written notice releasing Recipient from this Agreement, or
- The above-described trade secrets are no longer trade secrets.

8. No Rights Granted

Recipient understands and agrees that this Agreement does not constitute a grant or an intention or commitment to grant any right, title or interest in Discloser's trade secrets to Recipient.

9. Warranty

Discloser warrants that it has the right to make the disclosures under this Agreement.

10. Injunctive Relief

Recipient acknowledges and agrees that in the event of a breach or threatened breach of this Agreement, money damages would be an inadequate remedy and extremely difficult to measure. Recipient agrees, therefore, that Discloser shall be entitled to an injunction to restrain Recipient from such breach or threatened breach. Nothing in this Agreement shall be construed as preventing Discloser from pursuing any remedy at law or in equity for any breach or threatened breach.

11. Attorney Fees

If any legal action arises relating to this Agreement, the prevailing party shall be entitled to recover all court costs, expenses and reasonable attorney fees.

12. Modifications

This Agreement represents the entire agreement between the parties regarding the subject matter and supersedes all prior agreements or understandings between them. All additions or modifications to this Agreement must be made in writing and must be signed by both parties to be effective.

13. No Agency

This Agreement does not create any agency or partnership relationship between the parties.

14. Applicable Law

This Agreement is made under, and shall be construed according to, the laws of the State of _____.

15. Signatures

Discloser:

_____

By:

_____

_____

Title:

_____

Date: _____

Recipient:

_____

By:

_____

_____

Title:

_____

Date: _____

Agencies

Agencies

State Offices Providing Small Business Help

Alabama
Economic and Community Affairs
401 Adams Ave
PO Box 5690
Montgomery, AL 36130
(800) 248-0033* (205) 242-0400
www.alalinc.net/
partner.cfm?Location=secretary

Alaska
Division of Community and Business
Development
Department of Community & Economic
Development
PO Box 110809
Juneau, AK 99811-0804
(907) 465-2017
www.dced.state.ak.us/cbd/

Arizona
Department of Commerce
3800 North Central Avenue
Suite 1500
Phoenix, AZ 85012
(602) 280-1300
www.az.gov/webapp/portal/
topic.ysp?id=1158

Arkansas
Small Business Information Center
Industrial Development Commission
State Capitol Mall
Room 4C-300
Little Rock, AR 72201
(501) 682-5275
www.sosweb.state.ar.us/

California
Office of Small Business
Department of Commerce
801 K Street, Suite 1700
Sacramento, CA 95814
(916) 327-4357 (916) 445-6545
www.ss.ca.gov/business/business.htm

Colorado
Economic Development Commission
1625 Broadway, Suite 1700
Denver, CO 80202
(303) 892-3725
www.state.co.us/gov_dir/sos/index.html

Connecticut
Department of Economic and
Community Development
505 Hudson Street
Hartford, CT 06106
(203) 258-4200
www.state.ct.us/ecd/

Delaware
Development Office
PO Box 1401
99 Kings Highway
Dover, DE 19903
(302) 739-4271
www.state.de.us/corp/index.htm

District of Columbia
Office of Business and Economic
Development
Twelfth Floor
717 14th Street NW
Washington, DC 20005
(202) 727-6600
www.dcra.org

Florida
Bureau of Business Assistance
Department of Commerce
107 West Gaines Street, Room 443
Tallahassee, FL 32399-2000
(800) 342-0771* (904) 488-9357
www.dos.state.fl.us/doc/index.html

Georgia
Department of Community Affairs
100 Peachtree Street, Suite 1200
Atlanta, GA 30303
(404) 656-6200
www.sos.state.ga.us/corporations/

Hawaii
Small Business Information Service
2404 Maile Way
Room A 202
University of Hawaii
Honolulu, HI 96819
(808) 956-7363
www.hawaii.gov/dbedt/index.html

Idaho
Economic Development Division
Department of Commerce
700 W. State Street
Boise, ID 83720-0093
(208) 334-2470
www.idsos.state.id.us/corp/
corindex.htm

Illinois
Department of Commerce and
Community Affairs
620 East Adams Street
Springfield, IL 62701
(800) 252-2923* (217) 782-3235
www.commerce.state.il.us/bus/
index.html

Indiana
Ombudsman's Office
Community Development Division
Department of Commerce
One North Capitol, Suite 700
Indianapolis, IN 46204-2288
(800) 824-2476* (317) 232-8891
www.state.in.us/sos/bus_service/

Iowa
Bureau of Small Business Development
Department of Economic Development
200 East Grand Avenue
Des Moines, IA 50309
(800) 532-1216* (515) 242-4720
www.sos.state.ia.us

Kansas
Division of Existing Industry
Development
700 SW Harrison, Suite 1300
Topeka, KN 66603
(913) 296-2741
www.kssos.org/

Kentucky
Division of Small Business
2400 Capitol Plaza Tower
Frankfort, KY 40601
(800) 626-2250* (502) 564-7670
www.sos.state.ky.us/

Louisiana
Department of Economic Development
Office of Commerce and Industry
PO Box 94185
Baton Rouge, LA 70804-9185
(504) 342-5365
www.lded.state.la.us

Maine
Business Development Division
Department of Economic and
Community Development
State House 59
187 State Street
Augusta, ME 04333
(800) 872-3838* (207) 287-2656
www.state.me.us/sos/cec/cec.htm

Maryland
Division of Business Development
Department of Economic and
Employment Development
217 East Redwood Street
Baltimore, MD 21202
(800) 873-7232 (410) 767-3316
www.dat.state.md.us/

Massachusetts
Office of Business Development
1 Ashburton Place, Room 301
Boston, MA 02202
(617) 727-8380
www.state.ma.us/sec/cor/coridx.htm

Michigan
Michigan Jobs Commission
Ombudsman's Office
201 N. Washington Square
Lansing, MI 48913
(517) 373-9808
www.michigan.gov/emi/1,1303,7-102-
115---,00.html

Minnesota
Small Business Assistance Office
Department of Trade and Economic
Development
500 Metro Square Building
121 E. 7th Place
St. Paul, MN 55101-2146
(800) 652-9747 (651) 297-9706
www.sos.state.mn.us/business/
index.html

Mississippi
Mississippi Development Authority
PO Box 849
Jackson, MS 39205
(601) 359-3349
www.ms.gov/frameset.jsp?URL=http%
3A%2F%2fwww.mississippi.org%2F

Missouri
Small Business Development Center
300 University Place
Columbia, MO 65211
(573) 882-0344
http://mosl.sos.state.mo.us/

Montana
Business Assistance Division
Department of Commerce
1218 Sixth St.
Helena, MT 59601
(800) 221-8015* (406) 444-3797
www.state.mt.us/sos/biz.htm

Nebraska
Existing Business Division
Department of Economic Development
PO Box 94666
301 Centennial Mall South
Lincoln, NE 68509-4666
(402) 471-3747
www.nol.org/home/SOS/htm/
services.htm

Nevada
Nevada Commission on Economic
Development
Capitol Complex
5151 S. Carson St.
Carson City, NV 89710
(702) 687-4325
http://sos.state.nv.us/

New Hampshire
Small Business Development Center
108 McConnell Hall
University of New Hampshire
15 College Road
Durham, NH 03824
(603) 862-2200
www.state.nh.us/agency/agencies.html

New Jersey
Office of Small Business Assistance
Department of Commerce and
Economic Growth Commission
20 West State Street, CN 835
Trenton, NJ 08625
(609) 292-2444
www.state.nj.us/njbgs/services.html

New Mexico
Economic Division
Department of Economic Development
1100 St. Francis Drive
PO Box 20003
Santa Fe, NM 87503
(505) 827-0300
www.edd.state.nm.us/about.htm

New York
Division for Small Business
Department of Economic Development
1515 Broadway
51st Floor
New York, NY 10036
(212) 827-6150
www.dos.state.ny.us/corp/
corpwww.html

North Carolina
Business and Industry Division
Department of Commerce
Dobbs Building, Room 2019
430 North Salisbury Street
Raleigh, NC 27611
(919) 733-4151
www.ncgov.com/asp/basic/business.asp

North Dakota
Small Business Coordinator
Economic Development Commission
1833 E. Bismark Expressway
Bismark, ND 58504
(701) 328-5300
www.state.nd.us/sec/

Ohio
Small and Developing Business
Division
Department of Development
77 S. High Street
Columbus, OH 43215
(800) 248-4040* (614) 466-4232
www.state.oh.us/sos/

Oklahoma
Oklahoma Department of Commerce
PO Box 26980
6601 N. Broadway Extension
Oklahoma City, OK 73126-0980
(800) 477-6552* (405) 843-9770
www.state.ok.us/

Oregon
Economic Development Department
775 Summer Street NE
Salem, OR 97310
(800) 233-3306* (503) 986-0110
www.sos.state.or.us/corporation/
corphp.htm

Pennsylvania
Bureau of Small Business and
Appalachian Development
Department of Commerce
461 Forum Building
Harrisburg, PA 17120
(717) 783-5700
www.dos.state.pa.us/corp/corp.htm

Rhode Island
Business Development Division
Department of Economic Development
Seven Jackson Walkway
Providence, RI 02903
(401) 277-2601
www.sec.state.ri.us/submenus/
buslink.htm

South Carolina
Enterprise Development
PO Box 1149
Columbia, SC 29202
(803) 252-8806
www.callsouthcarolina.com/

South Dakota
Governor's Office
of Economic Development
Capital Lake Plaza
711 Wells Avenue
Pierre, SD 57501
(800) 872-6190* (605) 773-5032
www.sdgreatprofits.com//

Tennessee
Small Business Office
Department of Economic and
Community Development
320 Sixth Avenue North
Eighth Floor
Rachel Jackson Building
Nashville, TN 37219
(800) 872-7201* (615) 741-1888
www.state.tn.us/sos/service.htm

Texas
Small Business Division
Department of Commerce
Economic Development Commission
PO Box 12728
Capitol Station
410 East Fifth Street
Austin, TX 78711
(800) 888-0511 (512) 936-0100
www.tded.state.tx.us/smallbusiness/

Utah
Division of Business and Economic
Development
324 South State St., 5th Floor
Salt Lake City, UT 84114
(801) 538-8700
www.utah.org/dbcd/welcome.htm

Vermont
Agency of Development and
Community Affairs
The Pavilion
109 State Street
Montpelier, VT 05609
(800) 622-4553* (802) 828-3221
www.sec.state.vt.us/corps/
corpindex.htm

Virginia
Small Business and Financial Services
Department of Economic Development
PO Box 798
1021 E. Cary Street
11th Floor
Richmond, VA 23206-0798
(804) 371-8106
www.state.va.us/scc/division/clk/
index.htm

Washington
Small Business Development Center
Krugel Hall, Room 135
Washington State University
Pullman, WA 99164-4727
(509) 335-1576
www.secstate.wa.gov/corps/default.htm

West Virginia
Economic Development Authority
1018 Kanawha Blvd. E., Suite 501
Charleston, WV 25301
(304) 558-3650
www.state.wv.us/sos/

Wisconsin
Department of Commerce
201 West Washington Avenue
Madison, WI 53717
(608) 266-1018
www.commerce.state.wi.us/

Wyoming
Economic and Community
Development Division
Commerce Dept.
6101 Yellowstone Road
Cheyenne, WY 82002
(307) 777-7284
http://soswy.state.wy.us/corporat/
corporat.htm

---

*In-state calling only.

Source: National Association for the
Self-Employed, *USA TODAY* research,
updated by Nolo.com.

State Unemployment Tax Agencies

Alabama
Department of Industrial Relations
649 Monroe Street
Montgomery, AL 36131
334-242-8371

Alaska
Employment Security Division
P.O. Box 25509
Juneau, AK 99802-5509
907-465-5912

Arizona
Department of Economic Security
3225 N. Central Avenue
Phoenix, AZ 85012
602-248-9354

Arkansas
Employment Security Division
P.O. Box 2981
Little Rock, AR 72203
501-682-3253

California
Employment Development Department,
MIC-90
P.O. Box 942880
Sacramento, CA 94280-0001
916-653-1528

Colorado
Department of Labor and Employment
1515 Arapahoe, Tower 2,
Suite 400
Denver, CO 80202-2117
303-603-8235

Connecticut
Employment Security Division
Labor Department
200 Folley Brook Blvd.
Wethersfield, CT 06109
860-566-2124

Delaware
Department of Labor
Division of Unemployment Insurance
4425 North Market Street
Wilmington, DE 19809-0950
302-761-8353

District of Columbia
Department of Employment Services
500 C Street, NW, Room 501,
Washington, DC 20001
202-724-7462

Florida
Department of Labor and Employment
Security
107 East Madison Street
Tallahassee, FL 32399-0211
850-921-3108

Georgia
Department of Labor
148 International Blvd.
Atlanta, GA 30303
404-656-4309

Hawaii
Department of Labor and Industrial Relations
800 Punchbowl Street
Honolulu, HI 96813
808-586-8927

Idaho
Department of Employment
317 Main Street
Boise, ID 83735
208-334-6385

Illinois
Bureau of Employment Security
401 South State Street
Chicago, IL 60605
312-793-1918

Indiana
Division of Workforce Development
10 North Senate Avenue
Indianapolis, IN 46204
317-232-7698

Iowa
Department of Job Services
1000 East Grand Avenue
Des Moines, IA 50319
515-281-8200

Kansas
Department of Human Resources
401 Topeka Avenue
Topeka, KS 66603
913-296-5025

Kentucky
Division of Unemployment Insurance
P.O. Box 948
Frankfort, KY 40602
502-564-6838

Louisiana
Office of Employment Security
P.O. Box 98146
Baton Rouge, LA 70804
504-342-2992

Maine
Maine Department of Labor
P.O. Box 309
Augusta, ME 04332-0309
207-287-1239

Maryland
Office of Unemployment Insurance
1100 North Eutaw Street
Baltimore, MD 21201
410-767-2488

Massachusetts
Department of Employment and Training
19 Staniford Street
Boston, MA 02114
617-727-5054

Michigan
Employment Security Division
7310 Woodward Avenue
Detroit, MI 48202
313-876-5131

Minnesota
Department of Economic Security
390 North Robert Street
St. Paul, MN 55101
612-296-3736

Mississippi
Employment Security Commission
P.O. Box 22781
Jackson, MS 39225-2781
601-961-7755

Missouri
Division of Employment Security
Box 59
Jefferson City, MO 65104
314-751-3328

Montana
Unemployment Insurance Division
P.O. Box 1728
Helena, MT 59604
406-444-2747

Nebraska
Division of Employment
Box 94600 State House Station
Lincoln, NE 68509
402-471-9839

Nevada
Department of Employment, Training, and
Rehabilitation
500 East Third Street
Carson City, NV 89713
702-687-4599

New Hampshire
Department of Employment Security
32 South Main Street
Concord, NH 03301
603-228-4045

New Jersey
New Jersey Department of Labor
CN 947
Trenton, NJ 08625-0947
609-292-2810

New Mexico
Employment Security Department
P.O. Box 2281
Albuquerque, NM 87103
505-841-8568

New York
State Department of Labor
State Campus, Building 12
Albany, NY 12240
518-457-4120

North Carolina
Employment Security Commission
P.O. Box 26504
Raleigh, NC 27611
919-733-7395

North Dakota
Job Service of North Dakota
P.O. Box 5507
Bismarck, ND 58502
701-328-2791

Ohio
Bureau of Employment Services
P.O. Box 923
Columbus, OH 43216
614-466-2319

Oklahoma
Employment Security Commission
Will Rogers Memorial Office Building
Oklahoma City, OK 73105
405-557-7135

Oregon
Employment Department
875 Union Street, NE
Salem, OR 97311
503-378-3257

Pennsylvania
Department of Labor and Industry
Labor and Industry Building
7th and Forster Street
Harrisburg, PA 17121
717-787-2097

Rhode Island
Department of Employment & Training
One Capitol Hill
Providence, RI 02908-3688
401-277-3688

South Carolina
Employment Security Commission
P.O. Box 995
Columbia, SC 29202
803-737-3070

South Dakota
Department of Employment Security
P.O. Box 4730
Aberdeen, SD 57401
605-626-2312

Tennessee
Department of Employment Security
500 James Robertson Parkway
8th Floor, Volunteer Plaza Building
Nashville, TN 37245-3500
615-741-2346

Texas
Employment Commission
101 East 15th Street
Austin, TX 78778
512-463-2699

Utah
Department of Employment Security
P.O. Box 45288
Salt Lake City, UT 84145
801-536-7755

Vermont
Department of Employment Security
P.O. Box 488
Montpelier, VT 05602
802-828-4242

Virginia
Employment Commission
P.O. Box 1358
Richmond, VA 23211
804-371-6325

Washington
Employment Security Department
P.O. Box 9046
Olympia, WA 98507-9046
360-902-9554

West Virginia
Unemployment Compensation Division
112 California Avenue
Charleston, WV 25305-0112
304-558-2675

Wisconsin
Department of Industry, Labor, and Human Relations
P.O. Box 7942_GEF 1
Madison, WI 53702
608-266-3177

Wyoming
Employment Resources Division
P.O. Box 2760
Casper, WY 82606
307-235-3201

State Sales Tax Agencies

Depending on the nature of your occupation and the state in which you live, you may have to pay state sales taxes. Check with your state sales tax office for the current requirements. If sales taxes are required, you'll have to fill out an application to obtain a state sales tax number, also called a seller's permit in many states. (See Chapter 5, Section A2c.)

The following states have no sales tax: Alaska, Delaware, Montana, New Hampshire and Oregon.

Alabama
Department of Revenue
Sales and Use Taxes
P.O. Box 327710
Montgomery, AL 36132-7710
Phone: 205-242-1490

Arizona
Department of Revenue
Licensing Section
1600 West Monroe
Phoenix, AZ 85007
Phone: 602-255-2060

Arkansas
Department of Finance and
Administration
Sales and Use Tax Section
P.O. Box 1272
Little Rock, AK 72203
Phone: 501-682-7104

California
State Board of Equalization
P.O. Box 942879
Sacramento, CA 94279-0001
Phone: 916-322-2010

Colorado
Department of Revenue
Sales and Use Tax Division
1375 Sherman Street
Denver, CO 80261
Phone: 303-534-1208

Connecticut
Department of Revenue Services
92 Farmington Avenue
Hartford, CT 06105
Phone: 203-566-8520

District of Columbia
Department of Finance and Revenue
Sales and Audit Division
P.O. Box 556
Room 570 North
Washington, DC 20044
Phone: 202-727-6566

Florida
Department of Revenue
Sales and Use Tax Division
5050 West Tennessee Street
Building K
Tallahassee, FL 32399-0100
Phone: 904-488-9750

Georgia
Department of Revenue
Sales and Use Tax Division
P.O. Box 740390
Atlanta, GA 30374-0390
Phone: 404-656-4065

Hawaii
Department of Taxation
TaxpayersÔ Services Branch
P.O. Box 259
Honolulu, HI 96809
Phone: 808-587-1455

Idaho
State Tax Commission
800 Park Boulevard
Boise, ID 83722
Phone: 208-334-7660

Illinois
Department of Revenue
RetailersÔ Occupation Tax
101 W. Jefferson Street
Springfield, IL 62796
Phone: 217-782-7897

Indiana
Department of Revenue
Sales Tax Division
100 N. Zenith Street
Indianapolis, IN 46204
Phone: 317-233-4015

Iowa
Department of Revenue and Finance
Taxpayer Services
Hoover State Office Building
Des Moines, IA 50319
Phone: 515-281-3114

Kansas
Department of Revenue
Sales Tax
P.O. Box 2001
Topeka, KS 66625
Phone: 913-296-2461

Kentucky
Revenue Cabinet
Sales Tax Division
P.O. Box 1274
Station 53
Frankfurt, KY 40602
Phone: 502-564-5170

Lousiana
Department of Revenue and Taxation
Sales Tax Division
P.O. Box 201
Baton Rouge, LA 70821-0201
Phone: 504-925-7356

Maine
Bureau of Taxation
Sales Tax Section
P.O. Box 1065
Augusta, ME 04332-1065
Phone: 207-287-2336

Maryland
State Comptroller
Sales and Use Tax Division
301 West Preston
Baltimore, MD 21201-2383
Phone: 410-225-1300

Massachusetts
Department of Revenue
Sales Tax Division
Room 200
100 Cambridge Street
Boston, MA 00204
Phone: 617-727-4490

Michigan
Department of Treasury
Sales, Use, and Withholding Taxes Division
Treasury Building
Lansing, MI 48922
Phone: 517-373-3190

Minnesota
Department of Revenue
Sales Tax Division
Mail Station 1110
St. Paul, MN 55146-1110
Phone: 612-296-3781

Mississippi
State Tax Commission
Sales Tax Division
P.O. Box 1033
Jackson, MS 39215
Phone: 601-359-1133

Missouri
Department of Revenue
Sales and Use Tax Bureau
P.O. Box 840
Jefferson City, MO 65105-0840
Phone: 314-751-4450

Nebraska
Department of Revenue
Taxpayer Assistance
P.O. Box 94818
Lincoln, NE 68509-4818
Phone: 402-471-5729

Nevada
Department of Taxation
Revenue Office
Capitol Complex
Carson City, NV 89710-0003
Phone: 702-687-4820

New Jersey
Department of Treasury
Division of Taxation
Taxpayer Information Service
Office of Communications
CN 281
Trenton, NJ 08646-0281
Phone: 609-588-3800

New Mexico
Department of Taxation and Revenue
P.O. Box 630
Santa Fe, NM 87509-0630
Phone: 505-827-0834

New York
Department of Taxation and Finance
Technical Services Bureau
Building 9, Room 104
W.A. Harriman State Office Building Campus
Albany, NY 12227
Phone: 518-457-1250

North Carolina
Department of Revenue
Sales and Use Tax Division
P.O. Box 25000
Raleigh, NC 27640
Phone: 919-733-3661

North Dakota
State Tax Commission
Sales and Special Taxes Division
600 East Boulevard Avenue
Bismarck, ND 58505
Phone: 701-224-3470

Ohio
Department of Taxation
Sales and Use Tax Division
30 East Broad Street, 20th Floor
Columbus, OH 43215
Phone: 614-466-4810

Oklahoma
Tax Commission
Business Tax Division
2501 N. Lincoln Boulevard
Oklahoma City, OK 73194
Phone: 405-521-3279

Pennsylvania
Department of Revenue
Bureau of Business Trust
Dept. 280901
Harrisburg, PA 17128-0901
Phone: 717-783-0312

Rhode Island
Department of Administration
Division of Taxation
One Capital Hill
Providence, RI 02908-5800
Phone: 401-277-2950

South Carolina
Tax Commission
Public Assistance
P.O. Box 125
Columbia, SC 29214
Phone: 803-737-4788

South Dakota
Department of Revenue
Sales Taxes
700 Governors Drive
Pierre, SD 57501
Phone: 605-773-3311

Tennessee
Department of Revenue
Sales Tax
Andrew Jackson State Office Building
500 Deaderick Street
Nashville, TN 37242
Phone: 615-741-3581

Texas
State Comptroller
Taxpayer Assistance
P.O. Box 13528
Austin, TX 78711
Phone: 800-252-5555

Utah
Tax Commission
Taxpayer Assistance
160 E. 300 South
1st Floor, South Center
Salt Lake City, UT 84134
Phone: 801-530-4848

Vermont
Department of Taxes
Business Tax Division
P.O. Box 547
Montpelier, VT 05601-0547
Phone: 802-828-2551

Virginia
Department of Taxation
Sales Tax
P.O. Box 6-L
Richmond, VA 23282
Phone: 804-367-8037

Washington
Department of Revenue
Taxpayer Information and Education Section
P.O. Box 47470
Olympia, WA 98504-7470
Phone: 206-753-5525

West Virginia
Department of Tax and Revenue
Sales and Use Tax
P.O. Box 1826
Charleston, WV 25327-1826
Phone: 304-558-3333

Wisconsin
Department of Revenue
Sales and Use Taxes
P.O. Box 8902
Madison, WI 53708
Phone: 608-266-2776

Wyoming
Department of Revenue and Taxation
Sales Taxes
122 W. 25th Street
Cheyenne, WY 82002
Phone: 307-777-7961

Patent and Trademark Depository Libraries

Alabama	Auburn University Libraries	334-844-1737	
	Birmingham Public Library	205-226-3620	
Alaska	Anchorage: Z.J. Loussac Public Library	907-562-7323	
Arizona	Tempe: Noble Library, Arizona State University	480-965-7010	
Arkansas	Little Rock: Arkansas State Library	501-682-2053	
California	Los Angeles Public Library	213-228-7220	
	Sacramento: California State Library	916-654-0069	
	San Diego Public Library	619-236-5813	
	San Francisco Public Library	415-557-4500	
	Santa Rosa: Bruce Sawyer Center (not a PTDL, but useful)	707-524-1773	
	Sunnyvale Center for Innovation	408-730-7290	
Colorado	Denver Public Library	303-640-6220	
Connecticut	Hartford Public Library	860-543-8628	
	New Haven	203-946-8130	
Delaware	Newark: University of Delaware Library	302-831-2965	
District of Columbia	Washington: Howard University Libraries	202-806-7252	
Florida	Fort Lauderdale: Broward County Main Library	954-357-7444	
	Miami: Dade Public Library	305-375-2665	
	Orlando: Univ. of Central Florida Libraries	407-823-2562	
	Tampa: Tampa Campus Library, University of South Florida	813-974-2726	
Georgia	Atlanta: Price Gilbert Memorial Library, Georgia Institute of Technology	404-894-4508	
Hawaii	Honolulu: Hawaii State Public Library System	808-586-3477	
Idaho	Moscow: University of Idaho Library	208-885-6235	
Illinois	Chicago Public Library	312-747-4450	
	Springfield: Illinois State Library	217-782-5659	
Indiana	Indianapolis: Marion County Public Library	317-269-1741	
	West Lafayette: Purdue University Libraries	765-494-2872	
Iowa	Des Moines: State Library of Iowa	515-242-6541	
Kansas	Wichita: Ablah Library, Wichita State University	316-978-3155	
Kentucky	Louisville Free Public Library	502-574-1611	
Louisiana	Baton Rouge: Troy H. Middleton Library, Louisiana State University	225-388-8875	
Maine	Orono: Raymond H. Fogler Library, University of Maine	207-581-1678	
Maryland	College Park: Engineering and Physical Sciences Library, University of Maryland	301-405-9157	
Massachusetts	Amherst: Physical Sciences Library, University of Massachusetts	413-545-1370	
	Boston Public Library	617-536-5400	Ext. 265
Michigan	Ann Arbor: Media Union Library, University of Michigan	734-647-5735	
	Big Rapids: Abigail S. Timme Library, Ferris State University	231-591-3602	
	Detroit Public Library	313-833-3379	
Minnesota	Minneapolis Public Library and Information Center	612-630-6120	
Mississippi	Jackson: Mississippi Library Commission	601-961-4111	
Missouri	Kansas City: Linda Hall Library	816-363-4600	
	St. Louis Public Library	314-241-2288	Ext. 390
Montana	Butte: Montana College of Mineral Science & Technology Library	406-496-4281	
Nebraska	Lincoln: Engineering Library, University of Nebraska	402-472-3411	

Nevada	Reno: University of Nevada-Reno Library	702-784-6500,	Ext. 257
New Hampshire	Concord: New Hampshire State Library	603-271-2239	
New Jersey	Newark Public Library	201-733-7779	
	Piscataway: Library of Science & Medicine, Rutgers University	732-445-2895	
New Mexico	Albuquerque: University of New Mexico General Library	505-277-4412	
New York	Albany: New York State Library	518-474-5355	
	Buffalo and Erie County Public Library	716-858-7101	
	New York Science, Industry & Business Library	212-592-7000	
	Rochester: Central Library	716-428-8110	
	Stony Brook: Melville Library at SUNY	516-632-7148	
North Carolina	Raleigh: D.H. Hill Library, North Carolina State University	919-515-2935	
North Dakota	Grand Forks: Chester Fritz Library, University of North Dakota	701-777-4888	
Ohio	Akron: Summit County Public Library	330-643-9075	
	Cincinnati and Hamilton County, Public Library of	513-369-6971	
	Cleveland Public Library	216-623-2870	
	Columbus: Ohio State University Libraries	614-292-3022	
	Toledo/Lucas County Public Library	419-259-5212	
Oklahoma	Stillwater: Oklahoma State University Library	405-744-7086	
Oregon	Portland: Paul L. Boley Law Library, Lewis & Clark College	503-768-6786	
Pennsylvania	Philadelphia, The Free Library of	215-686-5331	
	Pittsburgh, Carnegie Library of	412-622-3138	
	University Park: Pattee Library, Pennsylvania State University	814-865 4861	
Puerto Rico	Mayaguez General Library, University of Puerto Rico	787-832-4040,	Ext. 2022
Rhode Island	Providence Public Library	401-455-8027	
South Carolina	R.M. Cooper Library, Clemson University	864-656-3024	
South Dakota	Rapid City: Devereaux Library, South Dakota School of Mines and Technology	605-394-1275	
Tennessee	Memphis & Shelby County Public Library and Information Center	901-725-8877	
	Nashville: Stevenson Science Library, Vanderbilt University	615-322-2717	
Texas	Austin: McKinney Engineering Library, University of Texas at Austin	512-495-4500	
	College Station: Sterling C. Evans Library, Texas A & M University	979-845-5745	
	Dallas Public Library	214-670-1468	
	Houston: The Fondren Library, Rice University	713-348-5483	
	Lubbock: Texas Tech University	806-742-2282	
Utah	Salt Lake City: Marriott Library, University of Utah	801-581-8394	
Vermont	Burlington: Bailey/Howe Library, University of Vermont	802-656-2542	
Virginia	Richmond: James Branch Cabell Library, Virginia Commonwealth University	804-828-1104	
Washington	Seattle: Engineering Library, University of Washington	206-543-0740	
West Virginia	Morgantown: Evansdale Library, West Virginia University	304-293-2510	Ext. 5113
Wisconsin	Madison: Kurt F. Wendt Library, University of Wisconsin	608-262-6845	
	Milwaukee Public Library	414-286-3051	
Wyoming	Casper: Natrona County Public Library	307-237-4935	

State Trademark Agencies and Statutes

Alabama
Ala. Code § 8-12-6 to 8-12-19 (1984)
Secretary of State
Lands & Trademark Division
Room 528, State Office Building
Montgomery, AL 36130-7701
334-242-5325

Alaska
Alaska Stat. 45.50.101 et seq.
Department of Community and
Economic Development
Div. of Banking, Securities and Corporations
P.O. Box 110807
Juneau, AK 99811
907-465-2521

Arizona
Ariz. Rev. Stat. 44-1441 et seq.
Office of Secretary of State
1700 W. Washington St.
Phoenix, AZ 85007
602-542-6187

Arkansas
Ark. Code A. §§ 4-71-101 thru 4-71-114
Secretary of State
State Capitol
Little Rock, AR 72201-1094
501-682-3409
FAX 501-682-3481

California
Cal. Bus. & Prof. Code § 14200 et seq.
Secretary of State
Attn: Trademark Unit
State of California
1230 ÒJÓ Street
Sacramento, CA 95814
916-653-4984

Colorado
Colo. Rev. Stat. §§ 7-70-102 to 7-70-113
Colorado Secretary of State
Corporations Office
1560 Broadway, Suite 200
Denver, CO 80202
303-894-2251

Connecticut
Conn. Gen. Stats, 621a §§ 35-11a et seq. and
622a §§ 35-18a et seq.
Secretary of State
Division of Corporations, UCC
& Trademarks
Attn: Trademarks
State of Connecticut
30 Trinity St.
Hartford, CT 06106
860-566-1721

Delaware
6 Del. C. § 3301 et seq.
State of Delaware
Department of State
Division of Corporations
Attn: Trademark Filings
Townsend Building
P.O. Box 898
Dover, DE 19903
302-739-3073

Florida
Fla. Stat. ch. 495.011 et seq.
Corporation Records Bureau
Division of Corporations
Department of State
P.O. Box 6327
Tallahassee, FL 32301
904-487-6051

Georgia
O.C.G.A. §§ 10-1-440 et seq.
Office of Secretary of State
State of Georgia
315 W. Towers
2 MLK Drive
Atlanta, GA 30334
404-656-2817

Hawaii
Hawaii Revised Stats. § 482 et seq.
Department of Commerce and
Consumer Affairs
Business Registration Division
1010 Richards St.
Honolulu, HA 96813
808-586-2744

Idaho
Idaho Code §§ 48-501 et seq. (1979)
Secretary of State
Room 203
Statehouse
Boise, ID 83720
208-334-2300
FAX 208-334-2282

Illinois
Ill. Rev. Stat. 1987, ch. 140, §§ 8-22
Illinois Secretary of State
The Index Dept., Trademark Division
111 E. Monroe
Springfield, IL 62756
217-524-0400

Indiana
Indiana Code § 24-2-1-1 et seq.
Secretary of State of Indiana
Trademark Division
Rm 155, State House
Indianapolis, IN 46204
317-232-6540

Iowa
Iowa Code ch. 548
Secretary of State
Corporate Division
Hoover Bldg.
Des Moines, IA 50319
(515) 281-5204

Kansas
K.S.A. § 81-111 et seq.
Secretary of State
Statehouse Bldg., Room 235N
Topeka, KS 66612
913-296-4565

Kentucky
K.R.S. 365.560 to 365.625
Office of Kentucky Secretary of State
Frankfort, KY 40601
502-564-2848

Louisiana
La. Rev. Stat. Ann. 51:211 et seq.
Secretary of State
Corporation Division
P.O. Box 94125
Baton Rouge, LA 70804-9125
504-925-4704

Maine
10 M.R.S.A. § 1521-1532
State of Maine
Department of State
Division of Public Administration
State House Station 101
Augusta, ME 04333
207-287-4190

Maryland
Md. Ann. Code Art. 41, §§ 3-101 thru 3-114
Secretary of State
State House
Annapolis, MD 21404
301-974-5531

Massachusetts
Mass. Laws Ann., Ch. 110 B, § 1-16.
Office of Secretary of State
Trademark Division
Rm. 1711
One Ashburton Place
Boston, MA 02108
617-727-9640

Michigan

Mich. Compiled Laws §§ 429.31 et seq.
Michigan Department of Commerce
Corporations and Securities Bureau
Corporation Division
P.O. Box 30054
Lansing, MI 48909
517-334-6302

Minnesota

M.S.A. §§ 333.001-333.54
Secretary of State of Minnesota
Corporations Division
180 State Office Bldg.
St. Paul, MN 55155
612-297-1455

Mississippi

Miss. Code Ann., § 75-25-1 (1971)
Office of Secretary of State
P.O. Box 1350
Jackson, MS 39215
601-359-1350

Missouri

Missouri Rev. Stat. 1978 §§ 417.005 et seq.
Office of Secretary of State
Attn: Trademark Division
P.O. Box 778
Jefferson City, MO 65101
314-751-4153

Montana

Mont. Code Ann., §§ 30-13-301 et seq. (1985)
Office of Secretary of State
Montana State Capitol
Helena, MT 59620
406-444-3665
FAX 406-444-3976

Nebraska

N.R.S. 1943, ch. 87 §§ 87.101 et seq.
Secretary of State
State Capitol Bldg.
Lincoln, NE 68509
402-471-4079

Nevada

Nev. Rev. Stat. 600.240 et seq.
Secretary of State of Nevada
Capitol Complex
Carson City, NV 89710
702-687-5203

New Hampshire

RSA 350-A
Corporation Division
Office of Secretary of State
State House Annex
Concord, NH 03301
603-271-3244

New Jersey

N. J. Stat. § 56:3-13.1 thru 56:3-13-15
Department of the Treasury
Division of Revenue
TM/SM UNIT
PO Box 453
Trenton, NJ 08625
609-530-3600

New Mexico

N.M.S.A. 57-3-1 thru 57-3-14
Secretary of State
Capitol Bldg. Rm. 400
Santa Fe, NM 87503
505-827-3600

New York

N. Y. Gen. Bus. Law § 360 et seq.
Secretary of State
Department of State
Miscellaneous Records
162 Washington Avenue
Albany, NY 12231
518-473-2492

North Carolina

N.C.G.S. § 80-1 et seq.
Trademark Division
Office of Secretary of State
300 N. Salisbury Street
Raleigh, NC 27611
919-733-4129

North Dakota

N.D.C.C., ch. 47-22
Secretary of State
State Capitol
Bismark, ND 58505
701-328-4284
FAX 701-328-2992

Ohio

ORC, ch. 1329.54 thru 1329.68
Secretary of State
Corporations Department
30 E. Broad St., 14th Floor
Columbus, OH 43215-0418
614-466-3910

Oklahoma

78 Okla. St. Ann. § 21 thru 34
Office of the Secretary of State
State of Oklahoma
101 State Capitol Bldg.
Oklahoma City, OK 73105
405-522-3043

Oregon

ORS 647.005 thru 647.105(i) and 647.115
Director, Corporation Division
Office of Secretary of State
158 12th Street N.E.
Salem, OR 97310-0210
503-986-2200

Pennsylvania

54 Pa. Cons. Stat. Ann. § 1101-1126
Department of State
(Purdon 1987 Supp.)
Corporation Bureau
308 North Office Bldg.
Harrisburg, PA 17120
717-787-2004

Puerto Rico

Title 10, Laws of P. R. Ann. § 191-195
Secretary of State of Puerto Rico
P.O. Box 3271
San Juan, PR 00904
809-722-2121, Ext. 337

Rhode Island

R. I. Gen. Laws §§ 6-2-1 thru 6-2-18
Secretary of State
The Trademarks Division
100 No. Main St.
Providence, RI 02903
401-222-3040

South Carolina

S. C. Code Ann. § 39-15-120 et seq.
Office of Secretary of State
P.O. Box 11350
Columbia, SC 29211
803-758-2744

South Dakota

SDCL ch 37-6
Secretary of State
State Capitol Bldg.
500 East Capitol
Pierre, SD 57501
605-773-3537

Tennessee

Tenn. Code Ann. § 47-25-501 et seq.
Secretary of State
Suite 1800
James K. Polk Bldg.
Nashville, TN 37219
615-741-0531

Texas

Tex. Bus. & Com. Code § 16.01 thru 16.28
Secretary of State
Corporations Section, Trademark Office
Box 13697, Capitol Station
Austin, TX 78711-3697
512-463-5555

Utah

U.C.A. 70-3-1 et seq.
Division of Corporations
& Commercial Code
Heber M. Wells Bldg.
160 E. 300 South St
Salt Lake City, UT 84111
801-530-4849

Virginia

Va. Code § 59.1-77 et seq.
State Corp. Commission
Division of Securities and Retail Franchises
1220 Bank Street
Richmond, VA 23209
804-271-9051

Vermont

§ 9 V.S.A. §§ 2521 thru 2532
Vermont Secretary of State
Corporations Division
Redstone Bldg., 26 Terrace St.
Mail: State Office Bldg.
Montpelier, VT 05602-2199
802-828-2386

Washington

R.C.W. 19.77.010 et seq.
Corporations Division
Office of Secretary of State
Republic BuildingÑ2nd Floor
505 E. Union St
Olympia, WA 98504
206-753-7120

West Virginia

W. Va. Code § 47-2-1- et seq. and § 47-3-1 et
seq.
Secretary of State
Corporations Division
State Capitol
Charleston, WV 25305
304-558-8000

Wisconsin

Wisconsin Stat. § 132.01 et seq.
Secretary of State
Trademark Records
P.O. Box 7848
Madison, WI 53707
608-266-5653

Wyoming

W.S. §§ 40-1-101 et seq.
Office of Secretary of State
Corporation Division
Capitol Bldg.
Cheyenne, WY 82002
307-777-7378 ∎

Index

CATALOG

...more from Nolo

	PRICE	CODE

BUSINESS

	PRICE	CODE
Avoid Employee Lawsuits	$24.95	AVEL
The CA Nonprofit Corporation Kit (Binder w/CD-ROM)	$59.95	CNP
Consultant & Independent Contractor Agreements (Book w/CD-ROM)	$29.95	CICA
The Corporate Minutes Book (Book w/CD-ROM)	$69.99	CORMI
The Employer's Legal Handbook	$39.99	EMPL
Everyday Employment Law	$29.99	ELBA
Drive a Modest Car & 16 Other Keys to Small Business Success	$24.99	DRIV
Firing Without Fear	$29.95	FEAR
Form Your Own Limited Liability Company (Book w/CD-ROM)	$44.99	LIAB
Hiring Independent Contractors: The Employer's Legal Guide (Book w/CD-ROM)	$34.95	HICI
How to Create a Buy-Sell Agreement & Control the Destiny of your Small Business (Book w/Disk-PC)	$49.95	BSAG
How to Create a Noncompete Agreement	$44.95	NOCMP
How to Form a California Professional Corporation (Book w/CD-ROM)	$59.95	PROF
How to Form a Nonprofit Corporation (Book w/CD-ROM)—National Edition	$44.99	NNP
How to Form a Nonprofit Corporation in California (Book w/CD-ROM)	$44.99	NON
How to Form Your Own California Corporation (Binder w/CD-ROM)	$39.95	CACI
How to Form Your Own California Corporation (Book w/CD-ROM)	$34.95	CCOR
How to Form Your Own New York Corporation (Book w/Disk—PC)	$39.95	NYCO
How to Form Your Own Texas Corporation (Book w/CD-ROM)	$39.95	TCOR
How to Get Your Business on the Web	$29.99	WEBS
How to Write a Business Plan	$29.99	SBS
The Independent Paralegal's Handbook	$29.95	PARA
Leasing Space for Your Small Business	$34.95	LESP

Prices subject to change.

	PRICE	CODE
Legal Guide for Starting & Running a Small Business	$34.99	RUNS
Legal Forms for Starting & Running a Small Business (Book w/CD-ROM)	$29.95	RUNS2
Marketing Without Advertising	$22.00	MWAD
Music Law (Book w/CD-ROM)	$34.99	ML
Nolo's California Quick Corp	$19.95	QINC
Nolo's Guide to Social Security Disability	$29.99	QSS
Nolo's Quick LLC	$24.95	LLCQ
Nondisclosure Agreements	$39.95	NAG
The Small Business Start-up Kit (Book w/CD-ROM)	$29.99	SMBU
The Small Business Start-up Kit for California (Book w/CD-ROM)	$34.99	OPEN
The Partnership Book: How to Write a Partnership Agreement (Book w/CD-ROM)	$39.95	PART
Sexual Harassment on the Job	$24.95	HARS
Starting & Running a Successful Newsletter or Magazine	$29.95	MAG
Tax Savvy for Small Business	$34.95	SAVVY
Working for Yourself: Law & Taxes for the Self-Employed	$39.95	WAGE
Your Limited Liability Company: An Operating Manual (Book w/CD-ROM)	$49.99	LOP
Your Rights in the Workplace	$29.95	YRW

CONSUMER

	PRICE	CODE
Fed Up with the Legal System: What's Wrong & How to Fix It	$9.95	LEG
How to Win Your Personal Injury Claim	$29.95	PICL
Nolo's Encyclopedia of Everyday Law	$29.99	EVL
Nolo's Pocket Guide to California Law	$24.95	CLAW
Trouble-Free Travel...And What to Do When Things Go Wrong	$14.95	TRAV

ESTATE PLANNING & PROBATE

	PRICE	CODE
8 Ways to Avoid Probate	$19.95	PRO8
9 Ways to Avoid Estate Taxes	$29.95	ESTX

	PRICE	CODE
Estate Planning Basics	$21.99	ESPN
How to Probate an Estate in California	$49.99	PAE
Make Your Own Living Trust (Book w/CD-ROM)	$39.99	LITR
Nolo's Law Form Kit: Wills	$24.95	KWL
Nolo's Simple Will Book (Book w/CD-ROM)	$34.99	SWIL
Plan Your Estate	$44.99	NEST
Quick & Legal Will Book	$15.99	QUIC

FAMILY MATTERS

Child Custody: Building Parenting Agreements That Work	$29.95	CUST
The Complete IEP Guide	$24.99	IEP
Divorce & Money: How to Make the Best Financial Decisions During Divorce	$34.99	DIMO
Do Your Own Divorce in Oregon	$29.95	ODIV
Get a Life: You Don't Need a Million to Retire Well	$24.95	LIFE
The Guardianship Book for California	$34.95	GB
How to Adopt Your Stepchild in California (Book w/CD-ROM)	$34.95	ADOP
A Legal Guide for Lesbian and Gay Couples	$29.99	LG
Living Together: A Legal Guide (Book w/CD-ROM)	$34.99	LTK
Using Divorce Mediation: Save Your Money & Your Sanity	$29.95	UDMD

GOING TO COURT

Beat Your Ticket: Go To Court and Win! (National Edition)	$19.95	BEYT
The Criminal Law Handbook: Know Your Rights, Survive the System	$34.99	KYR
Everybody's Guide to Small Claims Court (National Edition)	$24.95	NSCC
Everybody's Guide to Small Claims Court in California	$26.99	CSCC
Fight Your Ticket ... and Win! (California Edition)	$29.99	FYT

	PRICE	CODE
How to Change Your Name in California	$34.95	NAME
How to Collect When You Win a Lawsuit (California Edition)	$29.95	JUDG
How to Mediate Your Dispute	$18.95	MEDI
How to Seal Your Juvenile & Criminal Records (California Edition)	$34.95	CRIM
Nolo's Deposition Handbook	$29.99	DEP
Represent Yourself in Court: How to Prepare & Try a Winning Case	$34.99	RYC

HOMEOWNERS, LANDLORDS & TENANTS

California Tenants' Rights	$27.99	CTEN
Deeds for California Real Estate	$24.99	DEED
Dog Law	$21.95	DOG
Every Landlord's Legal Guide (National Edition, Book w/CD-ROM)	$44.99	ELLI
Every Tenant's Legal Guide	$26.95	EVTEN
For Sale by Owner in California	$29.95	FSBO
How to Buy a House in California	$34.95	BHCA
The California Landlord's Law Book: Rights & Responsibilities (Book w/CD-ROM)	$44.99	LBRT
The California Landlord's Law Book: Evictions (Book w/CD-ROM)	$44.99	LBEV
Leases & Rental Agreements	$29.99	LEAR
Neighbor Law: Fences, Trees, Boundaries & Noise	$26.99	NEI
The New York Landlord's Law Book (Book w/CD-ROM)	$39.95	NYLL
Renters' Rights (National Edition)	$24.99	RENT
Stop Foreclosure Now in California	$29.95	CLOS

HUMOR

29 Reasons Not to Go to Law School	$12.95	29R
Poetic Justice	$9.95	PJ

IMMIGRATION

Fiancé & Marriage Visas	$44.95	IMAR

RESEARCH & REFERENCE

SENIORS

SOFTWARE

**Call or check our website at www.nolo.com
for special discounts on Software!**

Order Form

Name

Address

City

State, Zip

Daytime Phone

E-mail

Our "No-Hassle" Guarantee

Return anything you buy directly from Nolo for any reason and we'll cheerfully refund your purchase price. No ifs, ands or buts.

☐ Check here if you do not wish to receive mailings from other companies

Item Code	Quantity	Item	Unit Price	Total Price

Method of payment

☐ Check ☐ VISA ☐ MasterCard
☐ Discover Card ☐ American Express

Subtotal	
Add your local sales tax (California only)	
Shipping: RUSH $9, Basic $5 (See below)	
"I bought 3, ship it to me FREE!"(Ground shipping only)	
TOTAL	

Account Number

Expiration Date

Signature

Shipping and Handling

Rush Delivery—Only $9

We'll ship any order to any street address in the U.S. by UPS 2nd Day Air* for only $9!

* Order by noon Pacific Time and get your order in 2 business days. Orders placed after noon Pacific Time will arrive in 3 business days. P.O. boxes and S.F. Bay Area use basic shipping. Alaska and Hawaii use 2nd Day Air or Priority Mail.

Basic Shipping—$5

Use for P.O. Boxes, Northern California and Ground Service.

Allow 1-2 weeks for delivery. U.S. addresses only.

For faster service, use your credit card and our toll-free numbers

**Call our customer service group
Monday thru Friday 7am to 7pm PST**

Phone	1-800-728-3555
Fax	1-800-645-0895
Mail	Nolo
950 Parker St.
Berkeley, CA 94710

**Order 24 hours a day @
www.nolo.com**

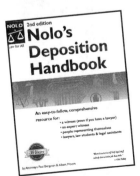

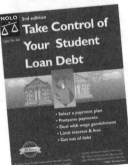

Remember:

Little publishers have big ears.
We really listen to you.

Take 2 Minutes & Give Us Your 2 cents

Your comments make a big difference in the development and revision of Nolo books and software. Please take a few minutes and register your Nolo product—and your comments—with us. Not only will your input make a difference, you'll receive special offers available only to registered owners of Nolo products on our newest books and software. Register now by:

PHONE
1-800-728-3555

FAX
1-800-645-0895

EMAIL
cs@nolo.com

or **MAIL** us
this registration card

fold here

Registration Card

NAME _____ DATE _____

ADDRESS _____

_____

CITY _____ STATE _____ ZIP _____

PHONE _____ E-MAIL _____

WHERE DID YOU HEAR ABOUT THIS PRODUCT? _____

WHERE DID YOU PURCHASE THIS PRODUCT? _____

DID YOU CONSULT A LAWYER? (PLEASE CIRCLE ONE)   YES   NO   NOT APPLICABLE

DID YOU FIND THIS BOOK HELPFUL?   (VERY)   5   4   3   2   1   (NOT AT ALL)

COMMENTS _____

_____

_____

WAS IT EASY TO USE?   (VERY EASY)   5   4   3   2   1   (VERY DIFFICULT)

We occasionally make our mailing list available to carefully selected companies whose products may be of interest to you.

❏ If you do not wish to receive mailings from these companies, please check this box.

❏ You can quote me in future Nolo promotional materials.
Daytime phone number _____.

WAGE 4.0

Nolo in the NEWS

"Nolo helps lay people perform legal tasks without the aid—or fees—of lawyers."

—USA TODAY

Nolo books are ..."written in plain language, free of legal mumbo jumbo, and spiced with witty personal observations."

—ASSOCIATED PRESS

"...Nolo publications...guide people simply through the how, when, where and why of law."

—WASHINGTON POST

"Increasingly, people who are not lawyers are performing tasks usually regarded as legal work... And consumers, using books like Nolo's, do routine legal work themselves."

—NEW YORK TIMES

"...All of [Nolo's] books are easy-to-understand, are updated regularly, provide pull-out forms...and are often quite moving in their sense of compassion for the struggles of the lay reader."

—SAN FRANCISCO CHRONICLE

fold here

Place
stamp here

Nolo
950 Parker Street
Berkeley, CA 94710-9867

Attn: WAGE 4.0